John Mortimer Murphy

Sporting Adventures in the Far West

John Mortimer Murphy

Sporting Adventures in the Far West

ISBN/EAN: 9783337177997

Printed in Europe, USA, Canada, Australia, Japan

Cover: Foto ©Andreas Hilbeck / pixelio.de

More available books at **www.hansebooks.com**

SPORTING ADVENTURES

IN

THE FAR WEST

By JOHN MORTIMER MURPHY

ILLUSTRATED

NEW YORK
HARPER & BROTHERS, PUBLISHERS
FRANKLIN SQUARE
1880

Entered according to Act of Congress, in the year 1879, by

HARPER & BROTHERS,

In the Office of the Librarian of Congress, at Washington.

PREFACE.

Having been a wanderer for nearly seven years in the Far West, a part of the time being ere railways were known there, and when very few whites, except the troops, were found in regions which now boast of thousands, I devoted particular attention to studying the fauna of the country, especially the game, whether it was fur, fin, or feather.

My object in preparing this work has been to give the general characteristics, the haunts, habits, and the best method of hunting the largest class of game; and as my facts are derived from personal experience, and from that of some of the most famous scouts and hunters I met in the West, I hope they'may be found generally accurate.

The contests between men and the fiercer creatures which are related were, when I do not speak personally, heard around the camp-fire or in the Indian's wigwam, and one or two were culled from Western newspapers.

Having no desire to pose as a Nimrod, I may say that some of my hunting was as much for the purpose of studying the *feræ naturæ* as for killing them, and that their life was frequently more pleasing to me than their death.

I have combined incidents in some chapters, notably the buffalo and the prairie-wolf, my aim being to give somewhat similar experiences which might, perhaps, be interesting when united, but tedious and unimportant if related separately.

THE AUTHOR.

CONTENTS.

CHAPTER I.
HINTS TO SPORTSMEN.

Hints to Sportsmen.—Best Game Regions of the United States.—Profusion of Animal Life.—Advantages of the Far West as a Hunting-ground.—Best Quarters.—Inconveniences of Farm-houses for Large Parties.—Character of Guides.—Resent all Assumption of Superiority on Account of Title or Wealth.—Anecdote of their Independence of Character.—Action and Reaction.—How to select Guides.—The Best Animals for Hunting Expeditions.—Tents to be used.—How and when to pitch them.—General Instructions about Camp Life.—What Foods and Medicines to use.—Bedding and Clothing.—Stoves.—Fires, and how to build them.—How to make a Fire without Matches.—Lamps. —Best Clothing for Hunting.—Treatment of Boots.—How to prevent the Feet from Blistering.—Moccasins and Slippers.—Rubber Goods.— Under-clothing.—An Antidote for Fever and Ague.—How to prevent the Insect Plague.—Picketing Horses.—Necessity of Vigilance.—How Sentinels should be Posted.—How to detect the Approach of Objects. —Weapons should be Convenient.—Thieves.—Best Fire-arms.—Bullets.—Breech-loading Shot-guns for Forest Shooting.—Woodcraft.— Lost in the Forest.—Necessity of Observation.—Value of a Compass. —How to track or trail Animals in Flight.—How to procure Water.— Telling the Weight, Size, and Movements of Animals by their Tracks. —Use of a Field-glass.—Qualities of a Successful Hunter.—Characteristics of Best Nimrods.—Difference between Field and Target Shooting .... Page 17

CHAPTER II.
THE GRIZZLY BEAR.

The Grizzly Bear.—Its Haunts, Habits, Size, and General Characteristics. —Fear of the Human Voice.—Its great Strength and Courage.—Fight between a Bear and Buffaloes.—The most Effective Means of killing it.—Anecdotes of Men killed and wounded by it.—Best Weapons for stalking it.—Is said not to touch a Man if he pretends to be Dead.— Examples.—How three Indians captured One.—Great Warriors and Grizzlies.—Value of Claws.—Judge Blank brings a Live Grizzly into Camp in a New Way.—Grizzly Bill.—Two Indians treed.—Subsequent Death of One.—A New Mode of killing a Grizzly in the West.—Its

Intractability and Selfish Nature.—How Mexicans capture it.—Is frequently killed by Hunters and Sportsmen single-handed.—My First Grizzly.—A Hunt after a Grizzly with Indians.—I am treed.—Death of a Warrior.—The Funeral Ceremony.—The Body subsequently devoured by Wolves.—A Comrade and Myself kill one in Wyoming.—A Grizzly invades the Camp.—The Midnight Alarm and Hunt.—I wound a Cub, and am chased by the Dam.—The Retreat.—Indian Anecdote of the Affection of a Grizzly for her Young.—Horseback Hunt with Greasers in California.—Our Trophies.—Death of a Horse, and wounding of its Rider.—We lasso Two Cubs.—Which is the King of Beasts—the Lion or the Grizzly?...Page 40

CHAPTER III.

THE BLACK BEAR.

The Black Bear.—Different Varieties.—Their Haunts, Habits, and General Characteristics.—Affection of Mothers for their Cubs.—Gravid Females never seen.—Migrations of the Bear.—Character of its Flesh. —Its Game Qualities.—Abundance of the Animal in the West.—The best Dogs for chasing it.—How to Hunt it.—Its Acuteness of Nose and Expertness in Swimming.—Captured by Steamers frequently in Puget Sound.—Why it is not Hunted much.—A Hunt with Indians.— The Scenes and Incidents of a *Potlatch*.—Capture of several Bears. —Tripped up while Stalking a Male.—Explosion of Gun.—A Rude Raft, a Wild Ride, and a Collision with a Barricade.—A bad Ducking. —I kill a Bear, and receive a bad Wound in the Arm.—A Canoe Trip, and a Hard Bump.—Reach Camp, and have my Wound dressed.—Return of the Hunters.—An Indian Festival.—How Indians cook Young Bears.—I am mistaken for a Bear by Hunters, and shot at.—Anecdotes of Men attacked by Bears.—A Bear-hunt which results in being Treed.—The Release, and Death of the Besieger.—How a Doctor captured a Bear.—Water *versus* Courage.—A Public Singer and an Imaginary Bear.—The Remuneration given for keeping his Adventure silent.. 75

CHAPTER IV.

THE COUGAR AND LYNXES.

The Cougar.—Variety of its Names.—Size, Weight, Strength, Color, and General Characteristics.—Its Peculiarities when treed.—How Farmers kill it.—Anecdotes of its Courage.—A Fight with a Wolf and a Bear. —Desperate Struggle between a Cougar and an Unarmed Man in Oregon.—Two Kittens captured.—Death of the Dam.—A Wild Cougar plays with a Man in Washington Territory.—His Fright and Escape.— An Episode in Minnesota.—My First Cougar.—A Weird Funeral Ceremony among the Digger Indians.—Why the Californians are called Tar Heads.—My next Capture, and another Form of an Indian Funeral.— A Hunt in the Cascade Range.—Death of a Cougar.—My Companion wounded.—Legend of an Enchanted Lake.—A Cougar cripples an Indian.—Dangerous Character of the Animal.—The best Time for hunting it.—A Night Hunt, and its serious Result.—Death of Two Cougars. —Other Members of the Cat Family.—Difference between Lynxes and true Cats.—How to distinguish them.—Lynx-hunts.—I kill Four in one Month.—Characteristics of the Genus.—Lynx-hunting as a Sport...Page 106

CHAPTER V.

THE GRAY WOLF.

The Gray Wolf.—Number of Species of Wolves.—Difference in Colors.— The Size of the largest Variety.—Its Courage.—Captures of small Dogs from the Indians.—A Pack kills Two of our Dogs.—Retaliation.—Indians eat the Wolf.—Sagacity of the Animal in Hunting.—How a Pack drives Deer.—Stratagems resorted to.—Satellites of Herds of Buffaloes and Antelopes.—What Wolves live on.—Useful Scavengers.—Their harmless character to Man.—Famishing Wolves attack an Indian.— Result.—Afraid of a Child.—Yelps when wounded.—Their Size and Character when Food is plentiful.—How they are killed.—"Wolfers," and their Mode of Work.—Their General Character.—Sudden Wealth and Poverty.—A Lucky "Wolfer."—A Hunt with a "Wolfer."—His peculiar Breed of Dogs.—Their Speed and Stubbornness.—Six Cubs captured, and Two Wolves killed.—Pursuit of a Coyote.—Affection of a Mother for her Young.—How Wolves run when pursued.—Different Breeds of Dogs fit for Wolf-hunting.—How it is hunted in Portions of the West.—A spirited Wolf-chase.—How Wolves act when Trapped.— The Future of Wolf-hunting in the West........................ 138

CHAPTER VI.

THE PRAIRIE WOLF.

The Prairie Wolf.—Origin of its Name.—Its Position among the *Canidæ*. —The connecting Link between the large Wolf and the Fox.—Its Burrows.—Peculiarity of its Barking.—Its Form and Color.—How it is looked upon by Plainsmen.—Where it is very Abundant.—Hunting it on Horseback.—Its Speed.—Best Dogs for Hunting it.—Its Numbers make it difficult to be Hunted by one Pack of Hounds.—The Heaviness of its Brush.—When it runs best.—Best Horses for the Chase.— Leaves a Screaming Scent.—Dashes after it with Hounds and Horses. —Kill Six in One Day.—Run into Encampments of War-parties of Indians.—Rapid Retreat.—A Severe Fight with the Red Men.—A Chase on the Plains of the Columbia.—The Meet.—Mongrel Dogs and their Love of Fighting.—At Cover.—Start.—Two Coyotes.—The Pursuit.—Killed by Indian Dogs.—A Mongrel Greyhound brings One to Bay, and it is shot.—I shoot One.—Looking for my Party.—A Meet and a Run.—Surprised by Indians.—Whites *versus* Indians in the Chase.—Seven Coyotes killed.—Fun and Confusion.—Falls and Laughter.—The Relation of Indian Dogs to Coyotes.—Their Character for Hunting.—Future of Coyote-hunting............................ 161

CHAPTER VII.

THE BUFFALO.

The Buffalo.—Number of Species.—Difference between them.—The gigantic Buffalo of prehistoric Times.—Fierce Aspect of the modern Bison.—Courage of the Male.—Social Character of the Species.—Mothers have Little Affection for the Calves.—Fight between a Grizzly Bear and a Small Herd of Bulls.—A Bull rescues a Calf from a Pack of Wolves.—Another tries to protect a Cow from a Hunter.—A New Mode of capturing Calves.—Buffaloes in a State of Domestication.—Favorite Habitat of the Buffalo.—Character of the Buffalo Grass.—Sufferings of the Animals in Winter from Hunger.—Why Old Bulls leave the Herds.—Use of the Buffalo to the Indians.—The Flesh of the Buffalo.—A Custom of the West.—How the Wolverine feasts on dried Buffalo Meat.—Cunning and Courage.—Pemmican.—The most Delicate Parts of the Buffalo.—Cows better than Bulls.—Vitality of the Animals.—Best Weapons for hunting them.—American Horses *versus* Mustangs.—Opinion of Old Hunters.—Faults of Mustangs in running Buffaloes.—The Various Systems employed for killing the Buffalo.—Great Annual Slaughter of the Animal.—Indians dressed in Wolf-skins attack the Buffalo.—Why they use Arrows instead of Fire-arms.—Hunts of the Half-breeds of British America.—Mean Devices of the Whites.—How Thousands are destroyed Annually.—The Camp and the Night Alarm.—Shooting at Antelopes.—Stalking Buffalo Skulls.—Gambols of Herds.—A Dash after a Herd, and what came of it.—An Alarm of Indians.—Opinions of a Party of Teutons about Jokes.—The Result to me of my Day's hunting.—A Spirited Chase in the Republican Valley.—Wolves and Number of Quarries killed.—A Thousand Hunters and Thousands of Buffaloes in Motion at the same Time.—Howling Wolves and bellowing Bisons.—An Alarm of Sioux.—The Retreat.—Panic-stricken Pawnees..Page 192

CHAPTER VIII.

THE MOOSE.

The Moose.—Its Range in the West.—Its Form, Haunts, and Habits.—The Rutting Season.—Cries of the Animal.—How Males are lured within Rifle Range.—Calling as an Art.—How to make a Call.—The best Callers.—Young Bulls easily inveigled.—The best Time for Calling.—The Moose as a Browser.—Difficulties in stalking it.—Acuteness of its Nose and Ears.—How experienced Hunters quarter the Ground.—Its Haunts in Summer.—Hunting it in Winter.—Dogs and Snowshoes.—The European and American Species.—How the Latter can be Domesticated.—Hide-hunters.—A Moose-hunt, and its Result.—A Charge.—Lost in the Forest.—Trying to find Camp.—A Welcome Moose-call.—Rescued.—A Hunt on Snow-shoes.—Episodes.—Number of Moose killed.—Difference in Size and Habits between the Eastern and Western Species.—Large Antlers.—Moose-hunting as an Art.. 244

CHAPTER IX.

THE ELK, OR WAPITI.

The Wapiti.—Its Range, Haunts, Habits, and Gait.—Fierce Contests between the Males.—How they may be detected by the "Shaking."—Courage of the Elk.—Two Men charged by a Couple in Oregon.—The Escape.—Novel Mode of killing it in the North-west.—Thousands never saw Man.—When started, said not to stop until it crosses Water.—How Herds run when in Flight.—Their Speed and Endurance.—The Elk as a Roadster and Saddle Animal.—Hide-hunters.—Great Slaughter of the Animal.—Why Hinds lead the Columns.—How to Hunt it successfully in the Forest and on the Plains.—Dr. Carver's Great Feat.—The best Weapons.—How to Shoot on Horseback.—The most Exciting Run I ever had after it.—Bagging a Stag.—Pursuit of a Hind, and why she was Captured.—Escape of a Fawn.—Surprised by Indians.—The Assembly.—Our Plans and Stratagems.—A Running Fight.—Loss of the Indians.—Find Refuge in a Chasm.—Death of one of our Men.—He is mutilated, and burned to Death.—Our Retreat.—Suffer from Hunger.—Loss of our Camp, and Escape of the Camp Guard.—Where we found Safety.—A Scalp Dance.—Unusual Abundance of large Game.—We kill sixty Elks in Colorado.—Lassoing Fawns.—Visions of the Sport..................................Page 266

CHAPTER X.

THE MULE DEER.

The Mule Deer.—Its Haunts and Habits.—General Characteristics.—Origin of Name.—Weight, Size, and Appearance.—Why it is called the Jumping Deer.—Fire-hunting.—Herding of Bucks.—Hunting with Hounds.—Stalking.—Migrations of the Animal.—Large Numbers killed by Hunters.—A Hunt in the Bitter Root Mountains.—Wailing of Squaws.—A Visit to an Indian Cemetery.—Disappearance of the Mourners.—A Retreat.—Wolves.—Sit up all Night.—Fear of Indians.—A Visit from them in the Morning.—Our Preparations for their Reception.—Mutual Recognition.—The Trapper's Story.—Visit the Indian Camp.—The Pipe of Peace.—Speeches.—A Buffalo Dance.—Revisit the Burial-ground.—Mode of Burying the Dead.—Mourning Songs of Squaws.—Change Camp.—Number of Deer captured, and how we Bagged them.—Wolves attacking a Stag.—Death of Five of them.—Change Quarters.—Hunting Does and Fawns.—Why these keep to the Foot-hills.—Our Success with them.—Another Visit to the Indian Camp.—An Aged Couple deserted.—How Indians treat Old People.—Their Fate... 292

CHAPTER XI.

THE BLACK-TAILED AND VIRGINIA DEER, AND THEIR VARIETIES.

The Black-tailed and Virginia Deer, and their Varieties.—Range of the Black-tail.—Misapplication of Names.—Size, Speed, and Jumping

Power.—Character of its Flesh.—Its Abundance.—Great Numbers slaughtered Annually.—Objection of Pot-hunters to Hounds.—Best Kind of Dogs for hunting it in the Forests.—Packs in the North-west. —Use of Deer-hounds.—Where to find the Black-tail.—The White-tailed Deer.—Its Haunts and Habits.—Difference between it and the Black-tail when running before Hounds.—Its Intrusive Character and Abundance.—How Farmers keep it away from their Crops.—Antipathy between Sheep and Deer.—Fondness for Salt and Sulphur Springs.—Best Weapon for hunting it.—The Spotted and White Deer.—The Former a Great Pet.—The Latter supposed to be a Wandering Spirit by the Indians.—Where found.—The Virginia Deer.—Its Feeding-grounds.—Best Time for stalking it.—How to stalk it.—The Dwarf Deer.—Its Haunts, Habits, and Numbers.—Different Methods of hunting Deer.—A Day's Hunting in the Woods with Hounds.—Number Captured.—A Fortnight in the Forests of Washington Territory.—Our Camp and Hunting Experience.—Extraordinary Abundance of Fur, Fin, and Feather.—Incidents of Sport and Camp Life.—Merry Times.—Attacked by a Buck.—Lost in the Forest.—Actions of a Man when lost.—How I reached Camp.—Excursions after Fin and Feather.—Homeward bound.—A Grand Hunt-ball.—The Ball-room and the People.—An Original Band.—The Terpsichoreans, and now they were put through their Figures.—Ball-room Scenes and Repasts.—A Hunt-dinner.—Rambling once more.—A Pleasant Reminiscence...Page 323

CHAPTER XII.

THE ANTELOPE, OR PRONG-HORN.

The Prong-horn.—Its Haunts, Range, and Abundance.—Character of its Food.—Its fear of Woods.—Its Position in Natural History.—General Characteristics.—Strange Growth of its Horns.—Its Glandular System. —Is easily Tamed.—Sterility when Domesticated.—Its Speed.—Coursing it with Greyhounds.—Vigilance of the Animal.—A Herd on Guard. —Best Means of stalking it.—Great Curiosity of Males.—Weeps when wounded.—Twenty-four killed by one Dog.—A Day's Coursing on the Laramie Plains.—Lassoing Fawns.—The best Dogs for the Chase.— How experienced Hounds hunt the Antelope.—Stalking and its Result.—Playful Fawns.—Stags and Wolves.—Fate of the Antelope.. 363

CHAPTER XIII.

THE ROCKY MOUNTAIN GOAT.

The Rocky Mountain Goat.—Position in Natural History.—Its Classification.—Supposed to be a Goat-antelope.—Its Appearance, Haunts, and Habits.—Character of its Hair.—Vigilance of Sentinels.—Its Nimbleness.—Fear of the Lowlands.—Getting Scarce.—Flocks in Flight.— First Introduction to the Goat.—A March with Indians.—A Stalk in the Cascade Range.—Its Result.—Disappointment.—A Ram killed.— Skin spoiled by a Fall.—A Hunt in Montana.—Sharp Terriers.—Their use in stalking.—Trophies and Tramping.—Opinion of an old Hunter on Goat-shooting.—A successful Stalker's Faculties.—Charging Goats. —The use of Dogs in hunting them........................Page 381

CHAPTER XIV.

THE BIG-HORN, OR MOUNTAIN SHEEP.

The Big-horn, or Mountain Sheep.—Its Haunts and Habits.—Characteristics required to Hunt it successfully.—Its Caution and Vigilance.—Order of a Flock in Flight.—Hunters' Tales of its Nimbleness.—Pugnacity of the Males.—Contest between a Wolf and a Big-horn.—Size of Rams.—Measurement of Horns.—The Rutting Season.—Flocks of Old Rams.—Best Time for Hunting them.—Stalking Exercise.—A good Rifle.—Usefulness of a Field-glass.—Indian "Sheep-eaters."—Pemmican.—My First Hunt.—A Kill.—Stalk a Flock.—Detected.—The Assembly.—Result of a Fusillade.—Tedious Chase after an Old Ram.—I get Butted over.—A tardy Capture.—Flavor of wild Mutton Cutlets. —Dogs for Sheep-hunting.—A Hunt in the War Eagle Mountains.—Our Success.—A Cougar scared. — "Dancing" Sheep.—Big-horns waiting for their Leader.—Adventure of the Guide with a War-party of Indians. —Defeat of the Latter.. 394

CHAPTER XV.

FOXES.

Foxes very Numerous in the West.—Hunting-clubs.—Various Species and Varieties of Foxes. — Difference between the American and the European Red Fox.—Size, Color, Characteristics, and Value of Fur of the Prairie, Cross, Black, Silver, Swift, and Arctic Foxes.—Difference between the Red and the Gray Fox.—The Latter trees, but rarely runs to Earth.—A true Woodland Animal.—Its Food.—Is being superseded by the Red Species.—The Dwarf or Island Fox.—Lives on Insects.—Fearlessness and Numbers.—Cause of its Diminutive Size.—Value of Fox-skins in Commerce... 418

CHAPTER XVI.

HARES.

Hares.—Their Abundance.—The "Jack Rabbit."—Mark Twain's Opinion of its Speed.—Marvellous Tales of Pioneers.—What constitutes an Oregon Mule.—Coursing-clubs.—California Greyhounds.—Characteristics of the Water-hare.—Swims like a Retriever.—How it escapes its Pursuers. — The Swamp-hare. — Its Peculiar Appearance. — Measurements.—The Washington, Prairie, California, Wood, and Sage Hares, and the Smaller Varieties.—Peculiar Character of Baird's Rabbit.—The Males suckle the Young.—Dissection by a Surgeon.—How Indians and Whites capture Hares.. 426

CHAPTER XVII.

THE RACCOON, OPOSSUM, AND SQUIRREL FAMILIES.

The Raccoon, Opossum, and Squirrel Families.—Number of Species.—How Hunted.—Two Negroes and a Coon Stew.—Best Way of Shooting Squirrels..Page 436

CHAPTER XVIII.

FUR ANIMALS.

Haunts, Habits, and Mode of Capturing the Wolverene, Mink, Fisher, Marten, Ermine, Musk-rat, Skunk, Badger, Land and Sea Otter, Fur-seal, Beaver, and Showtl.—An Unpleasant Adventure while after Fur-seals.—Enormous Destruction of Fur Animals.—Latest Statistics.. 442

ILLUSTRATIONS.

	PAGE
Moose-calling	*Frontispiece*
Grizzly Bears	41
Necklace of Bears' Claws	50
Lassoing a Grizzly	73
Black Bear	76
Indian Dance	85
The Puma, or Cougar	107
Concŏlor—The Puma	111
Gray Wolves	139
Prairie Wolves	162
The Wolf	166
Coyotes	169
A Wolf-hunt on the Prairie	189
American Bison	194
The Herd moving toward Water	201
Kaiowa Buffalo Chase	211
Buffalo-running	237
Buffalo-hunting	240
The Moose	245
Snow-shoe	261
Moose-hunting	264
Wapiti Deer	267
The American Deer	293
Virginian Deer	325
Feeding-ground of the Antelope	364
The Big-horn	395
River Scene, Montana	416
The Fox	419
The Hare	427
The Rabbit Warren	433
The Raccoon	436
The Squirrel	440
The Wolverene	442
The Ermine	448

	PAGE
Musquash, or American Musk-rats	449
The Badger	450
The Otter	451
Fur-seals at English Bay, St. Paul's Island	455
The Seal	456
The Beaver Trap	459
The Beaver	460
Bulls Quarrelling	467

SPORTING ADVENTURES

IN

THE FAR WEST.

CHAPTER I.

HINTS TO SPORTSMEN.

Hints to Sportsmen.—Best Game Regions of the United States.—Profusion of Animal Life.—Advantages of the Far West as a Hunting-ground.—Best Quarters.—Inconveniences of Farm-houses for Large Parties.—Character of Guides.—Resent all Assumption of Superiority on Account of Title or Wealth.—Anecdote of their Independence of Character.—Action and Reaction.—How to select Guides.—The Best Animals for Hunting Expeditions.—Tents to be used.—How and when to pitch them.—General Instructions about Camp Life.—What Foods and Medicines to use.—Bedding and Clothing.—Stoves.—Fires, and how to build them.—How to make a Fire without Matches.—Lamps. —Best Clothing for Hunting.—Treatment of Boots.—How to prevent the Feet from Blistering.—Moccasins and Slippers.—Rubber Goods.— Under-clothing.—An Antidote for Fever and Ague.—How to prevent the Insect Plague.—Picketing Horses.—Necessity of Vigilance.—How Sentinels should be Posted.—How to detect the Approach of Objects. —Weapons should be Convenient.—Thieves.—Best Fire-arms.—Bullets.—Breech-loading Shot-guns for Forest Shooting.—Woodcraft.— Lost in the Forest.—Necessity of Observation.—Value of a Compass. —How to track or trail Animals in Flight.—How to procure Water.— Telling the Weight, Size, and Movements of Animals by their Tracks. —Use of a Field-glass.—Qualities of a Successful Hunter.—Characteristics of Best Nimrods.—Difference between Field and Target Shooting.

THE higher order of game animals are now so scarce in the United States east of the Missouri River that sportsmen can have little real hunting until they go far to the west of that noble stream; but if they would enjoy it to an unusual extent they must cross the Rocky Mountains;

for in the vast area lying between that chain and the Pacific Ocean may be found nearly every species of game indigenous to the North American Continent, and several whose habitat is confined to that region alone. Among the latter may be mentioned the grizzly and black bears, the mountain sheep and goat, several species of deer, besides cougars, wolves, foxes, and many smaller quadrupeds. Of the entire area, Montana, Wyoming, Idaho, Oregon, and Washington Territory, with their towering mountains and extensive plains, dense forests and treeless plateaus, are by far the best hunting-grounds, as they possess all the elements of soil and climate necessary for the sustenance of a large and varied faunal life, and their population is yet so limited that it has little effect on the increase of the *feræ naturæ*. These countries can be approached in variety and abundance of game only by the tangled jungles of India, or the impenetrable woods of Africa; and as they, including Utah, embrace an area of nearly six hundred thousand square miles, or about five times that of the United Kingdom of Great Britain and Ireland, it is evident that they will afford a splendid field to true sportsmen for many years to come. In their profusion and variety of game birds and fishes they have no rivals in any quarter of the globe; hence it may be safely stated that the entire region extending from California on the south and west, to British America on the north and east, is without a peer as a recreation-ground for those who love the ecstatic excitement of the chase, or the quiet, meditative pleasure of angling. The advantages which the Far West possesses over all other places to the lovers of the rod and gun are, that the expense of reaching it is comparatively small; that game is unusually abundant; that life is generally safe there now from the attacks of savages, fierce animals, irritating insects, poisonous serpents, or deadly diseases, by taking ordinary precaution; that trusty and experienced guides are easily procured, and at a nominal sum; that an outfit complete in every detail may be obtained in a town of any importance; that a rapid means of travel are always at command; and, finally, that no matter how irregularly persons may roam in pursuit of game, they are within a few days' march of civilization and the highways of communication with the outer world.

Those who visit the country in search of the denizens of the forest and the stream, the mountain and the plain, should, if they wish to be unusually successful, or desire to satiate themselves with the delights of hunting and fishing, be prepared to camp out, or take up their quarters in farm-houses some distance away from large settlements. The latter is much the cheaper plan, and may do well enough for single individuals or very small parties; but it has its disadvantages in the fact that the surrounding country is hunted in a short time, that the accommodations are often of a poor character, and are sometimes difficult to find; for the owners of cabins frequently object to receiving strangers, and especially those from the city, who are supposed to be exceedingly fastidious in their tastes; and, finally, the Nimrods are hampered in the freedom of their movements and actions, and are never so much at their ease as they would be if they were snugly quartered in their own tents or wagons, or even extended under the umbrageous shelter of a spreading tree. The inconvenience is all the greater if persons are accompanied by dogs, horses, and a large hunting paraphernalia; but if not, and they only desire a few days' hunting or fishing in a place, and they do not care about making very large bags, a farm-house may afford them all the comforts they want, and will at least save them no small sum for camping outfit and the means of travelling.

Some of the guides in the country are prepared to accommodate a few followers of the chase; but it is often the case with them that familiarity breeds contempt; hence they do not work so well, in many instances, as they would if their *protégés* were less familiar with them. One word may be said here of these Western guides, and that is, that they will bear no high-handed dictation or any assumption of superiority over them by those under their guidance;

and though they may not resent it personally, they will in many other ways, by causing a person's hunting exploits to be few and far between, and to make him tramp many weary miles over rugged mountains, through precipitous canyons, and over tiresome plains, for no other purpose than to thoroughly fatigue him, so that he may be glad to take a rest the next day. If he is kind, genial, and openhearted, however, they will do almost anything for him, and will leave no effort untried to make his experience of the chase as pleasant as possible.

I remember meeting a party of English tourists once in Nebraska who were out on a buffalo-hunt; and although they were travelling three days, and had met herds of buffaloes every day, they were not able to get a shot at one; but, with characteristic pluck, they were still following the moving throngs, hoping to be able at some time to have a dash on horseback after them. As they had two good scouts and some experienced wagon-drivers with them, I was rather surprised at their ill luck, but my surprise ceased when I spoke of the matter to the leader of the expedition. His explanation, which was made with many expletives, and in exceedingly vigorous language, was, that the tourists, who knew nothing about the business on which they were engaged, were constantly dictating to himself and his companions what they should and should not do in the most frigid and supercilious manner; that they never spoke to them except to give some command or make an impatient inquiry; that they kept entirely to themselves both in camp and on the march, and never once offered to share the contents of their flask with them; that their English servants were even as consequential as their masters, and evidently looked upon them (the guides) as barbarians and mudsills, and would obey no order unless it came from "mawster;" and that all, when by themselves, were overheard running down the country in every way. "'Tain't likely," was the scout's comment, "that we're going to trouble ourselves much about —— of that sort, so we drive the buffaloes away before they get up to Bill and myself; and if they keep up their foreign style as they have done, they won't get any nearer to a buffalo than they have so far for the fortnight for which they engaged us." As two friends and myself were in the region on a buffalo-hunt, we asked the gentlemen to join us for a day or two if they wished, and to leave their teams and guides in camp, and we hinted that they could kill all the animals they would care to; but they, in a frozenly polite manner, refused our invitation, on the ground that they had their own tents and guides, and could not accept favors from unknown strangers. We became frozen ourselves after that assertion, inasmuch as we thought it to be too egotistical in manner; so we left them at once, and, on returning to town a week afterward, heard that they had come back without killing a buffalo, although they had seen them in immense numbers.

I met the same party subsequently in Wyoming, and all expressed themselves delighted with their luck in that region; and some became as enthusiastic as their temperament would permit them in describing the quantity of game they had killed, and the wonderful scenery of the country. Their good fortune was due, however, to their former experience; for they soon learned that Western men cared very little for mere titles or wealth, and paid no more personal respect to their owners, when they were arrogant, than they would to the simplest citizen. They were, in fact, sometimes spoken of in the most disrespectful manner in their own hearing; and this taught them that they were not of as much consequence as they deemed themselves to be; so, accepting the facts, they made themselves as agreeable to those who accompanied them as cultured gentlemen could, and the result was such an amount of pleasure and successful hunting as they had never anticipated. I mention this incident for the purpose of showing how differently foreign tourists are treated by those very independent guides, when they, in the language of the latter, " put on lugs," and when they are genial, and act the part of " hail fellows well met."

In selecting guides for a protracted hunt, a good plan

would be to make no contracts with them except for their personal services, and to obtain wagons, horses, and mules from other parties, as the former often charge unusually heavy prices for their teams, and furnish the poorest animals in their herds in the bargain. The majority, however, are honest, and will do all in their power for their patrons; but these are generally off the highways of travel, and are themselves ardent followers of the chase. The services of a good guide ought to be obtained for two or three dollars per day, and if an Indian, for one dollar; and a team and driver ought not to cost more than thirty dollars per week, or five dollars per day. If it is intended to continue the hunt for any lengthened period of time, the best method would be to purchase whatever wagons and animals may be needed, as they can be sold again when the season is over for nearly as much as they cost in the first instance. Good mustangs can be obtained at from fifteen to sixty dollars each; but mules are dear, they being rather scarce beyond the Rocky Mountains. In the majority of cases it would be better to use pack animals for transporting the baggage, as this gives greater mobility, and they can traverse mountainous regions which wagons cannot even enter. For travelling over hills or any rugged country, mules make the best riding animals, as they are hardy, patient, and sure-footed; but a mustang or an American horse is better for the plains, its gait being much more easy and regular than that of the long-eared quadruped.

The best tent for camping purposes, during the summer at least, is the wall tent, with fly attached, as that is convenient to pitch, easily folded, can be readily ventilated during sultry weather, and is of a shape that enables beds to be put up with little trouble. It should be made of duck heavy enough to keep out rain and the fierce rays of a noonday sun; and poles for it should always be carried along, as their weight is nothing in comparison to the delay and annoyance of cutting new ones at every encampment, even where wood is plentiful; whereas in many places it is so scarce that not a vestige of it is visible for miles. In selecting a camp, the first requisites are that wood, water, and grass should be convenient, if it is intended to remain there any length of time; if not, the second element is the first matter that should receive attention, and all others, except personal safety, should be sacrificed to it. It is, fortunately, plentiful enough in the hunting regions west of the Rocky Mountains, and if it takes its rise in a granite formation it never runs dry. When a tent is pitched, its back should always be toward the wind, if there is no shelter convenient; but if there is, advantage should be taken of it. It should occupy, if possible, a knoll, or the crest of sloping ground; and if a storm is threatened, a trench a few inches deep should be dug all round it to drain away the rain; and the earth ought to be placed against the lower part of the sides to prevent their being lifted up by the wind or saturated with water. On a mountain, it ought to occupy the lee of a rock or a bluff, and in a forest, should be placed amidst the shrubbery; for if pitched under a tree, the latter is liable to be hurled down by a fierce gust of wind, and to do the occupants some injury. This rule does not apply, however, to the dense woods of Oregon and Washington Territory, as wind-storms are rare in that region, and the most violent that ever blew seem incapable of tearing up the arboreal giants that cover the ground there for an area of many thousands of square miles.

If the camp is located near a river, care should be taken that it is not inundated during the freshets which occur in all of them in May or June, and in many of them after a heavy rainfall. To provide against such an accident, it should be established some distance away from the banks, and, if possible, on sloping ground or a crest. No hard-and-fast rules can be followed in all cases; hence persons must depend on their own judgment as to where it would be best to pitch a camp; so the precautions given are only to suggest that where it is convenient they might be followed to advantage.

It is necessary that persons should make themselves as comfortable as they can in camp, if hunting would not become a toilsome labor, instead of a buoyant, virile pleasure. I would, therefore, intimate to sportsmen to take as much variety of condensed food with them as they think necessary for the trip, for it is not only palatable, but it is almost necessary to health, and is, besides, exceedingly portable. Condensed milk and coffee, pressed tea, sugar, self-leavening flour, dessicated eggs, some canned fruits, crackers, pepper, salt, and onions, pickles, ham, pork, beans, and potatoes, should form the larger portion of commissariat of all expeditions; and when to these are added edible wild roots and herbs, and succulent fresh meat and delicious trout, a party may live as happily in the wilderness, and thrive better than if they were quartered in the best hostelry in the world.

The cooking utensils should include a kettle, a frying-pan, a pot, a broiler, and a teapot; and the table appendages should embrace tin plates, tin or plated cups, knives and forks, spoons, a pepper and salt box, and a sirup caddy; and the whole, when not in use, should fit into a compact kit made of tin or wood.

If an open fire is used for cooking, it should always be built to the leeward of the tent, to avoid accidents; and if the wind is baffling, and blows the smoke and sparks in every direction, it ought to be made in a hole dug in the ground. Two pieces of wood having a crotch at one end, and placed at opposite ends of the fire, with a cross-stick connecting them, make an excellent crane on which to suspend a pot for boiling; and if one is hungry, and wishes to satisfy the craving of the appetite at once, he may do it by thrusting a sharp-pointed bit of wood through a piece of meat, and holding it in the blaze for a few moments. A slice of venison cooked in this manner, and sprinkled over with pepper and salt, makes a delicious tidbit, as the juices are retained in it.

In camping out, one should carry four heavy blankets for bedding, as the nights in the region adjoining the Pacific Ocean are always cool, owing to the rapid radiation of heat after sunset—the result of the absence of clouds. Some people prefer to sleep on the ground rolled up in their blankets, and with their feet toward the fire, to the softest couch; but I have found that a bed or a hammock is the most comfortable, and the safest also, as its height prevents snakes and other crawling things from becoming unwelcome bedfellows. An excellent, convenient, and exceedingly portable bed, which can be rolled up into a very small compass, is now made in New York specially for camp purposes; and this I found to fully supply all the requirements of such an article, as it has a gentle slope from head to foot, so that one does not need a pillow, and it may be set up in less than a minute.

I have also found an air-bed made of rubber very convenient when I could not pitch a tent and was compelled to sleep on wet ground; but I thought it too heavy for transportation, unless I was travelling by canoe, and my cheeks often ached in trying to fill it. It has its advantages, however; and if a person had the means at command for carrying it, he would find it a matter of difficulty to get any bed to equal it in comfort, it being both soft and water-proof. If one must sleep on the ground, a rubber blanket should be placed upon it to keep out the dampness; and with another over the woollen blankets he may repose soundly, even while the rain pours down upon him.

The most comfortable means of keeping warm in a tent either night or day, and also the readiest for cooking food, is to use a neat camp-stove made of sheet-iron, which has a length of about two feet, a breadth of thirteen or fourteen inches, a height of, say, fifteen inches, and contains an oven nine or ten inches in length, and occupying the whole width of the apparatus. There should be two holes in the top for kettles, and their covers ought to be saucer-shaped, to prevent them from being warped by the heat. The pipe should be made in small sections, for the sake of portability; and where it passes through the tent the hole should be protected by a plate of sheet-iron or tin, to prevent the camp from being set on fire. This will not only keep the tent heated in the coldest weather, but will minimize the danger of a conflagration from vagrant sparks, and will enable a person to cook several dishes at the same time. Those who have used it would scarcely do without it, as it makes camp pleasant on the rawest and dreariest days and nights, and it is almost a necessity to the culinary department. All hunting-parties should carry one at least, and they would soon learn to prize it at its full value. It need not necessarily do away with the open-air fires, as the latter are often useful in keeping skunks, wolves, bears, flies, snakes, and other prowling creatures away from the camp; and persons may, as of yore, seat or stretch themselves on the ground beside it, and relate tales of dangers passed, and adventures by flood and field.

To make a good fire of this character, a back-log, or perhaps three or four of them piled one on the other, and retained in their position by stakes driven into the ground, is needed; and two or three large stones should be placed under the fuel in front, in order to give it the draught necessary to cause it to burn freely. The Flat-head Indians make one by placing the butts of the logs in the centre and resting them on one another, thus giving them a pyramidal form; and under these they place moss, bark, and twigs, which burn rapidly as soon as they are set on fire; and as they communicate their heat at once to all the wood above them, the result is a splendid fire in a very short time. Not having any matches with which to ignite the fuel, the red men frequently do it by firing powder into dry moss, punk, or grass, and waving it back and forth in the wind until it burns freely, or by revolving rapidly between their hands a piece of hard wood inserted in a small aperture cut in dry, soft wood. They can obtain a fire by the latter means in less than a minute sometimes; but in many cases it takes much longer, especially if the material is damp. As wood is always wanted, every camp should have an axe; and a hammer, saw, auger, nails, rope, twine, and needles will be found useful. A lantern is also a necessity; and a mechanical lamp which burns any kind of oil, and does not require a glass chimney, will be found exceedingly convenient on some occasions, especially if reading at night is any pleasure; and it is, for one frequently gets weary of the same class of tales when repeated too often. This lamp can also be used for cooking a steak, or boiling a tea or a coffee pot, which it does in a few minutes; and as it cannot be blown out by any ordinary breeze, and the oil cannot be spilled, it is well adapted to tent life.

Persons should always carry a generous supply of matches, and, to preserve them from dampness, they ought to be packed in a bottle or a rubber bag; for they are very precious things when the place where they may be purchased is many miles distant. Soap and towels should also be abundant, especially the former, for a bath in the limpid stream after a hard day's toil is a luxury indeed, and, if taken in the morning, it acts both as a mental and physical invigorator.

The clothing of a hunter who would be successful ought to be of a dull, neutral, or pepper-and-salt tint, so that animals may not be startled by the presence of any unusual hue, and that he may the more readily conceal himself in timber, on the prairie, or amidst mountain crags. Light colors are better than very dark ones, as the latter contrast strongly with the ground or foliage, and are therefore more readily seen; whereas a drab, a butternut, or a light brown can scarcely be distinguished at any distance from many natural objects in the surrounding landscape. For working in the woods in spring or summer, the former tints are preferable to all others; but for the autumn, or even for mountain shooting, the "pepper-and-salt" cloth, or some kindred material, is by many persons deemed the best. The clothing worn should be made loose, so as to give freedom of movement, and the older it is, consistent with comfort and appearance, the better it is; for one does not care for it then so much, and he "roughs" it without any compunctions of conscience about a tailor's bill; and if it should get torn into shreds he feels that he has not lost much.

Good heavy boots or shoes are indispensable for long walking or heavy climbing, and they also should be free to the feet, so that they may not blister them, or produce heart-aching corns, which always pinch most when most inconvenient. Should the shoes get wet, the soles and uppers ought to be oiled well with castor-oil before being dried; and should they blister the feet, the inside of the stockings should be coated with common yellow soap; and this, when repeated a few times, will both harden the pedal extremities and prevent them from blistering for many weeks at least. An extra pair of boots or shoes should always be carried, also slippers or moccasins. The latter, if smoke-tanned, are, in my estimation, the best, as they are easy and pliable to the feet, do not harden and shrink after a wetting, and may be used even for travelling over a country where rocks and briers are not common. An overcoat, a rubber cape and leggings, and a rubber blanket or two should form a portion of every Nimrod's wardrobe when out in the wilds; for the former is often useful even on summer nights, and the latter are necessities during the prevalence of a rain-storm, or to act as preventives against the dampness of the ground or the atmosphere, if one is compelled to sleep in the open air; and he often is, or he sometimes wishes to do it. Warm under-clothing is a necessity, even if the outer is light, and should be made of flannel, to prevent the too rapid cooling of the body after great or severe exertion; and in order that it might be always fit to wear, that and all other materials of the wardrobe should be carried in a water-proof bag.

As the majority of people, no matter how robust they may be, are sometimes liable to light attacks of illness, it is fair to infer that those who cross the Rocky Mountains in search of fur, fin, or feather may at one time or other become indisposed, owing to a change of climate, water, or some other cause; it might, therefore, be well to suggest to them to take some simple medicines with them, so that they might be used promptly in case of need. These may be confined to a few cathartic pills, a diarrhœa mixture, a diuretic, sal-volatile, salve, court-plaster, sweet-oil, a bottle of ginger, and the fluid extract of hamamelis to allay the irritation of fly-bites, and to bathe contusions or slight wounds with. Should such a calamity occur to a person as to be bitten by a rattlesnake, a generous dosing of whiskey until he is drunk is the only effective remedy against the poison, and that is thoroughly effective; hence the extract of rye, wheat, or corn is no unimportant part of a campaigner's pharmacopœia. Hot lemonade is an excellent preventive of fever and ague—a fact which I have thoroughly proved in several cases; and if it is mixed with a strong dose of good Holland gin, it may banish the disease within a few hours. A wine-glass of this mixture taken twice a day acts both as a tonic and as an opponent of that most disagreeable malady; and I am free to say that few persons who try it will find it ineffective.

Fly-bites may be prevented by applying a light coating of tar and sweet-oil to the face and hands; and if disturbed by flies around the camp-fire, one should move to the smoky side; but if he uses tobacco, he might light his pipe on any side and enjoy the pleasure of hearing their song, while he knows they dare not come near him.

To avoid fleas, boughs of trees should be used for a bed on the ground instead of hay or straw, and all dogs should be banished the tent and forced to keep in their own domiciles, if they have one; if not, to lie around the fire, or in some extemporized shelter.

In taking care of horses, it is necessary that they should be hobbled with side lines, or picketed, while grazing, to prevent them from straying away or being stampeded by any cause. The picket-ropes for each animal should be thirty or forty feet long, and be attached to an iron ring in a stout leathern headstall, and to a swivel-ring in an iron pin which is driven almost to the head in the ground, and so firmly planted that a horse, in its wildest terror, could not withdraw it.

A strict watch should always be kept over the animals; for there are thieves, both white and red, in some portions of the region who would not hesitate a moment to steal them if it could be done without actually risking their lives. This statement is true to only a limited extent, for there are other parts of the country where they might be left for years, and no person would probably molest them. Vigilance is, however, a virtue which will be well repaid there, and it should be exercised to the fullest extent. If encamped anywhere in the vicinity of an Indian settlement, a guard should be mounted at night and kept up until daylight. The reliefs might be changed every two hours; and this short time, even if there is no danger, could be employed to good advantage in keeping the fire burning brightly, or in preventing the intrusion of thieving quadrupeds. Sentinels wishing to note the approach of objects can do it best by lying on the ground, face downward, and looking toward the horizon; and by applying the ear to the ground, the advance of bodies can be heard when some distance away, and, after a little experience, their character and route may be pretty accurately surmised.

A guard should never stand up in sight of the camp when on duty at night, as he is more likely to be seen by foes than he is to see them; and he ought, if possible, to be placed on some crest overlooking as large a tract of country as it is convenient to survey, or take up his position in a tree. He should be under shelter where it is available, and he ought never expose his full outline in any case. In a region where Indians are very active or threatening, the guards should be increased, the animals picketed in camp or tied up every night, the wagons placed in such a manner that they could be used for cover in case of attack, and the camp so situated that it could be assaulted only at a serious disadvantage to the assailants. It should be protected as much as possible by crags, bluffs, or woods; for though it may be safe from the red men, it is often endangered by the causeless stampede of terror-stricken steeds, which gallop madly over everything, from tent to man.

Weapons should always be kept ready for prompt use in case they might be needed, and every man ought to know at once where to place his hand on his own, even in the darkness.

All these precautions may be unnecessary; yet it would be well to pay some attention to them when parties are camping out, and are traversing new or dangerous ground, as a detachment of white or red thieves might consider a raid upon a camp a profitable enterprise, and nothing proves so efficacious an antidote to their avariciousness as a few prompt and well-delivered bullets. In ordinary hunting expeditions there is very little danger of being attacked by anything fiercer than a wounded animal, and that in very rare instances; so that, except under very unusual circumstances, life is as safe there as it would be in the heart of a great city, if not safer.

Sporting dogs of all kinds can be utilized in every quarter of the country; but the most valuable are pointers, setters, and hounds. The greyhound can be employed in coursing hares and antelopes; the deerhound, for following on open ground the lordly elk, burly moose, or swift and cunning white-tailed deer; the terrier, for routing foxes and badgers from their burrows, or measuring its strength against them in deadly combat; while the beagle, harrier, fox and otter hound will find all the work they wish to do, and more than they may care for, almost every day in the year.

The weapons required for the chase in the region are a rifle, a breech-loading shot-gun, a heavy revolver, and a good hunting-knife. The rifle should be of large calibre, not less than forty-five at least, and its trajectory should be as flat as possible; for in shooting at rapidly moving game one cannot stop to elevate the rear sights; and even if he did, he might raise the wrong one, in his hurry and excitement, and shoot either over or under the quarry. It is, besides, a difficult matter to estimate distances in that country, even with an extensive experience, owing to the clearness of the atmosphere, which causes all objects to seem nearer than they actually are. For shooting on treeless plateaus at a distance of three hundred yards and under, I have found the Express rifle to be the best of arms, as I used the same sight, with the exception of its being a little coarser, at objects one hundred and fifty yards away that I did at those only fifty, and I found very little difference between my accuracy at both ranges. The double Express has one fault, however, and that is that both barrels do not shoot with equal precision, and, in hunting, a person sometimes forgets which barrel he is shooting; so fails to allow for its peculiarities, and the result is often a serious miss. A single-barrelled weapon is devoid of this fault; but then it is not so convenient as the preceding, especially where one desires to plant his bullets rapidly in the body of a running animal that may get out of range before a second ball can be inserted and aim taken. The former, even with its failing, may therefore be said to be the better of the two. I have found the Winchester magazine or repeating rifle very convenient for general shooting; but that also had its faults, not the least of which was that the bullet would sometimes tilt as soon as it reached the breech from the magazine, at seemingly the most critical moment; and ere it could be extricated and placed in its proper position, the game would probably be out of sight. I was compelled to leave a buffalo hunt on two occasions on account of this serious defect in its working, and I have several times lost a deer through the same cause. Another fault that it possessed for shooting heavy game was that the charge of powder it carried was too small, and, as a matter of course, its driving power was not great enough to give hard-killing animals a fatal wound; but it atoned in some respect for this by the rapidity with which it could be fired when the magazine was full. I understand that it has been improved very much recently, so the failings I mention may exist no longer.

Some excellent single-barrel sporting rifles are now made, both in Europe and the United States, which are quite accurate up to four or five hundred yards, and carry powder and ball enough to kill a large animal within that distance. These are very useful weapons for hunting the grizzly bear, mountain-sheep, wild goat, and buffalo, which are sometimes rather difficult of near approach, and such denizens of the woods and coppices as the moose, elk, deer, black bear, and cougar.

The most effective weapon that I ever used was a fifty-calibre Springfield rifle, which was resighted so that its point-blank range was one hundred and fifty yards. This was almost as accurate at three hundred yards as it was at half the distance, and I have killed a wolf with it nearly four hundred yards away. As the greater number of animals are killed within three hundred yards, a rifle that can be depended upon up to that distance is good enough for all practical purposes; but it should have no rear sights. Some hunters west of the Rocky Mountains use a "buckhorn" or an ivory sight; but I have found that an ordinary sight, nickel-plated at the inner tip, was equally as good, and was less liable to injury if made rather long, and fastened well.

Explosive bullets are now used by some sportsmen in their encounters with bears, cougars, buffaloes, and the larger species of deer; but, as at present made, they cannot always be relied upon to explode when wanted, and they are sometimes rather dangerous to the carrier. When well made, however, and not so sensitive as to explode on merely touching the animal, they are not only comparatively safe, but the most merciful and effective missiles known for killing heavy game, as they destroy them at once. Yet I would not recommend them.

A very good word may be said in favor of the hollow bullets, as they are certainly superior to the solid in making a large wound and in paralyzing the game; but they have the fault of want of very deep penetration unless they are fired at short range and with high charges of powder, one hundred and twenty grains at least being required to give them force enough to kill large animals at a distance of one hundred and fifty or two hundred yards. Like the explosive shells, they are also difficult to procure in the Far West, and this forces one to cast them himself. That they possess decided advantages over the conical ball at short ranges, is undoubted; hence those who do not care to try long shots would find them very effective, and would lose less game with them than they would with the conical bullet fired with ninety-five grains of powder.

For forest-shooting a rifle cannot be compared to a good breech-loading gun charged with buckshot, as a single ball is liable to be swerved from its course by trees and matted shrubbery. One may fire at a deer with a rifle several times in the dense woods and miss it, whereas he may tumble it over at once with a dose of buckshot, as some of the charge is likely to hit in a vital part. The best gun that I know of is a ten-bore, weighing from nine and a quarter to ten pounds, and having a length of barrel of thirty-two inches; for that can stop anything that runs in the forests less tenacious of life than a grizzly bear, and it is equally useful for shooting fur or feather.

I prefer good wood-powder to any other, as I have found it to make a good pattern, to have excellent penetration, to be cleaner than the ordinary powder, and to make less of a report, and little smoke. The latter two characteristics are most desirable, as the detonations do not startle game, and a person's aim with the second barrel is not obscured by smoke.

Every sportsman ought to have some knowledge of wood-craft and the characteristics of the animals he wishes to hunt. The latter is necessary to success, and the former to enable him to make his way through regions unknown to him; for it is as disagreeable as it is a serious matter to get lost in a dense forest or on a trackless prairie. In North-western America, where settlements are often few and far between, and there are no roads to indicate a person's course, it is almost maddening to find yourself wandering stupidly about in an aimless manner, and not knowing which way to turn to reach camp or a cabin. I was lost twice in the forest, and once on the prairie; and I remember vividly how I wandered about, now wading deep and rapid streams, plunging headlong through marshes that threatened to ingulf me at every step, clambering like a squirrel over felled and slippery trees and up steep bluffs, dashing down precipices with the celerity of a mountain goat, or rushing through heavy shrubbery, that lashed my face incisively, with almost the ease of a startled fawn. I was only a short distance from camp on these occasions, yet I could not find it, although I moved around it in a circle. One cause of this was that it was night, and that I could not tell by leaves, trees, or footsteps where I was going; I was, therefore, compelled to sleep alone in the lonely forest and amidst wild animals more than once—incidents by no means pleasant. Had not my companions been better backwoodsmen than I was, I would in all probability have been lost, for I was in a portion of the forest where it would have been almost impossible to track me, and where I must have died of hunger. I learned from these incidents not to travel in unknown forests without a compass; to take bearings of all the prominent landmarks, and the peculiarities of the trees on my route; and not to depend on the sound of a horn to lead me to camp in a region covered with woods and seamed by canyons, as the latter cause an echo to sound in every direction, and to repeat it from so many quarters at the same time that one gets bewildered. I have been much in the forest since then; and though I have sometimes had to grope my way through it in doubting fear, yet, by carrying a compass, I was always enabled to reach my destination in time enough to prevent any apprehensions about my safety. It may be all well enough for persons who know a piece of woods as well as they do their own kitchen, to smile at the caution of those who carry a compass to guide them back to camp; yet I, for one, would advise the sporting novice to pay no heed to their criticisms, and to consider life, or even the danger of getting lost, of much more importance than any idle ridicule. I would, therefore, never move out without one, even if it were only for a distance of a few miles, unless I was familiar with the country.

After some experience in wood-craft, and learning to be a

careful observer, one may find camp in the densest forest almost as easily as he would in a glade. The first thing in starting out in the morning is to note the position of the encampment and its immediate surroundings, paying particular attention to any peculiar or prominent landmarks, streams, tarns, or rocks, and the direction in which they lie from it. The region traversed during the day, if one is alone, should also be impressed on the memory; or it might be "blazed" at intervals, by scoring trees with a knife, breaking the boughs of some of the shrubbery, or dropping a stone here and there, so that they might be readily seen in case the return was made by the same route. A person ought also to carefully scan the principal trees, and remember any individuality they might possess; as, for instance, on which side the moss grew thickest— generally the north, and on which side the boughs were longest and most abundant — always the south. If one thinks he is lost, he should retrace his steps as carefully as possible, and that he can readily do in the woods; and if night overtakes him ere he can reach camp, he should not get alarmed, but make himself as comfortable as he can under the circumstances, and wait for daylight to continue his work.

As the most cautious and careful of persons may sometimes be compelled to make a temporary shelter for themselves away from their companions, it would be well to always carry a supply of matches in a pocket for the purpose of building a fire, as that is useful in many ways, besides its heat and cheerfulness.

If the trail becomes indistinct, it may be followed by raising the eyes and allowing them to glance a little way ahead; then any impressions on the ground or leaves, or any disarrangement of the grass and shrubbery, is readily seen. The scanning glance should be rapid, as the line is likely to become blank to the gazer if it is looked at steadily for any length of time. Another fact that may be noted is, that wild animals — and as for that the domestic also — run against the wind when startled; and if one knows from what direction that blows, he may be able to extricate himself from his dilemma in a short time.

In the woods bordering the Pacific Ocean water is generally abundant, so that a person need not suffer from thirst; yet if he should by accident be in a section where it is scarce, he may obtain enough to allay his craving by digging a small hole in a marshy spot, filling it with grass, then applying to it any hollow tube, and using the mouth for a suction. A refreshing drink may also be obtained from maple or birch, if one has only a knife with which to scar them. If one cannot find water or camp by searching on the ground, he might be successful by climbing a tall tree and surveying the landscape before him. If he seeks the former, he may discover it by noting a break in the forest; if the latter, by the smoke of the fire, which is nearly always kept burning. I have found a good long lariat useful for climbing the gigantic trees of the Pacific, as the boughs are so high up and the trunks so thick that no ordinary person can reach their summit without some such assistance as the lariat gives; and it is exceedingly useful for swinging at once out of the reach of an angry bear.

In trailing animals, one may, after a little experience, tell their size by the spread of the feet on the ground; their weight, by the depth of the impression made; the speed at which they moved, by the intervals between the paces; the length of time since they passed over a spot, by the freshness of the tracks; and whether they were startled or not, by the condition of the grass, leaves, or soft ground.

If they have been wounded seriously, it may be detected by drops of blood, or by the irregular and straddling character of the gait; hence it may be said that a habit of close observation of the imprints on the earth will reveal to one the names of animals that visit a region, their motives in travelling, and their condition and numbers, almost as readily as if he saw them before him.

All game quadrupeds should be hunted up wind, seldom across it, and never down, as scent is to them what sight is to birds and feeling to mankind. The best time for pursuing them is the early morning or late evening, as they rest during the day.

A good idea would be to carry a field-glass. I have found it of great use in many cases, and have seen game with it that otherwise would be lost to us. This is especially true in hunting on the mountains and prairies, as many animals look so much like their surroundings that, even when in motion, they cannot be seen at any great distance.

No person should start out in the morning without partaking of something to eat, even if it were only a biscuit or a cup of tea or coffee, as any of these fortifies the stomach against the chills of the morning, and prevents the nausea of hunger. I have known several sturdy and enthusiastic sportsmen to be injured by their habit of starting out at daybreak to kill something before breakfast, not that it was wanted, but that they wished to make their list large during the trip or the season. They may be able to defy the laws of nature for awhile, but I have found they were the first to succumb in the long-run.

To be a successful Nimrod, one must be patient, cautious, and persevering; mere dash is of little avail, except under favorable circumstances, and they are not common in hunting large wild animals. The best hunters that I have known were exceedingly keen in sight and hearing, and were close observers of the ground and the haunts and habits of animals; not that they possessed these qualities in any extraordinary degree naturally, but that their constant exercise developed them to the fullest extent. These men were not by any means the ideals of the novelist — tall and thin, of an iron frame, and with muscles like steel springs; nor were they so taciturn that one could not get a sentence out of them except by a great deal of persuasion. Neither were they always indulging in hyperbole when they did speak, or execrating the whole red race; many of them were, on the contrary, simple and unpretentious men, who were as sociable as men could be, and who bore no sort of resemblance, either in form, manner, language, or expression, to Leatherstockings or any of his ilk. They could not hit an acorn many miles away, nor did they perform heroic feats in hugging a grizzly bear to death or killing every animal they fired at; yet they could give an excellent account of themselves in a hunt lasting a week or two, or even a whole season.

Another thing may be asserted—namely, that the best shots at game may be of no account in firing at a target. Both systems are entirely different; for he who may be an excellent long-range rifleman may be of no use in the field, and is liable to be beaten by a man who does not know the first principles, in theory, of rifle-shooting, and cannot tell a Vernier sight from a sardine box. To be a successful hunter requires practice more than anything else, but, of course, a naturally good eye and the bump of calculation are valuable adjuncts to practice; yet I am free to say that any ordinary person can become a successful hunter in time, provided he has the ordinary five senses and sound limbs, if he has practice.

CHAPTER II.

THE GRIZZLY BEAR.

The Grizzly Bear.—Its Haunts, Habits, Size, and General Characteristics. —Fear of the Human Voice.—Its great Strength and Courage.—Fight between a Bear and Buffaloes.—The most Effective Means of killing it.—Anecdotes of Men killed and wounded by it.—Best Weapons for stalking it.—Is said not to touch a Man if he pretends to be Dead.— Examples. — How three Indians captured One. — Great Warriors and Grizzlies.—Value of Claws.—Judge Blank brings a Live Grizzly into Camp in a New Way.—Grizzly Bill.—Two Indians treed.—Subsequent Death of One. — A New Mode of killing a Grizzly in the West. — Its Intractability and Selfish Nature.—How Mexicans capture it.—Is frequently killed by Hunters and Sportsmen single-handed. — My First Grizzly.—A Hunt after a Grizzly with Indians.—I am treed.—Death of a Warrior.—The Funeral Ceremony.—The Body subsequently devoured by Wolves.—A Comrade and Myself kill one in Wyoming.—A Grizzly invades the Camp.—The Midnight Alarm and Hunt.—I wound a Cub, and am chased by the Dam. — The Retreat. — Indian Anecdote of the Affection of a Grizzly for her Young.—Horseback Hunt with Greasers in California.—Our Trophies.—Death of a Horse, and wounding of its Rider.—We lasso Two Cubs.—Which is the King of Beasts—the Lion or the Grizzly?

THE grizzly bear (*Ursus horribilis* or *ferox*) ranges from Mexico in the south to British America in the north, and from the Rocky Mountains in the east to the hills adjoining the Pacific Ocean south of the forty-second parallel of north latitude in the west. In size, strength, and ferocity it is the monarch of the American animal world, and even man himself has to yield it undisputed sway in many cases. It differs from all its family not only in ponderosity of proportions, but in courage, fierceness, and intractability, and in being more strongly carnivorous, with the exception, perhaps, of the polar-bear. It also ranks far above them in the enormous size of its soles, the length of its claws, and the breadth and depth of its head; but it is inferior to them in length of tail, and in the quality of its fur and flesh. I have heard of some that attained a length of nearly nine feet and a weight of thirteen hundred pounds, but these were far above the average in size. I have seen some that measured seven feet in length, and weighed over nine hundred pounds when in good condition, and these were thought

GRIZZLY BEARS.

to be rather large in the Rocky Mountain region; but I should judge that those found in warmer climates, such as Southern California, Arizona, and other places, were not only larger, but also fiercer, than their northern kindred.

The forehead of the grizzly is broad, flattish, and nearly on a line with the nose; the ears are longer than the tail, and are more arched and conical than those of the black bear; the legs are thick, and very powerful; the claws are exceedingly long, ranging from two and a half to six inches, and project some distance beyond the hair of the foot; and the foot has a length of about eighteen inches. The claws are very sharp, and so dense that they cut like a keen sabre when the animal uses them; and, to make them as effective as possible, nature has made the fore claws double the length of the hinder.

The grizzly has an erect mane between the shoulders; a dark dorsal stripe from the occiput to the tail; a lateral one on each side along the flanks, but nearly concealed by the light tips; and the intervals between the stripes are lightest in hue. The hairs on the body are a brownish-yellow, with hoary tips occasionally; the muzzle is pale; the parts around the ears are dusky; the legs are inclined to be darkish in hue; and the tail is so short as to be hidden by hair. The presence of this giant may be known long before it is seen, by the size of its footsteps, and especially by their great width.

This is the bear of the mountains, as its congener is of the forests and lowlands; yet it is not confined in its habitat to rugged regions, but goes wherever food is to be found. It is a denizen of nearly all the States and Territories west of the Rocky Mountains, but it is not met farther north than the forty-second parallel on the Cascade Range, or about the junction of Oregon and California. It roams to British America, however, in another direction, by following the lower chains that trend northward from the Rocky Mountains, and is as abundant in some portions of that country as it is farther south.

It hibernates during the winter in the northern regions; yet it is not unusual to see an old male out in search of food during the coldest weather, but I doubt if one ever saw cubs or gravid females. To encounter the animal during these expeditions in search of pabulum is a dangerous matter, as it will not hesitate a moment to attack anything living, from a man to a mouse; and the one is of about as much consequence to it as the other, for it can crush the former at once with a blow from its powerful paw or the pressure of its massive jaws. It will, in ordinary cases, avoid an encounter with man, unless startled suddenly or cornered; but when it is hungry, angry, or suffering from petulance during the rutting season, it seems to lose its fear of everything, and to be ready to fight without the least provocation. When surprised, it rises with a deep, gruff, bass-drum-like "huff, huff," that recalls the giants of the fairy tales; and when it commences an attack it charges vigorously. Notwithstanding its clumsy form, it can run rapidly, owing to its enormous strength, and woe betide the man who cannot then find a tree convenient, for that is his only refuge, if he is alone, as the grizzly cannot climb, owing, according to the assertions of the Indians, to the form of its claws. It can climb trees when young, however; so its great weight may have something to do with its inability to accomplish such a feat at adult age. Should a man seek safety even in a tree, he is liable to be made a prisoner for several hours, for the bear will not, it is said by hunters, leave until night sets in or it becomes hungry.

Should a person meet it suddenly when he is alone, he should not run unless he could do so with some assurance of success, for it is almost sure to pursue if it is at all within convenient distance. The best thing in that case would be to try the effect of a few screams, for, great and powerful as the grizzly is, it is very much afraid of the human voice, and often flees from it. It has been known to turn tail and run, even when preparing to attack, on hearing the terrified screams of a man; and I heard of a woman in Siskiyou County, California, who caused a female grizzly and her two cubs to beat a rapid retreat by shouting lustily at them when the former began to show signs of being dangerous. An unusual noise of any kind is liable to alarm it, if it is not hungry; but such means of driving it away cannot be relied upon, and the only efficacious mode of circumventing it is to avoid an encounter, or to give it the contents of a heavy rifle. Even with the latter, one is not always sure of victory, for it is probably one of the hardest animals in the world to kill. I have known it to carry away several ounces of lead and then outrun its pursuers; and I knew one to be hit with ten heavy bullets before relinquishing its spirit. This tenacity of life is accounted for by its great strength, thickness of hide, powerful and strongly resistant muscles, and the form of the skull, which affords good protection to the brain.

Its strength may be inferred from the fact that it has been known to kill two combative buffaloes in Montana, in about as many minutes, by strokes of its huge forepaws, and subsequently to drag a heavy bull, which must have weighed at least twelve hundred pounds, a distance of several hundred yards, and bury it in a hole which it excavated with its claws. It can kill a man with one fair blow, and can crush him as it would an egg-shell, should he ever get locked in its embrace; while it can tear the hide off the thick-skinned buffalo with a sweep of its cimeter-like claws.

I have heard old hunters say that the most effective way of killing this Western monarch is to shoot it in the chest when it rises on its hind-legs to survey an adversary previous to advancing to the assault, as one is then almost sure of reaching a vital part, or at least of crippling it so much as to prevent it from running rapidly. A shot in the lungs is certainly sickening, if not paralyzing, and is liable to produce internal hemorrhage. A person should not attack the animal with impunity, however, unless he is in company with others, and is well armed, for it is as fierce as the lion when aroused, and is far more dangerous; as it will pursue a hunter vigorously, if it can run, should he wound it, whereas the other is content with a bound, and, if it misses its object, to wait and crouch for another.

The number of persons who have lost their lives through

their foolhardiness in attacking the grizzly at a disadvantage, or with poor weapons, is by no means small; and were it not for the fact that others sought safety in convenient trees when pursued, it would be much greater. A man in Northern California who attacked the animal single-handed, and at close quarters, was supposed to have been killed by it with a single blow of its paw; for when found by his friends a few days after, he was scarcely recognizable, as the flesh was torn off the scalp, face, and chest, the ribs were crushed in, and the arms and thighs were broken.

Another man, who formed one of a party of hunters who were out in search of deer in California, encountered a grizzly suddenly while passing through a coppice in which manzanita formed the undergrowth. The bear was eating the berries of this shrub, of which it is very fond, and will travel far to procure, and strongly protested with muffled, thundering huffs, at being disturbed during its meal. The hunter being dazed by the suddenness of the meeting, and terrified by the growls, knew not what to do at first; but after a short hesitation he concluded to face about and hasten out of the shrubbery, and, acting on this impulse, he tore through it at his highest speed. The bear, which had made no threatening demonstration before that time, seemed to have been aroused into fury by the noise and action of the fugitive, so after him it ran. The race was a short one, for the enormous weight of the grizzly carried all obstacles before it, and the man was overtaken inside a distance of one hundred yards, and hurled to the earth with one blow. The fall stunned him for a few moments, and, when he recovered his senses, he found that he was being dragged away by the arm, the bear evidently having decided to bury him for future use. Though sick at heart from the pain of his arm and his forcible passage through the bushes, he concluded to keep quiet, hoping that something would turn up to give him an opportunity of escaping, or, if the worst came to the worst, to enable him to extricate himself from a living grave. He had been dragged along only a very short distance when the bear came to a deep canyon; and as it could not carry him conveniently down this steep without changing its hold, it let go the arm and seized him by the neck. This was too much for the equanimity of the stoic, so he gave a loud and piercing yell of terror that rang all over the coppice, and was echoed and re-echoed in thundering tones by the rock-bound precipice and the adjacent woods. This unexpected alarm caused the bear to drop its prey suddenly and to scamper away panic-stricken; and to be sure that it did not return, the hunter gave another unearthly yell, which was thundered in every direction by the trees, shrubs, and rocks. Wild with joy at his miraculous escape, he jumped to his feet, but, on arising, he found himself so stiff and sore that he could scarcely move, while his left arm hung limp and useless at his side. Making the best of his way out of the woods, he reached camp, and there fell in a swoon, which must have lasted some time, as he could not remember anything until he found one of his comrades bathing his face and trying to arouse him. An examination of his body proved that the bones of the forearm were broken, but that there were no injuries on the back beside some deep flesh-wounds which bled freely, and the temporary paralysis of a few muscles.

Using their rude surgery, the hunters stopped the bleeding, and, leaving him in camp, they started out the next day in search of the assailant, and returned in the evening with a four-year-old female dragging at the end of their lariats. As she was supposed to have done all the harm, her head was cut off and given as a trophy to the victim of her anger, and, if he is not now dead, it adorns his cabin in Humboldt County.

A man whom I knew well was killed by a grizzly in the Sierra Nevada Mountains. He also was out in search of deer in Butte County, and, meeting a bear, attacked and wounded it, then followed it into the dense shrubbery, where he must have been killed at once by a sudden blow; for, when found, he displayed no injuries except that the head was crushed, and the scalp torn off by the Mamaluke cut of the claws.

I knew another who was so severely injured in a contest with one that he is to-day a cripple, and can scarcely lift a hand or a foot, while one eye is completely gone. He also wounded the animal, but was not able to escape from it, and were it not for the timely arrival of two companions he would have been killed.

I heard of two Piute Indians who were surprised by a grizzly while out picking blueberries, and were killed so suddenly that they hardly knew what hurt them; and of a Blackfoot, in Montana, who was attacked on horseback by one; but he, fortunately, escaped with only a serious wound, by deserting his steed. The numbers of casualties resulting from encounters with grizzly bears might be extended to a volume, for many of the early pioneers of the Pacific Coast, who lived by hunting or trapping, had an experience of them, and not a few gave their life as a forfeit for it.

The incidents given will, however, show that it is no animal to play with, and that, unless one is prepared for a contest of life and death, he ought to give it a wide berth, should he not have a decided advantage in every way. To encounter it, then, with any degree of success, one needs the most approved weapons; and they should be heavy enough to kill it at once, or to give its nervous system such a shock as would deprive it of all power to do harm. A hollow bullet fired from an Express rifle will often kill it immediately, if planted in a vital part; but it is more likely to merely sicken it, or to incite it to mad deeds of violence. A good bone-smasher is a heavy, solid, and spherical bullet fired from an Express rifle. Shells are also good; but they are dangerous to handle, and are, in too many cases, ineffective, as they explode as soon as they touch the body; and even if they enter, one cannot be sure of their bursting. They are, besides, difficult to procure, and are, in my estimation, almost as dangerous to the hunter as to the hunted. A capital rifle for stalking the grizzly would be an eight-bore, carrying twelve drachms of powder; or a No. 12, carrying six drachms, might be found convenient. The objections to these are, that they are too cumbersome for general shooting, and too heavy to be carried about except on particular occasions. A good fifty-calibre Express rifle may, therefore, be said to be the best for general purposes; and if one can use that to good advantage he need have little fear of grizzlies, if he will only manage to keep them at a safe distance for a run before commencing the attack. For my own part, I should not care to get nearer than one hundred yards at least, and a few feet more might not be disagreeable, if there were to be a fight for supremacy, and trees were scarce.

The grizzly will not, it is said, touch a man if he remains motionless on the ground, and does not breathe loudly; and so generally is this believed that the Indians have a saying that a man lying down is medicine to a bear, but the trappers say that "Ephraim" is good medicine only when you let him severely alone; and their general instruction to novices is not to fight him except in self-defence.

As a proof that the grizzly will not injure a man who pretends to be dead, a tale is told of Tarpello, a Snake Indian, who was knocked down and wounded in the back by one of these giants; but on falling he took excellent care to lie perfectly still, and to bury his mouth, nostrils, and eyelids in the deep alkali dust, so that his breathing could not be perceived. The grizzly, after sniffing at him and rudely pawing him about for awhile, must have concluded he was dead, for it retreated without doing him any further injury.

When it entered the shrubbery the wily red man arose, and started for home as fast as his legs would carry him, and told his wondering spouses, children, and kindred of his miraculous escape. The tale spread all over the village in a short time; and when the medicine-man heard it, he predicted that the lucky man had such strong medicine that he would yet capture his assailant, and, to strengthen his power, the whole tribe was ordered to commence the bear-dance immediately, and to keep it up until the next morning. The mandate was promptly complied with, and each brave, donning his bear mask or skin, danced as he had never done before, while the vocal appeal of all to the great bear spirit to be kind to them was sung with the greatest *esprit*. As soon as they had imitated all the attitudes and cries of the bear with mouth, hands, and feet, Tarpello jumped into the bounding circle and roared and danced like a mad man, or bear; but every time he attempted to escape he was driven back, no matter how sudden his onslaughts were, nor how varied his stratagems. When the dance was over, the doctor told him his medicine power and heart were so great that he would kill his foe and bring joy to the whole tribe through his prowess, if he would only follow his advice; and this he promised to do. Having received his instructions, he and two of his kindred started after their burly foe, and, having found its lair, they laid a line of powder toward it from three directions, and perching themselves on trees to the leeward, awaited the arrival of the dreaded brute. Toward nightfall it was heard approaching; and having allowed it to get comfortably settled in bed, they fired the powder-trails, then ran for shelter to a large crag that lay on the route in which the villanous saltpetre was not placed. The powder, when ignited, spluttered along rapidly and set the grass and dry twigs on fire; and it was not long before the blaze reached the lair and sent "Ephraim" out in a tremendous hurry, and thoroughly frightened. Making for the only pathway free from fire, it ambled rapidly onward; but on reaching the rock on which its enemies were concealed, it was checked suddenly in its course by having blazing pine knots thrown before it. Before it could decide what the new danger was, it received volley after volley from the repeating rifles of the Indians, who were guided in their aim by the lighted torches, and it soon laid a corpse at their feet. Highly elated with their success, they dragged the carcass to camp on an improvised sledge made of boughs, and held a carnival over it for two or three days. All the members of the tribe celebrated the victory by a feast on the body, and by indulging in dances; while the slayers related their deeds with all the extravagant language of their race. This daring act made them famous at once, and they were conceded to be the highest type of warriors. From that day forth they always wore a necklace made of the claws of the bear as a proof of their bravery and importance.

An Indian who can wear such ornaments is considered to be an invincible warrior; hence one of his highest ambitions is to slay the monarch of the mountains, and to decorate his inodorous neck with its weapons of warfare. I remember distinctly with what, to me, seemed ludicrous dignity or gravity, a Sioux chief once pointed out a string of ugly-looking grizzly claws that hung around his dirty

NECKLACE OF BEARS' CLAWS.

neck, and then to the anklets of the same material that encircled his blanket-clad legs, and in what a heroic tone he assured me that he had killed their former owner himself, and was now considered to be unrivalled as a brave. He thought that if the Great Father in Washington knew he was so great he would send him plenty of meat, flour, tea, coffee, and sugar, and keep him from the necessity of going out buffalo-hunting to keep his family from starvation. He wished me to tell the Great Father who he really was, and what were his wants; and when I, to test the generous phase of an Indian's nature, volunteered to do so on condition that he gave me the prized trophies, he rejected my offer at once, and said he would not part with them on any account; he would rather lose his favorite wife first. When he saw that I seemed indifferent to the matter, he said that if I could procure him permission to hunt in the Republican Valley he would give me one claw; and when I told him I would not have such articles, as I could get them, if I wished, by simply going on a hunt myself, he looked rather astonished, if an Indian can express that feeling, and grunted out an "uch" of disapprobation, as if he thought I was lessening his importance.

A Nez Perce sub-chief whom I met in Idaho was also exceedingly proud of a necklace of the same material which he wore, and strutted around among his compeers as if he felt that none could approach him in dignity and courage.

Hunting the grizzly has its comic side sometimes as well as its tragic, though the former is too often the result or sequence of the latter. I knew a man in Wyoming named Grizzly Bill—an individual who was equally fond of a joke and a hunt, but who had a thorough contempt for cold water. All the temperance lecturers in the world could not induce him to look with favor on "Adam's ale," and he had a standing joke which was uttered many times a day when he was in a certain humor. This was, "Look here, boys! don't drink water; you oughtn't to. You know that it rots boots; and if it rots boots, what will it do to a man's stomach? Let's have a drink, boys." When he had become well acquainted with John Barleycorn, he was always willing to tell how he received his sobriquet, and he told his tale with such inimitable and unctuous humor that an anchorite would laugh at it. Detailed in a few words, it was, that while out "prospecting" for gold one day in the Wind River Mountains, he was suddenly startled out of his wits by the muffled roar and the charge of a grizzly bear. Not knowing what to do under the circumstances, he did what most men would do—he fired at the animal, then ran for it. As the bear was closing on him, he sought safety in the first tree he met, and that was a young fir. Climbing up this with all the speed of terror, he was comfortably seated on the strongest branch before his pursuer reached the foot. The latter then commenced a regular siege by placing its paws against the tree, looking savagely upward, and growling spitefully at intervals. Bill, feeling safe, took matters philosophically until he began to get hungry toward evening, when he commenced hurling epithets at the besieger, and told it in vigorous language that it was of mean descent, and was anything but a "gentleman" of a bear. This having no effect, he tried to hit it in the eye with cones; but this act only increased its anger, and caused it to shake the tree violently, as if it would like to shake him down.

Having used up all the cones within his immediate reach, Bill tried to get at some others, and this produced a catastrophe he had not expected, for the bough on which he had been sitting had been steadily giving way under his weight; and when the pressure was removed from the strongest to one of its weakest points by his movements, it gave way at once, and he went downward with lightning speed. He thought, of course, that it was all up with him; but when he reached the base of the perch, instead of falling into the jaws of the grizzly, he came plump on its head. The sudden onslaught and shock terrified the bear so much that it fled with the utmost precipitancy, nor did it halt until it reached a place of safety. Bill felt so joyous at this unexpected piece of good fortune that he commenced dancing vigorously, and, after doing several double-shuffles and a breakdown, he picked up his rifle and returned to camp, highly elated with his adventure. He told his comrades the story, but they would not believe it until they saw the broken tree and the bear-tracks. They, of course, told it to others, and Bill received his name. When a little merry he would boast good-humoredly that he was the only man in the Territory that had defeated a grizzly with his feet alone, and would defy anybody else to accomplish the same feat.

The Earl of Southesk relates a somewhat similar incident of two Indians who were treed by a grizzly in British America. The tree in which they took refuge was a mere pole, having only one lateral branch, and on this the first one up seated himself, while his companion had to try and hold on around the trunk with his arms and legs. Such a state of things could not, as a matter of course, last long, and the wretched man below, as his strength was giving way, felt that there were only a few minutes between himself and eternity. When he thought of his wife and young family, he burst into tears and lamentations, and was looked upon with contempt for doing so by the individual safe above. The fatal moment came at length, when his strength was exhausted, and abandoning himself to what he could not prevent, he closed his eyes and slipped helplessly down the tree; but, fortunately for him, the bear was on a line beneath him, and he fell on its back. This was a most unexpected meeting to the grizzly, and the result was that it fled in the wildest panic. Seeing the coast clear, the "percher" came down, and accompanied the grizzly-driver to the encampment; but the latter, fearing that his actions had been anything but heroic, and that he would be an object of ridicule among his people if they were described, offered his companion several presents if he would preserve secrecy about the matter; and this he promised, but not until after he had stripped the poor fellow of everything he possessed. A few months later the percher got drunk, and went all over the camp proclaiming his companion's disgrace, and ridiculing him. The latter was so incensed at this outrage that he procured a rifle, and going to where the scandal-monger was uttering his sentiments, shot him dead before all his auditors. These two incidents might prove that the most effective means of routing a grizzly is to go up a tree and tumble down on it suddenly; yet I would not advise any person to try it.

Judge—we may say Blank—of San Francisco, a famous Nimrod and lover of good wine, had an adventure once with a grizzly that displayed both humor and courage. Having been elected one of a select few that were going out for a week's shooting among the grouse and quail, he was asked to be ready to join the party at a very early hour in the morning, so that a camping-place could be reached in the afternoon. He agreed on condition that a generous supply of a certain fluid was taken along, and, his proposition being accepted, everything was made ready for a prompt start. The night before starting he attended a ball, and before morning was so much under the influence of his favorite beverage that he tumbled in the mire several times on his way home, much to the detriment of his evening-dress and opera-hat. He had scarcely entered his room before a carriage called to take him to the rendezvous, and, despite the earnest protestation of his friends, he insisted upon going in the costume he wore, or not at all. As his wit and humor were much needed to enliven camp in the evening, he was taken as he stood; and the party having united, they started for the mountains about forty miles distant, and there pitched the camp, and lighted a fire at once to prepare supper. While that was being cooked, a Spaniard approached the group and stated that there was a grizzly a few rods off in the bushes. He was asked why he did not kill it, and he nonchalantly replied that he had lost no bears. The judge, who was dozing near the ashes, jumped up when he heard grizzly mentioned, and said that he would bring it into camp.

His seedy appearance and the quaintness of his hunting costume caused his companions to greet his heroic boast with roars of laughter, and to chaff him unmercifully; but his mettle was up, and with a half-drunken leer he said he would prove it; and, seizing an empty shot-gun, he strode into the shrubbery. He was not gone more than twenty minutes before a tremendous commotion was heard in the bushes, and they were seen to sway in every direction. The party were alarmed at once, and all seized their weapons and prepared for some unknown danger. They had hardly taken their positions before the bushes parted, and out came the judge minus a hat, and running with such speed as to cause his hair and coat-tails to flow backward in rigid lines. As he approached his bewildered companions, he shouted at the top of his voice, " Clear the track; here we come, the *bear* and *me*, d—n our souls!" They did clear the track, and the limb of the law rushed through the fire, nor did he stop until he had run a good half-mile to the rear. A few yells and shots checked the pursuing Bruin, and caused it to retreat; so the foolhardy Blackstone escaped without suffering any greater injury than a good scare, and being made the butt of many a joke. When the party returned to town, the escapade of the judge was told to all his friends; and they decided at once that the bear pursued him to get some of the wine out of him, as it knew that he generally carried enough for himself and the four largest grizzlies in the country, and it was resolved to have a share of it if possible.

They tell some humorous tales in the West of how men have killed grizzlies. One man, on being attacked, took out his whiskey-bottle and gave the bear a smell of its contents, and it fell dead at once, after giving a long howl of agony. This story is intended to show the vileness of the stuff sold in certain sections of the country; and a vender of strong fluids, if not liked, is sometimes called a grizzly-killer. Another man was said to be so ugly that a bear, on seeing him, committed suicide by hurling itself into a precipice; and a ranting, long-winded, dreary preacher was said to be so strong in lungs and larynx as to be able to blow a grizzly into eternity in three howls.

Notwithstanding the dangerous character of the animal in its wild state, it is capable of being tamed, if taken young, and, if treated kindly, will follow one about like a dog, until it learns to know its strength; and then it is apt to assert its will and power at inconvenient times. I have seen several of them in a state of semi-domestication in some places on the Pacific Coast, but in no instance would they bear too much familiarity when they reached adult age; while they were the deadly enemies of anything in the form of flesh, from a dog, pig, or chicken to a rat. When the male and female are caged together they indulge in the most unseemly family quarrels, and fight viciously for the least morsel of food. The former is a most ungallant brute, and the embodiment of selfishness. From what I have seen of its character, I should say that "bearishness" was a much more appropriate word for expressing the lowest type of self-interest than that homely old word "hoggishness," for the *suidæ* are exceedingly generous compared to the grizzly. Its mode of living when wild is not such as to arouse our sympathy either, as it preys on the most wretched little creatures, such as ants, mice, rats, and squirrels, and, not content with destroying them, it devours their small stores of nuts and roots. Like its black congener, it is also fond of berries, honey, and the pomona, and will risk its life to obtain either. As few persons—perhaps no one—make a business of hunting this animal, it is not often shot, as it is only occasionally met with, and, in most cases, accidentally. It is not, fortunately, very common; and as it avoids the haunts of man, it does not do much harm to the farm-yard.

Those who go out for a grizzly hunt make it a matter of sport, if I except the Indians, and, if they seek its abode, it is for the purpose of adorning themselves with its claws, and boasting of their prowess. They catch it sometimes in pitfalls; and the Sioux formerly chased it on horseback, when they found it on open ground, and filled it with arrows or pierced it with rude lances. The Mexicans of California formerly captured it most deftly with lariats; but to do this several were required. Their first movement was to charge past it, if it stood erect, and lasso its paws, and, if successful in this, they entangled it in their lariats, and used their active mustangs to drag it to a convenient spot, where it was either killed or safely penned up until it was wanted for a contest with a fierce bull. These contests were once popular, and were the great feature of holidays, but they are now becoming rarer, owing to the advance of civilization and the interposition of the law.

For one man to kill a grizzly single-handed is no ordinary event, owing to the quantity of lead it can carry, the promptitude with which it can generally retreat to cover or charge its foe, and to the often inaccessible haunts which it frequents; yet it is done occasionally by experienced hunters. A small party of English gentlemen killed seven last year in Colorado; two sportsmen killed six in Dakota in a month; and I knew a hunter in Montana to kill one with an army revolver by firing at it from a tree. Numbers are poisoned annually in several parts of the West, especially in Colorado, Montana, California, and British America; hence they are getting scarce in the more frequented sections of the country, and the survivors keep to regions remote from settlements, except during unusually severe weather, when they make raids on farm-yards. They are almost as abundant as ever, though, in Dakota, Montana, Wyoming, and Idaho; but the sooner they begin to decrease in these Territories the better will farmers and stock-raisers like it, as they are considered anything but pleasant acquaintances.

I have hunted the grizzly occasionally, but generally in company with others; and while we killed one now and then, yet no person could tell which had given the death-shot, so that none could claim the honor. I bagged a large male myself one time, but it was done in such a prosaic manner that the only interesting thing about it was the death. I was passing through a rugged precipice, trying to stalk a band of mountain sheep, and, on reaching a small abutment of loose rocks, I saw grizzly lapping up some water beneath me. Taking deliberate aim at his head near the ear, I fired, and a few moments later he fell over as stiff as a stone. On examining him, I found that the bullet had entered the brain through the ear, and produced death almost immediately. The whole thing was so simple that I scarcely felt a thrill of pleasure on gazing at my trophy, and I left it where it fell, in the most unconcerned manner, until my hunt after the sheep was over, and then I had it sent for by the pioneer at whose house I was stopping.

Grizzlies are most destructive visitors to a camp—a fact which I learned on more than one occasion. The most disagreeable visit that I ever received from one, however, was during a trip I was making with a party of Indians who were on their way to a pow-wow of their tribe, which was called to meet a newly-appointed agent and hear his statements. The band which I accompanied consisted of twenty men, with their squaws and children, and many horses, and that was commanded by a now famous sub-chief, who was said to be equally great in the hunting-field and on the war-path. Our route led over vast treeless prairies and densely wooded hills, until the evening of the second day, when we reached a mountain four or five thousand feet high. Selecting a beautiful glade for a camp site, the *tepees* were soon erected by the squaws, mine being pitched a short distance to the right of the front line. In this I placed little delicacies not used by the red men, namely, condensed milk, tea, coffee, and sugar, and some biscuits, and left them there confidently, while I accompanied the braves on a hunt after deer, as we had no fresh meat for dinner. When we returned late in the evening we found the squaws and children in a state of commotion, and, on inquiring the meaning of it, learned that a male grizzly had visited the camp during their absence in search of wild roots and fruits, and had destroyed several parcels of dried beef, torn some of the tents, and killed two combative curs.

On hearing this, I rushed to my *tepee* to see if my little stores were injured, but, on reaching it, I was disgusted and enraged to find all my delicacies either eaten up or trampled into an indiscriminate mess on the ground. The cans of condensed milk, a bag of biscuits, and all the sugar had been devoured, and the other articles were strewn about in the mud, so that they were of no use to me. On seeing this condition of affairs, I called on the chief, and learned from him that several of his tribe had lost all their pemmican, and were actually without any food, except the few roots and berries gathered by the squaws, and their share of the venison just brought in. All were so angry at the action of the burly prowler that they decided to have his head if possible; but for fear he would visit the camp during the night and inflict any more damage on the remaining food, or on man and beast, they concluded to pitch the camp in a deep chasm a short distance away. Into this we marched, accordingly, after dinner; but we experienced much difficulty in getting the horses to the bottom, owing to the steepness of the walls and the difficulty of getting a foothold. On reaching the base, the *tepees* were soon erected, and, when this was done, the horses were let loose to pick up such herbage as they could find during the night.

The inmates of the encampment then retired to rest, and I should judge that they were soon asleep, as I saw no one stirring about; but I found it impossible to woo gentle slumber, owing to the strangeness of my surroundings. The chasm was, in the first place, so deep and gloomy that the darkness was fairly inky in hue, and so dense that all that could be seen were the shadowy walls and the twinkling stars, which seemed to be unusually far away. A turbulent river roared past the camp with such power and velocity that the air appeared to vibrate; and, to increase the din, several ospreys, which occupied islets in the stream, screamed in the loudest manner at intervals, as if they objected to the intrusion on their domain. The whole scene, which was weird in the extreme, and seemed to belong to another planet, or to the land of the ogres rather than to this earth, impressed me so much that I could not sleep, so I laid and tossed on my hard couch on the ground all night. I often sighed for the morning, and was delighted on seeing the first gray glimmering of the dawn in the sky above. On noticing this, I seized my rifle, and started out to find my mustang, for I was rather afraid that he might have tumbled into the river during the night, as it hugged the banks so closely in some places that there was no shoreline, and not even a talus, owing to the strength of the current. Groping my way to the right of the camp, I followed the courses of crags or the few open spots where a long, dank grass grew in profusion, and in half an hour reached a rock which gave me a good view some distance up the river. I waited there until the light was strong enough to enable one to note objects distinctly, and when that time came I saw the horses huddled together on a sort of cape that jutted a considerable way out into the stream. On approaching them, I saw that they were trembling with fright, and, on looking for the cause of it, I beheld a large object crouching on the ground about sixty yards away, and, on gazing at it intently for a short time, I concluded that it was either a bear or a cougar, and that it was feasting on something. Taking deliberate aim at it, I fired, and, when the report died away, I could hear the gruff "huff, huff," of a grizzly; but ere I could load the second time it had disappeared behind a mass of crags.

The shot had alarmed the camp and brought the armed warriors rushing toward me, and, in response to their inquiries, I told them in one word what was up. Calling the dogs, we followed the bear, and were soon on its tracks, passing on our way a partially eaten mustang. The route led us up the precipice and into a piece of woods, and there the trail was lost by both dogs and men. Being resolved to have the animal if possible, the men deployed, and were soon carefully examining every fallen leaf and blade of grass in search of Bruin's footsteps. While engaged in this business, I was startled suddenly by the abrupt yelling of a pack of curs directly behind me, and, on bounding round to see what it meant, was thunderstruck to see a huge male grizzly bearing down on me, while the dogs yelped and barked around him, yet took excellent care not to go too near him. I had just time enough to jump behind a young fir when he went tearing past me through the undergrowth, but before he had proceeded ten paces I gave him the contents of my breechloader, a large army rifle. I must have struck him badly, for he turned round and charged me viciously; and as no other means of escape then presented itself to my mind, I scrambled up the tree near which I stood with all the speed that the fear of a horrible death could impart to limbs that were neither old nor weak.

I had not reached a perch before my foe was at the base

of the tree, but I was beyond the reach of his jaws; and this gave me such a feeling of safety that I turned my head round to gaze at his position. I could see his huge jaws agape, and hear his hot breath come out in gasps, as if he were severely wounded; and on noticing these incidents I scrambled on a strong bough, and seated myself on it with a feeling of pleasure one can only know who has been in the same position. On looking down once more, I saw the dogs worrying my besieger; but he seemed to take little notice of them, and to devote all his attention to my situation. In a few moments more he was in full retreat, however, for on every side of him were howling Indians who were plying bow or rifle as rapidly as possible. The raising of the siege induced me to descend at once, and, picking up my rifle, which was uninjured, I loaded it, and joined in the chase with five others. Not finding any opportunity to fire to good advantage, I reserved my fire; and fortunate did this prove for a heedless brave in a short time, for while the grizzly was rushing through a dense piece of shrubbery, this young warrior placed himself directly in front of him at less than thirty paces, and fired straight into his face; but he must have missed his aim, for the bear charged him with open mouth, and, before he could escape by running, overtook him, knocked the rifle out of his hand, and, seizing him by the shoulder, bore him to the ground face downward. The brave drew his knife promptly, and, turning partially round, began to use it on the neck and chest of his huge captor; but he was evidently getting the worst of it, for the bear was using teeth and claws with a vigor that must soon have finished him had not aid arrived.

While both were struggling fiercely in this contest of life and death, the chief and myself appeared on the scene from opposite quarters, and, rushing toward the foe, I delivered my fire at his heart at a distance of a few paces; and before he could relinquish his hold to face us, the chief gave him the contents of a revolver in rapid succession in the head, and he fell over dead, after giving one or two violent gasps. The fallen man was picked up more dead than alive, as his arm and chest were fearfully lacerated, his face was one mass of blood, and his side had the flesh torn off from the arm to the abdomen. He was a most ghastly object to gaze at, and, as his limp form was borne away, I did not expect to see him reach camp alive. When re-enforcements arrived several lariats were sent for, and with these the fallen monarch was dragged near the canyon, and left there while we went to get some breakfast. When that was finished, the bear was skinned, and the flesh distributed equally among all the hunters; but it became a delicate question as to who should receive the claws. I relinquished all pretensions to them, however, in the promptest manner, and this was reciprocated by the chief giving me the hide. The claws were then divided between the chief and the wounded warrior; and the latter, I know, felt as delighted with them as if he had captured the scalps of several of his foes.

As the injured man could not be moved, it was decided to rest one day to see if he would improve; and if not, to leave him behind and push ahead as rapidly as possible to make up for lost time. A second reason for remaining a day longer in camp, though it was only mentioned incidentally, was to procure meat; for the destruction committed by the grizzly had placed several on very short rations, and his flesh could not supply the loss. The women were commanded to secure wood for the fires, and while they were engaged in that work the braves went on a deer-hunt. Their success was greater than could be expected, owing to the abundance of the animals and their unsuspicious character, as most of them had probably never seen man; so twelve mule-deer were brought into camp in the evening. When we began to draw near the wigwams we heard the wailing of women, and this announced to us at once the fact that the young brave was dead. On entering the canyon, I noticed that all the female friends of the deceased were grouped around his tent and howling fearfully, while his aged father and his brothers sat apart in gloomy silence.

Every person in camp visited the *tepee* of the young man and took a last glance at his features; but they were so ghastly that I was glad to hasten away and forget their expression. No person indulged in a word of condolence to his parents, and the only comments I heard made by the men was a simple " too bad." As the chief would not wait another day in camp, the friends of the deceased dug a rude grave, and placed him and all his paraphernalia in it, without any other covering than his clothes. When this simple and hurried ceremony was over, two of his mustangs and three dogs were killed, and their skins placed on a pole above the grave, in order that he might have some useful animals in the happy hunting-grounds. To spend another night in this wild chasm was anything but a pleasant anticipation to me, yet there was no avoiding it, so I made up my mind to bear it as philosophically as possible. Disagreeable as the previous night had been, I found the second much worse; for not only were the same noises in operation, but they were increased by the moaning of weeping women, the guttural gabble of men grouped around the camp-fires, and occasionally by the melancholy howling of packs of gaunt wolves that prowled over the ground above in search of food. I did manage to get a little sleep, however, late in the night, but, when roused in the morning, I felt as weary as if I had not closed my eyes.

After a hasty breakfast, the camp was struck and the march resumed, but not a word was uttered by anybody about the name or fate of the deceased; but what struck me as most curious was the apparent absence of all signs of grief on the features of his kindred, for they laughed and chatted as gayly as if they had never known a sorrow, and certainly not one so recent. We reached the pow-wow two days after, and remained in attendance for three days; and after a lot of useless talk and idle ceremony had been indulged in between the Indians belonging to the reservation, the agent, and a superintendent of Indian affairs, we turned backward on our route, and reached once more the old camp near the chasm; but the band would not pitch their wigwams there, owing to their belief that it was a fatal spot, and was haunted by the spirit of the brave. Being anxious to see again the place that had so deeply impressed itself on my memory, I descended the chasm and visited the grave; but, on reaching it, I was horror-stricken to find that the wolves had scraped up the body and eaten it. I saw that the remains of the mustang killed by the grizzly had also been devoured by the same hungry creatures, and could then readily understand why some of them are one mass of sores in some portions of the West. The sightless, fleshless skull of the brave, with its long, lank hair, was so displeasing a sight to me that I was glad to beat a retreat, and get out of the savage chasm to the gentle glade and generous forest above. When I reached camp I did not mention a word of what I had seen to anybody, but on arriving at our destination I told it to the chief; but he manifested no feeling whatsoever in the matter, and did not even make a comment, although I was very careful not to use the name of the brave, knowing how scrupulous they are about referring to the dead.

A comrade and myself killed a grizzly one day in Wyoming by running it down on horseback, but not until after we had planted its body with bullets. While riding toward a frontier post we espied the bear pottering about a few cotton-woods that grew on the bank of a small stream. On seeing it, we dashed forward, firing; and both found, when we got to within seventy or eighty yards of it, that our bullets evidently went wide of the mark, for, instead of attempting to run away, it raised itself on its hind-legs, as if it were willing to face all foes in a sparring or wrestling match. The attitude was so gravely ludicrous that I was forced to laugh at it; but my companion, who could see nothing funny in it, thought he could see a good chance for a shot, and he availed himself of it by sending a bullet somewhere into its body. This seemed to impress upon it the idea that mere attitude was nothing, and that its visitors were not pleasant creatures to know; so it concluded that discretion was the better part of valor, and, acting on this idea, it moved toward the open ground at a rate of speed that surprised me. We started in pursuit, and kept delivering our fire at its back and head, being afraid to range ourselves on its sides for fear we might shoot each other. Finding this mode ineffective, we concluded to rush past it, one at a time, and shoot at it with our heavy revolvers, then wheel back and give a return fire. I moved first, through the courtesy of my companion, and delivered two shots in rapid succession at its sides, hoping to cripple it, and wheeling back on the opposite side, after running about a hundred yards ahead of it, got in two more. These forced it to halt and growl terribly, as if in pain. My companion did exactly as I had done, and we repeated the movement until we had emptied our revolvers. The animal had staggered three or four times, charged twice, and fallen once, while this fusillade was taking place, and finally halted, one of its shoulders having been broken. This was the opportunity we wanted; so, taking deliberate aim at its head with our rifles, we fired, and it fell dead in its tracks. An examination proved that it had eight bullets in it, one of which was in the heart, one in the fore-shoulder, two in the skull, and the remainder scattered over the body. Those in the brain were what had slain it, for one of them entered the occipital region and broke the bone. We found it to be a full-grown male, but it was very thin. My companion skinned it rapidly, and kindly gave me the hide; but, notwithstanding all my pains with it, some red man is now probably using it, as it was captured, with other cherished articles, by the Indians during one of their raids on a wagon-train.

While accompanying a party of Indian scouts in the Government service, on another occasion, I had a most unheroic contest with a grizzly, and one which might be left untold but for the fact that it proves the affection of the female for her cubs. After a hard day's march, the camp was pitched in a pine forest on a high hill, and, when supper was over and the horses were picketed, all retired to rest except one vedette and a horse-guard of two men.

As we were thoroughly tired, we slept so soundly that no noise could be heard, for even the drowsy sentinels who relieved each other were too fatigued to indulge in talk. Suddenly, about midnight, several rifle reports were heard in rapid succession; and thinking this an attack by the red foes of whom the expedition was in search, we rolled out of our blankets, seized our arms, and prepared for a contest of life and death, for we did not care to lose our scalps without making the enemy pay dearly for them. After the first alarm was over, inquiries were made as to the cause of the firing, and we learned from the guard over the horses that a grizzly had been prowling about the camp, and they were afraid that it would attack themselves or the animals under their charge, unless they shot at it and drove it away. After receiving a severe reprimand for raising a needless alarm, and firing without consulting their superior officer, the encampment was once more in sound repose. On awaking the next morning, we concluded to go in search of the disturber of our sleep, and to secure its hide as a forfeit for its daring. An examination of the ground was first made, and that revealed the tracks of a female and her two cubs; and this caused us to feel somewhat elated, as we hoped to have some stirring amusement. Selecting eight men for the hunt, and leaving the remainder in camp, much to their disgust, we followed the trail until it was lost in the dense shrubbery. This forced us to spread out, and each commenced a search for himself. I was on the extreme left of the party, and my course led me along the banks of a deep canyon and through heavy timber. While standing listlessly near a large crag, and almost despairing of meeting any bears, I saw a cub about six months old groping about on the outer margin of some undergrowth. Thinking that it was alone, I fired at it, and hit it, I fancy, in the abdomen, from the jump it gave; and, before it could move off, I delivered a second shot as it wheeled around, and tumbled it over. Presuming that I had mortally wounded it, although it was growling and groaning fearfully, I advanced at a run to finish it; but I had not gone twenty yards before I saw the dam sniffing around it and caressing it. She evidently thought something had injured it, for, on lifting her head, she gazed about as if in search of a foe. Seeing me standing in plain sight — for I halted on seeing her — she charged me promptly and fiercely. I fired at her once, but I suppose I missed her; and not having time to reload, I broke for the shelter of the chasm. Dashing, or rather tumbling, down its side at a headlong pace, I was soon at the bottom and clambering up the opposite side; and on reaching the crest I looked around for my pursuer, but she was not visible. The firing brought some of the party to my aid in a few minutes, and, thus re-enforced, I went in search of the cub; but, on reaching the place where it lay, we found only a large pool of blood, and a zigzag trail of the same material which led into the heaviest part of the undergrowth.

Knowing that the dam was exceedingly fierce at the treatment of her offspring, and not caring to meet her in the dense shrubbery, it was deemed the wisest plan not to pursue her; for we did not want to have any dead or wounded men to dispose of, and we were anxious to resume the march in order to get some tidings of the red foe who was then on the war-path, and whose movements we were employed to watch. I learned on that occasion from an Indian hunter that the female, when she is accompanied by her cubs, is much more dangerous than the male, even in the rutting season, and that she will boldly face anything living that may approach or threaten her darlings. As an instance of this, he related the case of a friend of his who captured a cub about two months old, and was hastening homeward with it, when he was suddenly arrested by hearing some animal tearing through the bushes behind him. Looking around, he saw a female grizzly bounding toward him at her best pace, her eyes all aflame with rage, and her mouth frothing. Knowing that he could not escape her if he stuck to his prize, he threw it on the ground and fled; but the mother did not stop in her course on account of meeting her cub, and pursued him until he disappeared from her sight in a precipice. Feeling safe there, the red man halted to ease his breathing, and he could then hear the loud yet gruff calls of the mother to her cub. He felt so thankful for his hairbreadth escape then that he never tried cub-stealing again, for, in his opinion, an enraged grizzly mother is as bad and fierce as the spirits of evil.

One of the pleasantest chases after grizzlies that I ever enjoyed came off in Southern California. The party, myself excepted, was composed of Greasers, or native Californians, and two Mexican Spaniards. As the hunt was organized for the special purpose of driving the bears out of a section of country where they were committing sad havoc among sheep, we selected the best and most experienced mustangs to be found in a large area, and, arming ourselves with rifles and revolvers, we started for the foot-hills from our rendezvous at 5 P.M., and encamped that night under the shade of some oak-trees, having built a rousing fire to keep away all quadrupedal intruders. After supper we devoted ourselves assiduously up to midnight to puffing cigarettes, singing songs, and relating hunting experiences. The last "story" was told by a swarthy old veteran, and according to that he had killed a bear single-handed with only a hunting-knife, by simply evading a blow of its paw, and then cutting its jugular vein before it could meet his attack. Having slept soundly, we awoke promptly at 4 A.M., and, after partaking of a light breakfast, we loaded our rifles and revolvers, and saddled our steeds, and were in motion in less than an hour.

Deploying in skirmishing order, and in the form of a crescent, we advanced toward a coppice of oaks half a mile in front, which grizzlies were known to frequent. We were accompanied by a dozen mongrel dogs of many breeds, and they were taken by one of the party to the top of a hill, so that they might drive the quarry toward us. He took the precaution to keep to the leeward of the copse, for if even the daring grizzly caught the odor of humanity, it would sometimes think it the better part of valor to beat a rapid retreat. The captain of the skirmish-line gave us orders how to move by the wave of his hand, and all obeyed most promptly. On reaching the wood, we held the reins tighter, grasped the saddle closer with our legs, and placed the barrel of the rifle in the crook of the left arm. This was no sooner done than the dogs gave tongue; the chorus became loud, then broken and general, and in a few minutes after a splendid male grizzly emerged from the bushes, about one hundred yards distant. When he saw the circle around him he hesitated a moment; but the noise of the dogs soon decided his movements, and he made for the opening in front. Bang went a rifle, followed in a second by another. My horse, which had been restless, now showed undoubted terror; he wheeled, and was making for the rear at his best pace; but when I got the reins out of my mouth and into my hands, I gave the Spanish bit a touch that nearly threw him on his haunches, and, wheeling him, I made for my place in the crescent. I found my mustang was not alone in his fright, for I saw two more making their best strides for home. When I reached my position, Bruin was making for that direction, as it was the only opening left. I fired at him twice in rapid succession; but at this moment my mustang became alarmed again at the object approaching, and wheeled to the rear. He had not gone far ere I checked him; caused him to make a demi-volt, and got another shot. Bullets were whizzing thickly around his bearship at this time, and he did not go five yards farther ere he fell, groaning, to the ground, and bleeding profusely. Two revolver-shots in the head finished him, and our prize lay outstretched before us in all his inanimate majesty. Who killed him? Every one was willing to bet or swear that he had hit him, yet, on examining the body, only three bullets were found, though fifty must have been fired. The whole time occupied by this contest did not exceed ten minutes, yet it would seem as though a small army was firing, so rapidly were the leaden missiles poured forth.

After the death the assembly was sounded by a loud halloo, and the runaways returned, swearing, as only Spaniards can, at their ill-luck and their cowardly steeds. Having dragged the bear into some bushes, we reformed our line, and moved in an oblique direction to the right, where the manzanita grew thickly. The dogs had scarcely entered the shrubbery ere a simultaneous yelp made us all halt, and in a few moments a female broke cover; but seeing the number of enemies surrounding her, she re-entered the bushes and made for a ravine on the right. Her course was marked by the swaying of the shrubbery, so to the right we all started at the best speed of our horses, intending to head her off. We had scarcely proceeded half a mile ere we struck a canyon, and into this we had the chagrin of seeing our game hurl herself, for she apparently went to the bottom at one stride. That she was not injured, however, was proved by the yelping of the dogs, which pursued her for over a mile; but I may add that they took very good care not to go too near her.

As we could not do much in the heat of the day, we concluded to return to camp and await the morrow for the resumption of our sport. During the evening, while lying around the fire, everybody was telling just how he missed or hit the bear; but who hit him is to this day a mystery, for the greater number insisted that their bullets struck just where the holes were found. Whoever reached the vicinity of the heart, however, was the champion. The action of our veteran mustangs was accounted for on the ground that Bruin emerged too suddenly, so did not give them time to think. This may have been the cause, but to me it looked like want of courage and experience. Our camp was the scene of hilarity that evening, and the song, "*Hermosa esta la noche*," was sung many times over, and with immense gusto, as all were pleased with the success achieved.

We started out the next morning at six o'clock, and worked up a piece of woods half a mile from the coppice of the previous day, but it proved a blank draw. While we were passing from this to another promising country, we espied a grizzly and her two cubs playing together in a dell in the most affectionate manner; and as we felt sure that they could not escape, we watched their ludicrous and clumsy antics for some moments with keen interest. When weary of that, the dogs and a huntsman were sent to the windward in order to drive the animals to the leeward, where we posted ourselves. As soon as the hounds came in sight of the bears they set up a tremendous yelping, and charged them boldly; but they reckoned without their host, for the entire party stood boldly at bay, and did not make even an effort to avoid their canine foes; and when the dogs came to close quarters the cubs drew near their dam, and all raised themselves on their hind-legs, as if they were willing and ready for the contest.

The dogs tried to get a nip at them, but their effort was in vain, for their ungainly opponents met them in every direction, and frequently charged them in return; but their canine caution and nimbleness enabled them to escape all blows and attempts at a hug. The old grizzly finally became so angry at their pertinacious annoyance that she rushed suddenly at one that approached very close, and, giving him a sweeping blow with her paw, killed him as easily as she would a mouse by crushing his skull. While she was engaged in this affair, half a dozen of the dogs surrounded the cubs and gave them several severe nips, which caused them to howl fearfully, and their cries brought the dam back in a hurry to aid them; but before she could come up, one of the youngsters had killed another of its opponents by breaking his spinal column with a blow, and then biting it through and through. As the entire pack was threatened with destruction if the contest continued, we advanced at a gallop to the scene, and calling the dogs away, though not without much trouble, we opened fire on the old one only, as we wished to lasso the youngsters. When the latter saw the numerous enemies surrounding them they tried to escape into a copse close by, and the mother attempted to follow them; but two or three bullets in her body caused her to stop and face about to deliver battle to her foes. Her eyes fairly gleamed with fury on seeing the men and horses galloping about her; and whenever a cavalier came any way near her she charged him boldly, but only to receive a shot from him or some other person near by. Bullets rained around her from rifle and revolver; but they seemed to have no other effect on her than to rouse her into fury and cause her to charge whenever she had the chance.

A man named Diego Gonzales, becoming incensed at the inefficacy of the fire, or her magical vitality, rode close up to her, as his mustang was well trained, and delivered his fire within ten yards of her face; but he had scarcely discharged his rifle before she bounded toward him; and before he could wheel and get away, she had thrown horse and rider to the ground by one desperate blow. The fallen man drew his revolver, so as to sell his life as dearly as possible; but before he could use it half a dozen men jumped off their terrified mustangs and ran toward her, and, opening fire on the huge beast, they killed her ere she could transfer her attentions from the steed to the rider. When these were examined, we found that the horse was so severely injured that he could not live, while the rider escaped with only a severe contusion of the under side and leg, and the crushing of the ankle-bone. To rid the poor horse of his misery, as his neck and face were horribly cut, he was shot, and Gonzales was taken on a rude litter to camp by four men. The remainder of the party started out after the cubs, and, with the aid of the dogs, we soon found them concealed in a dense growth of manzanita. The party separated on finding them, in order that each might capture one, but, at my request, it was decided not to shoot them there, but to drive them out and capture them alive if possible. When the proposition was agreed to, four of us went after one, and the rest after the other. Driving our cub into open ground, the lariats were soon whirling about its head, and in less than five minutes we had it bound legs and head, so that it could not move either. The other party being equally successful, we placed all our trophies in three wagons and returned to our rendezvous, at the house of Gonzales, as he was

LASSOING A GRIZZLY.

too much injured to be able to indulge in any hunts just then, and all wished to show him how much he was respected. I left the neighborhood a few days afterward, but I learned from a correspondent that over twenty grizzlies were killed in that section during the season, though the greater number were poisoned.

A final word might be said about the position of the grizzly in the animal world. Naturalists have called the lion the "king of beasts," but they evidently knew little of the grizzly at the time they made this decision. If strength and courage are considered as recommendations to royalty in the quadrupedal world, then I think the grizzly ranks above the lion. I have not seen the former perform the feats said to be accomplished by the latter, of trotting away with a heifer in its mouth, as it does not generally carry its prey in that manner, as the *felidæ* do; but I have known it to kill an elk weighing five or six hundred pounds, and, in devouring it, to turn it over with the greatest ease. It, so far as my experience and information go, drags its prey along the ground if heavy, but if light it has been known to carry it between its forelegs. In magnanimity of character, if carnivorous animals can possess such a trait, it is equal to the so-called "king of beasts," for it has been known to wound a buffalo severely, then let the poor creature escape. That it has killed two and three buffaloes at a time with strokes of its huge paws is a well-authenticated fact; and it has been, to reiterate, known to drag a heavy bull, that must have weighed from twelve to eighteen hundred pounds, a long distance. I doubt if a lion can do this, and I am rather inclined to think that in a contest between both animals the grizzly would prove the victor. Sportsmen, unless provided with heavy rifles, would therefore do well to beware of it; for there is not a year, I suppose, that some men are not killed by it, owing principally to their own foolhardiness in attacking it with light weapons, or without the aid of companions.

CHAPTER III.

THE BLACK BEAR.

The Black Bear.—Different Varieties.—Their Haunts, Habits, and General Characteristics.—Affection of Mothers for their Cubs.—Gravid Females never seen.—Migrations of the Bear.—Character of its Flesh. —Its Game Qualities.—Abundance of the Animal in the West.—The best Dogs for chasing it.—How to Hunt it.—Its Acuteness of Nose and Expertness in Swimming.—Captured by Steamers frequently in Puget Sound.—Why it is not Hunted much.—A Hunt with Indians.— The Scenes and Incidents of a *Potlatch.*—Capture of several Bears. —Tripped up while Stalking a Male.—Explosion of Gun.—A Rude Raft, a Wild Ride, and a Collision with a Barricade.—A bad Ducking. —I kill a Bear, and receive a bad Wound in the Arm.—A Canoe Trip, and a Hard Bump.—Reach Camp, and have my Wound dressed.—Return of the Hunters.—An Indian Festival.—How Indians cook Young Bears.—I am mistaken for a Bear by Hunters, and shot at.—Anecdotes of Men attacked by Bears.—A Bear-hunt which results in being Treed.—The Release, and Death of the Besieger.—How a Doctor captured a Bear.—Water *versus* Courage.—A Public Singer and an Imaginary Bear.—The Remuneration given for keeping his Adventure silent.

THE black bear (*Ursus americanus*) is found all over the United States, but it is more abundant in the wooded regions beyond the Rocky Mountains than in any other part of the world; so he who would revel in bear-hunts to his heart's content should seek that country, and spend a season amidst its extensive forests and towering mountain ranges. There are supposed to be two or three species of this animal in the West, but, so far as I could learn, they are all one, the only difference between them being confined to variety of hue; and this is undoubtedly the result of climate and *habitat*.

I have seen on more than one occasion dams accompanied by cubs which displayed distinct colors; some being black, others brown, or a dark cinnamon, and even a piebald color is not uncommon in some sections of the country.

The cinnamon bear is thought by many persons to be larger and fiercer than the black; but such is not my experience, for the largest one of the former that I saw killed did not exceed five hundred pounds in weight, and I knew several of the black variety found in Alaska to turn the scales at six hundred pounds. Some hunters in the Rocky Mountain region call the grizzly the cinnamon bear when its pelage becomes somewhat light in hue at certain seasons; but it is not generally called so, as it is an easy

BLACK BEAR.

matter to distinguish between both species. The common cinnamon variety is not, in my opinion, any more inclined to be fierce than the black, and I have yet to see the first man who has been attacked by it without provocation. A further proof of the three varieties being one species may be deduced from the fact that their claws are of the same form and length, that their fur is of the same texture and length under the same circumstances, and that the flesh of one tastes exactly like that of the other, all things being equal. I have been explicit in making these statements, because some writers, and even some experienced hunters, have assumed that the cinnamon is a modified grizzly, and is equally as dangerous, and as ready to fight without cause. My experience of it is, however, that it has the same habits as its black congener; that it is no more dangerous; and that it will flee from the presence of man unless it is wounded, very hungry, or laboring under the excitement of the rutting season; and even then a lusty shout is liable to scatter a regiment of its tribe.

The American bear has forty-two teeth, and I have heard or read that it has one tooth more than the European species. It is naturally sluggish in character, and keeps to the densest parts of the woods, where the shrubbery is most profuse. Its usual haunts are caverns or hollow trees, and in these retreats it passes away a large portion of its time in dozing and sleeping. It is ever on the alert for foes, however, and unless the hunter approaches its lair from the leeward, he is liable to be detected by the apparent sluggard. It is omnivorous in taste; and it seems to matter little to it whether it eats ants, grubs, eggs, berries, roots, grapes and fruit generally, or mice, moles, squirrels, and other small animals. Its presence may be readily detected in the woods during the summer by the large number of berries stripped off the bushes, and the torn condition of the soil where it has been digging for roots. In the Far North-west it frequents thickets where a species of buckthorn (*Frangula purshiana*) grows, and devours its fruit with great gusto, though to man it proves a violent cathartic. I have seldom known a bear to attack other animals of large size unless provoked to do so by hunger, and, when that was appeased, it relapsed into its usual harmless condition. This quiet disposition is readily accounted for by its dental formation; for that proves at once that nature intended it to live principally on fruits, vegetables, and roots. Its greatest weakness of appetite seems to be a fondness for honey, and, to obtain that, it will face the attacks of all the bees on earth, even if they should cause its muzzle to swell to the size of a small balloon. Having a very sweet tooth, it is also attached to sugar, and I have seen two of them fight in the most vicious manner for a lump so small that an ant would almost scorn to notice it. I used, at one time, to enjoy keenly sending a brace of cubs racing up a tree for a piece of sugar or honey; and when they reached the spot in which it was concealed, they would commence growling, moaning, and quarrelling if they did not secure it at once. Whichever got it first ran away with it; but the other resented such selfishness, and attacked its companion energetically for displaying such a low trait. If they were not fighting about sugar, they were sure to be about something else, especially if it was anything edible. To give one food and overlook the other would cause the neglected one to indulge in moaning growls of rage and envy. The opposite sexes quarrel as readily as the males during feeding-time, for gallantry seems to be an attribute foreign to a bear's nature. Whatever affection the animal may possess belongs entirely to the female, for she is kind to her young, and will sometimes fight bravely in their defence, or sincerely mourn their loss should the hunter kill them. The only time when she is really dangerous is when she is accompanied by her cubs; for she will then fight if surprised suddenly, cornered, or wounded, or if she thinks any harm is intended toward them.

The female brings forth her young late in December or early in January, the period of gestation commencing in October, and lasting generally about one hundred and twelve days. When in this condition she retires to a tree-top or a cavern, and there remains until the cubs are able to move about briskly enough to flee to her if attacked by wolves or other foes. So carefully do the mothers secrete themselves at a certain season that I never heard of a pregnant one being killed, nor did I ever see one, to the best of my knowledge. During unusually cold seasons in the north the bears migrate to the south, where food and warmth may be procured; but in these migrations even, when many are shot, no person could say that a gravid animal was seen, though females were frequently found among the throngs.

The animal cannot be attacked at close range with impunity during these excursions, for hunger and cold make it rather desperate. As its fur is valuable, however, professional hunters slay it at every opportunity, and sometimes follow groups for two or three days together. Its flesh, which is succulent and fat from June to the period of hibernation, becomes lean and dry during the migration, so that it is not much sought for as an accessory to the larder. Should its winter rest even be undisturbed, the flesh is leathery and disagreeable when it reappears in the spring, and continues in that condition until the wild roots and fruits are ripe, when it fattens up in a short time.

During its hibernation the bear is said to suck its forepaws so much that they are very tender when it arouses itself from its torpor; and it is even said by some telescope-sighted hunters to close the *anus* with clay, to prevent the passage of any element of nutrition that could support existence while in its dormant state.

As a game animal, when in good condition, the bear may be classed with the fox or badger; for while it is harder to kill and more difficult to find, it is equally as harmless to man if he will not throw himself into its embraces, and assume that he can whip his weight in wild-cats. While it is a dangerous opponent at close quarters, owing to its weight, size, and strength, the sharpness of its teeth and claws, and its hugging propensity, yet its power may be overcome by seizing it by the throat near the root of the tongue, and pressing the fingers heavily on it; and this soon produces spasms of the glottis, which suffocate it in a short time.

Bears are interesting and playful creatures about a house until they are a year old, but after that time they are troublesome, and liable to get into mischief on every occasion. They are so numerous in certain sections beyond the Rocky Mountains that several of them form accessories of towns and cities, and even of farm-houses; and in all cases they seem to be pampered pets. I have seen as many as eight tied around a house in Oregon, and five near another house in Washington Territory; and I knew a half-hunter and half-stock-raiser in Wyoming to have seventeen cubs in his stable at a time. He kept them for sale, however, and those that he did not dispose of were killed for their hides and flesh. He informed me that he could catch as many cubs as he wanted in February and March, by killing the dam, but that they were not worth the time and trouble devoted to their capture.

To kill a bear in the Atlantic States is considered quite a feat; to kill twenty of them is not considered much by any experienced Nimrod west of the Rocky Mountains. The reason for this discrepancy in the feelings of the chase is, that while the animal is very scarce in one division of the country, it is very abundant in the other. Even in portions of the Southern States, where it is still common, a bear-hunt is a gala event, and armed and mounted men and numerous dogs take part in it, much the same as they would in a wolf-drive in Russia or a boar-hunt in the Ardennes. I have hunted it in the Far West, not because I wished to do so specially, but because it came in my way when in search of other game, and I thought it better than nothing. I have on a few occasions formed one of a party organized specially for a chase after it; but I soon learned that we could not find it sometimes when we most wanted it, and that, when found, it offered little or no sport unless it was shot when running, or while trying to fight its way through a pack of dogs.

To hunt it successfully, a person should be accompanied by dogs trained specially to pursue it. These ought not to be large, fierce creatures, that would attack it boldly and fight until it resulted in the death of either; they should, on the contrary, be lithe, active, and high-tempered, and pugnacious enough to nip at it whenever they get the opportunity, and discreet enough to avoid a blow or a hug. Large, rough-coated terriers make capital bear-dogs, as they have endurance, mettle, a keen nose, and sufficient combativeness to assail any animal that runs on four legs; and of these I do not know any better breed than that peculiar to Ireland. Any dogs having a good nose, speed, and activity would do, however, if trained to the business, as they can detect Bruin's strong odor from amidst that of any of the *Feræ naturæ*, and follow it with little trouble, and often with the keenest interest.

The bear, when cornered by dogs, generally seeks safety in a tree, if it is any way near; and there it remains in false security until the hunter arrives on the scene and brings it down with a bullet planted in its heart or brain.

Experienced dogs keep away from the foot of the tree when their master opens fire on "Cuffey;" and when that individual tumbles to the ground they take excellent care not to go too close, for fear of receiving a blow that would soon end their earthly career. They should, however, be prepared to attack it in the legs and flanks whenever it attempts to escape, else it may prove indifferent to their barking, and attack the hunter with a fierceness by no means agreeable.

The Indian dogs make good lymers, and few bears escape them before being treed, so that a person is almost confident of bagging one, at least, while in their company, if any are aroused. A fifty-calibre Express-rifle is a capital weapon for hunting this animal; but in the woods I prefer a breech-loader carrying a heavy charge of buckshot, as some of that is almost sure of reaching its destination, whereas the bullet is liable to be swerved from its course by the undergrowth.

Bears, when they are special objects of the chase, should be stalked or hunted up wind, for "Cuffey"—the familiar name for the black bear, as "Old Ephraim" is for the grizzly—is keen of nose and ear, and will be out of the reach of its human enemy long before the latter knows that it is about. To show how sensitive it is in the nose, I may mention an incident that occurred to me in Washington Territory. Coming into Seattle one day from Washington Lake, I rested for a short time in the woods, using a fallen tree for a seat. While deeply engaged in a brown-study something startled me, and, on looking up, I saw a bear and two cubs a short distance away picking berries and searching old logs for grubs and the nests of ants. As I wished to study them, I moved quietly to one side and secured a perch to the leeward in a vine-maple tree. While seated there, I had a good opportunity of watching them; and so amused was I with their affectionate demeanor and joyous gambols, that I took no notice of the direction in which they were moving. In the course of perhaps half an hour they jumped on the log on which I had been lounging, but they had scarcely done so before they were off again and hastening into the forest at their best pace, as if they were thoroughly frightened. They must have got the odor left by my hand on the wood, or they would not have left such a good grub and ant ground as the log without searching it well, and feasting on its dainties. I have found that farmers, when setting traps for bears, could not get one to approach them until after the wind and sun, or dew and rain, had taken away the smell which the hands had left upon them.

Being cautious and vigilant, and "knowing," in the sense of cunning, the bear is no stupid, to be slain without some exercise of the perceptive qualities, unless it is taken at a great disadvantage. I have known it to be captured in Western rivers by steamboats and canoes; and one of the pleasantest runs that I ever had after it was in a canoe, on the Chehalis River, in Washington Territory. It is even found swimming Puget Sound, which is an inland sea; and it is no uncommon occurrence to see it using the currents of streams in its autumn migrations from the high cold mountains to the sheltered forests and warm climate of the coast. It takes boldly to the water when necessary, and seems to think little of swimming several miles, and at a good pace too. It is no rare occurrence for a steamboat to capture one while it is swimming Puget Sound, and I heard of a boat that ran down two in one day in the Snohomish River, a stream emptying into Possession Sound.

The animal is so common everywhere in the dense forests of the North-west that it seems somewhat odd that large numbers are not killed annually for their flesh alone; for a bear steak, though by no means the tenderest of meat, is still palatable to the most dainty of appetites. One reason for their immunity from attack is due to the fact that they do not trouble the farm-yard much, and that their hide does not bring much of a price in the West, though it is costly enough in the retail market. They commit a raid occasionally, however, on the farm-yard, but it consists principally in stealing a young pig or a lamb, or upsetting an apiary; but in the majority of cases they pay dearly for such temerity, for no effort, from poison to rifle, is spared to get rid of them.

The Indians formerly hunted them for their skins, which were sold to the fur companies; but since the great companies have left the country, little attention has been paid to this business south of British America. The red men kill them occasionally now for their flesh and hide, and for their claws, which are highly prized for necklaces.

A friend and myself, while wandering through Washington Territory, found ourselves one day among a tribe of Indians on the Skagit River; and as they were preparing for a grand *potlatch*, or distribution of gifts to their friends in other tribes, we concluded to wait and see the ceremony. Not caring to share the cabin or wigwam of any of the sons of the forest, through fear of making the acquaintance of the numerous crawling creatures that live in them with the owners, we pitched our camp under the shelter of a spreading spruce near the middle of the encampment, and made ourselves as comfortable as circumstances would permit. Being guests, in an informal way, of the chief, we left all our *ictas* in camp, except our rifles, revolvers, and knives, and roamed around among the different huts or mat wigwams, paying visits of curiosity and ceremony, as we wished to ingratiate ourselves with the people.

We were received with the usual stoicism of the Indian nature; and were it not for our efforts to pronounce their terribly guttural dialect, which caused them to laugh heartily, it is doubtful if we could have induced them to look kindly upon us under the circumstances, as they do not care to have white men see their meetings, or *potlatches*, for fear they might ridicule them. We managed, however, to make ourselves at home with them; and our intrusion was not, after awhile, considered to be very disagreeable. The day after our arrival the neighboring tribes began to pour in — men, women, and children; some coming on horseback, some afoot, but the greater number arrived in canoes, which held from four to a dozen persons. When all were assembled they were welcomed by the chief, and the ceremony of distribution commenced late in the afternoon. The highest dignitaries among the visitors received presents in accordance with their dignity; some receiving a pair of blankets, and others old muskets, revolvers, cheap knives, pieces of cloth, deer-skins, bear-skins, strings of colored glass beads, copper bracelets, and ear-rings, and so on, until all the presents were exhausted.

No person was forgotten, from the highest to the lowest, and the result was that all were as happy as children. Not a little merriment and good-natured rivalry was manifested when a miscellaneous collection of articles was thrown among a throng of men, women, and children, for they commenced struggling for them as ravenously as a body of boys for pennies. This ceremony lasted for four days; and to make it as interesting as possible, the evenings, up to midnight, were devoted to speech-making, gossiping, and feasting and dancing, in which all, except the very aged, joined with an alacrity and light-heartedness one would not expect from a people so taciturn and unimpressible.

The camp presented a very picturesque appearance during the night; for the fires, which blazed in every direction, were surrounded by shadowy human groups who were enjoying themselves with song and story, or the gross feast, while numbers of men could be seen in various directions jumping around in a circle and grunting like pigs. This they called dancing, and they apparently enjoyed it.

The last dance on the programme for the night was in honor of the animal kingdom; and this my friend concluded to join, as he thought the previous Terpsichorean evolutions rather ridiculous, and therefore funny, and he could not see any fun going on without wishing to take a part in it. When the circle was formed he took his place in it, thoroughly resolved to grunt and jump as well as any

INDIAN DANCE.

of his red companions. While waiting for the signal to start, two men wrapped up in bear-skins rushed into the middle of the circle from a *tepee* close by, and, giving an unearthly yell, commenced jumping, first to the right, then to the left, keeping time to their heavy stamping by deep abdominal grunts. Those around them went through the same movements, and I noticed that my friend acted his part as well as if he had been to the manner born. The two inside imitated the actions of the animal they were supposed to represent very well, in some cases; and whenever they pretended to break through the circle, those forming it played the part of dogs and hunters and beat them back. After indulging in this hard work for half an hour, all the Terpsichoreans bounded into the air suddenly, and gave a long, loud, and prolonged yell that was so blood-curdling and terrifying that my friend broke away at once, being actually startled out of his wits by its intensity and fierceness. The suddenness of his retreat and his blanched countenance caused me to laugh heartily; but when I learned that he knew too well what an Indian war-whoop was in reality, and had cause to remember it, my sense of ridicule was turned into sympathy, and I stopped teasing him.

This dance was followed by others in honor of the wolf, deer, elk, and other quadrupeds; but all were alike in character, except that the Terpsichoreans inside the circle wore the skin of the animal they represented, and sometimes imitated its voice and action. The pale-faced dancer could not be induced to take any further part in the ceremony, however, and the fun which he saw in it at first had all vanished.

We were awake the next morning at an early hour, and, seeing an unusual commotion in the encampment, asked what was going on, and were told that the *potlatch* would close with a grand feast, and that some of the braves were going out hunting, while others were bound on a fishing expedition. We asked permission to join the Nimrods, and it was readily granted by the simple word "*na-witka*" —yes—for the red men are sparing of words, except when they are extolling their own deeds.

The hunting-party, attired in all sorts of garments, from blankets and buckskins to the tattered remnants of a white man's clothes, or a simple shirt and a piece of cloth tied round the legs, looked more like scarecrows than anything else at a distance. Their head covering aided this appearance; for while some were bareheaded, others wore old felt-hats, skin caps, or the small painted baskets made of cedar roots or coarse grass, and three or four were decorated with "plug" hats that were shattered so much as to scarcely resemble the originals in texture or shape. They were accompanied by as motley a throng of dogs as ever was seen, even in an Indian village, some being large, powerful brutes, which showed indications of being descended from a more civilized stock than their kindred, while others were small, fox-like curs that looked as if they were degenerate coyotes. When everything was ready, we marched about seven or eight miles from camp in a body, and then separated, each man taking his own course. My companion and myself kept together, and took a position in the centre of the line, in hopes that we should have a chance shot at anything that fled from the flanks. The dogs were set to work the moment we parted, but we listened in vain for their opening chorus, and this induced us to try still-hunting, and to use our eyes instead of our ears. Moving onward cautiously through the dense and towering forest of firs, we often found it hard work to force our way through the matted undergrowth that grew in tropical luxuriance, or the masses of tall ferns, that towered above our heads in many places, and were so thick that we could not see five feet ahead of us. While groping through one of these forests of fern, a fine doe started up so close to us that I could almost have touched her with my gun, and before she could get away I planted a load of lead in her head. That was the first report heard during the morning; and it had scarcely died away before two Indians were beside me, as if they had risen out of the bushes, and making inquiries about what had been killed. On seeing it, they seemed to be satisfied; and taking out a knife, one of them cut it open, drew the *viscera*, and hung the carcass on a tree, which was "blazed," so that it could be readily identified. We then resumed our march, and in the course of twenty minutes heard the yelping and howling of the dogs.

"*Itsoot*"—bear—said one of the Indians who remained with us, and, rushing through the shrubbery at a pace we could not show, he soon disappeared from our sight. We tried to follow, but gave up the attempt in a short time, and walked on leisurely, excusing ourselves for our apparent laziness by saying that we would not kill ourselves running after a bear which we might not even see. We could hear the dogs yelping at intervals, first in one direction, then in another, and some distance away; but they suddenly began to approach us. This put us on our mettle; so we hastened forward, and reached an open piece of woods in a few minutes. As soon as we entered this we saw the dogs nipping at, and yelping around, a large dark object that was alternately charging and wheeling, and attempting to retreat. Making a strong spurt, we were soon near the pack, just as four or five Indians appeared from opposite directions. The bear, seeing new foes, broke away, despite the efforts of the noisy curs, and sought refuge high up among the branches of a fir that must have had an altitude of two hundred feet.

A shot or two caused it to lose its hold of the bough on which it was resting and to come tumbling to the ground, amidst a shower of branches, with a shock that killed it in a moment. The dogs became hilarious on seeing the death of the fugitive, and barked and jumped about in a most enthusiastic manner; but even in death they feared it; for, after nipping at it, they would jump away growling and grinning, as if they were being pursued. The quarry proved to be a female nearly full grown, and, by making a rough guess, we judged her to weigh over three hundred pounds. We subsequently learned that she was accompanied by two cubs, but that the dogs had treed them, and they had been killed before the mother was. Resuming the march, we were kept busily at work nearly all day, now shooting at a deer, next at a squirrel, a hare, a wild-cat, a wolf, a grouse, or whatever else came in our way, for the forest was well stocked with game. During the course of the afternoon I saw a bear and two cubs, and fired at one of the latter and hit it in the shoulder; but the mother, instead of showing fight, scampered away at her best pace, and left her youngster to the tender mercies of my friend, who finished it with a shot in the heart.

Our guns were kept busy at intervals for several hours on both fur and feather; but no plantigrade presented itself to receive our compliments until near four o'clock, when we came in sight of a burly male which was munching berries in a patch of buckthorn. We commenced stalking him by retreating as rapidly as possible for three or four hundred yards, then crawling carefully up from the leeward, so as not to give him our wind. After groping about among wet shrubbery and dodging behind trees for half an hour, we came to within fifty yards of our intended victim, and were getting ready to open fire on him, when a vine tripped me up, as I was trying to get a little nearer, and sent me sprawling headlong into a mass of apparently unfathomable briers that tore small lanes of blood through my face. When I fell, the bushes caught my gun so strongly that it was discharged within an inch of my nose; but I, fortunately, escaped any greater injury than having my mouth and eyes partially filled with fine grass, leaves, and particles of clay that were scattered about by the shot. By the time I had extricated myself from my thorny couch and picked out enough of the stuff in my eyes to enable me to gaze around, the bear and my companion had disappeared, and I was left to my own emphatic thoughts and exasperated feelings. Not knowing which way to move to find either quarry or friend, I started straight ahead, where I heard the dogs giving tongue, and in the course of twenty minutes reached the bank of a stream that was both deep and rapid. I tried to cross this in several places, as the dogs were yelping in the loudest manner on the opposite side, but I found the water too deep to wade and too turbulent to swim; so I was compelled to make a raft of two small trees which extended far out into the river, and whose branches were so closely entwined that they could not be easily separated. By pressing off the heavy ends with a lever made of a large bough, I got my rude bark afloat, and tried to push it across the stream; but the whirlpools were too numerous and the current too strong to enable me to do this, and it went rushing down the river at a pace almost sufficient to take my breath away. I found it extremely difficult to keep my position, as the eddies whirled the raft around so abruptly at intervals that the base, side, or top was alternately in front, but neither very long. I had ridden floating logs before in the pine-forests of Maine, Wisconsin, and Minnesota, and thought I was rather dexterous in the exercise, but on no former occasion did I experience such a wild ride.

Finding I could do nothing with my pole, it being perfectly useless in that mad current, I let the bark go wheresoever the water carried it, and devoted all my attention to retaining my seat. In the course of perhaps a quarter of an hour I reached a straight stretch of the river, and floated steadily down this at a rapid rate, but, on rounding a bend, I was startled to see before me an immense mass of fallen trees extending across the whole width of the stream. Fearing a collision, I tried to push my unmanageable raft ashore, but my efforts were in vain, and, before I could realize my situation, the rude craft went crashing into the obstruction with such force that I was hurled into the water with a velocity that sent me almost clean to the bottom at one bound. I came to the surface again in a hurry, however, but only to be caught in a whirlpool that dashed me against a tree with such power as to partially stun me, and cause me to feel as if my head and ribs were broken. In my wild anxiety to keep myself from the collision, I threw out my left hand, and, fortunately for me, caught a strong branch; and when I recovered from the confusion of the blow, I seized this with both hands and clambered on a tree, but not without difficulty, as the current was so fierce near the logs that it threatened to sweep me under them, especially when my body was partially out of the water, as it then exercised its full strength on my legs. I reached the barricade, however, in a short time, and on looking about for my gun, saw it safely lodged among the branches. This was a most pleasing surprise, as I expected that it was lost in the river, and I hastened to secure it with the utmost celerity. I next essayed to reach the shore; but the branches were so closely entwined that a passage was rendered almost impossible, and I had to take to the water to pass them, holding myself against the current by clinging to the trunks and boughs, and pushing myself forward with one hand at a time, as I was desirous of keeping my gun from getting wet.

After a toilsome and tedious effort I secured a foothold on the bottom, and crawled out on the bank, shivering, and as exhausted as a half-drowned rat. Undressing promptly, I wrung my clothes as dry as I could, and, after taking several good runs in the forest to dispel the chill from which I was suffering, I rehabilitated myself and started toward camp, as I did not know where to seek for other members of the party, not hearing sounds in any direction; and, to be candid, my dripping garments took away all the ardor of the chase. Scurrying along as fast as the matted shrubbery would permit me, I was lost to everything but seeking my quarters, when a sudden series of yelps a little to my right startled me into the liveliest state of activity, and into the most intense desire to kill something, if it were only a hare, to appease my disgust at the *contretemps* that had befallen me. The canine cries began to approach me gradually; and knowing by their tones that some large game was afoot, I dodged behind a tree and put myself in readiness to give it an unhealthy reception. I was in position only a short time before a large black bear, with mouth open, as if it were suffering from a wound, came tearing through the bushes to leeward; but, catching my wind, it halted abruptly, sniffed the air for a moment or two, then turned to flee, but before it could disappear I put a bullet into its thigh, and it fell on the ground in a heap, and growling terribly. Before I could fire a second time, a small army of Indian curs were waltzing, grinning, growling, and barking about it, and nipping it on the flanks; but after every successful bite they retreated backward rapidly, or turned tail and bounded away for a short distance.

The wounded animal tried to rise, but it could only succeed in dragging itself forward a few feet with its forelegs. I knew then that both hind-legs were broken, and this induced me to approach to close quarters to finish it; but I found this a matter of difficulty, as the dogs were grouped about it so densely that to shoot at it would endanger the life of some of them. I tried to kick them away, but when driven from one position they ran to another, and remained there despite all my yelling. One of them, finally, was bold enough to make a dash for the throat of the bear; but that wily animal, being too prompt for it, caught it in its jaws, and crushed it to death in five seconds, by breaking its spinal column. I rushed in to save the poor brute, and gave the bear a cut over the head with a keen-edged cimeter which I carried, but my blow was too late to preserve its life, and, when it dropped to the ground, its spirit had flown to the unknown canine world. I thought the blow was sufficient to cut the bear's head open, but I had not calculated on the thickness of the skull; and the result was that I only inflicted a severe wound, which made the animal so furious that it turned on me in the twinkling of an eye, and, before I knew what it was about, struck me so severely on the arm with one of its paws that the clothing was torn away from shoulder to wrist, and I received a wound which, though not deep, was long, and very painful. When I saw the blood streaming out I became fairly incensed, and drawing my revolver, a short forty-one calibre, carrying a large charge of powder and a long bullet, I fired at its head in rapid succession until I emptied every chamber, and when all were discharged the animal was lying dead. Some of the bullets went clean through the skull and came out on the opposite side; and one of them wounded a cur that would insist on keeping in the way, in the shoulder.

When the conflict was over, the ground was freely sprinkled with blood, and the bear's face was fairly covered with it, from the wound inflicted by the cimeter. I then turned my attention to my arm, and soon had that bound up, using my linen for a bandage; and when that was done I felt rather pleased with myself, as it was my first actual contest with the plantigrade, and I had come off better than I could expect. True, I had every advantage over the slain; but one forgets that in his pleasure at having killed a dangerous wild animal that has caused him any injury.

Before leaving the spot I commenced shouting for help, and in about fifteen minutes a young brave came up. I explained to him what had occurred, but he was content with saying "*masatchee itsoot*," which might be translated that it was either a bad or a dangerous bear.

As I wished to return to camp at once, I told him to have the animal brought in when his party returned home; but he objected to my walking to the village, and said he would take me down in a canoe which was concealed in the bushes below the jam of logs in the river. I accepted his proposal gladly, and was soon dashing down the stream at a headlong pace; but my misfortunes for the day were not over, for, in passing under a huge fir which stretched across the river, I did not stoop low enough, and received, as a consequence, a fearful bump in the forehead which almost threw me backward, and made me see a greater variety of vari-colored stars than are to be found in the firmament.

What with my arm and splitting headache, I was in anything but a pleasant mood; hence the wild and luxuriant forest scenery which was everywhere visible was lost to me. I was glad, indeed, when I reached the village, and had an opportunity of changing my garments and taking a stretch on the humble pallet of straw in my small tent. The young fellow who was so kind to me returned to his companions when I stepped ashore, but, before going, he told one of the women that I was wounded, and she gave me a glance in which there was more of curiosity than sympathy.

After resting for an hour or more, I went out to get some water with which to bathe my arm, as it was painful and very stiff; and while on my way to the river I met an old chief, and in response to his queries as to what ailed me, I told him, in a few words, in Chinook. He asked me to accompany him to his cabin and he would attend to the arm at once, so that it should not become inflamed. I accepted his invitation, and, on reaching his place, found that one of his three wives had been making a decoction of some herbs, she having heard of my accident from the woman to whom it was first told. When I entered, the women did not speak a word, and only lifted their heads once; and from this I deduced that curiosity was not a trait in Indian feminine nature. Their lord and master told them what to do, and when I had taken a seat near the smoky fireplace, the youngest unbound my arm and washed it copiously for ten or fifteen minutes with the prepared decoction. No one made any comments on the wounds; and when the bathing was over, the arm was bound up again, after having the leaves of some plant, not unlike dog-leaves, placed over the wound.

I waited in the chief's wigwam, or rather cabin, until evening, smoking and chatting; but when I heard that the hunters were coming in I went out to see them. The sight they presented was striking, and certainly worth beholding, for they were loaded with nearly all species of game found in the forest, from a bear to a squirrel, and from a grouse to a robin. They trooped in without any noise, or even the smallest demonstration of pleasure, and each party, as it arrived, placed its spoils in a common pile—though fur and feather were kept separate. The amount of game brought in was almost incredible for one day's work; but when I considered that the forests were fairly alive with animals, and that no foes threatened them except an occasional red man, I could readily understand the success of the party. The fishermen were also fortunate, and came in laden with the spoils of the river. My companion was among the last to arrive, and from him I learned that he had fired at and wounded the bear whose presence caused me to be tripped up, and had followed it to the river, where he lost it. Presuming that it had crossed over, he made a raft of a tree which extended partially across the river, by pushing the top off the bank; and seating himself on it, near the middle, the current swung the lighter portion around sufficiently to enable him to get to wading-ground, and then to the shore. On reaching the opposite side he heard the dogs giving tongue some distance below him, and hurried in their direction, but, before he could overtake them, they had driven their quarry across the stream, and followed it over. Not being able to recross, owing to the want of facility and the depth and strength of the current, he went hunting on his own responsibility, and managed to secure a deer before he joined a party of Indians. He excused himself for leaving me, on the ground that he did not see me fall, and mistook the report of my gun for an effort of mine to bag Bruin; and seeing him, a splendid male, bounding away, he forgot everything in the desire to tumble him over. The explanation seemed plausible enough, and nothing further was said about his deserting a friend in distress.

The young brave, known as Mowitch, or the Deer, who had proved a benefactor to me, saw that the animal which gave me the wound was brought in; and when the preparations for the feast were made, he skinned it, and gave me the hide and head, supposing that I would be glad to keep them as mementos of the occasion. I wondered at this considerateness on the part of an untutored Indian, as I had never before seen one of the race manifest it; but I learned subsequently that he was well educated, having been brought up in a mission school, and that his teacher had taught him the lessons of kindness which had made him even then famous in his own tribe for goodness. He could speak English well when he chose to do so; but it seems that he would not utter a syllable of it if the pale-faces with whom he came in contact spoke Chinook or his own dialect. The cause for this I did not learn; but my own experience among the red races living between the Missouri River and the Pacific Ocean, and between Southern Mexico and British America, has taught me to infer that Indians do not care to speak the language of the whites, except when compelled to do so from necessity.

This brave was even kind enough to give my companion

the heads and hides of the animals slain by us during the day, and to suggest that we could have all the antlers we wished if they were of any use to us. His offer was accepted with thanks, and by nightfall the door of our tent was surrounded by piles of skins and the heads of bears and deer.

The animals, bereft of their outer covering, were put into pots and boiled; but some, and especially the young bears, were placed in pits in which fires had been burning all day, and were covered with red-hot stones and earth and grass, so that none of the heat should escape. While the large game was being prepared for the feast in pits and pots, the feathered game was being cooked before the blazing wood-fires by the squaws, and the fish fizzled and steamed amidst heaps of hot ashes. Every feminine member of the encampment seemed to be busy in cooking for the great occasion; and while some baked unleavened cakes of flour or camas before the fire, others attended to the cooking of the wapato or wild-potato, and the boiling of certain herbs, which might be called greens in the general sense of the term, though, to be literal, they ought to be called thin grasses. When the grand dinner was ready, all hands "set to," as they say in Scotland, and were soon devouring the dainties with all the vigor that a keen appetite and a capacious maw could impart. Scarcely a word was spoken by old or young during the meal, they being too busily engaged in filling the stomach to devote any time to the pleasures of conversation. No person used a knife or fork, and plates were exceedingly scarce, for I only saw two among the entire lot, and these were used by the chiefs.

We roamed about among the various clusters, yet no person asked us to join in the festival, and we received no more attention than wandering spectres. We did not care for this, however, as we did not wish to accept their hospitality, our taste being too dainty to enjoy the gross food which they gulped down like so many wild animals. The novelty of the affair was highly appreciated, however, as the scene was exceedingly interesting, and would have delighted the soul of an artist; for in the same groups could be seen old men and women whose skins were like rumpled parchment, and whose bones were apparently so brittle that any attempt to use them in walking or other exercise would result in an instantaneous breaking, and young bucks and squaws who were ideal representatives of savage strength and beauty. The lurid glare of the fires on their faces; the darkness that reigned about them; the scantiness and tawdriness of their costumes; the mingling of all ages and sexes; and the crunching of bones or tearing of meat between the fingers, made such a scene as could not be witnessed outside the United States, in all probability, and one which even there would be worth travelling far to behold. Although my arm ached badly, I went about among the groups, and enjoyed the romantic strangeness of the picture they presented so much that it was long past midnight ere I retired to rest.

When the feasting was over, the young braves indulged in rude songs and dances; but the latter were all alike, consisting simply in jumping around in a circle and grunting as if they had a bad stomach-ache. Every dance wound up with a tremendous scream or war-whoop, in which all used the utmost power of their lungs to the best advantage. The squaws and old men looked on with approval at the Terpsichorean evolutions of the warriors, and the latter sometimes gave them a word of encouragement, or rated them for not performing a certain dance in a proper manner. Some of the braves related their own great deeds in the hunting-field, or those of their ancestors on the war-path, during the intervals between the dances, and these were frequently interrupted with the approbative intonations of "*naw*" by the auditors. When my comrade and myself left the encampment, the orators and Terpsichoreans were under full headway, and, I doubt not, kept up their frolic until morning, as they seemed bent on seeing it out. Their wild cries reached our tent occasionally during the night, and it was not until daylight appeared that they ceased; but even then we could hear the guttural tones of the gamesters as they droned out their "hu ha" in the game of "guess which hand holds the pebble." This childish game is played by opposite sides, there being from five to twenty on each side, and they continue it until they become weary or some of the members lose everything, even to the honor of their family. After these gambling contests some of the men are homeless, and perhaps wifeless, and cannot even claim their life if their opponents wish to take it from them.

When I arose the next day many of the visitors to the *potlatch* were leaving for home, but they departed without even saying good-bye to their hosts, so far as I could see. I do not know that they have even a word to express this sentiment; but they evidently, whether they have or not, care little for mere phrases, and depart without considering that a word or two would mar or make their welcome, as it does in civilized communities. When the majority of the guests had left we struck our tent, and, bidding the chief good-bye, secured a canoe to take us to salt-water in Puget Sound, whence we could find a sailing-vessel or a steamer to take us to our destination in Washington Territory. The run down the river was made in a short time, as the current bowled us along at the rate of eight or nine knots an hour, and our three paddles increased this speed considerably. On reaching Puget Sound, my companion wended his way northward to British Columbia, while I proceeded to Muckilteo, a fishing hamlet on the Sound, thence moved into the country, where I remained until my arm was in as good condition as ever. While stopping there I had an adventure with a bear that promised to be more dangerous than my last encounter. While trout-fishing one day, a bear, which was pursued by dogs, swam the river a short distance below me; and thinking I could get a shot at it with my revolver, I concealed myself in some tall bushes in order to be ready to pounce upon it the moment it struck land. Not hearing any noise, I began to poke my head above the bushes gradually, to take a glance about me; but the moment my hat appeared above the shrubbery two bullets went whizzing past me so close that I fancied I could feel their wind on my face. I dodged back in a second, and yelled out in stentorian tones what in the name of goodness such wise men were firing at. A shout across the stream informed me that I was mistaken for a bear, and, on emerging from my leafy covert, I asked if I looked like a bear. Two hunters laughingly informed me that I did not when they saw the whole of my body, but that my hat looked suspiciously like the head of the animal in the distance. The mistake was a natural one under the circumstances, but it came too near being a fatal one to me to make its repetition pleasant.

The hunt with the Indians may lead persons to think that an angry bear, even at its worst, is no great foe after all, and this would prove true were one well armed and ready to meet it, but such is not always the case; hence I would suggest to those in pursuit of the animal to be cautious at least, or disaster may follow. It may not be able to do a great deal of harm to a sturdy man, yet I have heard so many well authenticated accounts of the injury it has inflicted on them sometimes, that I believe them entitled to the fullest credence. As examples, I may quote the following incidents: A miner who worked on the Lummi River had his cabin invaded one evening by a bear, which was evidently attracted there by a deer that hung just inside the door. The man, on seeing the animal walk in so unconcernedly, yelled at it; but, before leaving, it seized a quarter of the deer, and was moving away with it in the most unceremonious manner, when the miner attacked it with an axe. The bear turned at once and made a desperate fight for life, using its powerful claws and teeth whenever it could close with the foe. The miner, after being severely bitten two or three times, and having his clothes and flesh torn, got a fair blow with the sharp edge of the axe at its head, and this stunned it. Following up his advantage, he got in three or four more in a few seconds, and soon had the satisfaction of seeing it drop dead at his feet. On examining his own wounds, he found that the left arm was severely injured, and that the flesh was torn rather severely on parts of the arms and thighs. As they were all flesh wounds, however, he congratulated himself on his escape; yet they were severe enough to lay him up for two months, and to make him go to the settlements for surgical aid and attendance.

A man whom I met in Montana was made a cripple for life by a bear because he shot one of her cubs. He was taking the young one away, when the mother overtook him and attacked him without a moment's hesitation. The struggle was a severe one; but the hunter finally caught her by the throat, and pressing on that part with all his might, soon reduced her to such a condition of weakness that he was enabled to take out a large pocket-knife which he carried, and to cut her jugular vein. When the contest was over, he was so exhausted from his wounds and the loss of blood that he fainted, and it was only by making the most strenuous efforts that he was able to get home. An examination proved that the animal had cut some of the tendons of the right foot and broken some of the ankle-bones, besides lacerating the arms and chest.

Another individual of whom I heard in Colorado followed a wounded bear into the undergrowth, and was attacked by it. His rifle being unloaded, he was unable to use any other means of defence than a knife; but before he could inflict any damage with that he was overpowered, and injured so severely that he died in two days after being brought home. When found by one of his neighbors he was apparently dead, nor did he ever recover consciousness, for the skull was injured in two places as if it had been struck with a hammer.

Accidents less serious than these frequently occur, but they are too often due to want of caution, and to supposing an animal killed when it is only wounded seriously enough to make it desperate.

The only instance in which I was chased by a black bear occurred in Washington Territory, and that taught me a lesson I have not forgotten. Having expressed a desire to an acquaintance, who farmed in summer and hunted in winter, to go on a "bearing" expedition, he kindly assented to my proposal, and made preparations for it by cooking plenty of food, and securing two mustangs, or *cayuses*, as they are called in the North-west, to transport our blankets and provisions out and our game back, as we intended to be absent two or three days. Our armament consisted of a muzzle-loading rifle which I carried, and a shot-gun borne by my comrade; our food was confined to boiled mutton and home-made bread; and our companions to two small, active, and noisy curs, which thought it necessary to bark at every bird and animal they saw. Having started at 6 A.M., we found ourselves about twelve miles from home by mid-day, and deeply immerged in a dense forest of those gigantic firs and spruces indigenous to the North-west. After resting for a few minutes to load our guns and to eat a simple repast, which was washed down with water, we went searching for bear "signs," and soon found them plentiful enough; for the berries were cleaned off quite a large patch of bushes, old logs had been stripped of their bark where they concealed grubs and ants, and some of the young trees contained marks of a large male's teeth, which was advertising his presence and portliness by placing his sign-manual as high upon them as he could reach. It is a peculiarity of the male that he will sometimes leave the impressions of his teeth as high up on some of the undergrowth as he can reach, as if he were desirous of making his dimensions known to other members of his family. What this signifies no one seems to know, though the surmises are many. Having noted these, the dogs, which had been previously kept at heel, were set to work to arouse the advertiser, and in less than ten minutes they were yelping in their loudest tone. I ran in one direction on hearing this notification, and my companion in the opposite, so that we might head off the game should it break from a straight course. After running for a few minutes, I saw a dark object dodging through the thick shrubbery; and judging from its size that it was the animal whose life I sought, I raised my rifle, pointed it as steadily as my palpitation would permit, and banged away. When the echo of the report ceased I heard a crashing of the bushes, and this was followed by a painful, vicious growl. Moving forward cautiously, and peering closely into the shrubbery, I saw the lover of berries stretched on its side and gasping violently, as if in the throes of mortal dissolution. This induced me to lay down my rifle, and seizing the fallen limb of a tree, which was large, crooked, and unwieldy, I gave Bruin a tremendous whack with it on the occipital region; but no sooner was the blow given than the animal sprung up and charged me. I raised the club to give it a second blow on the head; but the animal not only parried it with its paw, but broke it short in my hand. Being unarmed, I concluded to retreat; and I flatter myself that I did it in admirable style, for I clambered rapidly over felled trees of large dimensions, leaped the smaller ones, and tore through the thick undergrowth, which lashed my face with incisive sharpness, until, in a short time, I reached a clump of the many-trunked vine-maple, and up one of these I clambered with a speed of which I afterward felt proud.

The bear followed close on my track, and from its growls I expected to be in its embraces every moment; but the wound affected its coursing powers, and I was safe in my perch before it reached the foot. I felt perfectly safe where I was, as the trunk was too small for a bear to climb; and the protruding tongue and deep gasps of my pursuer proved that my leaden pill had sapped the vigor of its frame. Had I been a hero of the chivalric school I might have descended and ended the contest by a hand-to-hand encounter; but having scruples about risking my person or my clothes, I was content to remain where I was, and to shout for aid by yelling "hoo-oo-pee-ee," which the woods re-echoed many times. In a few minutes—though it seemed a long while to me—I heard an answering call, and, in a short time after, the yelping of the curs. Bruin, on hearing the latter, concluded that the wisest course would be to retreat, and this it did, though slowly and very laboriously.

When the dogs passed my prison I descended, and when my companion arrived I secured his shot-gun and started in pursuit of the jailer. I overtook it in a few minutes, the dogs having brought it to bay by nipping at it whenever it attempted to escape, and, on a good opportunity being presented, I let it have both barrels at short range in rapid succession, and it fell dead in its track. On looking for where I hit it the first time, I found that the bullet had passed through the anterior portion of the windpipe from side to side. This was what had saved me, as its breathing was too difficult to enable it to run rapidly, or even to climb well.

While out on that hunt we killed three adults and two cubs, but I took excellent care to avoid getting to close quarters with them, and to feel assured that they were dead before I tried any familiarity.

I have had some hunts after this animal which had their ludicrous side also. I was, on one occasion, running down the Chehalis River in a canoe, my companions being an Indian gondolier and a sporting Esculapius who was the surgeon on an Indian reservation. While rushing down in a swift current that bowled us along at the rate of five miles an hour, we came suddenly upon a young bear swimming across the stream. The doctor became excited at once, and ordered the red man to ply the paddle vigorously and get alongside it before it could reach the shore. He complied, and we were soon ranged beside it; but as we had no weapons except small pocket revolvers, and the animal was young, the doctor insisted that it ought not to be shot, but be captured alive. All parties being willing, the doctor, who was in the bow of the canoe, attempted to throw a rope around its head, and in his efforts to do so tilted the boat somewhat, lost his balance, and went headlong into the water on top of the bear. The latter gave a growl of terror and attempted to break away; but it somehow got entangled in the rope, so that when the disciple of Esculapius rose to the surface he found himself clinging to one end of the cord and the bear to the other, and both pulling in opposite directions. The scene was so ludicrous that even the stoical gondolier laughed heartily, and shouted, "*Closh doctol; hyas closh*"—well done, doctor; very well done. As the current was carrying them down the stream, and the doctor was puffing loudly, and the bear hoarsely screaming, we took the former aboard for fear of any accident—though not without some danger of getting a spill ourselves, owing to the lightness of the canoe—and, paddling toward the shore, we dragged the captive after us. Before landing, we found that it was too large to be made a pet of, so we killed it by shooting it through the head with our pocket revolvers, and gave the carcass to the Indian, who was delighted to have it. The doctor dried his clothes at an Indian hut before going to the reservation on which he was stationed; and, on reaching there, he took very good care not to mention a word about his accident, for fear of being made a target for ridicule.

I was out on another occasion after grouse with a public singer, and he, being unused to walking, stopped to rest in the woods while I trudged on in search of game. I had not been two minutes away before I saw him running toward me at his best pace, and shouting my name. Thinking he was being pursued by some drunken Indians, I cocked my gun and awaited developments. On reaching me, he said that a bear had jumped out of a burned tree-stump close by him, and had frightened him badly. I went back to the stump, but, although it was hollow, I could see no indications that a bear had inhabited it at any time, and I told him so. Assuming that he had been somewhat rash in his fright, and fearing the result if the tale were told to his acquaintances, he promised to sing all the way into town if I would not "peach" on him. I promised to comply on this condition, and the result was that he sung all the popular songs the entire distance. When we reached the outskirts of the town he wished to cease; but

I insisted on his singing as far as the hotel, or relating the story when we reached there, and he reluctantly consented. While passing down the main street his dulcet tones attracted the attention of several persons, and some who knew him must have presumed that he was laboring under some unusual mental excitement. A few called at the hotel to learn what ailed him, and these he told that he had shot a bear, and was so overjoyed at the matter that he had to indulge in singing to soothe his ecstatic feelings. The story passed current for awhile, but, unfortunately, the leading paper of the town heard the true story, and the exploit of the bear-hunting hero was announced in a column of double-leaded matter. He fell at once from his high estate as a Nimrod, and it took many an "I know you're thirsty, boys," to prevent the "boys" from inquiring about how it was exactly that he shot that bear, and how far the terrified animal ran before dying of fright at seeing him.

CHAPTER IV.

THE COUGAR AND LYNXES.

The Cougar.—Variety of its Names.—Size, Weight, Strength, Color, and General Characteristics.—Its Peculiarities when treed.—How Farmers kill it.—Anecdotes of its Courage.—A Fight with a Wolf and a Bear.—Desperate Struggle between a Cougar and an Unarmed Man in Oregon.—Two Kittens captured.—Death of the Dam.—A Wild Cougar plays with a Man in Washington Territory.—His Fright and Escape.—An Episode in Minnesota.—My First Cougar.—A Weird Funeral Ceremony among the Digger Indians.—Why the Californians are called Tar Heads.—My next Capture, and another Form of an Indian Funeral.—A Hunt in the Cascade Range.—Death of a Cougar.—My Companion wounded.—Legend of an Enchanted Lake.—A Cougar cripples an Indian.—Dangerous Character of the Animal.—The best Time for hunting it.—A Night Hunt, and its serious Result.—Death of Two Cougars.—Other Members of the Cat Family.—Difference between Lynxes and true Cats.—How to distinguish them.—Lynx-hunts.—I kill Four in one Month.—Characteristics of the Genus.—Lynx-hunting as a Sport.

THE cougar (*Felis concolor*) boasts a larger variety of names than any animal on the continent, being known as the puma, mountain lion, California lion, painter, and panther, besides the first mentioned; and some persons, in writing of sport in America, have made all these cognomens into distinct animals, and have gone so far as to give them different characteristics and varied degrees of ferocity.

The cougar is the largest of the *Felidæ* found in the United States, except the jaguar, or Mexican tiger (*Felis onça*); but that is confined in its northern range to portions of Texas, and is nowhere abundant, not even along the Brazos River. The former is quite common in the wooded regions beyond the Rocky Mountains, and its sharp, high screams in early morning frequently send the blood bounding through the veins of the wanderer amidst

THE COUGAR AND LYNXES. 107

forest depths. Though not often a dangerous foe until brought to bay or roused by hunger, owing to its natural cautiousness and timidity of character, yet its shrieks are so loud and penetrating that no person can hear them without feeling a thrill run through his body, and, if unarmed, without taking excellent care to avoid an encounter with it if possible.

An adult male weighs on an average from eighty to one hundred and fifty pounds; but in portions of the South,

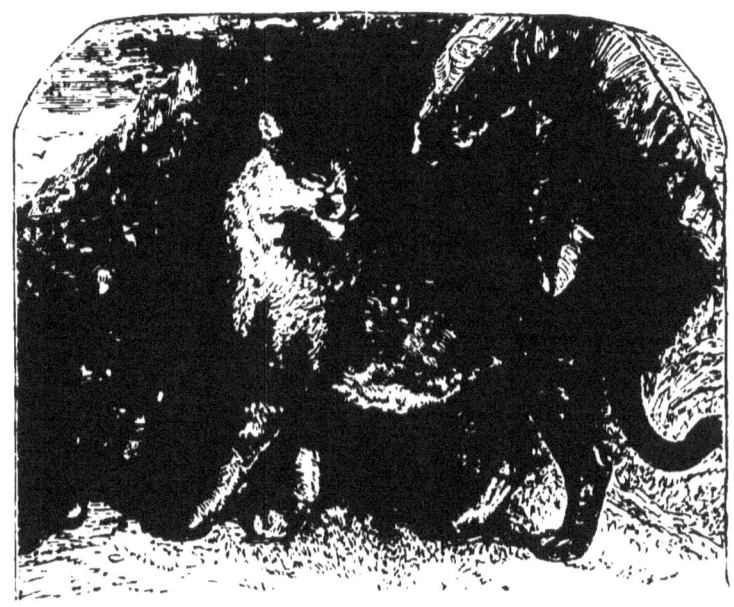

THE PUMA, OR COUGAR.

where the climate is favorable and food abundant, it attains greater weight than this. One shot near Elbow Creek, in Southern Florida, in December, 1873, measured nine feet four inches in length, and weighed two hundred and forty pounds. The skin of this monster is now, I believe, to be seen in the parlor of the Argonauta Rowing-club, at Bergen Point, New Jersey. The usual length of the cougar varies from four and a half to five feet, from nose to tail; but I have heard persons say that it sometimes attains a length of body of seven or more feet in portions of Florida and Texas. I have hunted in some of the best game regions of these States, and bagged a cougar occasionally; but I never saw one possessing such proportions, and I am rather doubtful if it exists, as that measurement would bring it up to the standard of the lion or grizzly bear. The two largest that I killed in the West measured, respectively, fifty-four and fifty-six inches, exclusive of the tail, and they were considered to be good-sized animals. The longest cauda measured was thirty-three inches, so that the animal had a total length of seven feet five inches. The height of the tallest one I ever killed was a fraction over thirty-one inches; the body was thirty inches around, and the head was a little more than twenty inches long.

Twenty-four hours after the death of the largest I had an opportunity of weighing it, and it turned the scales at one hundred and thirty-seven and a half pounds. This weight, when propelled by strong muscles, and placed in intense activity by rage, is no mean force for an unarmed man to encounter and vanquish; hence one cannot well blame the Indians for the fear of the animal they display, or their pride in killing one.

The color of the cougar is a brownish-yellow above, and a pale red or dusky-white beneath; the lower jaw and throat are white; and the whiskers, which are rather long, are white, and rise in a blackish base. It has no mane, nor any tuft on the extremity of the tail; its hair is soft and dense over the limbs and body; and the color is so much alike in both sexes that they cannot be distinguished by the looks of *pelage*.

The female brings forth her young in the spring, the number at a birth varying from two to four, and the period of gestation being about ninety-seven days.

The character of the cougar is like that of the cat family in general, whether wild or domesticated; and this may be summed up by saying that it is naturally timid and will flee before man, but is exceedingly fierce and daring when pressed by hunger, when wounded, or when defending its young. Affection for the latter is manifested only by the mother, however, for the male would destroy and eat them did he have the opportunity; and even the female is not always safe from his sudden and ungallant temper.

The favorite haunts of the cougar are amidst the deepest recesses of the forest, where it can obtain food and the close concealment so natural to its habits; and, being nocturnal in character, it seeks its prey principally at night, or early in the morning. It is seldom seen abroad during the day, unless severely pressed by hunger; and then it will go boldly anywhere and face man without a moment's hesitation, or make a raid on a farm-yard despite the protests of furious dogs. In the forests of the North-west, however, it is seldom compelled to risk its life to procure food, as it can obtain a plentiful supply without much trouble, owing to the abundance of deer, hares, squirrels, and other small animals, which it captures readily by bounding upon them suddenly from a tree or the thick undergrowth of the forests, where it always lies in concealment. Whatever it catches, let it be small or large, it first cuts open the throat and drinks the blood, and if its appetite is not then satisfied it devours the flesh; and should any remain over, it is carefully covered with leaves, to be kept for the next meal, or a "rainy day." When lying in wait for its prey, it seeks the shelter of a thicket or crouches on the lower branches of a tree; and the moment a hare, a deer, or even a wolf passes by, it jumps on its back, and, fastening its claws in the sides of the poor captives, cuts open the neck or throat in a few seconds. Its strength may be inferred from the fact that it can drag a deer, weighing perhaps one hundred and fifty pounds, a long distance, and can run quite rapidly with a large dog in its mouth. It has been known to kill a sheep, and without doing anything more to it than to drink its blood, bound away with the carcass at such a rate of speed that a man on foot found a difficulty in overtaking it. Should it commit depredations on a farm-yard, the farmer generally starts in pursuit with dogs and guns, or spreads strychnine over a piece of meat and places it in a spot where it will prove most effective. Numbers are destroyed annually by this means in the West, and, as a result, they are becoming scarcer in certain sections. When pursued, or startled on the ground, the cougar bounds for the densest thicket, or scrambles up the first convenient tree and conceals itself amidst the branches. Extending itself on a bough, it is sometimes difficult to find if it remains quiet; but it has a habit of swinging its tail from side to side, and of purring loudly if enemies approach its retreat, and these cause it to be detected when it otherwise would not.

Its courage is sufficiently great to induce it to face any foe, from bear to man, in a case of emergency. I heard an old hunter say that he once saw a fight between a black bear and a cougar, and that the latter killed its adversary in less than twenty minutes, by leaping on its neck and cutting the spinal cord with its lance-like teeth. Bruin did not die, however, without a severe struggle, and inflicting such injuries on the other that it would undoubtedly have died of its wounds had the hunter not shot it as it was crawling into the shrubbery. On examining it, he found that one of its hind-legs was broken, and the flesh torn off by a sweeping blow of the bear's paw, and that it also had a severe wound in the neck. The cougar was evidently the aggressor in this case, and was incited to the combat either by hunger or a desire to defend its young, as he found that it was a large female whose teats were full of milk.

He saw, on another occasion, a fight between a cougar and a wolf, and, according to his statement, it was one worth beholding, as they tumbled over and over each other, and caused the leaves to fly about as wildly as if two moose were engaged in a deadly contest. Knowing which one would win, he loaded his gun with buckshot, and, approaching them to within a distance of thirty yards, he fired both barrels at their heads in rapid succession, and killed them in their tracks. Both were full-grown, heavy animals, and that they were possessed of strength was proved by the number of wounds on their bodies, and the manner in which the ground was torn up.

A proof that the cougar is no mean foe to encounter may be illustrated by the following anecdote:

A farmer in Oregon was returning home one day from market at a rather late hour, but he had not proceeded half a mile from town before he met a large cougar on the

CONCOLOR—THE PUMA.

road. Being unarmed, he did not care to assail it; and as he did not want to retreat or take the trouble of flanking it by cutting across fields, he picked up a stone and fired at it, to drive it away; but, instead of complying with his desires, it crouched on the ground, as if preparing for a spring. Not liking its actions by any means, he gave a fierce shout; but, instead of fleeing, as it generally does, from the human voice, it bounded at him, and, striking him full on the breast, knocked him down. Then commenced a fierce struggle between man and beast. The latter caught the former by the upper part of the arm and fastened its claws in his breast; but he, being of a powerful frame, seized his foe by the throat and held it in a vise-like grip until it let go its hold. He held it in that position until he got on his feet, when he flung it away from him and attempted to escape, but the brute was not to be balked, and, before he ran three paces, it sprung upon him once more, and again a desperate struggle commenced, in which the man was getting the worst of it, as he was severely bitten in the arms, and his sides and chest were torn by its long, hooked, and iron-like claws. Seeing that his strength would soon be exhausted unless he could kill the animal, he made a desperate effort to choke it; but he was so weak from the contest and loss of blood that his efforts were futile. He had about given up all hope of his life, when he saw a large stone on the road; and seizing that eagerly, and despite the assaults of his fierce foe, he began to rain blows on the head of the latter with all his strength for several seconds. These caused it to loosen its hold on his arm and to drop to the ground, its face besmeared with blood; and when the farmer saw that, he hurled the stone with all his might at its skull and sent it crashing into the brain, killing it almost instantaneously. When the victory was won, he fell in a swoon from exhaustion and the loss of blood, and was in that condition when he was found by a neighbor of his who was going home in a wagon. Both the combatants were placed in the vehicle and taken back to town, for the man was so severely wounded that surgical aid was promptly required, and there he remained for two months before he was deemed sufficiently recovered to go home.

An acquaintance of mine, while out grouse-shooting one day, met two cougar kittens, apparently about three months old, and chased them at once. Finding they would be overtaken, they clambered up a young fir, and he followed in hot pursuit, and soon had them by the nape of the neck. He held them in that position while he searched in his pocket for a piece of twine with which to tie them, and during that time they were "youling" loudly and trying to break away. Having secured them, he was preparing to descend, when a new foe, in the form of their mother, appeared on the scene. She had evidently deserted them for a few minutes to provide them with provender, as she carried a large hare in her mouth. When she heard their cries, and saw them in the arms of a Philistine, she dropped the hare and bounded on to the lower limb of the tree, which must have been at least fifteen or twenty feet high. The hunter having left his gun on the ground, to enable him to climb with greater facility, was in a quandary, as he had nothing better than a pocket-knife with which to defend himself. He was a man of ready resources, however, and, not caring to risk his life or lose the youngsters, he concluded to await the onslaught of their protector. When she clambered, or rather sprung, to the next limb, he was enabled to reach her with his foot by clinging around the trunk of the tree, and, dropping the captives, he made a tremendous downward kick at her head. She raised on her hind-legs to parry the blow, so he missed her; but he struck the light branch on which she was sitting with such force that he almost severed it from the trunk, and caused the outer part to point directly downward. The result was much better than he anticipated, for the cougar lost her balance, and went crashing through the branches to the ground, a distance of perhaps thirty or more feet, and struck it with such vehemence that she was stunned. As soon as he saw her shooting downward he scrambled to the broken branch, and, seizing it with both hands, threw his full weight on it, and swinging himself sideways, tore it from its fastenings, and was soon on the grass, armed with an unwieldy but most effective battering-ram. Before the cougar could get ready for another spring at him—for the shock had evidently knocked much of the courage out of her, if it had not seriously injured her—he gave her two or three swingeing blows on the head to expel any remaining pluck, then ran for his shot-gun a few feet away. Seizing that hurriedly, he took aim at her eyes, which glowed so much with rage and hate that they were of a reddish-emerald hue, and planted two loads of No. 6 shot in them. The closeness of the range sent the pellets through the eyes into the brain, and she fell dead where she crouched. Feeling assured of her fate, he went up after the kittens, which were mewing terribly, and brought them safely down, notwithstanding their many protests with tooth and nail. As he could not carry both the kittens and their dam at the same time, he was compelled to leave the latter and go to an Indian encampment close by, and get a couple of *siwashes* to bring her in. While awaiting the return of the messengers he felt the stocking of one foot getting wet, and, on looking to see what was the matter, found that his leg was bleeding profusely from a wound which the slain animal had inflicted on him with her claws when he kicked at her. Binding that up, he engaged a canoe to take him home, and, as soon as he received his trophy, started off amidst the highest expressions of admiration that the Indians could give, as they looked upon his feat as a most remarkable one, and himself as a hero of no small magnitude.

The kittens were carefully housed and petted in every possible manner; but though playful when young, as soon as they became old enough to display their natural temper they were anything but playful or pleasant companions. They would bear no familiarity; and whenever they escaped, as they sometimes did, they would destroy fowls in the most indiscriminate manner, and apparently without any other purpose than to satisfy their bump of destructiveness, for they did not attempt to eat them. They were attached to no person, not even to him who fed them habitually; and as all the feeding and kindness in the world could not arouse a spark of affection in them, or overcome their propensity to destroy everything they could seize, even to the house-cat, they were shot before they were eighteen months old.

One of them escaped on one occasion, but its absence being detected in a few moments after, the dogs were sent in pursuit. They espied it heading for a copse some few hundred yards away, and announced the matter by a vigorous yelping. When it reached a deep but narrow stream that separated the woods from the house it plunged in boldly, clambered up the other side, and sought refuge in a tree. It was soon caught, however, and dragged back to the kennel a degraded, "youling" captive. This incident would prove that the animal will voluntarily take to water, and it is, I believe, one of the few species of the *Felidæ* that will do it; but my experience is that it will avoid it as carefully as any member of its family unless driven to it by stern necessity.

A proof that the animal in its wild state can be playful with man sometimes may be deduced from an incident that occurred in Washington Territory. A farmer, on his way to Olympia, the capital of the Territory, was passing one evening over the road that leads through the dense forests which stretch southward for miles from the town. These are almost of Plutonian darkness after the sun sets, owing to their density and towering altitude, so that one cannot see ten paces ahead. While walking leisurely along, he was surprised to feel something touch his leg, and, on looking down, was almost dazed to see a huge cougar rubbing its head against him, and purring pleasantly. Seeing that it was in evident good-humor, while he was defenceless in case of an attack, he moved onward in a sort of half-stupefied condition, for his heart was beating violently, and he dared not utter a sound through fear of arousing its anger. The animal accompanied him for a mile or more, and gambolled around him in the most playful manner, now running ahead for several yards, then bounding back and rubbing its head and side against him strongly, as a pet house-cat would. Knowing the treacherous nature of the brute, he expected every moment to be assailed; and the blood was often sent coursing violently and spasmodically through his body, and cold chills crept over him whenever he saw it plunging into the woods, then come leaping toward him at its best pace, and colliding with his legs so vigorously that he feared sometimes that he would be knocked down; and if such an accident occurred he was afraid that its natural instinct would prevail, and that he would be pounced upon. It began to get wearied after awhile of the gambolling, and kept closer to him; its tail also began to swing suspiciously from side to side, and its loud purring was occasionally transformed into a blood-curdling scream. Just as he was about giving up all hopes of getting rid of it quietly, he heard the rumble of approaching wheels, and taking courage from this indication of help, he gave a loud and prolonged yell, in which there was more of fear than defiance. The cougar was startled so much by this fierce and unexpected cry that it fled into the woods terror-stricken, and disappeared like magic in the shrubbery. When the driver of the wagon approached the man, he found him so weak from excitement that he could hardly speak, but he recovered himself after a little while and told his tale. He was driven to town, and, after taking a long pull at something stronger than tea, was himself again; but he will not to his dying day, probably, forget his agonizing half-hour with a cougar.

I heard of another instance in Minnesota, in which a cougar leaped from a tree upon the driver of a wagon who was carrying home some fresh meat from town. When the animal made the leap it knocked the man back in the wagon; but before it could do any more harm than to claw him severely, he tumbled out on the road at the tailboard, while his horses bounded away at full speed, carrying the assailant with them. They say the man was so frightened that he stayed in the road all night, with his nose stuck in the dust; and on being rallied about his courage the next day, he nonchalantly replied that he was not going to take any chances, and he would rather lie in the dust than in the stomach of a cougar.

The first time I had the pleasure of killing one of these fierce cats I was stopping at a rancher's cabin near the foot of the Sierra Nevada Mountains for a few days. While sleeping soundly one night after a hard day's hunting, I was startled suddenly by the barking of dogs, the cackling of fowls, and the squealing of pigs. Supposing some Indians or horse-thieves were making a raid on the house, I jumped out of bed and dressed as rapidly as possible; but, before that simple operation was finished, the clamor outside had ceased, except an occasional cackle.

The host next appeared on the scene armed with a rifle, and, giving me a loaded shot-gun, we went into the yard to see what the matter was. A momentary investigation revealed the condition of affairs; for near the corner of the yard we found the dead body of a magnificent dog, of which the owner was very proud, on account of his peculiar intelligence and affectionate disposition. He was a cross between a Newfoundland and a mastiff, and inherited the good qualities of both parents, being brave, kind, and faithful. His ribs were broken, and the abdomen torn away, so that the viscera protruded. "A painter did that," was the host's laconic expression; and after a long pause, as if trying to overcome his feelings, he vehemently asserted that he would have the cougar's hide before he was twenty-four hours older, or know why. A further examination proved that the brute had carried away a young pig about four months old, and had escaped by leaping a two-rail fence with it. There were several other dogs in the yard besides the one slain, but none had the courage, apparently, to attack the prowler, and the result was that the dead animal paid the usual forfeit of heedless bravery. We were aroused at daylight the next morning by the yelping of the dogs again, and, on rushing out, found that they were barking at a number of Digger Indians who were moving past the house toward a large piece of woods half a mile away. When we appeared on the scene one of the men approached the fence, and taking off his nether garment, the only one which he wore, except a battered, crownless tall hat, or "chimney-pot," as it is known in portions of the West, he handed it over to Mr. V——, and, with the simple word "keep," and some pantomimic gestures, he gave him to understand that he wished it kept until it was called for. Mr. V—— took it grudgingly, and, holding it as far away from his person as possible, told the owner that his wishes should be complied with, and he started away in lighter costume than that worn by the famous Georgia colonel, and that consisted of only a spur and a paper collar. After breakfast my host and myself armed ourselves, and, calling the dogs together, started on the trail of the cougar. The morning being fine, and the dew still on the ground, the two harriers that formed a portion of the small pack had little difficulty in following up the trail as far as a glade in the copse, but they lost it there. When we emerged on this we saw fifty or sixty Indians engaged in collecting brushwood and decaying felled trees, and making a large pile of them. On approaching them, V—— asked them what they were about, but no one answered. Thinking that they were preparing for a grand feast, and that they had perhaps called on his farm-yard for some tender chickens or turkeys, he moved toward the spot where their provisions were placed, and, after scanning them closely, saw among them a portion of the shote he had lost the night before.

Forgetting for the moment all idea of what he had been hunting during the morning, he began to rail at the Indians as thieves, and to assert that it was they who had stolen the pigs and sheep he had lately lost, while he was blaming it all on cougars. The man who had given him the trousers for safe-keeping, on seeing him pull out the remnants of the pig, whose body was drained of every drop of blood, approached him and said, "Mehali um find;" and pointing in the direction in which the squaw had found it, he led us to the edge of the copse to prove that he was right. When we reached the spot in the woods where the dogs had lost the trail, he pointed to a small pile of leaves and boughs, and, on scattering them, V—— found by the blood on the ground that the cougar had feasted on it there, and covered the remainder so as to keep it for another occasion. "If I had any strychnine in the house," said he, "I'd poison some fresh meat and put it in that place for the thieving brute; but as I have not, there is nothing left to be done except to come here to-night with the dogs and try and tree the old thief when he comes after his spare grub."

Our work being over for the time being, so far as the cougar was concerned, we devoted the day to deer-hunting, and returned in the evening with a splendid stag, which we killed while he was vaulting over a jam of fallen trees and branches seven or eight feet high. After a hearty dinner of venison, washed down with native wine, and a quiet smoke, we again started to hunt up the disturber of the previous night's repose. We marched direct to where it had secreted the remnants of the pig, and taking a position to the leeward in a dense thicket, we awaited its approach with intense anxiety, as V—— was most eager to avenge the loss of his faithful dog. We were concealed in shrubbery which grew with such luxuriance that the sky was scarcely visible, but we were well supplied with pine torches and matches; so that, should we find the object of our search, we could illumine its physiognomy long enough to enable one of us to shoot it. While discussing in a hushed tone how we should act under certain circumstances, our position was made distinct by a bright light that seemed to spread over a large tract of country. My companion thought the woods were on fire, and expressed his fear that it might extend toward his cabin; but when I reminded him that it came from the glade his apprehensions were calmed, if not dispelled. We waited half an hour after that for some signal of the approach of the quarry; but neither hearing nor seeing anything of it, we were becoming restless, when a fiery terrier started suddenly from covert and ran yelping to the windward. Its companions followed, and we followed all, and went scurrying and tumbling through the underbrush in our efforts to keep up with them. They suddenly halted, and when we approached they commenced barking up a tree. We lighted our torches, and swinging them in the wind to fan the flame, we espied, amidst the foliage of a sturdy oak, the gleaming green eyes of the cougar, and a tail that swung ominously to and fro in measured movement. As my companion, who was armed with a muzzle-loading rifle, desired to kill the animal himself, he fired first, but missed his aim, owing to the smoky glare of the light and his too great anxiety. While he was reloading, I fired at it with the shot-gun, which contained twelve buckshots in each barrel, and, hitting it in the head, I brought it to the ground. The fall alone from that height would have killed it; but, to be thoroughly sure, I let it have the second barrel right in the eyes as soon as it reached the earth, and that extracted whatever life remained in the body. My companion was highly delighted at our success, as he calculated that the death of the animal would be worth at least a hundred dollars a year to him, that being the value of the animals which he supposed he lost annually by its depredations.

Slinging the prize across his neck, after tying its legs, he led the march for home; but as the fire was still burning fiercely on our left, he began to get nervous about it, and concluded to see what the Indians were doing, as they have a habit of setting the woods on fire and destroying not only valuable timber, but also endangering farm-houses. Retracing our steps, we marched toward the glade, and, on emerging upon it, were so thunderstruck at the scene before us that we halted as promptly as if we had been shot, and gazed for several seconds in blank amazement, first at the bonfire, and then at each other. The scene was certainly enough to make any pale-face halt; for directly in the middle of the glade was a huge pile of blazing wood, and around this some fifty or more Indians of both sexes circled and danced and yelled and moaned. The shouts and bounds of the naked, dark-hued men and women, the cracklings of the flames, the showers of sparks, the brightly-lighted foreground, and the lurid glare that encompassed the shadowy woods in the background, produced a sight that seemed most strange, and recalled visions of the uncanny creatures that are supposed to dwell in deep and unearthly places. Loading our guns, we marched toward the fire, and, on approaching it, saw on the top the dead body of an Indian undergoing a process of cremation.

We knew then that we were spectators of a Digger funeral ceremony, and a literal dance of death, and I certainly was glad to have had an opportunity of seeing both. While looking on, he of the trousers asked for the cougar, that he might burn it on the funeral pyre with the body, as he would then be sure that his kinsman had entered the Spirit Land as a recognized true brave. He was told that if he would skin it he could have the carcass, and, without another word, he undertook the business. While he was engaged in this operation, we were watching closely the strange spectacle before us. The young men and women were wailing fearfully, and jumping around the pyre with all their might, but the aged and infirm were content with walking and moaning. When the cougar was skinned the carcass was thrown into the flames, near the corpse, amidst indescribable yelling, the butcher being the most vehement shouter or wailer. We spent half an hour gazing on this weird, wild scene, then returned home; I, for one, feeling as if I had been a spectator of some orgie among the fabulous creatures that inhabit subterranean abodes. Two days after this strange ceremony the dancers passed the house, and their heads and features were so bedaubed with tar that they bore a strong resemblance to veritable imps of darkness. I learned subsequently that it is a custom among the Diggers to mix the ashes left by the funeral pyre with tar, and to bedaub themselves with it as a sign of mourning; and as they do not remove it until it falls off through age, they look like ogres and ogresses for six months sometimes. This is the reason, I believe, that the Californians are locally called "Tar Heads," in contradistinction to the natives of North Carolina, who are known as "Tar Heels," on account of the large quantity of tar manufactured in the State.

The Indian who had left his trousers for safe-keeping quietly walked into the house and asked Mrs. V—— for them; but she, good woman, was so horrified at his appearance and costume that she ran out at the back-door screaming. The sad-eyed mourner, thinking he had done something wrong, retreated rapidly, and before I knew what he wanted, was out on the road, and staring at the house in a surprised manner. When I learned what he desired, I seized the prolongations with the tongs and handed them to him, and he received them with evident feelings of pleasure. He then asked for something to eat, and was furnished with a very large piece of fresh beef. Running a string through this, he slung it on his back and marched proudly away, though to me he presented a most ludicrous aspect; for his nether dirty-white garments were much too short for him, and were entirely devoid of the portion on which a person usually sits; his body was perfectly naked, but his head was covered with a battered and crownless "stove-pipe" hat, so that he looked like a "harmony" in black, dusky, and dirty-white.

As a curious coincidence, the next time that I was successful in bagging a cougar, I was also a spectator of an Indian funeral service, but it was the opposite of the previous one in character. During a visit that I made to the Snoqualmie Falls, in Washington Territory, I called at an Indian reservation which was under the charge of a self-denying missionary, who had devoted his life to the physical and spiritual welfare of the red man. While I was there a child belonging to one of the best young men in the tribe died, and the priest was sent for to bury her. I accompanied him to the little hamlet where a portion of the tribe dwelt, and as soon as we landed from the canoe, all its members marched to the shore, and each in turn touched the priest's hand as a sign of welcome, but no one spoke. When the greeting was over, the men and women assembled in a log-cabin, and squatted themselves on their heels around the coffin, or rather box, which was covered with white cloth. After prayers, and the sprinkling of the bier, all formed in procession, the head men being in advance, and they were followed by the young braves and squaws. The pall-bearers consisted of two relatives of the deceased, and they were preceded by a lad who rung a weird-sounding bell in measured time every few moments. When the procession advanced toward the grave, which was dug amidst the matted undergrowth of the forest, all commenced intoning a hymn in their native tongue, and that to me was the most pleasing, or, rather, the most picturesque, I had ever heard, as the weak and senile voice of the aged was contrasted with the deep bass of the young men and the clear tones of the squaws. When the grave was reached another prayer was uttered, another sad hymn for the repose of the soul of the deceased was sung, and the rude casket was placed in the earth amidst the dripping shrubbery. When the last sod was thrown on, the procession reformed and marched back to the hamlet, wailing the tribal song of death in prayerful words. The contrast between the solemn funeral ceremony of this Christian tribe and the barbarous Diggers made a marked impression on me, and caused me to remember the cougar-hunt of the two occasions in the most vivid manner.

After leaving the reservation, I engaged a canoe and two Indians to take me to the Falls; and as the trip was to occupy several days, I placed a store of provisions and arms aboard, in order to be prepared for all emergencies. We had to work hard during the day to pass over brawling cascades and to stem strong currents; hence, when night came, we were glad to go ashore and camp under the shelter of a gigantic spruce or fir. While I was soundly sleeping one night, an Indian jumped up suddenly, awoke me, and called my attention to an animal that was stealthily advancing toward us. Its movements were light and cat-like; and recognizing at once what it was, I seized the loaded rifle which laid beside me, and fired when I caught it in a position where the glare of the camp-fire fell full upon it. Not being more than thirty or forty feet away, I hit it in the shoulder, and the ball went crashing through it from side to side. One of the Indians then fired at it with a revolver, and he also succeeded in hitting it, the ball entering the skull. When we approached it the last gasp of life was leaving the body—a fact of which we were very glad, as I did not care to have any more shots in its coating than was necessary, for fear of spoiling it. We found it to be a two-year-old, in splendid condition, and unusually fat for its family in the wild state. It had, no doubt, been attracted to our camp by the savory smell of bacon, which the Indian cook had left uncovered in a pan near the fire; and though this was contrary to rule, yet I did not blame him when I saw what it had brought me.

During one of my short trips in the Cascade Range, I was accompanied by a stock-raiser, his two sturdy sons, and two Indians, who were civilized, in the sense that they lived in cabins, cultivated a few acres of land, had some cows and horses, and professed to be Christians.

We were out in search of big-horns, and took the red men with us, because they knew the mountains well and had killed several sheep in their time. We encamped the first night near a lovely tarn that was buried in a small, deep valley, which was gay with wild-flowers and green with generous grasses. Towering basaltic crags arose on one side, like huge sentinels intended to guard the vale, and on the other a coppice, composed of several varieties of trees, from pine to mountain maple, grew in wild luxuriance. The Indians objected strongly to selecting this beautiful spot for a camp, and on asking them their reason therefor they refused to tell, but they would not remain there, they said, for any consideration; and as we would not leave, they picked up their traps and departed for some other quarters. They rejoined us the next day, however, and hunted as assiduously as any of ourselves. On starting out, we went in pairs, and moved in opposite directions, so as to be able to head off any animals fleeing from one side of the valley or mountain to another, and, if necessary, to make a surround. My companion, who was the senior pale-face of the party, was accompanied by three large dogs used for hunting cattle and wild game, and they seemed to be equally expert in all. Moving toward the coppice, in order to work up the valley in the direction of the bluffs, we were soon beating the undergrowth to see if we could find game of any kind there. After quartering it for half an hour, the dogs, which were running wildly about in every direction, gave a loud yelp some distance ahead of us, and kept up the canine music for ten minutes, when it suddenly ceased. We hastened onward, and in about twenty minutes reached a narrow stream, and there found the dogs beating up and down in search of the quarry, but they made no effort to enter the water. Presuming from their actions that the game, whatever it was, had crossed the river, we waded through it to the opposite side, and the dogs, after a little work there, found the trail again, and declared it in the most vehement manner with their voices. We followed them up promptly for a quarter of a mile, and overtook them as they were grouped around a tree and barking violently. Peering through the foliage of the fir, we saw a large cougar perched on a low branch, its green eyes, like an emerald furnace, glowing with rage, and its tail swinging like a pendulum from side to side. We could hear its deep purring audibly, and inferred from this that it had little fear of its canine foes. It seemed to pay little heed to us, but concentrated all its attention and rage on the boisterous dogs, which disturbed its repose by their cries. As my companion feared that some of the latter might be injured if the animal was not shot dead, he asked me to fire at the same time that he did; so we both blazed away together, and the cougar came tumbling down amidst a shower of leaves and branchlets. When it reached the ground the dogs attacked it vigorously; but as its hip was only broken, it made a fierce fight, and placed one of its assailants on the peace list by tearing a large slice of flesh from the neck and shoulders with one sweep of its lance-like claws. This catastrophe caused the others to fight shy, and to jump at it only when it attempted to rise; and these tactics kept its attention so constantly engaged that it seemed to forget our presence completely. This proved anything but fortunate, for my companion, thinking he could finish it without any trouble, rushed in to place his revolver near its head; but before he could pull the trigger the animal turned on him suddenly, and raked his leg from hip to knee so severely with its paw that the flesh seemed to have been cut with a knife.

The man was so amazed at the suddenness of the onslaught that he did not move for a few moments; and were it not that the dogs attacked the brute boldly, and thus diverted its attention, he would have received a second wound, in all probability, before getting out of its reach. When he did move away it was in a hurry, and, seizing his rifle, he rushed in among the dogs, and placing its muzzle within two feet of the cougar's head, fired, and fairly blew the top of the skull off. When the animal was dead he began kicking it, and, having satisfied his vengeance, he turned to his wound, and with my aid bound it up. The injury, though painful, was not very serious, as no vein or artery had been severed; so he was able to walk back to camp, and even to help me in carrying the trophy at intervals. This accident caused a suspension of our hunting operations; and for fear it might prove to be more serious than it looked, we left the valley that afternoon and marched toward home. We reached a splendid camping-ground early in the evening, and there pitched our tent, as water and grass for our horses were to be found in abundance. While discussing the incidents of our trip over the post-prandial pipe, we asked the Indians, who were encamped close by us, why they would not remain near the lake the first night; and one of them, after much pressing, said it was because the valley was haunted. When asked to tell how, he said that a squaw who had been badly treated by her husband resolved on suicide, and one evening, when her tribe reached this valley and pitched their wigwams near the lake, she suddenly rushed forth from her *tepee*, and, plunging into the crystalline water, sunk to the bottom before any person could make an effort to save her. Her spirit was supposed to haunt the vale ever since, as several warriors had seen her frequently bound into the lake at sunset and disappear in a pyramid of foam. She had also, it is said, been heard chanting a mournful song, whose theme was the cruelty of her husband and her own sad fate. This tale had made the tarn famous among several tribes, to whom it was known as the Lake of the Squaw's Leap; and so implicitly did they believe in its truth that they could not be induced to camp in the valley on any account, or even to speak of the incident except with bated breath; for it is an article of faith among the red men that every time a dead person's name is mentioned he or she turns over in the grave, and punishes severely those who are guilty of such a sacrilegious act as to disturb the repose of the departed.

I asked the Indians if they ever had any personal encounters with a cougar, and they replied they had not, but that an acquaintance of theirs was attacked without any cause by one while he was searching in the woods for some strayed horses. The animal jumped at his throat and knocked him down; but as he was armed with a loaded single-barrelled shot-gun, he sent its contents into the brute's stomach, and this caused it to loosen its hold. Struggling to his feet, he attempted to run away; but, wounded severely as the cougar was, it leaped upon him once more, and another fierce struggle ensued, the Indian using his gun against the claws and fangs of his foe. After a desperate battle, in which the gun was destroyed, the red man came off victorious, but he was so badly wounded that his life was despaired of for several weeks. His strong constitution prevailed at length, however, and he recovered, but he was a mere wreck of what he had formerly been. In answer to another query, the most experienced replied that the cougar never chased its prey, but jumped on it from the concealment of a thicket or the bough of a tree, and he doubted if it could follow any animal by scent— a statement which I am rather inclined to believe, notwithstanding the assertions of some writers who say that it has trailed them as a hound would a hare or a fox. I heard of other incidents in the West which prove that the animal is very dangerous when hungry or wounded; but if it will attack man without any seemingly direct provocation, it is an easy matter to understand the motive therefor.

It is naturally so timid and cautious, and so far from large settlements, that it is only met by accident, unless a person enters the deep recesses of the forest; but in severe winters it leaves its concealment and makes bold raids on the sheep, pigs, calves, foals, and even the dogs of the farm. It is very destructive on such occasions, as it kills a great many more animals than it can eat, and frequently leaves the carcasses on the ground after it has extracted all the blood through the orifice which it cuts in the neck. It kills, in fact, for the sake of killing, even when gorged with food; and this propensity causes it to be thoroughly hated and feared by the settlers. Sheep-raisers who take their flocks to the mountains during the summer wage war to the knife upon it with rifle and strychnine; and the result is that it is disappearing as fast as the grizzly bear in some sections of the country.

During one of my rambles along the coast region in Washington Territory, I had an excellent opportunity of seeing how destructive it was to the farm, what great strength it possessed; and I also had the pleasure of killing one which had proved a perfect Thug to the denizens of the farm. While stopping at a lonely cabin that was buried in the forest, some seven or eight miles from any other dwelling, a cougar was so frequent a visitor to the sheep-pen that it killed eight lambs and four ewes in less than a fortnight. Their owner, becoming enraged, at length concluded to start out in quest of it, intending, if he could not kill it, to drive it some distance away at least by chasing it with dogs, or send it to visit some other neighbor whose hospitality it had not experienced. With these purposes in view, we armed ourselves one day, and taking four dogs with us which were taught to run mute when held in leash, we commenced scouring the woods, taking our course direct from the enclosure in which the pigs and sheep were usually kept at night during the winter. The dogs had scarcely entered the forest before they got on the trail of a thief that had been dining off young mutton the previous night, and following this up as rapidly as we could, we were soon forcing our way through dense shrubbery or scurrying over open ground. The dogs worked the trail admirably, and without giving a single whimper, for a mile or more, but they lost it at the base of a rocky chasm; nor could they carry it any farther, although they were harked back two or three times, and several casts were made in various directions. This induced me to look around me; and at the first glance I noticed that a huge flat bowlder, some ten or fifteen feet in height, rose abruptly upward from the ground where the scent had vanished, and I deduced from this immediately that the cougar had travelled as far as this, and closed its trail by bounding on the crag and seeking safety in the woods above. Presuming that it would be impossible for it to leap up there with a lamb in its mouth, we commenced searching around to see if we could find the remains buried anywhere; but after half an hour's diligent work we relinquished our effort, and decided that it must have performed that feat, else the lamb would have been carefully stowed away under leaves, branches, or dirt, somewhere in the vicinity of the rock.

We next commenced a search for footsteps among the terraces forming the upper portion of the chasm, and there found the slots of a cougar; but as they differed in size within a short distance of each other, we concluded that there were two of the same family in the neighborhood, probably two males, or they would have kept together, and that one of them used the canyon for its favorite line of retreat, while the other preferred the forest. We therefore decided to lie in wait for the former near its vaulting-place, and to attract it there by placing some fresh meat on the route it usually took on its foraging expeditions. Having formed our plans, we returned to the house and prepared two large pieces of venison for a bait, taking good care to wash them thoroughly, so as to take away the smell of the hands. We carried them to the trysting-place after supper, by running a piece of twine through them, and placed one several feet away from the top of the precipice, and the other near the base of the bowlder. We then sat down for a quiet and hushed chat, and kept it up until eight o'clock, when we separated, my companion going toward the summit of the chasm, while I kept at the base and to the leeward of the usual leaping-place.

We waited there patiently until after ten o'clock, but no cougar appeared, and the only noises that disturbed the brooding stillness of the night were the occasional hoot of the ghostly owl, the plaintive call of the whippoorwill, the croaking of frogs, and the whirring of the treelocust. Fire-flies were very numerous, and their transitory gleaming proved a welcome sight, as it illumined somewhat the inky darkness that reigned in the chasm. The lonely hours flowed on with slow paces to me, until the vigil began to grow from being monotonous to being exceedingly tedious. I was about despairing of meeting any cougar that night, when a sharp, fierce scream rung out in the precipice a short distance below me, and the rocks and trees taking this up, caused it to reverberate in stentorian tones for several seconds. It was so sudden and unexpected that it startled me violently; but when my first surprise was over I prepared for emergencies by noiselessly cocking my repeating rifle, and placing my knife more in front, so as to have it ready should it be necessary to use it. I then peered intently into the Cimmerian darkness in quest of the animal, but I could see nothing. I next extended myself flat on the ground and looked skyward at an oblique angle; but nothing met the vision except precipitous walls and masses of black clouds that were scurrying to the leeward before a stiff breeze, though in my cavernous retreat I could not feel a breath of it. After gazing for a few moments with such intensity as to strain my eyes and to make the eyelids somewhat sore, I noticed an animal emerge suddenly from some low shrubbery and come toward me with long, noiseless bounds. Thinking I was the object of an assault, I jumped to my feet promptly; and when the cougar, for such it was, passed by me within a distance of three or four yards, I fired at it almost without taking aim, and mingled with the report was the sharp yell of an angry, wounded cat. This was a pleasant but a dangerous predicament for me; and not caring for an encounter, I leaped back to the shelter of a rock and fired once more at the limping animal. There was no feline response to this detonation, so I moved forward to see what was the result of my fire. Before I had advanced a few feet I saw the cougar making vain efforts to leap up on the bowlder, and the moment I saw that I concluded it was my prisoner. Taking aim as carefully as I could in the darkness, I fired four shots in rapid succession, and, when the smoke cleared away, no cougar was visible. Not knowing whether it was dead or had escaped, I moved forward cautiously, with rifle cocked and ready for instant use, and when I reached the base of the crag I saw it extended at full length on its side. Lighting a match, I examined it cursorily, and found it was dead. Leaving it where it was, I clambered up the chasm to meet my companion and announce to him my good fortune, but he was nowhere visible. I began to call his name, but no response came. Wondering what could have become of him, I commenced groping about, thinking that he might have met with an accident; but after trudging up and down the terraces for half an hour I could find no trace of him. I then became really alarmed, and advanced to where the bait was placed, but that was gone. I divined from this that some animal had stolen it, and that he had started in pursuit of the thief; and this reassured me, as he was too good a backwoodsman to get lost, and too experienced a hunter to risk his life unnecessarily. After waiting half an hour, and shouting at intervals, I concluded that he was watching the object of his pursuit, and did not wish to answer my call for fear of spoiling his chances at bagging it. Another half-hour, and still no tidings of him, induced me to make an effort to find him; and as the moon then appeared from beneath a mass of clouds, I decided to track him if possible. When Luna's face was thoroughly clear, I bent low to the ground, and readily detected his footsteps on the grass and leaves, and by their length apart I knew he was running. As cats in flight generally keep a direct course, I concluded to follow a straight line; so I tore through the forest at a headlong pace, and called every now and then. When I had proceeded a mile or more I heard a weak cry, and, advancing toward it, found my friend lying in some brier-bushes, face upward, and a dead cougar not ten feet from him. Lifting him up, I asked what ailed him, and in feeble tones he told me that the animal had attacked and wounded him severely, if not fatally.

When placed on his feet, he found he could walk; so, with my aid, he tottered slowly home, but he was so weak that he could not carry his gun. After walking a seemingly interminable distance, we reached his house, and on looking at him by the light of the lamp he presented so ghastly an appearance that his wife screamed with fright. One side of his face was cut as cleanly and deeply as if it were done with a knife; his chest and left arm were torn sadly, and he had a heavy scar on the right thigh. After dressing his wounds, he was put to bed, and the next morning he was strong enough to be able to tell how he met with his accident. According to his statement, it was, that when he heard the scream of the cougar in the chasm he directed all his attention that way, thinking that if the animal passed me he could get a shot at it, or, if I needed assistance, that he would come to my aid.

When I ceased firing he was about to descend to see what luck I had; but, before doing so, he took a glance in the direction of his bait, and saw an animal running away with it. He followed in hot pursuit, and, on seeing it enter a clump of hazel-bushes, fired, without considering for a moment his chances of being successful in hitting it. He aimed better than could be expected under the circumstances, and struck it in the ribs; but the wound was only severe enough to make it angry, so it turned upon him at once. He delivered his second barrel hurriedly as it approached him; but he supposed he missed it, as it leaped upon him with as much vigor as if it had never been touched. He attempted to flee, but the brier-bushes tripped him up, and he fell flat on his face. He turned over promptly, however, and drew his knife, but the cougar was then upon him, and the struggle commenced. He used his knife blindly, striking wherever he could; but his aim was uncertain, owing to the hot breath of his foe, and its biting and clawing. He kept at the throat whenever he could get the opportunity, and was finally successful in causing the fierce brute to leave, in order to get breath; but it had gone only a few paces before it fell dead from loss of blood. He was so weak from the contest when it was over that he did not even have strength enough to crawl out of the briers, and he would probably have died there had he not received assistance.

The strength of the animal was so great, according to his assertion, that it used to turn him over on his side when it seized him by the arm and attempted to drag him away; but, owing to the matted mass of briers, it could not move him sideways, and it made no effort at any time to lift him up bodily and bear him away as cats generally do. But for the briers he thought he would have been killed under any circumstances; for when the animal pounced on his throat at one time, and its fierce breath almost suffocated him, it was compelled to let go its hold immediately, as one of the thorny stalks, which extended across his face, got into its mouth and pricked it so severely that it had to lift its head several times to get it out; for it stretched across the lower jaws, and was held there by having one of the cougar's own legs resting on one of the ground-ends. While the animal was trying to relieve itself of this disagreeable bit, the hunter used his knife on its throat to such good advantage that he forced it to retreat a few seconds later; and it was this fortunate accident that, undoubtedly, enabled him to kill his assailant and save his own life. It was a narrow scratch, however, which would have to yield first; and were it not for the brier-bush the hunter would, in all probability, have had to succumb, and be made into cat's meat inside of twenty-four hours.

I went after the slain animals the next day and brought them to the house, with the aid of a boy, by tying them on a drag made of the bough of a tree. On looking at them, I found that the one I had killed was a four-year-old male; but the assailant which had done so much damage to the person of the pioneer was a full-grown female that boasted exceedingly large and dense claws, and long, sharp fangs. Her face, throat, and abdomen were freely sprinkled with knife-thrusts, and her handsome hide was covered with blood from nose to flank. After being skinned, the remains were thrown to the pigs, and they went to feasting on the carcasses of animals which had often made a feast off one of their company. When I left the cabin its owner was on the high-road to recovery; but when I saw him a year later he presented a disagreeable sight, his face being as scarred as that of a Border Ruffian.

The cougar is, as must be apparent, no mean foe in a close struggle; so persons who do not care to spoil their handsome features would do well not to go too near it before its spirit has been expelled by the power of a heavy bullet. It may, for all that, be hunted for years before a man is attacked by it; but such good fortune is due more to accident than any amiability on the part of the quarry.

There are several other members of the feline race to be found in the West and South-west, but they are not so large, the jaguar excepted, as the celebrated "painter" of the pioneers. Those indigenous to the South-west, such as Texas, New Mexico, Arizona, and adjacent regions, are the jaguar, or Mexican tiger; the ocelot, or tiger-cat ($F.\ paradalis$); the eyra and yaguarundi; and a variety of the bay lynx, known scientifically as the $F.\ macalutus$. The Canadian and the bay lynx are denizens of the more northern regions; yet they are found far to the south on the Pacific Coast, much farther than on the Atlantic.

The lynxes, which are quite common in the region beyond the Rocky Mountains, may be readily known from the true cats by their physiognomy and anatomical construction. In the first place, they have only twenty-eight teeth, while the others have thirty; their skull is broader in proportion to size; the forehead is higher, and more arched; the skull is more capacious; the muzzle is broader; and the lower jaw is thicker, and more massive. They also have short, thick, and stubby tails; their feet are heavily furred; and they move along with short, straight bounds. The three recognized species in the Far West are the Canada lynx (*L. canadensis*), the bay lynx or red cat (*L. rufus*), and the *L. fasciatus,* which closely resembles the latter in everything except the color of the *pelage.* The former, which is the largest and heaviest of its genus, is a timid animal, and readily flees from the presence of man. It has large paws, slender loins, long, thick hind-legs, and a short, thick tail, which gives it an awkward if not clumsy appearance. The head and face are not unlike that of the domestic cat; the ears are erect, and tipped by an upright, slender tuft of black hairs; the legs are thick; and the toes are thick and furry, and armed with very sharp, curved, and awl-shaped claws, which are shorter than the fur. On the body and extremities the fur is hoary, most of the hairs being tipped with white; but on the middle of the back, on the crown of the head, and on the sides and legs, it is a pale wood-brown; and the tail is of the same color, except that it is tipped with black. The fur is close and fine on the back, but it is longer and paler beneath than above. The ordinary length of an adult is about thirty-eight inches, the height about seventeen inches, the tuft on the ears one and a half inches, and the tail, inclusive, about four and a half inches. Its color changes according to the seasons, so that one may be deceived in its appearance if he goes by hue alone.

If aroused by anger it spits like a domestic cat, and sets its hair up like a hyena. Its gait is by bounds, and with its back somewhat arched, and, when it alights, it comes down on all-fours at once. It is not swift, and any ordinary dog can overtake it in a short time. It swims well when forced to take to the water, but it avoids that element if possible, as it has all the objections of its race to a wetting. Its flesh, although white and tender, is flavorless, yet it is highly prized by some of the North-western tribes, and not a few pretend to think it superior to hare. Some of the French *voyageurs* and half-breeds call it the *loup cervier;* but why they do so I could never surmise, as it does not resemble the wolf either in looks, habits, or tones of voice. Neither is it dangerous to anything larger than a bird or a small quadruped; so all the tales told about its attacking men and killing them must be considered as approaching the fabulous. In the first place, one good blow on its back with a walking-stick would kill it immediately, and a rifle-ball or a dose of buck-shot is sufficient to send the spirit of the strongest to the feline world beyond this at once. Large numbers are shot or trapped annually for the sake of their skins, which command a fair price in the fur market; but they are not utilized as objects of the chase to any extent, as their first move is to seek safety in a tree, whence they are easily dislodged with a rifle or a bow and arrow.

A wounded catamount may sometimes turn on a man, but it cannot inflict much greater injury than giving him a severe scratching, and few experienced hunters care for such trifles. I have shot it occasionally after treeing it with dogs, but I never knew it to assault me, nor to make even a fierce fight against its canine foes; hence it offers but little sport; yet a person who bags his twenty-pound cat after a scramble through brake and brier feels not a little pleased with himself. Its congeners, the *L. rufus* and *L. fasciatus*, which resemble it in habit and character, are very common in the forests of the North-west, and commit sad havoc among the grouse, hares, squirrels, and other small animals on which they prey.

The latter is readily distinguished from the former by its rich chestnut color and soft, full fur, the other having a reddish hue, and a shorter and coarser fur. With this exception, both look remarkably alike—so much so, in fact, that an amateur naturalist would consider them to be the same species, and would attribute their different hue of coating to age, habitat, or the season of the year. An adult frequently attains a length of thirty-four inches, exclusive of the tail, which is about seven inches, and a height at the fore-shoulder of sixteen inches. Both varieties or species inhabit the same character of country, being generally found in the wooded borders of plains or valleys. If captured young, they soon learn to know the person who feeds them, and become somewhat attached to him; but they are such inveterate thieves, and so destructive to poultry, that they can only be kept in strong cages from which there is no possibility of escape, else they would soon prove most costly pets.

They resent the friendly advances of all strangers by humping up their back, depressing their ears, showing their teeth, and spitting fiercely, and should one approach too closely, they would even fly at him. As they make raids on the farm-yard occasionally, the farmers resort to poison to get rid of them, and not a few fall victims to the rifle or shot-gun. I killed four in one month in Washington Territory with the aid of dogs, and I never experienced any trouble from them — probably for the very excellent reason that I did not place myself in their way until they were rendered harmless. Cat-hunts are very popular with some persons, and especially those who have good dogs, as there is generally a fight and its accompanying wounds; but the result is in nearly all cases detrimental to the physical welfare of the bob-tailed feline. I can enjoy one on a moonlight night when I am with a jolly party and accompanied by a good pack, as it is full of quiet excitement, and frequently of ludicrous incidents; but it cannot, in my estimation, equal a bear or cougar hunt, and it cannot approach the bounding sensations produced by a dash after the fleet-footed stag when he is going at a view halloo pace.

CHAPTER V.

THE GRAY WOLF.

The Gray Wolf.—Number of Species of Wolves.—Difference in Colors.—The Size of the largest Variety.—Its Courage.—Captures of small Dogs from the Indians.—A Pack kills Two of our Dogs.—Retaliation.—Indians eat the Wolf.—Sagacity of the Animal in Hunting.—How a Pack drives Deer.—Stratagems resorted to.—Satellites of Herds of Buffaloes and Antelopes.—What Wolves live on.—Useful Scavengers.—Their harmless character to Man.—Famishing Wolves attack an Indian.—Result.—Afraid of a Child.—Yelps when wounded.—Their Size and Character when Food is plentiful.—How they are killed.—"Wolfers," and their Mode of Work.—Their General Character.—Sudden Wealth and Poverty.—A Lucky "Wolfer."—A Hunt with a "Wolfer."—His peculiar Breed of Dogs.—Their Speed and Stubbornness.—Six Cubs captured, and Two Wolves killed.—Pursuit of a Coyote.—Affection of a Mother for her Young.—How Wolves run when pursued.—Different Breeds of Dogs fit for Wolf-hunting.—How it is hunted in Portions of the West.—A spirited Wolf-chase.—How Wolves act when Trapped.—The Future of Wolf-hunting in the West.

WOLVES are unusually numerous throughout the whole of North-western America; and they seem to be equally at home on the prairie or in the forest, on the mountains or on the treeless plateaus, where shelter is often so scarce that they are compelled to form burrows for themselves under banks, or content themselves with a lair amidst crags.

There are, in reality, only two species in the country, the gray, timber, or prairie wolf (*Canis lupus var occidentalis*), and the coyote or prairie wolf (*Canis latrans*), but there are others which are classified as varieties on account of their distinctions in color. The difference in hue seems to be the result of climate and habitat, yet I have seen cubs of various hues in one litter. This might be the result of the association of differently marked animals; but in some instances this could not be the case, as only one variety frequented the country in which they were found.

There are five marked colors among them in the Northwest, and they are called from these the gray, white, pied, dusky, and black wolves; and to these may be added the red variety, which is indigenous to some southern regions. The white is the most northern in its habitat; south of this comes the gray and pied; while the dusky and sooty black are found largely in Southern Oregon, Northern California, portions of Washington Territory, and scattered throughout the whole area west of the Rocky Mountains. I have

GRAY WOLVES.

seen the latter principally in trappean countries, as if nature intended their color to harmonize with their surroundings, the better to enable them to secure food and escape enemies.

The American wolf differs in several points from its European congener; indeed, it resembles an Esquimau dog more than it does the latter. The main differences are that it has shorter ears, a broader forehead, a thicker muzzle, shorter legs, broader feet, and a finer fur, and denser and bushier hair behind the cheeks. The largest of the family is from thirty-four to thirty-six inches in height; is about four feet long; and weighs from ninety to one hundred and twenty pounds, and even more where food is abundant. The tail is carried straight, except when the animal is frightened; and then it crams it between the legs, like a terror-stricken cur, and carries it in that position for some distance if hotly pursued.

Large, gaunt, and fierce as it looks, it is one of the greatest cowards known, even when assembled in numbers, and seldom has the courage to face even a boy. When assailed by dogs it manifests a stronger desire to flee than to fight gallantly for life, and to show its teeth rather than use them. A couple of staunch hounds will cause one to scamper off in a tremendous hurry; and should they overtake and assail it, the probability would be that it would only snarl at them and try to escape, instead of closing and killing them at once, as it could readily do, owing to its weight, great strength, and long fangs. When it does bite, however, it inflicts a very severe wound, as its lancet-like teeth can cut clean through the leg of a dog; hence, hounds devoid of courage do not care to attack it after they have once felt its power, unless they are in sufficient numbers to make an assault successful. It does not show any fear of a single dog, unless it be a very large one, and does not hesitate a moment to gobble up an Indian cur and devour it in sight of its yelping, impotent kindred. I have known tribes to lose several dogs by these lupine prowlers, and they sometimes had the audacity to make a raid on the encampment for them and boldly bear them away to safe quarters, where they could eat them at their leisure.

While out on a hunting expedition along the Loup River, the wolves pounced on a valuable pointer and terrier belonging to our party, as they were on their way to visit some of their kindred in an Indian village, and actually devoured them in sight of our camp. We had so little fear of the scavengers assailing our dogs, when they crowded around the camp at night to the number of two or three hundred apparently, and their glittering eyes peered at us out of the darkness, that we did not molest them unless they threatened our edibles; but after that incident we kept them at a safe distance, and showed them no quarter wherever we met them. Though willing enough to scamper away before a small pack of hounds, a party of them treat a single dog, even of large size, with contemptuous indifference. I remember hearing a hunter telling me that he owned an immense dog, whose greatest pleasure was to fight with every one of his own species he met; and this propensity of his got him into many scrapes with their owners, for he was always the conqueror in a few moments. As he had never been defeated, he had such an overweening confidence in himself that he was ready to meet all foes; but the wolves taught him that he could not triumph over them as he had done over his civilized congeners. Felix, the canine hero, saw three wolves one day on a hillock; and thinking they afforded him an excellent opportunity for indulging in a victorious contest, advanced toward them with hairs bristled up like the quills of a porcupine; and they, on seeing his combative attitude, trotted away. This retrograde movement so encouraged him that he dashed after them at full speed, and whining with excitement; but when he was next seen he was retreating as rapidly as his legs could carry him, his tail was tucked between his legs, and he was ki-yi-ing fearfully, while the three wolves were ranged behind him, and giving him a good solid nip in the flanks every few moments, just to hear how nicely he could sing and see how fast he could run. His owner, seeing his plight, ran out to meet him, and drove his pursuers away; and this kindness Felix appreciated very highly, for he extended his tail and wagged it in the liveliest manner. That whipping made him a member of the canine peace society for the remainder of his life, for he was never afterward known to fight, or threaten to fight, any of his own species; and this saved his owner much unnecessary trouble.

The Indians who have lost their curs secure revenge by killing their destroyers, as they consider that one wolf is as good as four or five dogs; for not only is its skin valuable in trade, but its flesh is deemed to be palatable, and to be equal to that of the dog at least in gastronomic qualities.

When wolves hunt a large animal in packs they do not run together, in many cases, but secure positions on the routes which the quarry is supposed to take, and bound on it from cover. Their first movement is to hamstring it, and when that is done they have little difficulty in finishing it. It is no uncommon thing to meet old buffalo bulls in the spring, when they are weak and shedding their coat, with pieces of flesh actually torn out of their hams, the work of wolves; but in the autumn and winter these wounds are not so readily apparent, owing to the length of the hair. I have heard persons say that wolves give tongue when on the trail of a deer or other animal, but I cannot verify this from actual observation; for though I have seen them pursue several large quadrupeds, from the antelope to the elk, I do not remember hearing a whimper out of them while running, although they were noisy enough while waiting for something in the form of food to turn up.

When a strong pack chases an animal, it generally results in the death of the quarry, for wolves have speed, nose, strength, patience, and perseverance; and when a capture is made, it is very often the cause of a nice quarrel about a division of the spoils, and one in which ten or fifteen are frequently engaged at the same time. Their love of fighting is not very great, however, and they are glad to quit it for a mouthful of meat at the earliest opportunity.

It is amusing to see them try to capture an antelope or a buffalo, and the wiles to which they resort to obtain every advantage. One group may stand in front of the creature to attract its attention, while another steals around to the rear and attempts to cut the tendon by a sudden bound. If foiled in this, they break away promptly to avoid a thrust of the horns, while the others rush in; and by these cunning assaults they frequently obtain a feast in a short time.

When the quarry is disabled, they tear it to death, as it were. I have known them to eat a good-sized buck inside of ten minutes after its capture. They are constant attendants upon the herds of antelopes and buffaloes that exist on the plains of the West, and follow the latter in their migrations as far as the wintry regions of British America. When large game becomes scarce they manage to eke out an existence by preying on prairie-dogs, hares, ground-squirrels, badgers, foxes, and other animals, and such refuse as they may find in deserted camps and Indian villages. If farm-houses are convenient, they display their affection for the inmates of the farm-yard on every convenient occasion; but they are mostly attached to sheep, pigs, and calves.

Although they are the pirates of the plains, and the deadly foes of all animals they think they can destroy, yet they are very useful in that region, for they act as scavengers, and clear away the putrefying carcasses of hundreds of animals that die from various causes, and which but for them would make the plains a bed of pestilence at certain seasons.

Little can be said against them on account of their danger to man, for they seldom attack him, even when they are in overpowering numbers and starving; and in this characteristic they present a strong and favorable contrast to their European congeners. I have heard of only one corroborated case in which they attacked a human being, and that was under exceptional circumstances. During a severe winter, when the fall of snow was very great, an Indian hunter in Northern Idaho killed a deer one day, and while taking it home the smell of the blood attracted a pack of famishing wolves that were hunting in the woods. As soon as they overtook the man they jumped for the meat at once, and he, in trying to defend it, as he wanted it sadly for his own family, was attacked with the greatest fierceness; but before they could kill him he broke away, and sought safety in a huge fir, and there he remained until the next morning, when he was rescued by some of his tribe. The wolves remained under his perch all night, and howled dismally, as if bemoaning their loss; but as he had nothing except his bow and arrows with which to assail them, he did not have even the satisfaction of killing one. As their victory on that occasion was supposed to have emboldened them, the whole tribe turned out with their dogs and weapons, and destroyed several of them, and caused the remainder to flee to less dangerous quarters. I have only heard one hunter say that he was pursued by wolves, and that also seemed to be under unusual circumstances. According to his tale, an immense pack, which he estimated to number some hundreds, chased him for several miles over deep snow; and were it not for the speed and endurance of his horse, and the proximity of his house, he said he was almost sure they would have torn him to atoms, as they seemed to be in a famishing condition. The statement seems probable enough, but, so far as I could learn, the occurrence was exceedingly rare.

I have actually kicked them and pelted them with stones and dried buffalo chips, but I never knew them to display any more dangerous characteristics than to howl fearfully, or grin with pain as they trotted away. I did not even hear that they ever attacked horses or domestic horned cattle, probably for the reason that these animals will not bear any familiarity on their part, and charge them boldly whenever they come too close, or manifest any desire to feast on a colt or a calf.

In certain wooded portions of the West where food is abundant at all seasons, the wolf attains such a large size that some naturalists have denominated it the *Canis gigas*, as it frequently attains a weight of one hundred and fifty or more pounds; but when it reaches such dimensions it is generally timid, and keeps away from the abode of man, except on convenient occasions, when it takes a fancy to a lamb or a young porker. It often pays dearly for this thieving propensity, for the rifle and strychnine are sure to be ready for it the next time it visits the farm-yard; and if the farmer does not open on it, a bait sprinkled with the poison is almost sure to make it turn up its toes inside of three or four hours. This is the most effective means of destruction sheep-raisers can employ against it; and so effective has it been found that the animal has been decimated in large tracts of country where it was very numerous a few years ago.

A certain class of persons known as "wolfers" earn their livelihood by destroying it with poison. These men are a set of reckless nomads who live on the borders of civilization, and whose whole life seems to consist in braving cold, hunger, and sometimes death, for several months in the year, and spending the remainder in riotous debauchery. Those who make a business of "wolfing" do nothing else; and it is doubtful if the majority are useful for anything else. They commence operations as soon as the winter sets in, and continue it until late in the spring. Their equipment consists of strychnine, flour, bacon, tea, coffee, and sugar, and a few primitive cooking utensils; the edibles being intended for themselves, and the poison for the wolves. Travelling far away from the settlements, they pitch their camp in a region where the animals are numerous, and wood and water are convenient. Having established themselves, their first duty is to procure a bait; and whether it be a buffalo or a deer, they cut it up into large pieces, sprinkle it freely with strychnine, and scatter it about some distance from camp. The result is that from ten to eighty wolves may be found dead the next morning within an area of five hundred yards, and sometimes the number exceeds even this.

The carcasses are taken to camp, where they are skinned, and, being sprinkled with some more poison, are placed as lures where they will do most good; and so the slaughter is continued for several months, until scarcely one is left in a large tract of country. When the wolves eat the bait they become sick, and mad sometimes, especially if water is not near, and break away for the hills, there to die, and be lost to the "wolfer." Some persons who follow "wolfing" as an addendum to their regular trapping or hunting, sprinkle aniseed or assafœtida over the poison and drag the bait over an area of several square miles, dropping pieces here and there until camp is reached, when they scatter several about in various directions, or tie them to trees and rocks, at a snatching height, with strings, so that they cannot be pulled away. This is a very effective system, as the trail of the meat is easily followed by its pungent odor, and, when once the wolves get on its line, they seldom give up until they reach the end. As the poison produces a burning thirst, it would be well to have some water convenient to the bait at intervals; for, when once they have drunk this, they collapse immediately. If water is not near, they often run for miles to obtain it; and this necessitates a long walk in the deep snow, and freezing atmosphere, to get the remains.

Another means of poisoning them that is frequently employed is to bore or cut a hole in a deep block of wood and fill it with melted fat sprinkled with strychnine, and place these blocks on the ground at irregular intervals. When the wolves find them they must lap up the fat slowly, and before they have cleaned out one cavity they are, in the majority of cases, turned into corpses. A little aniseed or assafœtida scattered over the fat will help to attract the animals from afar, and lead them to blocks which they might otherwise miss. I have known forty coyotes to be collected in a space of three hundred yards by both these means, but I should consider the former the more preferable of the two.

Trapping is of comparatively little avail, owing to the cautiousness, sagacity, and timidity of all the wolf family, whether small or large; but if a trap is used, it should be the double-springed American make, as that will cling to anything.

Some men earn from five hundred to fifteen hundred dollars each in poisoning wolves during the winter and spring, and it is no unusual thing for a party of half a dozen to return to the settlements, after one campaign, with from six to twelve thousand cured skins; and as they realize from one and a half to two dollars each, it is evident that the business is profitable if the season is even indifferently good.

When the majority of these men receive their money they spend it in the most reckless manner, and when it is exhausted they disappear from the settlements, and are not seen again until the following spring, when they return to renew their debauch. Where they go to after their spree no person seems to know; but, from their character, one might infer that they wandered about like the animal with which they are so closely identified. A few of them, however, are wise enough to keep their money, and they soon retire for good from the business, or seek a more congenial occupation. I knew one "wolfer" to save up eight thousand dollars in five years, and when I last saw him he was a prosperous merchant in a Western city. Another, whom I met in Montana, was a man of intelligence, a keen sportsman, a good amateur naturalist, and a successful stockraiser. He cultivated a farm in spring and summer, and hunted in winter; but his greatest wealth, in his own estimation, consisted in an interesting family, and, after them, in his herds of mustangs and horned cattle. He had a thorough knowledge of the character of the wolf, and so much contempt did he have for it that he could only compare it to an Indian. Although he destroyed many with strychnine, yet his greatest amusement was to hunt them with a pack of half a dozen huge fierce hounds which seemed to be a cross between the deer-hound and the blood-hound. These were bred by a Scotch half-breed in British America, their parents having been obtained from an officer in the British army. They were powerful animals, which would run either by sight or scent, and any one of which was almost a match for a wolf either in strength or stride; but they were difficult to manage, being so intractable and bad-tempered that he dare not strike them without arousing their anger to such an extent that they were liable to attack him. This forced him to always go armed when hunting them, and to wear a sabre-bayonet, so keenly sharpened that he could cleave the head of one open with a blow if necessary.

Useful as he found them, he thought them too dangerous for his own safety, and he was trying to supersede them by a cross between the mastiff and deer-hound, or the foxhound and greyhound, as he thought these would be less irritable, more easily handled, and do their work equally as well as the fierce brutes which were then in his kennel, and whose sole reliable obedience consisted in not touching a dead wolf. I went on a hunt with him one day with this pack, and the moment they were let out of the rude stable they commenced baying and dashing about, as if they were overjoyed at the thought of a run. Both of us being well mounted, and armed with breech-loading guns charged with buckshot, we directed our course toward some rocky, wooded hills which loomed against the horizon about four miles to the north. Moving at a rapid gait, we were soon at their base, and the hounds, which seemed fresh and anxious, were set to work in a piece of shrubbery where a few wolves were generally found, especially during the cubbing season, as hares, antelopes, and other food were always to be procured in its vicinity. The hounds rushed through this as if it were a plain, and commenced quartering in every direction.

Beating back toward us, one gave tongue within five yards of our position, and a moment later we saw a large grayish object darting through the bushes, and the hound in full cry after it. The others soon joined in the chorus, and away all dashed for the hills. "That must have been a she-wolf," said my friend, "or the critter would not have stayed there so long when we were so near; it is, therefore, very likely that we may find the cubs where she started from." We accordingly commenced a search for them, and in a few moments found six little creatures, evidently about a month old, in a grassy cleft between two rocks. Tying them in couples by the legs, they were placed on the top of a huge bowlder to prevent them from falling into the jaws of the hounds; and, to keep them from tumbling down, a barricade was laid around them. Feeling assured of their safety, we prepared to follow the pack, but we had advanced scarcely one hundred yards before the canine chorus was heard approaching us a little to the right. "That wolf has played them a nice game," was the comment of my companion on hearing the baying. "How is that?" said I. "Why, she ran for the top along a dry ravine," said he, " where the scent is hard to follow; and as soon as she got there she forded a small stream and doubled back to her young ones, and the hounds have been puzzling over the trail until a few minutes ago, when they probably struck it by accident; but now they are going to push her hard; for she must either break from cover or double on her tracks, and in either case she will be overtaken in less than an hour." "What do you suppose she will do?" said I. "Why, she'll visit her nest," was the response, " and, finding the youngsters gone, will head for the plains; for a mother-wolf will not stop in a section where she has lost her cubs. If she leaves the forest, we may have a gallop after her over the plains, and you will then see what beautiful coursing a wolf can show, and what tact it will display in using cover, and in selecting the worst possible place for the scent to lie."

During this conversation the canine music was drawing rapidly near; so we prepared for a run by hurrying to the outer edge of the woods, and occupying such a position that we could see any object leaving it within a convenient distance. We had not taken our stand fifteen minutes, before the wolf broke cover so near us that we could have shot her if we wished; but as we desired to see a run, we allowed her to escape. Heading down wind, the terrified creature sped onward with immense strides, and we followed in hot pursuit. The hounds soon joined us, and, with foam-flecked mouth and lolling tongue, streamed past us at a pace I had never seen hounds equal. The fugitive kept her lead for two or three miles, although our mustangs were fresh and fleet, but the hounds finally began to gain upon her, the ground being open; she soon struck into a rough country, however, which was seamed by two or three small rivulets, and portions of which were dry masses of indurated clay that could scarcely produce a spear of grass, and over this she regained her lead by resorting to stratagems. She ran along the banks of a ravine, then into the water, moving down with the slow current, and, escaping some distance below, made for the hillocks of bare earth, or where the prickly pear grew thickest; and this trick she repeated until she passed all the streams. The result was that the hounds frequently lost sight of her, or were puzzled on the trail; and were we not mounted, so that we could see her movements, she would, in all probability, have escaped them, owing to the lead she obtained by these delays. We, however, were able to make a straight cast as soon as we overtook the pack; but they were so stubborn that their huntsman had some difficulty in getting them to obey him and leave their puzzling for the direct trail, they seeming to consider that they knew their own business better than he did. When one responded, however, the others followed its lead, and they were streaming away again in a short time with renewed energy. The chase continued over a rough piece of country for four or five miles, then into a beautiful stretch of gently undulating grass-clad prairie, and over this we had a splendid view of it, until it finally disappeared in a coppice of poplars. Our steeds were too much pumped to do more than keep in sight of the dogs after the first few miles; still, they had endurance, and we were able to follow at a hand-gallop during the entire run.

When we reached the coppice we found the wolf dead, and its throat torn open, while the hounds were lapping its blood. The swift creature had evidently sought rest and refuge there; and, having become stiffened by the halt, was unable to escape her merciless pursuers when they reached it. On examining her, we found that she was a splendid animal, evidently about four years old, and that she was in excellent condition for running, the suckling of the youngsters having relieved her of all unnecessary flesh, without having weakened her too much.

My companion having taken her skin and tied it on his saddle behind him, we called at a rancher's cabin to get two sacks in which to bring home the cubs, and, having procured these, we returned to the hill where the youngsters were concealed. On the way back he told me that wolves cubbed in May, and had from four to nine in a litter. The whole care of rearing them depended on the mother; and she was a good type of a faithful guardian and provider, and had strong maternal affection—as much, if not more, than the dog.

When hunted or startled by foes, she does not desert her young until the last moment, and she leaves them then apparently more for the purpose of protecting them than of saving her own life. She has the greatest fear of man, and he is probably the only enemy she will not face in defence of her young; yet, if they are able to run at all, she depends more on flight than fight for saving them. She will not, in fact, engage in combat if she can avoid it, unless it is with some animal she thinks she can overpower. She hunts much during the maternal period, and while her cubs are in the nest keeps them well supplied with edibles. The young join the pack as soon as they are able to run about well, and at the end of six months take part in the hunts and forays organized by their elders, and often acquit themselves creditably, especially in stealing from camps, and in coursing hares and ground-squirrels. At the end of twelve months they are trained hunters, and able to hold their own in cunning with any fox that ever lived. He also said that wolves were attacked by hydrophobia sometimes, and on such occasions they rushed madly about, biting and snapping at everything. They lose all fear of man then, and boldly enter an Indian encampment and fly at any person they meet. Any one bitten by them is said to be almost sure to die of hydrophobia; so his friends make preparations for his death at once, and see that he is tied in such a manner that he cannot injure others. An Indian has been known to escape the effects of a bite, however, by merely drinking a decoction of some herbs known to his tribe and bathing the wound in warm water. What this most potential herb was I could not learn, nor did my mentor ever hear its name even in the Indian vernacular.

Having returned to the cubs and tied them up in the bags, we started for home; but before we got out of the woods a young dog-wolf broke cover almost under our nose. How on earth he remained there undisturbed after the previous scouring of the region we could not understand, nor could we determine how his presence escaped the keen nose of the hounds. A look into his lair revealed the latter reason very promptly, for that contained some dead hares, one of which was scarcely touched. Having had plenty provision in the house, he had not stirred out during the night or the day, and his footsteps could not therefore be dogged. When he went away, however, he went in a hurry; for we both gave a tremendous shout that caused him to clap his tail almost up to the root between his legs, and to round himself into a hump, as if he had an elastic spinal column; but when he heard the baying of the hounds behind him he straightened out the hump, put his nose close to the ground, and scudded away with all the speed that deadly terror could impart. Out of the woods he broke, and over the plains, with the pack in full cry behind him. Being hampered by the cubs, we did not attempt to follow, but, on mounting a knoll, we had a fine view of the run until it vanished from our sight behind one of the long hillocks near which a rivulet ran. "Something is the matter with the wolves here just now," said my companion, "else they would not break for the open so soon; for they generally keep in the woods and rough places as long as they possibly can, and get away from shelter only when close pressed, and they see no other means of escape."

"But what about the first?" said I. "Oh! she was trying to lead the dogs away from her young," was the response. After thinking over their haste to escape from the woods for a few moments, he said he thought he could attribute it to the presence of Indians, and surmised that they were encamped higher up on the hill. This guess proved to be correct, for, on reaching an elevated piece of ground a little later, we saw a large party of the sons of the forest driving their mustangs out on the plains to graze. While jogging home, the mellow cow's horn, which the host used as a hunting-horn, was sounded at intervals to recall the hounds if the run was over, but not one answered the summons. When we were within three miles of the house, we came upon them suddenly as they were grouped around the dead wolf; but they displayed no signs of welcome on our approach, and sat sullenly in their position until their owner threw the slain animal on his horse. On resuming our march, we came upon a herd of antelopes; but the dogs paid no attention to it, as they were not, as a rule, allowed to chase antelopes, not being fleet enough to overtake them in a fair run. They were used on deer, however; but they went at such a pace in the woods that they frequently overran the scent, and their owner found it such a difficult matter to induce them to hark back that he was often annoyed by them. For open general running he considered they had few superiors, as their nose and pace were fairly good.

As they trotted home with us, they looked gaunt, bony, and listless; but when they espied a coyote some distance away, they were all animation at once, and, despite their hard day's work and the peremptory recall of the horn, they dashed after the creature in vigorous style, and with a wild burst of yelps that must have nearly startled the life out of it. The promenader, on discovering the canine group, closed to its work with a will, and was soon showing a clean pair of heels; but as both vanished rapidly in the twilight, we were unable to see much of the chase. The dogs returned about ten o'clock, having been evidently successful in the run, and after a dinner of wolf-meat were glad to retire to their couch of straw in the stable. Their owner told me that they remained out all night sometimes in pursuit of wolves; and if they traced a bear or panther, they would not leave it until he arrived on the scene, or hunger drove them away. They made their position known by loud barking, and this they would keep up for twenty-four hours if necessary. They got into trouble frequently, through their ardor in the chase, and some of them carried the wounds inflicted by the teeth or claws of an angry bear or panther; but they were so active, cautious, and supported each other so well in an attack, that the advantage rested with them, as a rule. While they were not close-quarter dogs, yet they were excellent "snippers" and good "fencers," and could escape the leap of a panther or the hug of a bear as well as any animals in the country; but their greatest delight was to collar a wolf and tear it to death. They did not always escape scathless from these contests, however, for in a life-and-death struggle their lupine foe was capable of doing a fair share of work with its long fangs. The fault he found with them was their temper and stubbornness, and the difficulty he had in managing them when once they got on the trail of an animal; otherwise he liked them very much for their work. They were good all-round dogs, that would do well at any game, and it seemed to me that they were well suited for general hunting in a country where there is so much variety and abundance of large animals.

The true wolf-dog, one that has the size, weight, strength, speed, courage, and endurance to cope alone with the large gray species, is not yet known in the West, and, until it is, persons must be content to hunt it with any dogs that will chase it and bring it to bay till the sportsman can finish it with his knife, rifle, or revolver. If the Irish wolf-hound is ever to be revived, that seems to be the country in which it will be brought to perfection, as everything there is favorable to its full development. If that animal is nothing more than a large deer-hound, however, as some writers assert, it cannot cope singly with a wolf weighing from one hundred to one hundred and fifty pounds, as it would lack weight and strength, though it might possess nose and speed. Boar-hounds would make better wolf-dogs than the famous Irish breed which are sometimes exhibited pictorially in sporting newspapers, and would be far more serviceable for general purposes.

Two of the best wolf-dogs I saw in the West were a cross respectively between a deer-hound and a mastiff, and a greyhound and a bulldog, with a dash of bull-terrier blood. When these two hunted together and managed to come in contact with a wolf, one seized it by the throat while the other seized one of its hind-legs, and between them both it was killed within the space of half an hour, or so seriously crippled that it fell an easy victim to the hunter's revolver. Though very brave and skilful fighters, they lacked speed to bring the animal to bay in a long run; and if they did not overtake it inside a distance of two or three miles, they generally gave up the chase, as they could not keep in sight, and they did not have sufficient nose to follow it readily by its scent. Their retirement from the chase is not to be wondered at, for I have known wolves to run twenty or thirty miles before a fast pack of foxhounds, and escape after all; but I have seen others run down in a sharp spin of five or six miles, although they had a good start. On a fine day, and with hard ground underfoot, a wolf will lead the fastest pack in the world a merry gallop; but during wet weather it shows to bad advantage, as its brush is so heavy that it is a regular mud-carrier; and this drags it down so much that it may be overtaken with a fast pack of fox-hounds in a run of a few miles over soft ground.

If the *barsee*, or Siberian wolf-hound, is all it is said to be, it would prove a capital dog for the West, as the climate ought to be well suited to it; and wolves are abundant enough to furnish it with all the exercise it wants, and to bring out its highest qualities.

One of the most intelligent dogs for still-hunting the wolf I saw anywhere was a combination of the wire-haired fox-terrier and the rough-coated colly, with perhaps a dash of the fox-hound or harrier. This creature would run mute and very slowly, and was as much under control as a well-broken sheep-dog. When a wolf was found in the woods, and its quarters were known, the hunter placed a piece of poisoned meat there, and the next morning, as a rule, he had another robe to add to his collection of peltries. This dog was owned by a stock-raiser and hunter, and nothing could induce him to part with it.

Several keen sportsmen keep a few hounds for the special purpose of wolf-hunting; but as they are no match in speed for their long-legged cousin, one or two greyhounds have to be used as auxiliaries, and when the quarry is getting too far ahead these are slipped, and they soon overtake it and keep it at bay, despite all its rushing and snarling, until the hounds and mounted huntsmen arrive.

If the wolf is young, the hounds are allowed to kill it themselves, in order to encourage them; but if it is an old one, it can inflict too much injury on light, weak dogs in a death-struggle to make the contest anything but interesting to their owner.

One of the most stirring hunting scenes imaginable is to follow a large pack of hounds in pursuit of a wolf over the level prairie on a fine morning in spring or autumn, and then to be in at the death. It has all the elements of the highest class of sport in it, and hounds and horses seem to enjoy it as well as the men. I recall distinctly such a hunt on the plains of Kansas. The pack consisted of fifteen couples of fairly fast fox-hounds trained to wolf-hunting, and two large Scotch deer-hounds, and they were followed by twenty men, who were well mounted, and armed with revolvers. When the quarry was driven out of a small coppice of poplars, it broke away over the prairie, with the hounds in full cry behind it, the deer-hounds being led by a leash beside one of the horses. Over the magnificent prairie, which extended in an unbroken line to the horizon like a vast flower-clad meadow, we dashed at the best pace of our fresh and spirited steeds, nor did we pull rein until we had covered at least ten miles, the pack being all that time going at their highest speed; but seeing that the quarry was still keeping its lead, and that there was a probability of losing it in a coppice a mile or two ahead, the deer-hounds were unleashed, and away they sped like a flash of gray light. A run of a few minutes placed them beside their foe, and they promptly brought it to a halt. It darted at them with open jaws, but they avoided its fangs, and when it tried to escape, one or the other bit it severely in the flanks. They worried it in this manner until the pack arrived; and when we reached the scene we could only see a struggling mass of dogs and flying hair, and hear an occasional yelp as some hound was severely bitten; but the struggle was soon over, and a splendid wolf lay dead before us, its head and throat being covered with scars, and its limbs broken. The spoils were then distributed among the equestrians; but that was a simple affair and easily done, for the first horseman in at the death received the brush, and the owner of the pack took the skin.

Some persons run down the animal with greyhounds trained to the business, and they keep it at bay until the hunters arrive, when it is killed with fire-arms. "Wolfers" resort to this method on the plains sometimes; but as they seek the hide only when it is in good condition, in winter and spring, they cannot use greyhounds to good advantage in the wild country they frequent during their expeditions.

In several merry spins that I have had after the wolf, both with and without the cheerful music of hounds, I have found the chase much more exciting than a run after a fox, as a person has no feeling for the fugitive, and he likes to practise his revolver on it as it scuds away. When mounted Indians pursue a pack of wolves, they make a surround, drive the animals into the centre, and then shoot away until they have slain all that have not run the gauntlet. They prefer to trap them, however, to any other mode of capture, as it is a saving of time and energy. A wolf caught by the leg will gnaw it off rather than be made a prisoner; but before attempting that it will try to run away with the trap, and, if successful in this, it will travel rapidly on three legs for days at a time, or until it dies of starvation.

There are so many wolves in the Far West, and there are so many good opportunities for driving them, that wolf-hunting must yet become a stirring pastime, one which will afford a virile pleasure, and, at the same time, prove of benefit to farmers and stock-raisers. As the animals can be pursued at nearly all seasons, and every farm is open to horsemen, wolf-hunting ought to become there what fox-hunting is in Great Britain; and doubtless it will be so when the country gets settled up, and people have a little spare time to devote to the pleasures of the chase.

Can the wolf be domesticated and made useful to man, is a question which might be asked here; and, from what I heard in the West, it seems probable that it can, for a hunter there had one that would chase a deer as well as any stag-hound, while it could also compare in pace with it, and had great endurance. It was so tame that it ran with a small pack of hounds which he owned, and so obedient that it answered his call promptly. He thought wolves had few equals for hunting large animals, such as the elk, or wapiti, moose, deer, wild-boar, and others, as they pounce upon the quarries and cut the hamstring, and, once crippled in that quarter, their formidable weapons are not very dangerous to their agile enemies. The lupine hunter does not always come off first best in a contest, however, as an incident related by a Western pioneer will show. This characteristic story was told to a party of men who were discussing the merits of wild pigs, and, as a type of the Westerner's descriptive power, is one of the best I ever heard or read. The speaker was one of those old farmers who lived some time in the wilderness, and he commenced his story in the following quaint manner: "One day, while passing along the bottoms, I seen such a sight of hogs as I never did see. Thar they stood, and squirmed, with their bristles up, and steam a risin' out o' their bodies, and their eyes a flashin', and teeth a champin'; a mass of bilin' mad hogs, who was a screamin' and a shakin' 'emselves with rage.

"What was a causin' of all this commotion I was not long in seein'. Thar, in the middle of the great convention of hogs, stood a big oak stump, about five feet high, and in the centre of the stump stood a big gray wolf, as gaunt, hungry-lookin' a critter as ever I seed.

"He was handsomely treed, and wasn't in a very pleasant fix, as he was beginnin' to find out. All about him was a mass of oneasy hair, fiery eyes, frothin' mouths, gleamin' teeth. Poor critter! thar he stood—his tail tucked close between his legs and his feet all gathered into the exact centre of the stump—and Jerusalem! wasn't he a sick-lookin' wolf? He seemed to be thinkin' that he had sold himself awful cheap.

"Right close about the stump and rairin' up against it was a crowd of some of the biggest and most onprincipled old sows I ever sot eyes onto. Every half-minit one of these big old she-fellows would rair up, git her fore feet on top of the stump, and make a savage snap at one end or t'other of the wolf, her jaws comin' together like a flax-brake.

"The wolf would whirl round to watch that partickerler sow, when one on t'other side of the stump would make a plunge for his tail; an' so they kept the poor, cowardly, cornered critter whirlin' round and round, humpin' up his back, haulin' in his feet and tail, and in every possible way reducin' his general average. I'll bet his entire innards was drawed up into a bunch not bigger'n my fist!

"Almost every instant thar was a charge made on him from some quarter, an' sometimes from three or four directions at once. Jewhittaker, wasn't it hurryin' times with him then!

"When he had a moment to rest an' gaze about, all he saw was them two acres of open mouths, restless bristles, and fiery eyes. His long red tongue hung out of his open jaws, and, as he moved his head from side to side, he seemed to have about the poorest conceit of his smartness of any wolf I ever seed. He had got himself into a nice pickle by tryin' to steal a pig, and he knowed it jist as well as if he'd bin human, and was ashamed of himself accordin'. No quarter could he expect anywhere in all that sea of open, roarin' mouths.

"Sich was the noise, and chargin' and plungin' and surgin' to and fro, that I hardly felt safe behind my tree one hundred yards away.

"I determined to try an experiment on that wolf. I raised my gun and fired into the air. At the report the critter forgot himself. He bounded from the stump with the crack of the gun, but he never tetched ground. Half a dozen open mouths reached up for him, and in them he landed. There was jist one sharp yell, then for a rod around was seen flyin' strips of wolf-skin, innards, legs, and hair; for half a minit was heard a crunchin' of bones, and then them old sows were lickin' their chops, rairin' up onto that thar stump and prospectin' about for more wolf.

"'Bout that time I concluded the neighborhood was likely to prove onhealthy, and I got up and peeled it for the nearest clearin's."

CHAPTER VI.

THE PRAIRIE WOLF.

The Prairie Wolf.—Origin of its Name.—Its Position among the *Canidæ*.—The connecting Link between the large Wolf and the Fox.—Its Burrows.—Peculiarity of its Barking.—Its Form and Color.—How it is looked upon by Plainsmen.—Where it is very Abundant.—Hunting it on Horseback.—Its Speed.—Best Dogs for Hunting it.—Its Numbers make it difficult to be Hunted by one Pack of Hounds.—The Heaviness of its Brush.—When it runs Best.—Best Horses for the Chase.—Leaves a Screaming Scent.—Dashes after it with Hounds and Horses.—Kill Six in One Day.—Run into Encampments of War-parties of Indians. — Rapid Retreat. — A Severe Fight with the Red Men. — A Chase on the Plains of the Columbia.—The Meet.—Mongrel Dogs and their Love of Fighting.—At Cover.—Start.—Two Coyotes.—The Pursuit.—Killed by Indian Dogs.—A Mongrel Greyhound brings One to Bay, and it is shot.—I shoot One.—Looking for my Party.—A Meet and a Run. — Surprised by Indians. — Whites *versus* Indians in the Chase.—Seven Coyotes killed.—Fun and Confusion.—Falls and Laughter.—The Relation of Indian Dogs to Coyotes.—Their Character for Hunting.—Future of Coyote-hunting.

THE prairie wolf, or coyote (*Canis latrans*), is found all over the open plains of the Far West, and ranges from British America on the north to Mexico on the south. Its technical cognomen is derived from its characteristic in barking, which is so different from the melancholy howl of the gray wolf, and its common name of coyote, from the Mexicans; but among them it is a wretched creature, little larger than a fox, and so timid that it flees from a cur. It is much larger, more active and energetic, in the North, and has all the qualities necessary to make hunting it with hounds and horses both interesting and exciting. It seems to occupy the position in size and character between the large wolf and the fox, and to be the connecting link between them. It resembles the wolf in bodily outline, appearance, and color, and, like it, hunts in packs;

but it approaches the fox in some of its habits. Like the latter, it lives and has its young in burrows, which it makes, if necessary, by digging with its claws; whereas the large wolf produces its young in caves, the clefts of rocks, under a tree, or in places where no digging is necessary. The voice also seems to be a combination of the long howl of the wolf and the yelp of the fox; but so distinctly marked is it from either, that, once heard, it is

PRAIRIE WOLVES.

never forgotten. The coyote has the strange peculiarity of making the cry of one sound like that of many; and should two or three try their larynx at the same time, persons would fancy that large packs were giving tongue in chorus. The cry seems to be divided into two parts. Its first begins with a deep, long howl, then runs rapidly up into a series of barks, and terminates in a high scream, issued in prolonged jerks.

This animal is larger than the fox, being about two feet

high, and, like it, has a long, slender, and rather sharp-pointed muzzle. The eyes, which are close together, are of a light-brown color; the ears are long and erect; the legs, especially the hind ones, are very long, compared to its size; the feet are also long; the pads are black and naked; and the tail, which is bushy, and more than half the length of the body, is tipped with white hairs. Its general color is an ochreous gray, which is much lighter on the abdomen than on the back and sides; and the long hairs on the neck, which it bristles up when angry, have a speckled appearance when it is in that mood. It hunts much at night, and its dismal howls may then be heard a long distance off. Its cry, which is so much execrated by those who feel that their life is not endangered by red foes, is pleasant music to those who have to traverse a country frequented by hostile Indians; for while it indulges in midnight serenades they know that their most deadly enemies are some distance away. Let its cries cease, however, and the plainsmen, who have been lulled to serene sleep by its weird howls, would awake at once, and make preparations for a struggle of life and death. Its voice has often been to hunters what the geese were to ancient Rome; and this characteristic has often been the means of saving its life, for it was looked upon more as a friend than a foe, notwithstanding its kleptomaniac propensities, and the natural antipathy of man to all its wild tribe. Its specific distinction of *latrans* is most appropriate, for a bigger barking thief it would be difficult to find, nor, at the same time, one more cowardly, for a cur will cause a whole pack to scamper away with the utmost celerity. It never attacks man, even when famishing; but should he leave any edibles convenient, it will steal them with greater cunning than ever fox displayed.

The Indians of Washington Territory have a tradition that it is a demon or deity, and therefore pay it much respect, and never, I believe, kill it, for fear of its bringing them "bad medicine," or ill luck. It figures largely in the myths of all the red men inhabiting the region bordering the Pacific Ocean, and occupies a position of prominence not accorded to any other animal. While it is common everywhere in the Far West, it is unusually abundant on the great plains of the Columbia east of the Cascade Range, as it finds plenty of food there in the innumerable sage-hares, ground-squirrels, badgers, and other small game that inhabit the country; while it enjoys a feast, that lasts for several months, off the myriads of dead salmon that strew the banks of the Columbia and its numerous tributaries during the spawning season. I have seen coyotes trotting up and down the shores of these rivers in large packs during the spring and summer, and fighting and snarling over any offal washed ashore by the waves.

It has so little fear of man in that region that it will impudently stare at him as he passes by, perhaps within revolver range; and should he fire at it and miss, the result might be that it would trot off a few paces, then turn about and gaze once more with an expression in which one might read, "I wonder who that is? what could he mean by making that noise? he evidently is no friend of mine, so I'll be off to safer quarters;" and, having come to this conclusion, it would quietly move off as if it were in no great hurry to display its fears. Should one repeat the fire, however, it would become a dissolving view, for, when put to it, few of its genus can make better time for a short distance, say from ten to fifteen or twenty miles. It has so little running to do in search of its prey in the Far West, owing to the profusion of animal life, that its full powers of speed have not been fully developed, and its wind is not good, if driven hard by swift-footed foxhounds, for more than two or three hours. I have myself, when mounted on a good horse, overtaken it in a run of fifteen or twenty minutes; but I must say that the pace was killing on my steed, and that I plied the whip occasionally.

One of my greatest amusements in a certain portion of California was to mount a horse belonging to a friend, and ride after coyotes until I lost or captured them. This horse, which was a great favorite of mine, although he would buck like a bounding rubber ball occasionally, and shy without the least cause every few minutes, and when I did not expect it, was a capital jumper—an unusual thing for an untrained horse in the West—and could run ten or fifteen miles at a slashing gait without showing much suffering. When I hunted coyotes I generally had one or two dogs with me; but I frequently went without them, as the quarries were so numerous that they were liable to start up at any moment near my feet. At the first view I would dash after them, and force them to their best pace for fifteen or twenty minutes; and I found that this soon produced its effect, and that I might expect to capture them at any moment if they did not escape me in the chaparral. When I drew alongside I let them have the contents of a large revolver; but I sometimes secured one by striking it on the head with a club or "waddy," or by lassoing it with a raw-hide lariat.

It may perhaps be needless to state that I lost many more than I captured, unless I was accompanied by the dogs, and even then I might say that I could count more escapes than captures. The only way to be sure of it is to use a greyhound; for that light-footed creature will soon bring it to bay, and enable the pack of hounds, or other dogs, to come up with it. If a person is well up in the run on such occasions, he will see a pretty bit of a scramble; for the coyote, when it sees no means of escape, will, like the traditional worm, turn on its foes, and use its sharp teeth to good advantage. A capital dog for hunting it would be a cross between the fox-hound and deer-hound, or the fox-hound and the German *ullmerhund*, or boar-hound; for the greyhound alone does not seem to have sufficient combativeness or destructiveness to face any animal that will make a vigorous resistance. I am rather inclined to believe that the latter cross would produce one of the best dogs for coyote-hunting in the West, as it would have strength and courage enough to face any game, and it ought

THE WOLF.

to have sufficient nose to enable it to follow a coyote, and the speed to overtake it also. A good pack of fast fox-hounds will drive it at a rattling pace, however, and, if the ground is open, may kill it inside an hour. I have known it to lead them for twenty or more miles without a check on broken, hilly ground, and escape in a chasm, yet I have frequently seen it captured in half an hour; but then the dogs were fast indeed, and got off close after it. I have seen several killed in a day by a small pack, but in such cases they were in unusual numbers, and rose up almost under the noses of the dogs. I have seen a small pack of seventeen or eighteen couples of coyotes rise out of burrows in the ground, apparently at once, and scud about in every direction, and in their eagerness to escape they sometimes ran into the mouths of the dogs. Where they are so numerous, the greatest annoyance is that the hounds separate, and the result is that there are perhaps a dozen runs going on at the same time instead of one.

If a coyote is started alone—not an unusual occurrence—the best means of securing a kill is to drive it as hard as possible for the first few miles, for, as in fox-hunting, it is the pace at the start that does the work, and causes it to succumb in a short time. Having a large brush, it soon tires on soft ground on a wet day, especially if the mud carries, for the tail is heavy, and soon drags it down. If nature intended it to escape by fleetness, she ought to have made it bob-tailed; for its present long caudal appendage is too cumbersome for its fore-quarters in a long run, and is a regular mud-carrier. When the animal is running uphill it also trails badly, and seems to almost counterbalance the advantage furnished by long hind-legs and staunch flanks. Over hard, broken ground, however, it does not seem to be so much of a drag-down, and the bearer can then travel at a rate that would put the best hounds and horses in Great Britain to their mettle to keep it in sight. The horses used in its pursuit should be compact, fleet, and enduring, and should also be prompt in movement—in a word, handy; for a coyote will often jump out of its burrow in the twinkling of an eye, and the steed that is not able to get under full headway in a moment is liable to remain in the background, unless it is unusually fleet of foot. Indian mustangs make capital mounts, as they have fair endurance, and can make a good spurt for a short distance, and can plunge into a gallop from a halt; yet some of the thorough-bred blood in them would enhance their value, as it would give them the speed they now lack except for a few minutes. Regular hunters would, to a certain extent, be useless in the West, as the country frequented by the coyote is so uneven, in many cases, that a run is often a scramble up hill and down dale, and, to clamber well, a horse seems to want some mustang blood in it, or the blood of those Kerry ponies which are said to be able to slide down a precipice with a rider.

With a good horse and a fast pack of hounds, few sports are more spirited than a coyote-hunt, as the run is, in nearly all cases, a break-neck one; for the animal leaves what might be called a screaming scent, and its flight is as straight as a bee-line, except under unusual circumstances. The male has one of the most vilely obscene odors imaginable; and if the wind is blowing from his direction when he is in flight, a person with keen olfactories can detect it, if close on. Although the coyote is generally captured by being trapped or poisoned, yet a few gentlemen of sporting proclivities have a dash after it occasionally on horseback, their ride being cheered by the stirring music of flute-voiced fox-hounds. Others keep mongrel greyhounds, which can overtake it in a spurt of two or three miles, if it has not received too much of a start; and they afford capital amusement, as the run is nearly always a straight one, for the animal doubles only when headed off or closely pressed. Those who poison it for its skin frequently scatter a little assafœtida over the bait, as it likes the smell of this, and will eat any meat on which it is placed with a ravenousness that only wolves or jackals can display.

It is sometimes rather dangerous to handle this animal when dead, for it is frequently covered with sores, produced by eating the corpses of Indians, which are often left unburied, or so lightly covered that they can be easily dug up. Persons should therefore be cautious about handling it without gloves.

The only danger one encounters in hunting it on horseback is, that in a headlong dash his steed may tread in the hole of a prairie-dog, badger, or ground-squirrel, and break its leg, or be thrown so violently as to pitch the rider several feet away on his back. This can be avoided, however, by a little caution, so that the sport is not so dangerous as fox or stag hunting in Europe.

A run is spoiled occasionally by the numbers of the animal, for, congregating as it does in large packs, it is no un-

THE PRAIRIE WOLF.

COYOTES.

common thing for the hounds to come suddenly upon one containing twenty or more, and then it is both amusing and annoying to see them break into a dozen or more groups and scamper away in different directions, with as many groups of hounds behind them. All the horns in the world could not control the dogs under such circumstances; so the riders have to follow some special pack, or sit idly in their seats and await the return. As a coyote rarely runs to ground, crosses heavy woods—though it may pass through a coppice—or doubles back, a person may imagine how tedious it must be to await the return of the hounds. I have known them to go so far that they did not get back to camp until late at night, and it was no unusual event for some of them to spend a night on the prairie.

A hunt would be more picturesque if there were many persons in the field, or if it were graced by the presence of ladies; but in that thinly settled country men and women are too busy to devote much attention to the chase, except for some practical purpose, such as supplying the house with meat, or their pockets with the money procured from the sale of peltries.

One of the most interesting runs that I ever had after the coyotes netted us six of them; but when we returned to the house in the evening, both hounds and horses were so badly used up that they were of little use for two or three days thereafter. The master of the hounds announced his intention to a few neighbors of having a grand coyote-hunt one day, and asked them to be participators therein; and they promptly returned an affirmative answer by coming personally the night before the meet. As there were not accommodations in the house for all, it was decided that some should sleep on the hay in the stable, and, with true Western contempt of idle luxuriousness, they all concluded to go there; and that matter being settled in a minute, the next was to decide at what hour in the morning we should start. Various hours were specified; but the matter was finally determined by a veteran, who was known as "an old settler," and therefore conspicuously important, when he said, with true Western politeness, "Gentlemen, I guess you all know more about coyotes than I do; but, if you'll take my good-for-nothin' advice, you'll go out as airly in the mornin' as you can, for coyotes are like the men that make money in the States—they stay awake all night a thinkin' how they'll beat other critters, and then they're up the first thing in the mornin' a tryin' to carry out all their nasty plans—I beg your parding, young gals, for sayin' 'nasty,' but that's my opinion o' coyotes; for I think they're only thievin' Injun dogs that can't be civilized. Now, if we get out in the mornin', we'll be sure to take 'em on the hop; and if we do, you'll have peltries enough " (addressing the M. H.) "to make up for the day's loss; and if we don't see 'em, why, we'll come home airly." The *pros* and *cons* of this statement were discussed fully, and it was finally decided that we should be up at daylight, and be on the coyote ground, three miles away, by four o'clock. The evening was spent in telling stories of hunting experiences about all sorts of wild animals, and I learned more on that occasion about the natural history of Western animals than I did out of all the learned works I had ever read. The intervals between the tales were filled up with music on the "pi-anor," as the "fust settler" called it, by the young ladies of the house—charming, independent, self-reliant, and domestic young ladies, who would do honor to any drawing-room in their easy, obliging behavior, and in their good looks; but I fear they would not pass muster in their dress, for it was a simple calico, made graceful by no other accessories than their good taste and Venus-like forms. It is a peculiarity, or I might say a feeling of paternal pride, in all Western men, that the moment they are able to purchase a piano they do it for the sake of the daughters, for, as they say locally, "boys are boys, and gals are gals;" and while one wants "a rifle, a dog, and a horse, the other wants nothing but a new dress or a hat, and a 'pi-anor.'" The boys are nobodies, the girls are everything; the former can hunt or fish, or be anything they please; the girls must be educated, and able to talk a little French and play the "pi-anor," else they are also nobodies. What with music, singing, story-telling, and the contents of a barrel, the evening was pleasantly spent, and by midnight we were all soundly sleeping.

We were awake before daylight, and had breakfast by lamplight; and after that we saddled our steeds, and each taking a spare horse with him, we were off by 4 A.M., and in half an hour after we were amidst the haunts of the prowling coyote. We had scarcely reached the ground before we espied a vagrant trotting about, and, getting after it close behind, we ran it for five miles at a rattling rate, and the hounds killed it on a knoll before we were within shooting range. The "blooding" they received seemed to have sharpened their appetite for more coyotes, for they were jumping about and giving tongue as if they were on a trail; but we supposed it was the buoyancy of their feelings at a prompt victory that caused them to indulge in such an unusual display of melody. Having skinned the slain animal, we moved down into the plain; and there the dogs found the scent so fierce that they raised their heads in the air, and went away at full cry. We could see nothing to cause this outburst; but before we had gone a few yards, out jumped from their burrows two dog-coyotes, and away we went after them. The hounds separated on the quarries, two couples following one, and three the other. I kept with the former, and in a run of less than seven miles had the satisfaction of planting a bullet in the fugitive's head as he swerved past me on a new tack, and the hounds, on coming up, found him dead, much to their astonishment, and, I should fancy, disappointment, as they were content with a few shakes, and a glance at me as if to inquire how it happened that he was dead. The other men followed the three couples, but they had to run for ten miles or more before they caught the runaway. As both divisions of the hounds were running in almost parallel lines, we had little difficulty in reuniting the pack; and when that was done we started off for new fields, after giving the animals a short rest.

Moving about two miles toward the north, we reached a long, rolling plain that extended for miles in every direction. Halting there, we changed horses, for each man had his spare steed with him. When the dogs were cast loose they could find no scent, the soil being light and gritty, therefore not well able to hold it; so we left there, and directed our course toward the eastward, where the grass was denser. A tramp of two miles led us into a region where the hounds found a sharp perfume, and away they went at a rattling pace; but they lost it inside of a mile, and so suddenly that we were surprised at it. We tried all means to strike the line again by casting about in every direction and harking back, but we could not find it. We then commenced searching the ground for a burrow, and, after working for perhaps ten minutes, one of the party found a deep hole on the banks of a rivulet, and, leading the dogs there, they gave tongue in the most clamorous manner. This proved that the quarry was there; and we were beginning to plan how we should get it out, when one of the dogs raised his voice a few yards below us, and, on looking around, we saw a coyote streaming away before him. We dashed after the quarry at our best pace, and as the horses were fresh we were soon leading the hounds. When we got within range of the fugitive we opened fire promptly with our revolvers, and, somebody hitting it in the flanks, tumbled it over, and before it could get away the hounds were upon it and throttling it to death.

After this kill, we concluded to turn homeward, and take our chances with meeting any coyotes on the way. We had proceeded scarcely three miles before we surprised a vixen out for a "constitutional;" but she evidently had little fear of us, for she did not attempt to move until she saw the baying hounds heading full for her. She then tore away at a stirring pace, but she was driven so hard that she ran to earth in the first burrow she met. This was a most unusual proceeding for a coyote, and we were rather surprised at it, but we concluded to have her, nevertheless; so one of our party was sent to a stock-raiser's cabin about a mile away to borrow a spade with which to dig her out. When he returned operations were commenced, and in less than twenty minutes we had her brush, and, a few minutes later, her skin. We were so delighted with our success that we were getting coyote-struck; but as our horses were badly blown, and were covered with foam, we concluded to give up any more hunting for the day; so, when we reached a small country store, where everything, from cloth to whiskey, was sold, we entered, and drank a bumper or two, and after hearty hand-shakes and several "good-byes," each wended his way homeward. I returned with the host and hounds, well pleased with my share of the spoils, as I had two brushes dangling from my horse's mane. When within five miles of the house, we started a splendid male, and the hounds, weary as they were, started after him; nor would they respond to the peremptory recall of the melodious cow's horn which their owner carried. Seeing that they would not return, we concluded to follow them, for fear they might get lost, or be captured by some lover of good hounds; so we jogged along at a steady canter, just close enough behind them to hear their cry. Their route led us over steep hillocks, up which we could only crawl, down precipitous ravines, where we had to pick our way, and across charming vales, gay with brilliant flowers and green with the richest of grasses.

The chase continued in this manner for an hour or more, when we at length got a glimpse of the hounds as they were entering a heavy piece of woods that crowned a hilltop. We followed them through this at a snail's pace, but, on reaching the other side, we saw the coyote running short, and this induced us to make a final spurt. Plying the spurs, we tried to close with the fugitive; but before we could do it we found ourselves in the midst of an Indian encampment, and the pack streaming away to the left on open ground. As the Indians were at that time supposed to be unfriendly, we did not know what was best to do at first—whether to dash through it unconcernedly, or turn about and beat a retreat; but after a halt of about a minute we saw that the women and children disappeared like magic in the *tepees*, and that there were no men about except a few old bucks, who stared at us in as much astonishment as Indians ever display; and knowing then that the braves were out hunting or on the war-path, we dashed through the village, revolver in hand, and followed the quarry. In a run of a mile or two we came suddenly upon a large pack of mongrels of all sizes and shapes, which were worrying our hounds, and, jumping into their midst, we soon scattered them by a few vigorous kicks, and sent them howling down the sides of a bluff. The rescue was evidently welcome to our dogs, for some of them were bleeding at the ears, and all were thoroughly exhausted. We found the coyote dead a few yards farther on, and, judging from his numerous wounds, we came to the conclusion that he had run into the Indian curs, and was killed by them before our dogs could overtake him. As we were rather suspicious of the friendliness of the red men, owing to the strange actions of the squaws and children, we collected the hounds together and hastened homeward as fast as our weary horses could carry us. Instead of retreating through the camp, however, which was the nearest route, we crossed a high, wooded hill, and on emerging on the other side, where we commanded an extensive view of the plain, were perfectly thunderstruck to see smoke and flames issuing from the scattered cabins, and to behold groups of horsemen dashing about in various directions. A momentary glance enabled us to decide what was the cause of these conflagrations; and when my companion turned round to me and said, "I think, old boy, our scalps will be lifted before we're many hours older," I confess I felt some qualms steal over me.

As time was of the utmost importance just then, we did not waste much of it in discussing what was best to be done, as my companion had resolved on reaching home as rapidly as possible, to try and save his family from the tomahawk of the red foes. He was very much afraid that they might have been there before him, and this made him almost wild with excitement and feelings of revenge; but on rounding a long, sharp spur of the hill, which gave us a good view of the vale in which his cottage was situated, he was delighted to see everything in its usual tranquil condition. Cheered by this welcome sight, we hastened onward as rapidly as possible, and in the course of half an hour reached the house. Leaping off the half-dead horses the moment we reached the door, he rushed in, still doubtful of the fate of his family; but on finding his wife attending to her business as usual, and the young children playing on the floor, he became as stoical as an Indian brave; and after kissing them all in the ordinary way, he asked his wife if she had seen any Indians about during his absence. She replied that she had not, except Joe, the half-breed, and he was hastening as fast as his horse could carry him to the mining hamlet ten miles away. In response to her query why he had asked such a question, he said that it was mere idle curiosity, as he had seen a party of them on his way back, and he did not know but they might be out on a horse-stealing expedition and pay his ranch a visit. Having lulled her suspicion by his coolness, he went to the stable and hitched two bell-mares and six stout mules to his wagon, and in this he placed a quantity of bed-clothing and some wearing apparel. When this was done, he told his wife that he was somewhat afraid that the red demons might visit the valley during the night or the following day, and he thought it best to take the family to a place of safety for fear of any accident occurring to them.

The wife, suspecting that something was amiss, did not utter a word; and at his request she wrapped the younger children as warmly as possible, and, placing them with the elder and a quantity of meat, bread, and flour in the wagon, she took her seat beside the eldest boy and drove the team herself, while we, armed to the teeth, rode on ahead on fresh horses to reconnoitre the route and look for Indian signs. After travelling about two miles in the direction of the mining village, we came upon the tracks of unshodden horses; and, after scanning them carefully, we decided that they were produced by four Indian mustangs which had come from the direction of the camp we had visited in the afternoon, and were going toward the north-eastern portion of the valley, where there were several settlers engaged in stock-raising. We deduced from this that the animals were ridden by four braves who were probably out on a reconnoissance to see if the presence of their tribe in the vicinity was known, and what opportunities were offered for making a raid on the settlement. The smallness of the party was evidently intended to allay suspicion; for the stock-raisers who have been harassed by the sudden attacks of the red men fly to arms on seeing them in any numbers, or finding the tracks of their shoeless ponies on the ground. Being assured of their purpose, we made a detour to the right and called at two farm-houses, and informed the occupants of the threatened danger, and what we had seen; and they soon joined us, leaving everything behind them except a little food and clothing. Thus re-enforced, we moved onward as rapidly as the teams could travel, the men keeping close to the wagons; but whenever we approached a house, two of the party rode off and notified its inmates of the alarming condition of affairs, and they too were on the march toward the mining camp as rapidly as possible. This place was selected as the head-quarters, owing to its strong position and the number of men there, and the fact that food and shelter could be procured there for a considerable length of time if the people could not return to their own homes.

When we reached the camp at eight o'clock, it was in a state of the greatest excitement, news of the danger having been brought there by the half-breed Joe, the information having been imparted to him by his cousin, an Arapahoe squaw. Men were running hurriedly about, and arming and mounting in hot haste, while couriers were being despatched in every direction to warn the distant stock-raisers and to rally the scattered miners.

The women and children, as fast as they arrived, were furnished with accommodations in their own cabins by the generous miners, and the armed men were assigned to detachments which were under the command of experienced Indian-fighters. About midnight we had fifty mounted and well-armed men ready to take the field, while twenty more remained in camp to guard the women and children—that number, with the re-enforcements which were sure to come in during the night, being deemed sufficient to protect the village from a whole tribe of Sioux. Each man who was to take the field having been supplied with bread and beef enough to last for three days, he tied them on his saddle, and, when everything was ready, all started out in a body about 1 A.M.; and, as the moon was shining brightly, we were able to gallop rapidly over the rolling plain, until we reached the previously mentioned spur of the hill, and there we halted to gaze on the scene of devastation, which was visible for miles toward the south. Houses were blazing or smoking in every direction as far as the eye could see, and their lurid glare illuminated the country for miles around. It was evident, from the course of the flames, that the raiders were working toward the south, and burning and killing on their way; but why they left the main settlement undisturbed was a mystery to many. The only cause that could be adduced was that the settlers toward the south had larger flocks and herds, and were also more widely scattered, so that they could not rally in sufficient numbers to make a stand of any consequence against the red fiends.

We gazed on the scene for an hour or more with a sort of fearful fascination; and during that time deep and vehement were the threats and execrations hurled at the treacherous foes who had created such havoc among a peaceable people. As we desired to be up at daybreak, we concluded to have a short nap, if possible; so each man picketed his horse and unloosed the saddle, but did not take it off, and, rolling himself up in his woollen blanket, was soon trying to woo gentle sleep. This was rendered impossible, however, by the yelping of coyotes and the melancholy howling of wolves, and, when we arose about daylight, I doubt if one person had enjoyed ten minutes of undisturbed repose. After a hasty breakfast, it was decided to send ten men back to the cottage of my host and let them watch the valley, while the remainder tried to surprise the Indian encampment we had visited the previous day. As soon as they started to return, the party that I was with moved off at a brisk trot, with scouts well advanced, and flankers stretching for a mile or more toward the wooded hills, to prevent any sudden assault from that direction. After proceeding about three miles, we heard firing in front, and, galloping up as fast as we could, found the scouts on foot, and skirmishing with a party of young braves. Our line was deployed in extended order at once, and each man advanced as he pleased. We found the Indians in stronger numbers than we expected, considering their movements the previous day; but as every man of our party seemed to be actually mad for revenge, their numerical superiority availed them little, and they were pushed backward gradually, notwithstanding the fact that they took advantage of every bit of cover, and seemed to rise out of the ground like grasshoppers. They tried to surround us two or three times inside of an hour, but a vigorous charge scattered them like chaff, and the survivors were glad to beat a hasty retreat to their own lines. Their yells and shouts, when circling around us, were fairly demoniacal in their intensity; but these had little effect on the pioneers who opposed them, as they had heard them too often to care much for them. After they were driven back to the wooded hill, they made a most determined stand, and poured out a deadly fire that killed several horses and wounded a few men. A party of our men on the left, who were on open, rolling ground, attempted to stop this by making a vigorous charge; but they were met by such a volley that they were compelled to halt and seek cover wherever they could find it. A few of the more advanced, who had their horses killed under them, used their trusty steeds as breastworks, and kept up the fight with a vigor and determination that only Western pioneers can display; and their fire was so destructive that a body of the Indians charged them several times on horseback, in order to capture them, but they were driven back with heavy loss each time.

The detachment which I accompanied worked around to the right until we reached a wooded knoll, and, under cover of this most welcome shelter, we reached the flank of the Indians and opened a fierce fire, which soon caused them to give way in the most precipitous manner. Our lusty cheers, on seeing this, were answered by the others, and, a minute later, by a rattling volley and a wild hurrah from the mountain side. The latter seemed to have fairly demoralized our foes, for they broke away from our front panic-stricken, and fled beyond the range of our rifles in a few moments. When we saw this we returned to our horses, and, mounting them in the twinkling of an eye, dashed to the left, and got several shots at some braves who were trying to escape from the forest, and these forced them back again, when they were received by other volleys delivered by concealed foes. Every Indian who was killed on foot was no sooner struck than he gave a wild yell, jumped high into the air, then fell back dead. These preliminaries to dying are, I believe, peculiar to the red race.

This attack decided the fate of the day; for the Indians fled in every direction, while we pursued them over hill and dale, dropping one every now and then. We were in hopes of reaching their camp before they could get it away, but in this we were disappointed; and, when we reached there, nothing was left of it but a few old *tepees*, and some poles and peltries which they could not carry off in the hurry of their flight. The noise of the firing had evidently warned the squaws of their danger, and, while the warriors were fighting, they took time by the forelock and escaped to safer quarters.

When our party had assembled once more, we found that the ten men who had been sent back to the valley returned on hearing the continuous fusillade, and, getting in rear of the enemy—a feat easily performed owing to the wooded character of the hill—had opened such a destructive fire on him from cover that he was compelled to retreat in a panic. Our loss in this affair was two men killed and eight wounded, while that of the Indians must have been four or five times as much, as our rifles were far superior to theirs, and our shooting was certainly far more accurate.

As soon as we felt sure that our foe had fled for good, a party was sent back to the mining village with the dead and wounded, while the remainder started toward the south to see what damage had been committed, and to learn if the tribe we had been fighting was that which had been raiding in that direction. We had not travelled far before we came to a smouldering wagon, and beside it we found a man and his wife, and, evidently, his two daughters, lying dead. They were terribly, unspeakably mutilated, and the horrible expressions of their features showed what an agonizing death they must have suffered. After burying these in the rudest manner, to prevent them from being devoured by wolves, we moved on, and at every few miles met indications of the savage fury of the demons who were scouring over the country. Every house was burnt, and amidst their ashes, or lying in the yards, were the mutilated remains of men, women, and children; not a person being spared, from the babe to the gray-haired old man. The scene was so sickening, and the destruction so wide-spread, that we were compelled to desist and turn our faces homeward; for it was evident, by the numerous tracks of horses' hoofs, that there were two bodies of Indians in the field, and that the one we were following was much the larger, and could not have numbered less than three or four hundred warriors. Fearing they might return through the valley, we made all possible haste back to prepare a warm reception for them, and, on reaching the mining hamlet once more, we found the tallest tree there graced by four dangling Sioux, who had been captured while trying to return to their own camp. They were evidently those whose tracks we had discovered the previous day; so their summary fate was the cause of some rejoicing.

The village was kept in a state of excitement for a week by the reports of scouts and reconnoitring parties, who reported the movements of several bodies of Indians that were hovering in the woods adjoining the valley on the north; but as they did not come any nearer, hopes were entertained that the severe lesson taught them would prevent any further trouble. Suddenly, one evening, a large war-party, driving an immense herd of horses, was reported to be advancing at a gallop from the east, and every available man present, except the camp-guard, went out to meet them, and, seeking shelter in a ravine, waited until the painted braves came within rifle-range, when they opened a deadly fire on them. This was evidently a most unexpected encounter to the red thieves, for they were thrown into a momentary panic, but they soon recovered themselves; and while some drove the horses away toward the right flank, the others opened a brisk fire to cover their retreat, and kept it up for half an hour, when they broke away terror-stricken. The cause of their flight was soon made evident by the appearance of a body of cavalry who had been pursuing them for several days; and on seeing these, the miners and ranchers ran from cover, mounted their horses, and dashed after the foe. A running fight was kept up for three miles, when a vigorous charge from opposite quarters finished the contest by scattering the Indians in every direction, and forcing them to leave nearly all their plunder behind. The captured horses were driven toward the village, while the cavalry pursued the fugitives, and kept them running until they sought the shelter of the Wind River Mountains, sadly depleted in numbers, and perfectly demoralized. I received, as the result of my coyote-hunt and subsequent Indian hunt, a slight flesh-wound in the side, and two months of as hard campaigning as any person would care to have; and these have so indelibly marked that chase in my mind, that I doubt if I shall soon forget it.

One of the most exciting, interesting, and laughable hunts after the coyote that I ever enjoyed came off on the great plains of the Columbia River, east of the Cascade Range. The region in which it occurred afforded ample scope for testing the pace, endurance, and cunning of the long-tailed quadruped, and also the sagacity of its very near and dear kindred, the Indian cur; for the former is frequently the size of the latter, and the two are more likely to play with each other than to quarrel, unless hounded on by man, or the coyote is too intrusive in its familiarity. I have known even the civilized dogs of the feminine gender, belonging to the pale-faces, to pay visits of courtesy and good-fellowship to the prairie roamers, and play with them by the hour; and, when the visit was returned, the guests were treated with becoming kindness and consideration. This would seem to be a proof positive that both species consider themselves close kindred; for I have never seen the domestic dogs display the same feelings toward the large gray wolf, and a fox was perfectly abhorrent in their sight.

Some of the Indian dogs resemble coyotes so much that it would be hard to distinguish which is which by form and color, and often in habits; and even the known half-breeds seem more inclined to take after the sire than the dam in every way. The latter have a keen nose, and, when trained, make excellent hunting-dogs; but they are not much in a tussle with a wild animal, and are anything but playfully sociable and affectionate with their human masters or their families.

On the occasion to which I refer, the hunt was organized for the purpose of enjoying a national holiday, clearing the coyotes out of a region in which they were becoming too numerous to be agreeable acquaintances of some of the denizens of the farm-yard, and to afford visitors a day's amusement. I stopped at the house selected for a rendezvous, and before daylight of the hunting morning was aroused from a sound sleep by a thundering knock at the door, the stamping of horses, the growling and fighting of dogs, and the strong language of men who were yelling at the combatants. These early arrivals being admitted, they were followed in such rapid succession by others that fifteen had assembled by five o'clock, and they were accompanied by as motley a lot of dogs as could possibly be got together. After a hearty though hasty breakfast, which was often interrupted by yells at the canine combatants, we mounted our steeds and started for cover at a good trot. The snarling pack, as they moved along, presented a sorry appearance, and looked perfect specimens of what a Falstaffian canine regiment ought to be. There were sheep-dogs, curs, mongrel pointers and setters, terriers, mastiffs, Newfoundlands, and hounds of all kinds and crosses, from the thorough-bred harrier to the half-blooded greyhound, besides the *oi polloi* of the dog world generally, whose family no one could make out. This miscellaneous rabble seemed to think that they were assembled for the special purpose of fighting, so they went at it vigorously whenever they had the opportunity. Were it not for the pace at which they were moving, and the many yells and curses hurled at them by their owners, half of them would evidently have been killed before we reached our destination.

A trot of three or four miles brought us to a scrubby coppice, in which firs, cotton-woods, alders, and willows were mingled together in confusion. Adjoining this was a stream, and back of it rose a series of the low terraces so characteristic of the trappean regions of the Pacific Coast. One of the party, who had two mongrel hounds that were used for hunting anything, from the bear and deer to a wild-cat, and which were said to be excellent "smellers," was appointed Master of the Hunt, out of respect to his dogs; and he, pleased with his new honor, went proudly forward with his pack and began to beat the excuse for a wood downward, while others took positions to the windward to check any movements in that direction by the quarry. A half-bred Indian, who was supposed to know more about coyotes than they did themselves, took all the dogs that he could induce to follow him to a treeless vale below the coppice; but his followers were evidently bent more on fighting than hunting, for our ears were soon regaled with snarling, growling, and yells, and the "cussing" of a disgusted whipper-in.

I had taken a position to the leeward of the vale with a party of four, who had half a dozen dogs with them that no amount of coaxing and patting could induce to leave the heels of their masters, and there we waited patiently for half an hour; but hearing no sound that indicated work, an impatient member of the group started off himself, stating that he could find a coyote quicker than all the assembled canine multitude. His assertion proved perfectly correct; for he was gone scarcely ten minutes before two ochreous-colored objects were seen stealing out of a burrow in the open ground a little way below us, as if they thought themselves too modest to face such a large company as ours. Their presence was a signal for a fierce yell of delight, and away went our party after them. This caused the prowlers to think we had some sinister designs against them, and to consider the enthusiasm of our greeting too demonstrative for their sensitive nature; so they gave a startled look of surprise, which lasted for a few seconds, and feeling assured that they were the great centre of attraction, became alarmed, and sped away at their best pace. The dogs, assuming that something was up, began to bark loudly; but when they were "hied" on they fancied that it was the signal to commence fighting, and at it they went, now rolling over and over each other, then breaking loose in order to overtake their masters. Two mongrels, which were too cautious to fight and too fleet of foot to be captured by the bullies, espied the runaways, and after them they went with sharp yelps. The quarries being checked to the leeward, headed up wind; but they had not gone far before they were stopped by another party of horsemen and their dogs. This forced them to take a middle course, so they bent their footsteps toward a series of wave-like hillocks that stretched far away to the north. Horses and dogs were now in full pursuit, and it was hard to tell whether the latter or the men made the most noise, for all were yelling or yelping. The chase led over the hillocks for a mile or two, then into a narrow valley, and up this the hunted turned their noses. This gave us a splendid chance for a run, and we resolved to utilize it, as we had no fleet dogs to bring them to bay. Putting spurs to our steeds, each individual now made a race of it, as every one was anxious to claim the first brush.

We had a good run of two miles or more over this pretty vale, when the coyotes again changed their course suddenly, and broke over the hills with, apparently, an army of dogs in pursuit. They had, in fact, almost run into an Indian village, and had, as a result, brought the large canine force, which always accompanies the red men, after them. The new pursuers were fresh; the coyotes were getting tired and scared; and the consequence was that they were soon overtaken and killed by their own nearest relatives, that follow man in his wanderings. The inglorious ending of our chase was a cause of much regret, as many were panting for the honor of wearing the runaway brushes. Having excommunicated all Indian curs in vigorous anathemas, our cavalcade returned toward the stream, as several of the party and the best dogs were left there; but before we had proceeded three miles we saw a dozen coyotes hastening rapidly away to safer quarters. A little farther on we met one at bay, a mongrel greyhound having overtaken it. When we rode up our dogs joined their comrade at once, and in two or three minutes a brush graced the saddle-bow of one of our party. As our horses were somewhat tired, we did not care to run them for awhile, so we jogged back to cover, and passed the time away by discussing the merits of dogs and horses. Some of the huntsmen were exceedingly angry at their dogs for their bad behavior and slowness of foot, and several, which were the most knowing and famous of their race in the world in the morning, according to the assertions of their owners, lost their character by that run, and were deemed worthless for coyote-hunting at least.

On approaching the stream, we saw some of our party on the hills above standing around in an attitude of expectation, and heard the cries of the two famous hounds—an indication that they had something in view. This caused us to scatter, in hopes that we might be fortunate enough to get a shot at anything started. I moved some distance to the leeward, and waited there patiently for half an hour; and my patience was soon rewarded, for a coyote came sweeping by me less than fifty yards away. As mustangs can jump into a gallop from a stand-still, I went in full pursuit at once; and so well did my *cayuse* ply his legs that I was soon within a distance that enabled me to use a revolver. To hit a small object in rapid flight is no small difficulty, even with a rifle, but to shoot it with a revolver is a matter of great difficulty, unless by accident; hence I must confess that I nearly emptied mine on the fugitive, and that it was only when I was close along-side that I tumbled it over with the last shot. A large pocket-knife ended its fate, and, slinging it over my saddle, I rode back to rejoin my comrades. None were in sight in any direction, however; and as I did not know the way home very well, I began to move in the direction where I supposed it was. After riding two or three miles, I met the entire party making preparations to go in search of me; but, seeing me in the flesh, they concluded to have another run if possible, for coyotes were more abundant than they expected, or even cared for. Moving toward the small vale over which we had enjoyed the first run, the hounds were set to work, and they soon gave tongue. A little later, and we saw some coyotes break cover near a rivulet, and after them we went, though at a rather slow rate, as dogs and horses were getting pumped. While moving forward at a heedless pace, we were almost startled out of our wits by seeing charging toward us in full cry a troop of mounted Indians.

We halted at once, not knowing what to make of the incident, and prepared for trouble, as we supposed that it was a war-party belonging to some tribe that had "broken loose" without a knowledge of the fact having come to our ears. Some of us had empty revolvers, and these we loaded at once, and dashed out of the valley and on to a knoll, without waiting for a moment to consider the character of the approaching cloud, except that it was not composed of whites; and having gained a position from which we could run or fight, we halted to reconnoitre. Our fears were soon dispelled, however; for no less a personage than an individual named Snake Jim, a sub-chief of the Snake tribe, rode up toward us suddenly as if he had risen out of the ground, and after a cheery " how !" informed us that some of the young braves of the village, who belonged to the Snake reservation, and had learned from the whites to have no fear of the "bad medicine" of the coyote, wanted to join in the hunt if there was no objection. He was positively informed that they would be welcome; and being re-enforced by about twenty braves and an army of their curs, we resumed our sport. Jim said he knew where there were several coyotes, and, under his guidance, we went to seek them.

A ride of two miles brought us to a deeply buried dell that was surrounded by huge basaltic bowlders, and in which hares seemed to be unusually numerous. Dividing our forces there, the red men occupied one position and the whites another. The dogs were then sent in, and they soon sent out two dozen coyotes, it seemed to me, and after them we all dashed right and left. The dogs were yelping, the Indians yelling, and using their bows and arrows, and the whites were shouting and firing their revolvers. The whole scene was one of excitement and wild hurrah, and reminded me of a sharp and close cavalry skirmish. Some of the men were "hieing" on their dogs; some got thrown by running their horses through the villages of ground-squirrels, and got heartily laughed at for their misfortune; while others were shouting at the red men to keep out of the way. It was a scene of fun and confusion, and the confusion was increased by the antipathy of the civilized dogs to their more barbarous brethren, and the efforts they made to hunt them instead of the coyotes. The riding and yelling and yelping was fast and furious, until four of the fugitives were killed by the Indians and three by our party; and having run by that time about six miles, we concluded to stop for the day, owing to the condition of our horses, and the fact that the coyotes were scared away from the neighborhood. During the last run the poor creatures were rushing madly through the canine lines in their effort to escape; but wherever they turned they met new foes in large numbers, so that those which got away were compelled to fight bravely for their liberty. We could have killed several more during the day if we wished, for they were scattered all over the country in small groups; but, our purpose having been accomplished, we

A WOLF-HUNT ON THE PRAIRIE.

returned home, well satisfied with our day's sport. On the way back we called at the small Indian village of mats; and I noticed there that many of the dogs running about were perfect fac-similes of the coyotes in all but color, and even barked so much like them that it would be hard to distinguish which was which. I learned there, also, that the coyotes frequently associated with Indian dogs at certain seasons, and that the products were wary, thieving, timid creatures, but often excellent animals for hunting game, and especially their own ancestors. Some of the best dogs in the country for mute hunting are these mongrels, and, if well trained, they are said to be invaluable.

Leaving the encampment, we wended our way homeward, and, after a pleasant evening with song and story, I retired to bed thoroughly tired, and highly pleased with the day's amusement. The pursuit of this animal, which is faster than any fox, will, no doubt, be fashionable in a few years, when gentlemen with sporting proclivities enter the country, and the sons of those now residing there learn to appreciate the pleasure it affords.

CHAPTER VII.

THE BUFFALO.

The Buffalo.—Number of Species.—Difference between Them.—The gigantic Buffalo of prehistoric Times.—Fierce Aspect of the modern Bison.—Courage of the Male.—Social Character of the Species.—Mothers have Little Affection for the Calves.—Fight between a Grizzly Bear and a Small Herd of Bulls.—A Bull rescues a Calf from a Pack of Wolves.—Another tries to protect a Cow from a Hunter.—A New Mode of capturing Calves.—Buffaloes in a State of Domestication.—Favorite Habitat of the Buffalo.—Character of the Buffalo Grass.—Sufferings of the Animals in Winter from Hunger.—Why Old Bulls leave the Herds.—Use of the Buffalo to the Indians.—The Flesh of the Buffalo.—A Custom of the West.—How the Wolverine feasts on dried Buffalo Meat.—Cunning and Courage.—Pemmican.—The most Delicate Parts of the Buffalo.—Cows better than Bulls.—Vitality of the Animals.—Best Weapons for hunting Them.—American Horses *versus* Mustangs.—Opinion of Old Hunters.—Faults of Mustangs in running Buffaloes.—The Various Systems employed for killing the Buffalo.—Great Annual Slaughter of the Animal.—Indians dressed in Wolf-skins attack the Buffalo.—Why they use Arrows instead of Fire-arms.—Hunts of the Half-breeds of British America.—Mean Devices of the Whites.—How Thousands are destroyed Annually.—The Camp and the Night Alarm.—Shooting at Antelopes.—Stalking Buffalo Skulls.—Gambols of Herds.—A Dash after a Herd, and what came of it.—An Alarm of Indians.—Opinions of a Party of Teutons about Jokes.—The Result to me of my Day's hunting.—A Spirited Chase in the Republican Valley.—Wolves and Number of Quarries killed.—A Thousand Hunters and Thousands of Buffaloes in Motion at the same Time.—Howling Wolves and bellowing Bisons.—An Alarm of Sioux.—The Retreat.—Panic-stricken Pawnees.

THE bison, or American buffalo (*Bos americanus*), is now confined to a few regions extending from British America to New Mexico, but it is nowhere abundant compared to what it was.

There are supposed to be two distinct species of the animal, namely, the common one which frequents the prairies, and the wood, or mountain buffalo, which is never seen on the plains, and cannot be induced to leave its forest home. The latter, according to Hind, is not uncommon north of the Saskatchewan region; but in the United States it is confined to the wooded mountainous regions of Montana, Dakota, Colorado, and Idaho. It differs from its lowland congener in being much heavier in body, having shorter and more robust legs, a soft and uncurled mane, a softer and finer pelage, and having the bump of cautiousness more largely developed, so that it is not unlike the Lithuanian aurochs. It can pick its way amidst crags and chasms with an agility worthy of a goat, and with much greater ease than one would give it credit for. Owing to the wild and sometimes inaccessible character of its haunts, it is not hunted much, so that little is known of its habits; but they do not vary much, in all probability, from those of its better known kindred, the difference being such as a person would expect to find between animals whose haunts are so totally distinct.

An adult male of the common species is about six feet high at the fore-shoulders; measures from eight to eight and a half feet in length; the horns are between twelve and thirteen inches in length, and the tail about twenty; and when the animal is in good condition it frequently weighs two thousand pounds, but the ordinary weight is between twelve and sixteen hundred pounds. Large and heavy as it is, it cannot compare with the prehistoric species of the West; for, judging from the fossil remains found, that must have been seven or eight times its size, and, if everything was in proportion, must have weighed several thousand pounds.

If Nimrods chased it, they must have been giants indeed, and worthy contemporaries of the mastodons, gigantic elephants, turtles, sloths, and other huge animals that roamed over the earth in the misty past.

The modern bison would be a good example to prove that appearances are often deceiving; for the novice, on gazing at its ponderous proportions, its large head covered with thick, matted hair, its shaggy mane a foot long, its sullen demeanor, its wicked eyes, which seem to glow into an emerald fire with rage and hate, and its sharp-pointed horns, would be apt to consider it one of the most dangerous of quadrupeds; yet the reverse is the case; for, unless wounded or cornered, it is one of the mildest, most harmless, and stupid animals on the continent. The only time in which it is liable to assume the offensive is during the rutting season, in July; for it is then exceedingly petulant, and the temper of the males is not soothed by their frequent though generally bloodless contests, and their long

AMERICAN BISON.

fasts, for wooing occupies the greater portion of their attention. They are more afraid of man than any other foe; and while they will take little notice of the wolf, cougar, or grizzly bear, one sniff of the former will cause thousands of them to flee for miles at their best pace. The males are by no means deficient in courage; for they will boldly attack a grizzly, and, if their horns are not blunted by rooting in the ground, are able to place that monarch of the Western wilds *hors de combat* occasionally.

The social character of the bison is much like that of the domestic cattle. It is gregarious in habit, and travels in herds which have been estimated to contain over one hundred thousand individuals, and to cover an extensive plain so thickly that it looked almost one mass of black dots at a distance. The herds are not so large now as they formerly were, yet they may, in some regions, still be compared to the "cattle on a thousand hills;" and few grander sights can be witnessed than to behold them in herds of many hundreds, moving north or south during their annual migrations.

The females commence bearing when three years old, and continue to be prolific up to an old age. They produce only one calf at a time, and drop that generally in April, though I have seen some in July that did not look to be more than two or three weeks old.

The mothers seem to have little affection for their young, and generally desert them at the first alarm; but the males are sturdy protectors, and carefully guard them from all foes. Calves run with their mothers until the latter are ready to increase the bovine population again, and after that they look out for themselves. When the females are about to become mothers they retire from the herd singly, and secrete themselves in some refuge where the young may be protected from wolves and other foes until they are able to run about; and when that time comes they rejoin the males, and the united company stroll over many long miles together.

When a herd is feeding, the cows and calves are in the centre, and the old bulls occupy the outer spaces, as if they intended to make an *abatis* of their horns to repel all adversaries. How effective a protection this *abatis* is, the wolves, which constantly attend the herds in large numbers, to see if they can pick up a calf or a wounded adult, know too well, for they never attempt to force it; and that the buffaloes consider it impregnable is evident by the contempt with which they treat their hungry attendants, and the closeness to which they will allow them to approach before they attempt to send them scampering away by a mere threat or a vigorous charge. Even a hungry grizzly has learned how dangerous it is, and has given its life as a forfeit for its ignorance and presumption. I heard an old hunter in Dakota relate how a male grizzly once attacked a herd in his presence. The huge bear commenced operations by boldly advancing toward a small herd of cows which was protected only by five or six bulls, the remainder of the stern sex being assembled in bachelor parties by themselves in other portions of the plain. As he approached the herd, the males closed up together, to make a protecting screen for those under their charge, and lowered their sharp-pointed horns almost to the ground. The grizzly halted to gaze at the reception prepared for him, and, after sniffing the air and gazing for a few moments, he concluded that he had little to fear, and advanced boldly to the assault. Before he reached the herd the most daring of the bulls charged him fearlessly; but ere he could reach him with his horns the bear struck him a powerful blow along the back with his huge paws, and killed him immediately by breaking the spinal column. Nothing daunted at the fate of their companion, the others charged vigorously, but two of them were overpowered in less than three minutes. The survivors plied their horns to such good advantage, however, that their powerful assailant was glad to crawl away with broken ribs and protruding *viscera*, only to fall a victim to the hunter.

The same man told me that he saw a pack of wolves chasing a young calf, apparently about two months old, on one occasion, and that the poor creature was so weak from loss of blood and hard running that it must soon have fallen a prey to its merciless pursuers had its life not been saved by a splendid bull, which charged down so suddenly upon the hungry throng that he hurled one of them into the air with a vehemence that killed it when it returned to earth, and caused the remainder to scamper away with the utmost celerity, as if they were panic-stricken. He then escorted his young charge away, and, although the prowlers followed them, they took excellent care not to go too near for fear of the consequences. The two had not travelled far before they met a herd, and this they joined, the youngster taking its place in the middle with the cows and calves. It is no unusual incident for wounded buffaloes to be protected from wolves by those that are not; and the bulls are certainly entitled to be classed in some characteristics with the knights of old, who fought for love, not gold. I saw a bull come to the aid of a wounded cow that was being pursued by a horseman, run with her for a mile or two, and change sides whenever the pursuer did, as if he would guard her from all danger. His gallantry would have been rewarded but for the fact that his companion was so badly injured that she could not live, and the hunter thought it better to kill her than leave her to be worried to death by wolves. Even cows show courage occasionally, especially if assembled in numbers, and boldly charge wolves that may threaten themselves or their young. I knew one to dash after a hunter who was trying to lasso her calf, and he only escaped her horns by killing her with a lucky shot just as she was about attacking him. It is a common idea among hunters that the cows have little affection for their calves, and that they will desert them in a moment if threatened by any danger. While this is generally true, yet there are some notable exceptions; and any person who has ever seen a mother lick and fondle her young one must know she has a deep feeling for it. I have known a cow which left her calf in a little dell come bounding and bellowing about our party to see if we had captured it, and, when she did not find it, go dashing back again in a state of the greatest excitement, and bellowing loudly for it.

A mother has even been known to charge headlong into a small valley in which her young one was concealed, on finding a hunter there, and cause him to run for his life; and another not only charged a body of mounted hunters, on suspicion that they had stolen her calf, but dashed wildly up and down, and circled round a flying column containing at least five thousand buffaloes, thinking it might be among them. When she could not find it, she fled over the plains in a crazed state, and uttered piteous calls for her darling at intervals; but no answer came back to her until she had disappeared over a hill in the horizon. Whatever may be said about their affection, it is certainly true that they are very careless mothers; for they leave their young without any hesitation in exposed situations, where they are liable to be attacked at any moment by wolves, and in this way many of them are destroyed annually; for the lupine prowlers are always vigilant, ready to eat at all hours of the day or night, and miss no opportunity of killing a young one even though they are not hungry. The calves themselves seem also to be very stupid creatures; for, instead of dashing off to join the herds and claim their protection, they frequently, especially if a little tired, merely poke their nose into a bunch of grass, and because they themselves cannot see, they fancy they are perfectly concealed from all foes. This idea is soon rudely banished, however, by the sudden onslaught of ravenous wolves, or the rifle and lariat of the hunter.

Lassoing calves is most interesting sport, as the creatures run well, course like a hare, and, when hard pressed, boldly charge the horses or riders, and even attempt to pierce them with their sharp but tiny horns; and, even when captured, they buck and plunge so violently that the attempt to lead them to a rendezvous is most amusing. Calves not older than a month or two will readily follow a horseman if they are separated from their dams; but when they get beyond that age they are too knowing not to distinguish the difference between their own kindred and the steed. Hunters who wish to obtain calves for menageries or private persons often resort to this method of capture, as the animals are more likely to live than if they were driven hard for several miles before being lassoed; and it is said that if a person breathes into their nostrils when they are caught they become tame at once, and will follow his horse for several miles like a dog. I have known them to follow horsemen out of a herd after a short run, and trot behind them for several miles without making an effort to escape.

Thousands of them are captured alive annually by being run down with horses, but the greater number die, owing to the severe manner in which they were chased, or else to their grief at being separated from their kindred and the nutritious grasses and freedom of the plains. I have seen a troop of cavalry lasso one hundred of them in two days, and bring them to the barracks; and although they had plenty of room in a corral to run about, and an abundance of hay and grass, few of them lived more than a week. The same mortality was noticeable among those captured by expert lassoers and regular hunters; so it is evident that they cannot stand much hardship.

The calves can be domesticated readily, if treated kindly; and when the bulls reach adult age they are said to be as good as oxen for ploughing, but they have the great fault of being stubborn; and when once they take it into their heads to go in a certain direction, nothing can prevent them except a wall or a bullet. One or two generations of domestication might break them of this habit, however, and they could then be made into valuable beasts of burden, while the cows would prove a valuable addition to the farm-yard. My own opinion is that the buffalo can be tamed easily, and vastly improved in physique, strength, and edible qualities, by careful feeding; for, in a wild state, its flesh is rather flavorless, and the stateliest bull cannot compete in power or pugnacity with one of his domestic congeners scarcely one-half his weight or age. The wild bull, that is, the domestic species, run wild, can defeat any two buffaloes in ten minutes, and a herd of wild cattle can drive twenty times their number of buffaloes in a very short time.

From experiments made in New Jersey, Virginia, Texas, and other portions of the United States, it has been found that the buffalo can be domesticated without much trouble, that its flesh can be greatly improved, and that the milk of the cow is rich and sweet, and yields more cream than almost any of the farm-yard species. The hide of the buffalo is also four times as valuable as that of the domestic race, and, by careful feeding, the fur is made longer and finer than it is when the animal runs wild. There is no doubt that the buffalo can be made a most valuable addition to our domestic animals, and it is rather a pity that some persons do not try it, and keep it from totally disappearing.

I have heard that buffalo bulls associate freely with domestic cows, and that their offspring is large and hardy, that their flesh is excellent, that the females are good milkers, and that they can be kept easily, as they are indiscriminate feeders, and anything but dainty in palate. Whether the cross would prove prolific is another question, but the probability is that it would, by paying careful attention to the laws of breeding. The cross is said to be very stubborn, however; but this fault could, no doubt, be eradicated without much trouble.

If the buffalo of India can be made useful to man, there is little doubt that its American congener also can; hence its domestication should be attempted by wealthy private gentlemen, stock-raisers, and even small farmers, and they would undoubtedly find their efforts crowned with success. Any pasture will answer its purpose, for it will thrive where any of the bovine species more dainty in appetite than a Texas steer would starve; and as it associates readily with the domestic species, it requires no unusual care.

The favorite habitat of the animal in its wild state is a rolling plain, where a short but very nutritious species of the *Graminæ*, known locally as the buffalo grass, grows in profusion. This is the most pugnacious grass known, for it will allow no rivals to intrude on its ground; but if they do, they are soon crowded out of existence. Like the bunch grass (*Festucca scabrella*), of which the buffalo is also fond, it cures on the stalk, and so affords pabulum to large numbers of quadrupeds throughout the year, for it is really the only thing they can depend on for food during the winter. The buffaloes that frequent the northern regions obtain it in winter by scraping away the snow; but during severe seasons, when the snow is deep and the crust hard, they cannot get at it, and the result is that many thousands starve to death. This is one of the reasons for their decimation, as much almost as their wanton

THE HERD MOVING TOWARD WATER.

slaughter by Indians, hide-hunters, and sportsmen. It is pitiful to hear the deep, gruff bellowing of the poor creatures then, as they wander over the snow-fields in search of food, or rush wildly about when almost mad with hunger.

A stranger who never saw a buffalo ground would know it immediately by the number of wallows it contains, and

9*

the numerous skulls that lie about in every direction. The latter are so deceptive that I have more than once mistaken them at a distance for living animals, and wasted valuable time in carefully stalking them. When this error has been committed a few times, however, a person learns to be more cautious and less enthusiastic, and to be sure that he is not laboring under a mistake before commencing his stealthy, crawling, and often fatiguing "still-hunt."

The wallows, according to Catlin, are made by the strongest bulls for the purpose of enjoying a bath. A veteran with ponderous horns, on reaching a spot where the earth seems damp, lowers himself on one knee, and plunging his horns, and at last his head, into the ground, makes an excavation into which the water filters from among the grass, forming for him, in a few minutes, a cool and comfortable bath, into which he plunges like a hog in its mire. Throwing himself flat upon his side in this delightful hole, he forces himself violently around, and, ploughing up the ground by his rotary motion, sinks deeper and deeper into the ground. Having cooled his sides, he stands in the pool till inclination induces him to step out, and give place to the next in power; and in this manner the whole herd pass through in turn, each one swinging its body around in a similar manner. When all have finished their bath, the hole is quite deep, and, once seen, its origin will always be known. It is evident that this excavating propensity must soon destroy the sharpness of the horns of the sturdier bulls, especially if the soil is of a stony nature; so that they have to yield their supremacy in a short time to the younger bulls, which have appendages with sharper points. It is supposed that the veterans are driven out of a herd by their jealous juniors, when their horns become too blunt to fight to good advantage; but this I should deduce to be a fallacy, inasmuch as the natural characteristic of the animals is to be social and peaceable. The actual reason why these old hermits quit their companions and seek comfort in solitude might be attributed to the waning or failure of their salacious disposition; for some of them look as if they entertained the sentiment, in a bovine form, that their only books were the cow's looks, and folly was all they taught them. I hope the spirit of Moore will pardon me for thus transposing and applying his rollicking ditty; but I thought it so appropriate to the circumstances that I could not help using it. These hermits are the specimens on which the wolves delight to dance attendance; yet they take excellent care to avoid their horns unless they are ill, or so decrepit as to be unable to make a strong resistance. Even when in vigorous condition, they sometimes yield their life to their gray foes, as the latter cut their hamstring by a sudden bound, and, once that is severed, they are soon transformed into wolf-meat.

Next to the lupine prowler, the Indian is the greatest lover of the buffalo; and no wonder, for to him it is house, food, clothing, and fire. Its flesh furnishes him with food; its skin with wigwams, lariats, reins, robes, and raiment; its dung—the well-known *bois de vache* of the Canadian voyageurs and half-breeds, and the "chips" of the plainsmen—with fire; and its bones often supply him with arrow-tips and other implements of the chase.

The statement so frequently made that the red man and the buffalo will disappear together is certainly true in a particular sense; for when the latter becomes so scarce as not to be able to supply the wants of the former, he will have to devote his attention to farming or stock-raising to obtain a means of subsistence; and as he cannot, or will not, do either of these, he must become a pensioner of the Government, and the result will be speedy starvation, or a war in which he will be decimated. In that case we shall know the typical Indian no more; and instead of the fierce, treacherous, and cruel brave, we shall have a sneaking, begging, poor wretch, who will, at an early day, be placed in the soil where his rude forefathers sleep, and his race will no longer be known on earth. The flesh of the buffalo has been the principal, one might say the sole, food of many thousands of Indians, half-breeds, trappers, and voyageurs for many years; and considering their thoughtlessness and their wanton destruction of all game at times, a person might wonder how it happens that the buffalo is so numerous as it is.

What these people do not eat fresh they dry, or make into pemmican. The drying process is simple enough. A number of poles, about four feet high, and having a crotch at the top, is inserted in the ground, and on these are placed light boughs, to make a platform. Under this platform, and about the middle, a shallow trench is dug, which is filled with green wood, so as to make as much smoke as possible. The flesh is next sliced off the carcass in long strips about two inches wide, and from half an inch to an inch in thickness, and is placed on the frame, after being immersed for a few seconds in boiling brine; but if salt is scarce the meat is dried without it. When the staging is carefully and evenly covered with the strips, the fire is lighted, and kept burning for two or three days, but never so brightly as to do more than make a dense smoke, as it is the dry air and sun that really cures the meat, and not the fire; for the sole purpose of the latter is to keep flies away, and to lessen the effect of the night dew. If ants appear, the upright poles are greased, and this causes them to retreat in a short time. The meat is often cured by merely hanging it on the boughs of trees, or on frames in long strips, and turning it around occasionally for two or three days. These platforms are frequently met with in the hunting regions frequented by Indians and half-breeds; and if they contain any pabulum, the wayfarer is permitted to take all he wants for present necessities but to pocket none for future use, for such is the recognized custom of the land.

The stages are frequented at all times by wolves, and sometimes by wild-cats, but they seldom get any of the contents. There is one creature, however, which is fortunate enough to feast off the stores, and that is the wolverene, one of the most daring, courageous, and cunning animals in the world. Instead of wasting its time in sniffing and sighing, or trying to climb the thin, upright stakes, it quietly goes to work and cuts a number of them down with the dexterity and rapidity of the beaver, its sharp teeth enabling it to do this in the course of a few hours. When several posts are cut away, the platform and its contents tumble down, and the wily animal enjoys a feast that would cause a hungry wolf to go into ecstasies. Should the latter attempt to become a participator of the good things procured by the other, however, it pays dearly for its presumption, for the wolverene allows nothing except its own kindred to be self-invited to its board. It is probably the most cunning animal on the continent, and a fox or a wolf is only a sucking dove compared to it. It defies traps, and, no matter how carefully a hunter may secure his bait, it will probably be taken away, and no result left for it. Meat buried deep under the snow for safe-keeping is stolen with a promptitude and ability that defies detection; but the experienced hunter knows at once who is the thief, and frequently does not attempt to follow in pursuit, for he knows how useless it would be.

This Western robber and glutton is a peculiar-looking creature belonging to the *Mustelidæ,* and is the largest of the genus. It is not unlike a polecat in form, but it is much heavier and more ungainly. It has a large head, which is carried somewhat lower than the upper portion of the body; the legs are short and massive; the tail is of medium length, black and bushy; the claws are sharp and dense; and its fangs are pointed and powerful. I have known it to enter a cabin and devour three or four pounds of pemmican, and get away from its pursuers, although three or four dogs joined in the chase.

This pemmican, which is made of meat dried, pounded, and mixed with melted fat and dried berries, forms the principal food of the wandering Indians, hunters, and voyageurs; but an inexperienced pale-face would find it a difficult matter to eat it with any relish unless he was almost starving. It frequently has a rancid taste that is sickening at first; but under the best of conditions it is anything but agreeable. I have been forced to eat it for want of something better on a few occasions; but whether it was made of the flesh of the mountain sheep, wild goat, or buffalo, it seemed to have the same flavor, differing only in various degrees of nastiness. The berries which it contains are intended to give it a sharp, sour taste, to counterbalance the nauseousness of the stale fat and the insipidity of the lean meat. The flesh of the buffalo is highly prized by some amateur sportsmen, on the principle, I suppose, that it is considered to have a gamy flavor, and to be therefore a dish fit for the gods; but I could never take kindly to it unless it was unusually tender, or I was very hungry. The tongue and hump are considered to be the most delicate parts, and many sportsmen will not eat any other. They do not, however, in my estimation, deserve the encomiums bestowed upon them. They are the best parts, it is true, but they cannot compare in succulency, flavor, or nutritive qualities with a good beefsteak, though I doubt if any steak ever tasted so well to a hungry hunter as they do after he has been on the prairies a few days or weeks. The cows and calves are much more palatable than the bulls; hence, the man who supplies his house with buffalo-meat selects them as a first choice whenever he can. They are also easier to kill than the males, though they too will often carry an enormous load of lead before falling. I have known an old bull to be perforated with fourteen bullets, and escape after all; and I saw a cow pierced with ten bullets, which were scattered all over her body, run for three miles, and fall only when she broke her leg by treading in the hole of a prairie-dog. The head is the worst place to aim at, as it is covered with a dense plastron of matted hair, which seems to absorb the ball before it reaches the skull, unless the rifle is of heavy calibre, or it is fired at close range. A twelve-bore is a capital weapon for buffalo-shooting, but it seems too inconvenient for use on horseback. In running them, I have found a large revolver a good weapon, as it is compact, and will kill readily at close range. The best buffalo-hunters burn the hair on nearly every one they slay, so close do they approach, and they generally aim for the spinal column or the ribs. The novice, in running them, might not do much better than to hit them in the fore-shoulder, for that soon causes them to halt, as the fore-quarters are so heavy that they cannot be sustained long by only one leg; and if wounded in that part, the hunter can finish them when he pleases. A very necessary element to attain success in hunting the buffalo is a fast and courageous horse that can be kept under control, and will not lose his head in a stampede or be afraid of ranging along-side a herd when it is in motion. For this purpose an American horse—as all horses are called that do not belong to the Indians, or, rather, that do not come under the head of *cayuse*—is preferable to a mustang, so far as my experience goes; for he has greater speed for a long run, is more intelligent, more tractable, and will go until he drops; whereas the other is liable to bolt at any moment, unless very well trained, and will often stop whenever he feels that he has done enough. I have been with a party that ran buffaloes for four days, at an average rate of fifty miles a day; and those who rode American horses killed more than those who rode mustangs, and their animals were also fresher when the run was over.

I heard of even a better case than this from an army officer, who is now on the high-road to fame; for he told me that he had ridden an average of fifty miles a day for ten days after buffaloes with two American horses, whereas some of his troopers, who were mounted on mustangs, could scarcely keep in sight of the herds after the fourth or fifth day. The most famous scouts and buffalo-hunters that I met in the West were dubious about using pure mustangs in a long buffalo chase, and I know for a fact that those deemed to be the most successful did not employ them. I have ridden mustangs in the chase on various occasions; but the greatest fault I found with them was their propensity to bolt suddenly at a right angle whenever a wounded buffalo assumed a threatening attitude; and if a person did not know this trick he was liable to be thrown, and left to face the fury of a fierce bull, or the hoofs of a maddened throng that a precipice could not swerve from their heedless course.

This habit of breaking away the moment a shot is fired may have its advantages; but they are more than counterbalanced by the disadvantages, and not the least of these is that a man does not feel secure of his seat for five minutes together in a headlong dash. Mustangs trained by Indians are also accustomed to run on the right of a herd, as that is the most convenient position for the red men in shooting their arrows; but it is not always so to the paleface, especially if he uses a revolver.

One of the surest means of bagging a large number of buffaloes is to remain about twenty or thirty feet behind a herd, so as not to scatter the animals, and rake them forward, so as to make a three-quartering shot through the ribs and lungs; for if a person crowded on them they would push away from him laterally, or break up into groups, and by this means give him as much trouble to tumble over a dozen as it would to kill three times that number. If a person has a fast and trained horse, all he has to do is to throw the reins on his neck and fire away, and he must be a poor shot indeed if he cannot claim several trophies in a run of twenty minutes. Experienced hunters kill one almost at every shot, or at least cripple them so much that they cannot escape, so are subsequently captured. Dr. Carver, the famous rifleman, and probably the best buffalo-hunter in the world, has killed sixty-three out of a herd in one run, and wounded several more; and it was no uncommon thing for him to kill thirty or forty in a run, and select his animals. I have hunted with him and other persons in the West, but I never knew one to even approach him in killing buffaloes or any other game when they were running at full speed.

The two methods of hunting the buffalo employed in the West is to stalk it and run it down on horseback. Which is the most sportsman-like method, sportsmen will readily discern without any comments. Hungry men and hide-hunters generally resort to the former, the true lovers of the chase to the latter. By the former system, all one has to do is to crawl to the leeward of a herd, taking advantage of every rise in the ground, and fire away when a good opportunity is presented; for buffaloes are such stupid creatures that the greater part of a herd may be destroyed before the remainder get out of range, provided they do not see or wind the hunter. This is how the hide-hunters make their enormous hauls, and rid a region of the animals in a short time. In a letter which I published in a prominent New York journal in September, 1874, I made the following statement about the destruction of the buffalo; but from what I have learned since, by experience, I should be apt to more than sextuple my estimate, and still be within the bounds.

"It is estimated that the 'hide-hunters' of Kansas, Texas, Colorado, and Southern Nebraska kill 50,000 each year for the skins alone; that the Indians kill three times that number, and that perhaps 10,000 more are killed by sportsmen and those pioneers who depend on buffalo for their winter meat; thus we have the enormous figure of 210,000 as the annual slaughter. But this even will not represent the grand total, for many calves are captured to be sold to menageries, museums, and to private gentlemen who desire such pets. I cannot approach a summary of the latter, but I think that from five to ten thousand would be an approximate estimate, though a low one. I have known instances where a hundred of these creatures were caught in a day by being run down, and not more than one-tenth were alive the next; for, though apparently strong, they cannot endure much hardship. By giving the figures in round numbers, we may estimate that a quarter of a million bison are destroyed annually. At this rate of destruction, they cannot last long; so the next generation will probably witness the decimation of the animal most characteristic of the fauna of North America—one with which the history of the plains, pioneers, and trappers is most closely blended."

This assertion may seem extraordinary, yet everything points to it as a fact; and although buffaloes still roam in millions over the Western plains, their fate is already sealed, as the hide-hunters kill even gravid females, and leave their carcasses on the prairie to feed carnivorous birds and quadrupeds.

I counted as many as thirty carcasses of cows one day in Southern Nebraska, and in each case the udder was full of milk. The Vandals in this heedless destruction were the hide-hunters, from whom no game is safe if they can only get a few pence for either the flesh or the skin. The death of over five million buffaloes in four years proves how successfully and assiduously these men work, and how stupid the bison must be. I have seen a small herd almost decimated by regular hunters before the remainder took the precaution to leave, yet they saw whence the deathly missiles came by the puffs of smoke. They would not have fled, in all probability, when they did, had not one of the men shown himself unintentionally; but the moment his head peered above the ravine in which he was stationed they swaggered away at their best pace.

The animals which are so much afraid of man show no fear of their satellites, the wolves; and this trait of their nature is used to good advantage by the Indians, for they sometimes dress themselves up in wolf-skins, and approach an unsuspicious herd from the leeward to within arrow-range, and, squatting themselves on their heels, ply their bows to such good advantage that they soon have a good stock of meat lying on the ground before them. They prefer using their swift and noiseless primitive missiles in such cases to fire-arms, as the noise of the latter is liable to scare the animals and produce a stampede that may last for two days. The rifle detonations are also liable to terrify other game and clear the country of it in a short time.

Their favorite mode of hunting now is to make a surround on horseback, and slay right and left until they become weary; and if this drives the buffaloes away, they follow them up as fast as the squaws can prepare the meat

KAIOWA BUFFALO CHASE.

and attend to the hides. I have seen some surrounds of the Sioux and Pawnees; and were the scene not made picturesque by the wigwams, the numerous and almost naked warriors, and excitement of galloping steeds and herds, I should say that it was not so inspiriting or successful as a drive organized by Western hunters and sportsmen.

The half-breeds of portions of British America organize regular hunts also, and on such occasions they take all their household effects with them. The women and children are stowed away in rude carts, and the men ride the mustangs which are to play so prominent a part in the chase. As the long cavalcade winds over the grass-clad prairie, made gay with many species of brilliant wild-flowers, it presents an inspiriting sight, and recalls, in a small way, the advance of an army. When it reaches the buffalo-grounds a camp is pitched in a convenient locality, close to wood and water if possible, and, after that is done, the leader takes his men to the leeward of a herd, and distributes them in such a manner that they may be able to drive it toward the encampment, in order to avoid as much trouble as possible in gathering up the meat. They sometimes place buffalo "chips" in such a manner on the prairie as to make them look like men, and, when the herd sees these, it breaks away from them, and heads perhaps for the camp, where another party of hunters is ready to receive it. When everything is arranged, the men close in gradually on the thousands of shaggy creatures that dot the plain, probably as far as the eye can see, and, on arriving within charging distance, they dash on at the best speed of their horses. Then commences a scene to which no pencil can do full justice. The alarmed throngs, on seeing their foes, break away in wild terror, the cows being generally at the head of the column, owing to their greater fleetness and lightness, and the calves being next to them, while the burly bulls close the rear and flanks. This terrified host causes the ground to fairly tremble beneath its weight, and the noise of its movements may be heard a long distance off, as it is not unlike the roar of an advancing hurricane.

When the hunters range along-side the crowding multitude they use rifle and revolver so rapidly that the noise sounds like the firing of a heavy body of skirmishers. They require few shots to kill an animal, one or two being generally sufficient; for their trained buffalo-runners carry them so close to the herd that a bullet can be planted in whatever portion of the body the hunter wishes. The result is that, in a run of perhaps twenty miles, a thousand or two animals may be lying on the ground, and in some instances double that number. When the recall is sounded, the horsemen return and devote their attention to the wounded, and soon put them out of their misery. The carts follow the hunters and gather up the meat, and the greater portion of that is, in a few hours, ready to be placed on the drying-stages, while the hides are being prepared for curing. When the expedition returns after the grand hunt, which sometimes lasts for weeks, its members have meat enough to feed them for several months, and many a buffalo-robe with which to provide clothing and luxuries for their families.

A good robe is worth from two to four dollars; so it will be seen that they can earn a handsome sum in a short time. A spring robe, when the animal has very little hair on its body, and it looks like a shorn poodle, is worth only one or one and a half dollars, yet the skin-hunters slay it even then, for this paltry sum, in large numbers.

The Indian hunts that I witnessed were something like the one described, except that they used short, powerful bows and heavy arrows in preference to fire-arms. The reason they gave for this was, that the former made no noise, and did not therefore terrify the animals so much as the latter would, or cause them to leave the country, and so make a long pursuit a necessity. By using arrows, they could hunt for several days within an area of twenty square miles, whereas the use of rifles would make them travel perhaps ten or twenty miles before they could find a herd; and it would then be so timid that to approach it might prove a difficult matter, and would certainly require great caution and the most careful stalking. Another reason is, that every man can tell what meat belongs to him by the private mark on his arrows; so all that the squaws have to do is to search for the arrows of their husbands, and commence an immediate dissection of the carcasses in which they are planted. If a precipice is convenient, the red men avoid all trouble by driving the herds toward it, and into this they tumble headlong; for they move at such a velocity, and are so crowded together, that the rear pushes the front downward, and all follow in the most stupid manner, though they may see the danger before them. Many thousands are destroyed in this way, and many more by being lost in quicksands, or swallowed up in the ice and turbulent currents of large rivers; so that fate seems to aim at their destruction.

One of the meanest devices ever instituted by man for their destruction is that practised by some persons south of the Platte River, in Nebraska. Streams being exceedingly scarce there, the poor creatures have to travel many miles sometimes to obtain water, and, when they reach it, they are so desperate from thirst that nothing except death can prevent them from having it. Hunters, knowing this, post themselves along the streams and kill them as they come to drink; but for fear their work by day should not prove effective enough, they build fires at night, and by this means keep the dying creatures away from the water for three or four days at a time. When, however, they can stand the pangs of thirst no longer, they rush for the precious fluid, preferring death to unbearable misery; and many sink, to rise no more, under the leaden hail of numerous rifles. Herd after herd is frequently slaughtered in this barbarous manner, until scarcely any remain in a large tract of country. The result is, that few, comparatively speaking, are now found there, though they could be counted by the thousands a few years ago.

I have had some exciting and pleasant runs after the buffalo on horseback, and I have stalked it on a few occasions; but the latter method seems to me to be little better than shooting cows, and not half so dangerous as an attack on wild cattle; hence it is scarcely worth mentioning; for all that is required to be successful is to seek shelter behind a knoll to the leeward of a herd and fire away to the heart's content, or until the animals get beyond range.

As nearly all buffalo hunts are alike, and differ only in minor details, such as a fall from a horse, or a charge from an angry or wounded bull, and perhaps a severe bruise, I shall tell how I secured my first two buffaloes, as my experience may prove of use to the novice in the chase. While halting for a few days at a little village in Nebraska, word was brought in that the buffaloes were moving toward the Platte River in immense herds, and that the country was black with them. This seemed to cause as much excitement among the men as if it were an announcement of an Indian raid; and all those who had horses and rifles or revolvers made preparations at once to have a dash at the strangers. In the hotel at which I was stopping was a celebrated hunter, Dr. Carver, and at his invitation I joined a party which he was to lead.

Not having a horse, I was advised to procure a buffalo-runner owned by the keeper of a livery-stable, and to him I accordingly applied, and made a bargain with him that I was to have his steed at the rate of four dollars per day, and be responsible for his value in case he was injured. At five o'clock in the evening he was brought to the hotel, and, when I gazed on him, I must say I was sorely disappointed; for he was small, ungainly in form, weedy, and boasted of very little flesh. He bore an old Mexican saddle on his back, and a rusty pair of reins and a curb-bit completed his trappings. After gazing at him for a few moments in silent disgust, I asked his owner if he could run a buffalo; and that individual told me, in the most emphatic terms possible, that he could, and was one of the best horses in the country for such a purpose.

Assured by his manner that the brute was really excellent, I mounted; and when the remainder of the party, ten in number, rode up, accompanied by a large covered wagon or prairie schooner, we moved off into the open country in the dim twilight. After marching until near midnight, we went into camp by simply halting, and after picketing our horses so that they could graze, we took our blankets out of the wagon, and, rolling ourselves up in them, we lay down to sleep under the shelter of the vehicle. Slumber was rendered impossible, however, by the sharp attacks of innumerable mosquitoes, whose "little bills" pierced through our heavy woollen blankets and clothes with apparently as much ease as if they did not exist. The first hour of retirement was devoted to tumbling about uneasily, in order not to have all the pricks on one side, and to blessing mosquitoes and all their race; but just as they were becoming unendurable, a fierce and sudden wind, to which the prairies are often subjected, came sweeping toward us with a howl of seeming rage, and in another moment our pests were swept away. The gale, though strong, was not very cold, and by cuddling close together we managed to keep warm enough to fall into a restless doze.

I had scarcely lost consciousness, however, before I was aroused by an alarmed shout of "Get up, boys; the Indians are coming!" The words were scarcely uttered before we were all thoroughly wide-awake and unrolled from our blankets. In searching for my boots, which were the only part of my vestments of which I had divested myself, I caught the man who was sleeping near my feet by the hair of the head, and gave it a strong pull in my haste to find what I wanted. This act must have thoroughly surprised him, and recalled visions of scalping to his mind; for he yelled out, "Holy Jerusalem! what is that?" This brought as a response a suppressed chorus of "Shut up, you d—n fool;" but the incident seemed so ludicrous to me that I chuckled heartily, notwithstanding the apparent danger. We were soon dressed, and, with rifles in hand, we ranged ourselves on one side of the wagon, prepared to sell our lives as dearly as possible. As the night was exceedingly dark, we were in hopes that our position might not be seen, and that the announced enemy might pass us by; but this hope was soon dispelled by hearing the clatter of many hoofs bearing directly down upon us. We cocked our rifles, and stood in breathless excitement awaiting the attack, yet hoping we should escape it, for we had the strongest objections to losing our scalps and having our bodies mutilated. The horsemen left the hard road when a few yards away from us, and galloped on to the grass. Supposing that our position was actually detected, we were thinking of opening fire, when they halted, and a strongly accentuated German voice called out, "Vell, poys, I dink ve'el gamp here; I see dere's oder poys here." The other boys were delighted at this unexpected turn of affairs; but, as soon as they were over their surprise, how they blessed that man's Dutch heart, and wished he and his party were transferred to a certain region where no winter climate is known! After a short but emphatic verbal battle, we learned that the strangers were a party of Germans from town who were out for a buffalo-hunt. After being taunted with not knowing a buffalo from a pig, and classifying any buffalo that would allow them to kill it as an idiot, a truce was declared, and we were once more rolled up in our blankets. The individual whose hair was pulled was then reviled for his scream of alarm, and he was told that he was anything but a wise man; and he, to retaliate, said that if he knew who made him scream he would put a bullet in him. "The d—n fool did it on purpose to skeer me," said he, "for he pulled out a whole handful of hair, and I thought my head would be histed off of my neck backward." As no person seemed inclined to acknowledge doing the deed, though nearly all except the right one were accused of it, we went to sleep once more, our lullaby being sung by the howling gale.

We were awake with the first streak of dawn; and after bolting a few mouthfuls of sandwiches and a cup of coffee, we saddled our steeds and rode away, the wagon bringing up the rear. We marched for three or four miles, but saw no signs of buffaloes where they were reported to be so numerous, and this caused some of the party to think the Indians had been pursuing them; and as the Sioux were then dangerous, and had been making raids on some of the settlements, it was deemed best that we should be cautious in our movements, and keep together as much as possible in a run, and, above all, to rally at once when the assembly call of "hoopee" was shouted. This matter being understood, we advanced slowly in search of the animals; but we could see nothing of them, though antelopes in large numbers were met, and the prairie seemed to be alive with birds. We also noted that the grass was not trampled; and deducing from this that the buffaloes had not come so far south, we put spurs to our horses and cantered on a few miles farther. On reaching a large meadow near the Platte River, we espied a cow and a calf grazing together. As they were the first seen, it was decided to capture them for luck, so two men were detailed to carry the resolution into effect. They galloped down through the long grass, which reached almost to the saddle-girths, and were soon beside the cow and running her hard. She coursed about in a lively manner, first in one direction, then in another, according as she was headed off, until she was finally brought to bay through sheer fatigue, and one of the men killed her with his revolver.

The calf had, in the mean while, broken away and headed straight for the low rolling bluffs or hillocks about two miles distant from the stream. This brought it across our path, so the leader and myself concluded to lasso it with some heavy ropes that we carried.

Starting in pursuit, we followed it down a trail, then up the bluffs; but I found that the famous buffalo-runner I bestrode was far behind in the chase, and that I could not even keep in sight of my companion. I therefore slowed down to a walk, and gave way to a vigorous rumination about the man who introduced me to his horse. While engaged in this unpleasant meditation I espied a calf a few yards away, and concluded to see if I could not have better luck with that than the previous one. Riding slowly toward it, and as much under shelter as the ground would permit, I approached it to within fifty yards before I was detected, then away we both went. After running about a mile, I drew close to it and made a throw; but the rope being heavy, and the wind blowing strongly against me, I missed, much to my chagrin. I lost nothing in speed, however, by the cast, and still keeping up the pursuit, and coursing the creature in every direction, I finally got a good throw, and caught it by the neck. Taking a few turns of the rude lariat around the horn of the saddle, I dismounted to secure my quarry, by tying its legs; but I had scarcely touched the ground before my steed, finding himself relieved of his load, broke away abruptly, dragging the calf after him for a few feet; but he soon released himself from that encumbrance and left the half-choked creature, the rope, and myself, on the open and, to me, unknown prairie, while he galloped away, swinging his tail, and turning round every now and then as if to see how I liked the predicament in which he had placed me. I did not like it by any means; and if he had been my property, and within close range, I fear he would not have lived for more than a second or two. I seized the rope before the calf could run away with it, and then commenced a tug of war between us; but, as I had the advantage, I was the victor in less than five minutes, for my antagonist was so choked that it had to cease its struggles. When I approached to upset it, by entangling its legs in the rope and then securing them, the vicious little creature charged me suddenly, and striking me full in the stomach with its head, it both doubled me up and tumbled me over, and, when I was down, attempted to gore me with its tiny horns. I was soon on my feet, however, and had my courageous little foe down by the rope trick, and, after tying its feet with a piece of string, I took off the lasso, intending to follow my horse and try its power on him. As he was some distance away, and the probability was that I would have to meet some of the party before I could catch him, I concluded to let the calf go free, for, if left tied, it would undoubtedly have fallen a prey to the wolves, as I could not, in all probability, have found it again if I went any distance away on a prairie where no mark existed by which I could identify the spot. I therefore released the creature, and was rewarded for my kindness by another charge; but I escaped that readily by volting to one side and allowing the assailant to rush past me and get away.

Starting out in pursuit of the runaway steed, a short tramp brought me to where he was grazing, but, on seeing me, he made a defiant attempt to kick up his heels a few times, and then started off; but, fortunately for me, he ran toward a farmer's wagon that was passing by a short distance off, and the driver captured him, and held him until I arrived. When I was on his back once more, I plied the spurs vigorously, and received in retaliation a series of buck jumps that threatened to break my spinal column. After a sharp contest of fifteen minutes, he acknowledged his defeat by moving onward at a smart gallop, and I was soon with my companians. I found that the leader had lassoed some calves, but that the others had not seen anything to shoot at except antelopes and prairie-dogs. Waiting until the wagon came up, in order to place the calves in it, we had a good opportunity of reconnoitring the surrounding country from a high bluff. We could see no buffaloes in our immediate vicinity; but far away, much farther than we cared to go, they dotted the landscape for miles in small herds. This induced us to change our route, and go direct for the highest bluffs, and, after the calves were stowed away in the wagon, we marched toward them. A walk of three or four miles led us into a splendid rolling prairie, over which the antelopes roamed in large numbers; and as we had few prospects of meeting what we sought, we concluded to test our rifles on them.

Taking a seat on the grass, we commenced popping away at all ranges, and, if we did not hurt them much we scared them a good deal, for they would stand and stare and wheel, then bound away with the fleetness of a greyhound. It was amusing to see the young approach us after being shot at, as if they could not understand that our firing meant danger, or else they were so blind that they could not see us while lying still, for motion seems to be one of the necessary conditions to their recognition of objects.

While amusing ourselves in this manner, one of our party noticed a number of trupials hastening past us, and he announced the event by jumping up suddenly and shouting, "I say, boys, there's buffaloes round yere somewhere, for there go the buffalo-birds; so we'd better be off." His suggestion was acted upon at once, and a few moments later we were following the route taken by the winged pilots. These, which are known in portions of the West as "buffalo-birds," are of a dark-brown color, and are really blackbirds. Flocks of them are nearly always found with the animals that have given them their name, and the two seem to get along well together, judging from the fact that the former may be seen perched on the backs of the latter and pecking away at the hide in the most familiar manner.

After riding about a mile, we saw a group of what we supposed to be our quarry a short distance away, and carefully approached it, but, on getting within range, found we had been stalking fleshless skulls that must have lain there two or three years at least. This proving a severe disappointment, we moved onward in silence. A short distance beyond this spot we saw two splendid herds coming from water, and, as they were advancing in our direction, we decided to await their approach. The usual impatience of delay was appeased, however, by watching the animals gambolling about in the most playful manner, and noting the mock contests of the unwieldy bulls. These would rush at each other as if about to engage in a deadly strife, but, after one or two pushes, they would break away and frisk about in the liveliest manner, as if they felt extremely happy. Others were rooting up the ground and scattering it about with their horns, and not a few were trying the quality of their voice in low, deep tones, which, if gruff, were not unmusical. The scene was full of life and interest, and we were enjoying it very much when the animals altered their antics by a sudden stampede, and went thundering to the windward. We were disappointed before; we were disgusted now, and our disgust was increased by seeing the "Teutonic Indians" of the previous evening rushing after them pell-mell, and, though far in the rear, keep firing at them with rifles aimed from the nose. The bullets could not reach half the intervening distance, yet they kept up the firing until they sunk from our sight behind a bluff. The imprecations hurled at such sportsmen by our party was a caution, and one went so far as to suggest that they should be pursued and shot at as nuisances run wild. The suggestion was not acted upon, however, and we wended our way in an opposite direction.

On reaching the top of a bluff, we espied a large herd grazing in a ravine; and to be sure this time that our labor was not in vain, we dashed across an intervening plain, crawled slowly up the declivity of the ravine, and when we reached the summit found that we were actually right on the herd. We dashed at it promptly as it tore away in a solid mass, and in a few moments our leader and the best mounted of the party were ranged along-side it and firing away for dear life. The experienced hunters cut off the rear-guard and turned it to the right; I followed the main column and tried to get a shot, but my famous runner would not take me close enough to enable me to shoot with any degree of accuracy. Seeing no other resource left, I threw the reins on his neck and commenced banging away at the herd in hopes that I might wound one, but, though watching closely, I could not even tell where the bullets went. My steed decidedly helped me in this ill-luck, for, as soon as he ceased to be directed by the reins, he swerved away at right angles, and in a few minutes carried me beyond rifle range. I was so furious that I felt like killing him; but I thought better of it, and turned back toward my party with feelings of shame and disgust. I had not proceeded more than a hundred yards before an old bull, with a splendid head, came rolling out of a ravine with a gait not unlike that of a sailor on shore, and attempted to cross my front. I fired at him, and planted a bullet in his shaggy forehead; but it had no effect upon him, apparently, for he kept up his swinging gallop at the same speed. I then started in pursuit, and commenced firing away, in hopes that I might give him a wound that would cause him to halt, as I had no confidence in the pace of my horse; but before I fired the third shot the bullet got jammed in the Winchester rifle which I carried, and no amount of pushing and "cussing" could extricate it, so I was compelled to halt to get it out. When I turned my attention from the gun to the bull, I saw him disappearing over a bluff, while my horse was going direct for home! Oh, how I blessed that buffalo-runner and the man who praised him! My misfortunes having reached a climax, I became stupidly calm in mind, and let the brute go his own course, without even attempting to punish him with the spurs. On my way back I saw the leader advancing, and driving a wounded cow before him, and by his side was a coal-black negro who rode a sorry excuse of a mustang. When he saw me he shouted to hurry up, and, on approaching him, he asked me if I had killed anything.

"Nothing," said I.

"Well," said he, "you mustn't go away from your first run with me without killing a buffalo; so you'd better tackle that cow, else you won't have any luck in your next hunt."

The thought was ignominious; but, being imbued with a small amount of the hunter's superstition, I concluded to become lucky in the chase, even at the expense of pride; so I opened fire on the poor creature, and in a short time caused her to halt, and a shot in the eye finished her, as it reached the brain. When brought to bay her eyes were a glowing emerald with rage, and she looked vicious enough to do anything, but, fortunately, she was unable to charge, else she might have gored me or the brute I rode, for he was too stupid or lazy to move off promptly even with a vigorous application of the spurs. I had killed my buffalo, to be sure; but, by Jove, in what a manner! I actually felt ashamed of myself; and this feeling was not allayed when I heard that she really belonged to the negro, he having wounded her first, but that she was taken away from him by my companion, on the ground that he did not belong to our party, and he wished to reserve her for me. "But how did you know that I would not be successful?" said I. "Because," said he, emphatically, "that wretched mustang you ride can't overtake a buffalo, and, if he did, he would run away from it. I know what he can do; but as there was no other horse left in town, I thought you could not do better than take him if you wished to join in the hunt; yet I had a hope he would prove better than he has. I know now what he can do, so you may have my spare runner for the next hunt." This assuaged my feelings of abashment somewhat, as it caused me to think that my ill-luck was not entirely my own fault; hence I took the brush at his suggestion, and left the remainder to the negro. When our party was assembled, I learned that they had killed only three cows for meat, but had captured four calves by lassoing them.

When the wagon drove up, we obtained some water from the barrel which it carried, and, after moistening our parched lips, we gave some to the horses. The best portions of the carcasses were then placed in the wagon, and on top of these the bucking, stubborn youngsters, which insisted on charging everybody that approached them.

While attending to this duty, which occupied some time, we descried a body of horsemen on a bluff two or three miles away; and as they appeared and disappeared a few times, it caused our party to think they were a marauding band of Sioux, and that we had better retreat at once if we would keep our scalps on our heads. The resolution was no sooner taken than it was carried into execution, and, after everything was ready, we hastened to the rear at a good canter. When we had placed a few miles between us and our supposed foes, we halted at the remains of a turf cabin, whose inmates had been killed and the hut burned down the year before by the treacherous red men.

After a rude though hearty meal, we resumed our homeward march, but we had not proceeded far before we saw another body of horsemen tearing down the plain in front of us. The men did not ride like Indians, and yet they were coming at a pace strongly indicative of a desire to head us off. We therefore halted, held a consultation, and decided to send two of the best mounted of the party in advance to reconnoitre, and to have them hasten back in case the strangers were foes, so that we might retreat to a good defensive position. They galloped away, and, after an absence of fifteen minutes, returned with a report that the supposed enemies were sheltered behind another dismantled cabin, whose inhabitants had met the fate of those of the previous one, but that they did not think they were Indians. Being assured of this, we galloped onward, but, on approaching the cabin, we left the road and moved on the grass-clad prairie, in order to deaden the footsteps of our horses. When we were within a hundred yards of it we gave a tremendous warwhoop, and rode on like the Six Hundred; and in a moment more we saw a party of white men, with well-bleached faces, peer from behind the cabin, and these we recognized at once as our Teutonic acquaintances of the previous night. When we rode up their features were still blanched, and they were in a violent state of agitation.

"Gott im himmel!" said one, "for vhat you scare us so? I nearly choked mineself mit a sandvich;" and, as he spoke, he was still slightly gagging with the remnants of a sandwich. His question was greeted with hearty laughter, for the fears displayed on the features of all looked ridiculous to us, who were not in their position. "Mebbe you call dot foon," said another, "but I call it tam fool foon mitout no joke." We were soon at peace, however, and, when the truce was declared, we learned from them that they had killed nothing, and that the cause of their hasty retreat was seeing a body of Indians. On comparing notes, we learned that both our parties had mistaken each other for the common foe; but we took excellent care not to tell them that we had run away for the same reason they had.

After a few pulls at their water-jugs, peace was ratified, and we jogged homeward together; but the way was made rather jolly by many lively sallies at their fears and sportsman-like qualities, all of which they took in the most simple earnestness, and answered in such a quaint manner that Hans Breitman, had he heard them, might have produced a capital work, did he take for a title their oft-repeated saying, "Mebbe you tink you make lots of foon of us; but I call dot tam fool foon!"

When I retired to bed that night I was so seriously lacerated, from hugging the saddle during the bucking and running, that I could hardly move, and, on awaking the next morning, I was so stiff and sore that I could not walk without presenting a ridiculous gait, so I stayed in bed. Notwithstanding the disagreeable condition of affairs, I laughed heartily at the scenes of the hunt, and treasure to this day my first buffalo-brush, as it recalls incidents I would not willingly forget. None that I have since won in a more glorious manner can approach it in value, in my estimation, and, whenever I see it, memory becomes active, and I am once more playing the part of a novice on the plains of the Far West.

My next brush was won in better style; yet I have reason to remember it. A large party of us started out for a hunt in the Republican Valley, and, as we intended to be absent some days, we took wagons and camping outfits with us, and a good store of food and ammunition, besides nearly every offensive weapon known on the continent. I was content to carry only a large, self-cocking revolver, and for a steed I secured a small, wiry, short-legged mustang, which was recommended to me as a capital buffalo-runner, he having been used specially for that purpose by a sub-chief of the Pawnees. As I was present when he was purchased, and heard the close-bargaining chief recommend him emphatically as *tickoree tuchnee*, or "very good," I felt satisfied that he was superior to my last mount; and he was accordingly bought for the sum of one hundred dollars after much haggling, and with the assumed regret of the high-minded vendor, who did not forget to tell us that he was a *layshawroo*, or chief, and had a straight tongue. I expected to accomplish wonders with him, and I did, but in a manner different to what I anticipated. I received with him as a present an old lasso (*ahshitscawree*) which looked as if it had seen many years of service; this I was, according to instructions, to tie around the horse's neck in the chase, and coil the remainder in my belt, so that if I got thrown I could catch my steed readily, and probably be dragged out of the way of danger, by clinging to it, as it would uncoil itself if I left the saddle unceremoniously.

When we reached our camping-ground we found that the buffaloes had moved to the southward of where they had been a few days previously, so we concluded to follow them. Our route led over an undulating prairie, which was richly carpeted with flowers and rich, succulent grasses, until the evening of the second day, when we reached the buffalo-grounds, and then our hearts bounded with joy on seeing the shaggy creatures, looking like so many black dots in the distance, scattered over a large area. We discerned, by their movements, that there was some commotion among those farther south; and after watching them attentively for an hour or more, we saw the dots unite in larger numbers and come toward us at a rapid pace. We inferred from this fact that they were fleeing before a large body of hunters, and that they would, in all probability, be so close to us the next day that we need not leave camp to enjoy all the hunting we wanted. In order to avoid their heedless, headlong rush, when stampeding, we concluded to pitch our tents in a grove of willows near the bank of the river, and not to picket our horses, but to tie them up to trees and cut grass for them, as we were afraid they might be injured by the advancing columns, should they approach our quarters.

After the camp was erected, we cleaned our arms, dined, and laid in a large store of wood with which to build fires at night to the leeward of the tents, in order to terrify the buffaloes should they attempt to enter the coppice in our vicinity. Everything being carried out according to the programme, we appointed sentinels, who were to remain on duty two hours each, and their business was to announce any danger to our position from the advance of the shaggy multitude, and to keep the fires burning. I was on duty about 2 A.M. when I heard the muffled roar produced by many hoofs galloping over grass; but as I could see nothing, although the moon was bright and the fires burned fiercely, I did not like to awaken my sleeping companions until I knew which way the columns were coming.

In about fifteen or twenty minutes I saw a black mass emerge from the horizon and come thundering toward our position with measured pace, and a few moments later I could detect the outlines of the buffaloes. Not knowing which way they were really heading, owing to the broad front of the column, and fearing they might be down upon us unless I was prompt in action, I fired my rifle, and in two minutes thereafter every member of the encampment was out, dressed and armed, yet not one of them had been aroused by the uproar created by the advancing hosts. Taking position to the leeward of the camp, we commenced firing at them as soon as they came within range, and banged away uninterruptedly for ten minutes, as we feared they might ride down our camp or stampede our horses, if they came too close. The firing soon produced its effect, for the herd divided, some going straight ahead, while others plunged into the river and crossed to the opposite side. They were so thick in some parts of the stream that the water looked fairly black with them; and through this they ploughed and rushed in the wildest confusion. This scene was as unusual to us as it was spirited, and we enjoyed it thoroughly. When they vanished from our sight all retired to bed again, except the sentinel on duty; but the novelty and animation of the scene prevented me from wooing gentle slumber for some time.

We were astir at daybreak the next morning, and, after

a hasty breakfast, vaulted into the saddles and started in search of the slain and wounded. We found them few enough, our fire having killed only six cows and seriously wounded another; but we discovered a solitary old bull roaming about half a mile away, and we soon had him among our trophies; not because he was deemed palatable, but that he had a magnificent head.

We next directed our course to the eastward of the camp, and after a ride of two miles came upon several small herds; but beyond these the prairie was almost covered with them. We halted and held a consultation, and it was then decided that our party should divide into three detachments, and that each should take one of the small herds and drive it, if possible, toward the main body, so that we might pick up the meat on the way to camp, and not waste any time in useless riding back and forth. That matter having been settled, the party to which I belonged approached to within a quarter of a mile of the column we had selected before being detected; but on seeing that we could get no nearer, we dashed after it. The race continued at a headlong pace for a mile or more before we were able to overtake the animals, and even then we could only range along-side the old bulls. As it was each man for himself, I chose a sturdy veteran that occupied the flank, and when I was within fifty paces of him I leaned forward and fired at his heart; but the ball must have struck his ribs, as he did not slacken his pace. I then brought the mustang closer to him and fired at the fore-shoulder, and, in doing so, I leaned to the right; but the explosion had scarcely taken place before my steed wheeled suddenly, and, it seemed to me, on his hind-legs alone; and as I had lost my balance by my attitude he went clean from under me, and I came on the ground with a thud that made me see as many stars as there are in the firmament in a few seconds, and caused me to feel as if my head were smashed. Instead of stopping to scratch it, however, and indulge in vehement language, which seems to be the usual and the proper thing to do under such circumstances, seeing that almost everybody does it, I had too lively a sense of danger to indulge in such delights; so I seized the lariat or trailing-rope, which was running out rapidly, and bolted after my steed in a half-dazed manner, for I felt as if I had half a dozen pieces of a head on me instead of a whole one. I did not go far, however, before I overtook him, and got into the saddle somehow.

It was a most fortunate thing for me that the bull did not charge, else I might have been gored to death. I learned from that accident to keep my balance, and not to touch the mustang with my feet—as his training had taught him to be guided by them, and to wheel to whichever side he felt their pressure.

I did not lose much time in getting under headway once more; and in five minutes I was beside the bull, which had fallen back to the extreme rear of the column. I tried to force my mustang close beside him, in order to get in a deadly shot; but that wary animal did not seem inclined to do so, but kept away at least thirty yards or more. I then tried running past the bull, and managed to accomplish that easily enough, and to deliver three shots in rapid succession at his shoulder. When I wheeled about I saw him stop, and noticed blood oozing from his nose, and when I got in front of him he charged me viciously with his head lowered; but the mustang was evidently prepared for this action, for he turned abruptly to the left, and by the time the enraged bull got to where he had been standing he was several yards away in another direction. I checked him in a few moments, however, and charged the veteran at full speed, and, rushing past him, gave him two shots in the head, and when I wheeled about again I saw him staggering; and in less than a minute he fell dead. I need not say I was glad of it, for my head seemed to be splitting, and I wished very much to see if it were whole or in parts. After a short examination I learned that there were no unusual indentations in it, and this put me in better humor than I had been.

Not seeing any wolves on the plain, I left my trophy

where it fell, and threw a handkerchief, containing my initials, over it, so that other hunters might know to whom it belonged; for I was most anxious to preserve the head on account of its size, the thickness of the matted hair, and the length and fulness of the horns. I next marked the position by taking bearings and noting the character of all surrounding objects — a precaution, I may add, which is rendered necessary if one would not lose the fruits of the chase; for in a region where one spot is almost exactly like another, one must closely scan every detail that would give it an individuality by which he could recognize it.

After marking the place carefully in my memory, I mounted and rode on, and, as I moved along, I noticed my companions running herds in every direction, and firing away for dear life; but as I wanted sport, not meat, I did not join them. When I reached the heavy columns, however, I concluded to have some runs alone, if the others did not come up within half an hour; and as they did not, I selected a herd which contained, I should imagine, about five thousand, and dashed at it from cover when within an eighth of a mile of it. The majority of this herd was evidently composed of adult bulls, which cannot at all compare in speed with the cows, calves, or the younger members of their own sex; hence I had little trouble in overtaking them. When I started in pursuit, the vast assemblage visible in every direction seemed to be in a state of commotion; and fearing I might get entangled in it, I ran to the front of the herd, intending to drive it away from the main body and push it toward the rolling ground to the right. When I reached that position, however, I found the work rather difficult, as the animals would not turn, but gave way laterally. I therefore concluded to kill one or two to see if that would have any effect, and, turning my mustang's head toward the herd, and not twenty paces away from it, I fired at the spinal column of the leading cow, and, fortunately, she fell dead at the first shot. Thus encouraged, I drew closer, probably to within ten paces, and brought another on her knees, and, plunging forward on her head, she was soon trampled to death; for the buffaloes crowd so closely together during a stampede that they have no room to swerve to one side; so on they must go, trampling everything before them.

The herd I was pursuing was so densely packed that it could be covered with a blanket, provided one could be found large enough; and, on looking toward the rear, all that could be seen through the heavy cloud of dust was a thicket of horns, for the bodies were almost concealed. Seeing that I could not turn it, I stopped the pursuit, not wishing to kill needlessly, as I had already secured some fine robes; yet I was anxious to get a few more of the best quality, and some burly heads for friends who were desirous to have them. As the column passed by me, I saw a splendid bull bringing up the rear, and ranging along-side him, I fired at his fore-shoulder at a distance of five paces, and brought him tumbling down. Riding close up to him, I placed my revolver against his back, fired, and breaking the spinal column, he fell dead in his tracks. This caused those behind to push away a little, and gave me an opportunity of firing at another fine animal; but as I hit him in the head, he went on with as much ease as if I had only struck him with a pebble. Not wishing to lose him, however, I followed, and in two shots brought him down, the last one having entered the heart.

I felt satisfied then, and rode out of the dust-cloud to let the remainder pass on in peace, and perhaps to relieve my mouth, nostrils, and eyes of their accumulation of dust. I soon learned that I had not done so too soon, for a few yards away another herd came thundering by; and had I remained in the cloud I would not, in all probability, have seen or heard it, and the consequence might have been disastrous to me. Even as it was, I had to fire at those on the flank toward me to make them give way to the left, as I was afraid they would crowd on me, and entangle me in their midst, and injure if not kill me. My efforts proved successful in a short time, and they left a large space of ground between us.

After I had marked the position of the slain animals, I rode back in search of my companions, and, on reaching a piece of rising ground, beheld one of the most spirited hunting scenes imaginable. The prairie as far as I could see was dotted with rushing herds, and running after them were several bodies of horsemen, while numerous puffs of blue smoke hung around them in clouds. I could see some fall occasionally, and knew that a havoc was being committed among them. It seemed a pity to destroy them so mercilessly; and on stating my opinion to a farmer at a later hour in the day, he responded to my sentiment by saying that he would be very glad to see the day that the buffaloes disappeared in the Republican Valley, as they ate up grass enough to support thousands and perhaps millions of domestic cattle, and they brought thieving Indians and unprincipled hide-hunters in their train; and between all three the farmers suffered more than their share of annoyance. He had no sentimental love for the shaggy quadruped, for, in his estimation, it "wasn't nothin' but a good-for-nothin' critter, that wasn't good for nothin' but to feed Injuns and eat up the food of the reg'lar cattle." Others in the same region held his opinion; so it is evident that the presence of the buffalo is not considered an unmixed blessing.

While walking back I noticed that wolves were making it rather lively for wounded animals, or those that strayed from the herds. I overtook one of the gray species, and as it did not attempt to escape, I dismounted and gave it a kick; but the poor brute was evidently sick, for it yelped with pain, but did not accelerate its pace. Knowing that it would soon be out of its misery, I did not molest it further, and passed on. In a short time afterward I noticed a pack of prairie-wolves chasing a calf that looked thoroughly pumped, and was bleeding from wounds in the nose, throat, and ears, while one eye was dangling down by a single muscle. On seeing me, they stopped short, and gazed at me with something akin to curiosity, and, before they were done scrutinizing, I dashed at them and emptied four chambers of the revolver in their midst. This caused them to scatter in a hurry; but I had the satisfaction of killing one and hitting another before they could get away. I slung the slain animal on my saddle, but allowed the wounded one to escape, as I did not wish to run my horse too much. Wolves of both species were quite common, and were feeding on dead buffaloes; but they did not dare go near the one on which my handkerchief was placed, their bump of cautiousness being too great to approach any strange object for fear it might mean danger to their physical welfare.

Soon after I had taken the brush of my first bull the wagons came up, and the drivers commenced loading them with heads and hides; but they only took the best portions of the meat. After pointing out to them the route the hunters had taken, I started off to rejoin the remainder of the party; but I had not proceeded far before I met a solitary old bull in a dry ravine, and, judging by his looks, he must have been a veteran indeed; for his head was covered with dense masses of hair, his horns were split and pointless, and the scars on his nose and hams showed that he had had many a contest with wolves. He did not see or wind me until I was fairly upon him, for the sight of the buffalo at the best is comparatively feeble; but when once he recognized my presence he bolted away at a good swinging gallop, which forced my horse to put on a good spurt to overtake him. When I ranged along-side him I fired at his spinal column; but the bullet striking him lower down, he no sooner felt its sting than he wheeled abruptly and charged me, and, before I could get safely away, he gave the mustang an upward raking blow in the flanks that scraped away some of the skin and brought the blood. This caused my steed to bound off at his best pace, and we were soon beyond his reach. Had his horn not been blunt, he would, no doubt, have seriously injured him, or perhaps killed us both. After running a short distance, I wheeled back, and set out after the assailant, which was making fast tracks over the prairie, and was soon at his flanks and firing away, raking him forward with every shot. He made two efforts to charge, but the mustang was too quick for him, and before he could wheel about we were out of his way. At the fourth shot he faltered for a few moments, swayed on his legs like a drunken man, then fell on his horns all in a lump. He was down only a short time, however, before he arose, and spreading his legs apart to steady himself, looked at me in the most frightfully ferocious manner that it is possible for an animal to assume. I saw that he was beyond all power for harm, however, for the blood was flowing from his nose and mouth, and his head was lowered; and, on noting this, I halted a few feet from him, and gazed at his ponderous proportions and impotent rage with a certain degree of fascination, for he was as perfect a picture of malignant ferocity as it is possible to conceive. His eyes were bloodshot, and of a glowing reddish-emerald hue; his mouth was open, and crimsoned with his life's fluid; and fury seemed to hiss out of his nostrils in streams of smoke and blood. His bearing was as defiant as his looks were revengeful, and he stood there an immovable living statue, for he was unable to advance or retreat. In a few minutes, however, his mien changed from that of a desire to annihilate a person to one of pain and weakness; and, after swaying and staggering for five or six seconds, he fell over dead. After marking his position, I rode on, mentally resolving to use a rifle of large calibre the next time I went after buffaloes; for I had come to the conclusion that a person could do better shooting with it, or at least more destructive work, than with a revolver, while it would also enable one to keep beyond charging distance.

After travelling a couple of miles I met a number of our party, who were wandering about, like myself, in search of experience and sport rather than hides and meat. Joining company, we moved toward the south, and in the course of twenty minutes reached a knoll that gave us a commanding view of a large portion of the surrounding country. We had been there only a short time before we noticed an im-

BUFFALO RUNNING.

mense column of buffaloes rising out of the horizon and come galloping toward us, and, a little later, we saw that it was pursued by a large band of Indians, who were plying their arrows as they only can. They carried the quiver slung over the shoulder; and so quickly did they draw the bolts from this, that one arrow was scarcely on its way before another was following it.

Knowing that they were friendly Pawnees, we decided to have a run with them; so, when the buffaloes drew near us, we dashed for the head of the column, and as it passed us emptied our weapons into it whenever we saw a stately bull that suited our fancy; and, when all had gone by, we wheeled about and followed them. I was more interested in the picture presented by the chase than in getting trophies, however, as it was full of life and animation. The maddened herd, the clouds of dust, the thundering of hoofs, the falling of the killed and wounded, the charging and wheeling of ponies, the showers of arrows, and the wild excitement of the nude Centaurs made as stirring a hunting scene as it is possible to conceive; and so interested in it was I that I permitted the animals to pass on, and remained behind to enjoy the grand spectacle they presented. After gazing at it for a sufficient time to enable me to appreciate its spirited character, I dashed after the fugitives, and was beside them in less than twenty minutes, and picking out the best heads.

While going at full speed, my horse put his leg into a prairie-dog hole, and, falling forward, pitched me headlong to the ground; and I had no sooner touched it than the revolver went off so close to my nose that some of the dirt ploughed up by the bullet went into my eyes and mouth. I was upon my feet in a moment, however, and, on looking for my horse, found him standing still, trembling with excitement and the violence of the fall; but as he had suffered no serious injury, I inferred that he had merely stumbled against the mound near the mouth of the hole.

My own bruises were confined to skinned knuckles and arms, and a few scratches on the forehead; and, after I had ascertained their extent, I vaulted into the saddle and started for camp, as I was a little bit shaken, and my horse seemed to be unsteady and nervous. After a refresh-

BUFFALO-HUNTING.

ing drink of water, which I procured in a thread-like brook, I moved south once more, and, on reaching the hillock from which I had started on the last run, saw herd after herd of buffaloes come thundering toward me. The many puffs of whitish smoke which hung over them proved that they were being pursued by white men, and the black dots on the prairie proved how destructive the shooting was. The picture presented by the advancing hosts might have been appreciated at any other time; but just then it was anything but agreeable, as I feared I would be entangled in their midst; for my horse was too tired to flee before them, and the columns were too wide to cross their front before they could reach me; so there was nothing left but to try and pass between two herds, or open a gap by scaring the animals with voice and weapon. When the multitudes came near my position some of the leaders winded me; and the moment they did so they gave way to the left, and they were followed by those directly behind, while others swerved to the right and divided up into groups. I darted into one of the lanes, and, by using voice and revolver, produced such an effect that the herds forced themselves farther apart, and left a space through which I rapidly retreated. On emerging at the rear, I found a party of hunters there at a full stop, evidently awaiting some exciting or important event; and when they saw me they asked if I knew of any man being killed in front. I guessed at the cause of their alarm at once, and told them I had not. "Well," said one, "there's some idiot there among the buffaloes, and he's been either shot or caught in the herds, and he's yelling like a pig under a gate. He seems to be a regular greenhorn, for if he doesn't want to be shot he ought to keep on the outside of a herd." "Never mind, Bill," said another, "if he's dead we can't help it, and if he ain't we'll find him. Let's be off; we can't afford to lose our buffaloes;" and, without another word, they started off in pursuit of the runaways. I did not care to explain matters to them, so I jogged toward camp, and reached it by six o'clock.

I found the greater number of our party there; and though several of them had been thrown, yet only one was severely injured, and he had his collar-bone injured by a fall. By seven o'clock all were assembled, and we sat down to a savory dinner, the chief part of which was buffalo humps and tongues; and most palatable they seemed to hungry men. After picketing our weary horses so that they could graze, all retired to bed except the solitary sentinel; but we could get little sleep, owing to the wild, melancholy howling of the wolves, and the deep bellowing of the buffaloes, which frequently approached close to our fires. We were up early the next morning, as we intended to bring in the animals we had killed; for to hunt on that day with our wearied steeds was out of the question.

After breakfast we sallied forth; but we had not proceeded more than two miles before we met a courier, who informed us that he had ridden from Kearney Junction, some sixty or seventy miles distant, to inform the settlers that the Indians were expected to make a raid on the valley, under pretence of coming there to hunt. He reported that a telegram had been received at Kearney the previous evening that a large body of Sioux were encamped south of Sydney, and that their destination was evidently the Republican Valley. This news caused us to feel somewhat alarmed; so we concluded to take what meat we could obtain in a couple of hours, and retreat into Kansas if the road to the north was closed against us. We therefore hastened our work, and in about three hours had four wagon-loads of meat and hides. Returning to camp, we struck tents at once, and set out on the march to Kearney Junction, and arrived there the next day just as a large party of panic-stricken Pawnees entered it; for they, like ourselves, had the utmost fear of encountering their worst foes: the most deadly hatred exists between both tribes, and they show no mercy to each other whenever they meet. On making inquiries at the telegraph-office, I learned that the marauders were stopped by some companies of cavalry, and were sent back to their reservation; but as I had had enough of hunting for the time, I did not return to the valley.

I heard it estimated in this town that there were over a thousand hunters, including the Indians, in the Republican Valley when we were there, and that every herd in the region was in motion at one time. This was evidently the scene I had witnessed, and grand indeed it seemed; it was one I certainly would not have missed for a good deal.

I passed through the same valley in 1874, when the crops were eaten up by grasshoppers, and persons had scarcely anything to live on but meat, and I then learned that buffaloes were not considered such nuisances as they had been; for, were it not for them, many of the inhabitants would have suffered from hunger.

I have followed the shaggy bison frequently since then, but no runs are so distinctly impressed on my memory as those of the first two expeditions, as they were my novitiate in buffalo-hunting, and gave me more experience than would a dozen ordinary runs in which there were neither mishaps nor disappointments.

A person does not always escape from a buffalo-hunt without any more serious injury than a fall or a few bruises, however, for it is no uncommon incident to have a man's horse ripped open by an angry bull, or himself trampled or gored to death. I saw an Indian on one occasion wounded so seriously by a bull that he died in twenty-four hours after; and I heard of an experienced hunter in Montana who got entangled in a large herd, and was carried along by it for some distance, only to meet his death by being pushed into a chasm by the wild crowd of animals behind him, and which followed him to the great spirit-land.

Buffalo-hunting has its comic side sometimes; but those who are participators in the comedy do not, as a rule, see the fun of the matter. To watch a man on foot legging it lively before a pursuing bull is certainly ludicrous to a spectator, for his face and eyes seem to fairly bulge out with fear, and he makes the most unnecessary leaps, and glances about him in the wildest manner to see how affairs stand. To watch a man holding on to a horse's tail while the animal bucked and circled and galloped to avoid the furious charges of an angry Taurus is mirth-provoking; and to see a novice, who is well mounted, riding like John Gilpin before a rheumatic veteran that can scarcely toddle along, is certainly sufficient to cause a smile; and that such scenes are not rare is evident from the number of stories floating about in the West. By using ordinary precaution, one can generally escape any disagreeable predicaments, however, if he is at all well horsed; for much depends on the intelligence, speed, and training of the steed. Dr. Carver, who killed five thousand buffaloes in one season, nearly all of which were shot from horseback, did not have a fall during that time; and as his horses were too well trained to withstand the charges of the bulls, he escaped without any serious accident. The pleasure of pursuing the buffalo will soon be unknown, however, as it is fast disappearing before the advance of the pale-faces; for where thousands upon thousands were found a few years ago, only a few small groups can now be seen; and they must soon join their predecessors, unless a law is passed to protect them.

CHAPTER VIII.

THE MOOSE.

The Moose.—Its Range in the West.—Its Form, Haunts, and Habits.—The Rutting Season.—Cries of the Animal.—How Males are lured within Rifle Range.—Calling as an Art.—How to make a Call.—The best Callers.—Young Bulls easily inveigled.—The Best Time for Calling.—The Moose as a Browser.—Difficulties in stalking it.—Acuteness of its Nose and Ears.—How Experienced Hunters quarter the Ground.—Its Haunts in Summer.—Hunting it in Winter.—Dogs and Snowshoes.—The European and American species.—How the Latter can be Domesticated.—Hide-hunters.—A Moose-hunt, and its Result.—A Charge.—Lost in the Forest.—Trying to find Camp.—A Welcome Moose-call.—Rescued.—A Hunt on Snow-shoes.—Episodes.—Number of Moose killed.—Difference in Size and Habits between the Eastern and Western Species.—Large Antlers.—Moose-hunting as an Art.

THE moose (*Alce americanus*), which is fast disappearing from its haunts in the Atlantic States and Canada, is still common beyond the Rocky Mountains, being found from British America to the mountains of Central Idaho, while it is very abundant in Alaska. It does not, in all probability, move farther south than the forty-eighth parallel of latitude, as I never heard of it in Oregon, and but very little in Washington Territory. The Lumni Indians, in the north-western portion of this Territory, say that it was formerly quite common in their section of country, but that it has moved farther into the recesses of the forests and higher up on the mountains since the advent of the white man. That they do not confound it with the wapiti, or elk, is evident from the fact that they have a different name for it, and readily recognize its horns as portrayed in works of natural history. I have heard that it is found extensively in the Cœur d'Alene and Kootenay Mountains, in Idaho, and is largely hunted by the Kootenay or Long-knife Indians—a wild tribe who inhabit these mountains, and make, or at least did make, it dangerous for a stray naturalist or Nimrod to seek knowledge or pleasure in their country. The red men capture it by means of pitfalls and traps made of fallen trees; but their most successful mode is to lie in wait near its watering-places and shoot it from under cover when it comes to drink. They never follow it for hours and days as their brethren in Canada do—for the simple reason that they can obtain

THE MOOSE.

food as good with much less trouble, and that they are thoroughly indifferent to such feelings as the enthusiasm of the chase. One thing may be said in favor of the Indian, and that is, that he seldom destroys the life of a valuable animal needlessly; hence, probably, the reason why he and all wild animals dwell in close proximity; whereas the presence of a white man will send them scampering off in a very short time, and the chances are that they do not return. To this fact might be attributed the expulsion of the moose from the vicinity of many places settled by whites on the Pacific Coast, whereas it is common near the encampments of some of the Northern red men. Its true range lies between the forty-eighth and sixty-fifth parallels; but I should say that, with the exception of those that roam as far as the Grand Coulee of the Columbia, few are to be found lower than the forty-ninth parallel. Its worst foes on the Pacific are the Blackfeet of Montana, who organize regular expeditions for its pursuit late in the autumn, and, it is said, capture or slay large numbers, they preferring its flesh to that of the buffalo.

This splendid animal differs from all its congeners in many features characteristic of the deer family, and this has caused naturalists to class it in a genus by itself. Its nose is, in the first place, covered with hair, instead of being naked as in other members of the *Cervidæ;* the nostrils are larger, being huge cavities; the upper lip is long, and prehensile; the ears are very large; the horns are palmated; the neck is short; the limbs are unusually long; the body is rather short; the tail is only rudimentary, and both sexes have a thick, shaggy mane. It is the largest member of its family on the continent, a full-grown stag or bull being from four to four and a half feet in height at the shoulder, and weighing from eight to eleven or twelve hundred pounds, although its body seldom exceeds seven feet in length. Its antlers, which distinguish it so much from its kindred, attain a weight of from forty to sixty pounds, measuring from root to tip, along the curve, from four to five and a half feet, and they are about the same distance apart at the points. They do not arrive at perfection of proportions until after the fifth year, when the palm is frequently twelve inches in width. A male calf produces only two small knobs the first season; but in the second these attain a length of seven or eight inches, and in the fourth they are sufficiently developed to become palmated. The antlers are cast in December or January, and appear above the skin in March or April; and so rapidly do they grow that, though they are in the "velvet" in July, and so soft as to bleed very easily, yet by the latter end of August they are hard and full-grown, and their adult owner is then ready to test their eighteen points against all rivals in love. It is only the male, as a rule, that is furnished with these powerful weapons, yet cases have been known in which they also adorned the female.

The latter, which is much smaller than the male, brings forth her young in May, the number being confined to one at a birth for the first two years, but after that she has two at a time. The calves remain with their mother long after she has ceased nursing them, and, if a herd is together, form a permanent portion of it. Gravid females always secrete themselves in the densest portion of the forest early in the season while carrying their young, and remain there until September, when they course over it in search of mates, and cause it to resound with their wild, erotic cries. The period of gestation is about eight months, and the calves are so strong at their birth that they are able to run about in a lively manner in the course of a few days. The mother is much attached to them; but the same cannot be said of the sire, for he is sometimes their worst foe until they are able to take care of themselves.

The rutting season commences in September, and lasts six or seven weeks, and during that time, whenever the males meet they engage in desperate and often deadly encounters. They are so busily engaged in fighting, roaring, and wooing during this period that they fade to skeletons, for they eat very little; and the haughty monarchs that stalked through the forest in September so conscious of strength and proud of mien, skulk through it in November, ragged, dingy, listless, and starved-looking wretches. They that would boldly face man, if necessary, a few weeks before, would not now fight a cur; and their only desire seems to be to mope and hide themselves in the thickets.

During the running season the woods resound with the cries of the animals that are in search of mates, and persons who can imitate the call of the female can then lead many a bull to destruction through it. This siren-like cry consists of a series of low, deep grunts that end in a wild, loud, prolonged, and hideous roar, which may be heard a distance of two or three miles on a fine night. The males, on hearing this, rush toward it from all parts of the forest; and should they meet, dire is the result to some of them. The female looks on during these contests in the most disinterested manner, then quietly strolls away with the victor, as if to prove the correctness of the adage that "the brave deserve the fair." Some old Indian hunters are excellent callers; but it requires natural aptitude for imitating sounds, and a long experience to become proficient in the art. The best apparatus for "calling" is a tube or trumpet made of the flexible bark of the birch. This is generally about an inch in diameter at one end, and four or five inches at the other, and is eighteen or twenty inches in length. One who can use this properly may deceive any erotic male that runs in the forest; but let the least false intonation be uttered, and even the most unsophisticated youngster would detect the imposition, and keep far away from it. One of the great secrets in "calling" is to know how to modulate the sounds so that the cautious lover may be lured to within close range; for a person cannot afford to waste any lead on him, or he might never see him again.

The "calling" commences in September, and is practised only on moonlight nights during the running season; for the animals will not respond to it in the daytime, and it would be useless to try it on dark nights, as they could not be seen in the gloomy forest at any distance, large as they are. The weather ought also to be favorable, as the "call" is then heard more readily, and the chances of getting a good shot are greater. The males respond to it more promptly in the earlier than in the later portion of the season, and the young are more easily inveigled than the adults, whose experience has taught them that "all that glitters is not gold." The unsophisticated youngsters are sometimes lured within range by merely striking a tree with an axe or a rifle; but no old one can be deceived by such a simple device.

The short neck, long forelegs, and elongated prehensile lip prove that the moose is a browser, and not a grazer; hence we find it only in extensive forests, where it can obtain shelter and a variety of choice food. It is very fond of dainty shrubs and the tender shoots of young trees; but its favorite pabulum is the maple, which is, on this account, known as moose-wood in portions of Canada and the United States. Being naturally timid and wary, the moose frequents the deepest recesses of the forest, where even the most light-footed hunter can hardly approach it undetected, for its huge ears and nostrils warn it instantly of danger. One would scarcely credit, without proof, the distance to which it can wind or hear a person in the woods; and this makes stalking it a laborious, and, too often, an unsuccessful enterprise. The most experienced hunter cannot circumvent it under ordinary circumstances; for should he crush a dead stick under foot, brush against decayed leaves or branches so as to rustle them, or be to the windward, he could not hope to capture it unless he ran it down in the snow. Its sight is by no means acute, and it cannot compete with any of its congeners in this characteristic. This is evidently due to the dense and gloomy haunts which it generally frequents, and where intensity of vision would be useless; but this defect is atoned for by such keenness of nose and ear that its loss must be little felt.

When browsing, the animal makes a very devious path that winds in every direction; and, when it is done feeding, it lies down to the leeward of its trails, with its head to the windward.

A hunter acquainted with its habits would not, therefore, follow its tracks, but would carefully quarter the ground against the wind, keep a sharp lookout, and move almost as noiselessly as a cat. If persons are hunting together, they are liable to bag one by these means, especially if there is a stream or a lake in the vicinity.

Moose may be sought for around woodland tarns in summer, as they frequent them to avoid the attacks of flies, which are their greatest pests, and to feed on the yellow lily. In searching for them, the water ought to be carefully scanned, as they are often almost wholly immersed in it, the only part appearing above the surface being the nose, eyes, ears, and the antlers, the latter looking like snags at a distance. In the winter, when the ground is covered with snow, herds of females, calves, and young bulls are found together in "yards;" but the old males like to wander about by themselves, or to form small bachelor parties.

A moose-yard is simply a feeding-ground, the paths through the snow being formed unconsciously by the animals while browsing. It is generally found where deciduous trees are numerous, as the animals like to nibble at these in the daintiest manner. After the first heavy fall of snow they seldom change their ground; but if the fall is light they frequently do so, and three yards may sometimes be found within five miles of each other, especially if young trees are numerous, and the herds are large. When the young trees have been plucked of their shoots as high as the moose can reach, they ride them down with their long forelegs, and straddle them until all the tender portions have been eaten off.

When startled by hounds or hunters, the bulls throw the antlers as far back as their straight, short necks will permit them, and, with noses in air, dash through dense forests and matted thickets with great ease, while their limbs are so long that they can step over fallen trees without breaking their gait. They are by no means so handsome in looks or graceful in motion as their kindred, the wapiti; and their fore-shoulders, which are higher than the haunches, and their ridge-like withers give them a most ungainly aspect. When running, they make a clattering sound with the horny points or spurs of the hoofs, and so distinct a slot or track that it may be readily noticed even on dry grass, as the hoofs are long and sharp-pointed, and the fore are shorter and less tapering than the hinder ones. This form of hoof prevents them from running well through deep, crusted snow, and the result is that they are readily captured, for they break through it easily; whereas their cousin, the caribou, with its expansive, broad-pointed, and rounded hoof, can travel over it with facility. This fault or defect in the moose is probably one reason why it has not been domesticated in Northern countries, as the reindeer has, although it has many advantages over the latter in size, strength, and speed.

Its congener in Sweden, the European elk, was formerly employed as a beast of burden, but the State authorities forbade its use after a time, owing to the fact that its superior speed frequently enabled criminals to escape. As a forest traveller the moose has no superior and few equals, and its endurance is something extraordinary. Were it domesticated, it would be found an invaluable aid to the farmer, as its support would cost very little, its flesh and hide can be used, and it has apparently the strength of any ordinary horse. It is easily tamed if captured young, and is inclined to be confident and affectionate if kindly treated; but during the rutting period the males are liable to be headstrong and pugnacious, if not dangerous. One generation of domestication might, however, eradicate these qualities, and render it as docile as a cow. It would make a capital steed for mounted scouts or couriers in a rough or wooded country; but I would rather be off its back if any manœuvres were to be executed, or any firing took place.

The usual methods of hunting this monarch of the *Cervidæ* is to stalk it, "call" it within range during the rutting season, run it down on snow-shoes during a heavy fall of snow, or drive it with dogs until it is brought to bay in a snow-bank, or is exhausted. The first two methods are legitimate sport, as they bring out the qualities of the hunter; but the last two are merely taking advantage of the animal's inability to travel in deep snow, then assassinating it.

The Indians of the Far West capture it by means of pitfalls, lying in wait near its haunts and shooting it as it passes them, and by grand drives, in which probably two or three hundred warriors are sometimes engaged. Some of the Indians of the Territories and portions of British America have an annual drive, in which they slaughter the poor creatures in large numbers; but they, unlike the wretched white "skin-hunters," utilize the meat for making pemmican, and the hides for making clothing, snowshoes, and moccasins; whereas the latter leave the carcass to rot on the ground, taking only the hide. They also destroy without regard to sex, and gravid females and calves are slaughtered as readily as old bulls. These hides bring, in winter, when the coat is inclined to be dark and the inner hair close and woolly, from four to five dollars; and for this sum men travel weary miles and destroy some of the finest animals on the continent with a recklessness of consequences worse than barbarous. If the destruction continues as it has been carried on heretofore, the animal will soon be a memory of the past, and will be known only through works on natural history.

I have not had as much experience in hunting it as other large game; for in the Far West, where it is common, it was dangerous to frequent its haunts a few years ago, owing to the enmity of the Indians against all intruders on their preserves, and the fact that white men could only follow it with safety in large parties, as it was a stranger in places settled by them.

I have followed it in several portions of the continent, however, from Maine to Western British America; but I must say that the hunters I accompanied were more frequently unsuccessful than otherwise, owing to its extreme caution and speed, and the wooded and often mountainous character of its home. All my expeditions were not failures, however, and I have enjoyed some delightful sport with it that atoned for laborious days and nights spent in its vain pursuit. In Idaho and Montana, where it is still quite numerous, sportsmen who are strangers in these countries must take guides and camping outfits with them; and if they do not slay dozens of moose, they will at least have the pleasure of beholding some of the wildest and grandest scenery on the continent.

On one of my moose-hunting excursions I accompanied a rancher, who seemed to devote as much attention to the chase as to farming, and an Indian who did odd jobs about his place. This trusty retainer had the usual antipathy of his race to continuous labor; so I have a suspicion that he was kept more for his fondness of the chase than for any other reason. He was also an excellent shot, a close observer of the haunts and habits of animals, and could skin them as rapidly and cleanly as the most expert butcher, while he was deemed unrivalled as a curer of their hides and as a maker of beaded moccasins.

Reaching a position in the dense forest where "signs" were numerous, we selected the shade of a large fir-tree as a site for a primitive camp, built a fire there, and, after supper, devoted ourselves to puffing tobacco-smoke until the moon began to creep from under a mass of clouds. This was the signal for us to commence operations, so we loaded our rifles, and, the Indian taking a light axe and a hunting-knife with him, we marched about a mile from camp. We could hear at intervals, as we advanced, the short, guttural sounds of the bulls, and the wild, prolonged roar or call of the cows. When we reached a good position, where the undergrowth was heavy and the space in front open, the hunter and myself sought shelter in the shrubbery close together, while the Indian climbed a tree; and, as soon as he was comfortably seated on a branch, he commenced calling with such exactitude that I could only tell his cry from that of a cow by its proximity. After waiting patiently for half an hour, we heard his summons answered by deep grumblings from two directions close by; and, on hearing these, he lowered his call, making it deep and subdued, as if the female were in a most loving frame of mind; and this was repeated three or four times in different keys, being now loud, fierce, and emphatic, anon sinking into a low, long-drawn grunt. A few minutes later, and two splendid bulls came crashing through the forest from opposite directions, about two hundred yards away. Both reached the open space at nearly the same time, and just as the deceptive red man was giving vent to a low and most loving grunt. On seeing each other, they forgot the call of love, however; and after gazing sternly at one another for a few moments, and uttering cries of defiance, they charged at full speed, and, meeting with a clanging thud, were soon engaged in a desperate fight. They struggled and pushed, and tried to get every advantage of each other, but they were too evenly matched for either to win an immediate victory. Their horns clashed and gave forth a dull sound not unlike that produced by men fencing rapidly with foils; but this was frequently drowned by the tearing up of the ground, the scattering of the leaves, the crashing of bushes, and the deep grunts of the combatants.

The contest was waging about five minutes, perhaps, when the Indian ran up to us and said that we might be able to kill both if we could steal upon them unawares. We accordingly crept out of the thicket, and, advancing as noiselessly and as rapidly as possible up wind, got within thirty yards of them undetected, for they were oblivious of everything but the struggle, and, securing a shelter behind a tree, and in a position where the moonbeams streamed in clearly, we took aim at them while their antlers were locked, fired, and when the smoke cleared away we saw one on his knees, and the other trying to unlock the entangled horns. I fired at the latter twice in rapid succession, and had the satisfaction of seeing him stagger, then fall over on his side. On approaching them, we found the shoulder of the first one to be broken; but, as he was not dead, the Indian finished him in a few moments by giving him three or four blows on the head with the axe.

Both animals proved to be in excellent condition, and were evidently full grown, as one boasted eighteen points on his antlers, and the other sixteen. Having "drawn" them, we covered them with boughs and leaves, marked their position, then sallied out for new trophies.

Moving onward cautiously, a walk of two miles or more brought us into a charming coppice of foliaceous trees of several varieties; and as it had the appearance of being a favorite feeding resort of the moose, we decided to halt there and test our luck. It was also recommended to us by the density of the coniferous forest in front, from which issued at intervals the hideous roars and nightmarish grunts of the animals. Having satisfied ourselves about the advantage of the copse as a cover, I went to one end, and my companion to another, while the Indian took up his quarters in a tree-top about three hundred yards behind and nearly equidistant from us.

When he had established himself comfortably he commenced his deer lay of love, and grunted and roared out his erotic strains for two hours with a perseverance and artistic finish most highly commendable; but neither cautious veteran nor impulsive young bull came within rifle range, although they answered him vigorously several times from various directions. Thinking that the animals might have winded me, and therefore kept away, I threw up a leaf, and saw from its course that I was to the leeward of the majority of the vocalists who had answered the call; so I decided that being winded was not the cause of their non-appearance. As the vigil was becoming wearisome, and I was getting sleepy, it being past midnight, and the moose seemed indifferent to the red man's persistent appeals, I concluded to start for camp; but before I had made up my mind to move, a sturdy young bull came dashing through the forest, and, on coming into an open spot, stopped suddenly, bent his long head forward to catch the exact direction of the sweet strains, and commenced sniffing the air, as if trying to detect the presence of a foe.

He was scarcely forty yards from me, and, feeling rather nervous about him, I fired just as he attempted to advance, but I only succeeded in breaking one of his forelegs. When he recovered from the shock and surprise he bolted at once for the heavy forest, and, as I did not want to lose him, I followed in hot pursuit. I found this hard work, however, as I could only catch a glimpse of him occasionally; and the only real guide I had to follow his course was the crashing of the boughs and bushes. Realizing the truth of the old adage that a stern chase is a long one, even after a wounded moose, I concluded to cut to the right in a straight line, as he seemed inclined to keep more in that direction than in any other, and to head him off, or at least to induce him to halt by stopping the noise behind him; and acting on this idea, I tore through the woods as rapidly as possible, and after running about what I should judge to be a mile, I emerged on a glade, but, on scanning it, I could see nothing animate there. I walked over a portion of it, and scrutinized the ground for "signs" as carefully as the pale moon would permit me, but I could find no indications of the presence of a moose. Feeling sorely disappointed at my want of good-luck, I concluded to go back to camp; but, on re-entering the forest, I could not tell in which direction it lay. I started, however, toward where I supposed it was, and wandered about for two hours, yet I seemed as far away from it as ever. Realizing the fact that I was actually getting lost in an unknown forest, my feelings were anything but cheerful, and I began to upbraid my own thoughtlessness for daring to follow an animal in a region of which I knew nothing, and did not even take the precaution to note. I did not know what to do. To rest, I could not; and to keep wandering aimlessly about I felt to be worse than useless, as every step might take me farther away from succor. After thinking the matter carefully over, I concluded to stop where I was until morning, if I could not get a response to some shouts, and try to retrace my footsteps by the tracks they had made. I commenced hallooing accordingly, but after keeping it up at intervals for half an hour, I stopped it, and resigned myself to fate.

Feeling fatigued, I sat down beneath a huge fir, placed my head against the trunk, and was soon fast asleep; and when I awoke the next morning the bright rays of the sun were streaming through my leafy chamber. On arising, I felt quite stiff, the night dew having chilled, and my unusual position cramped me. Giving myself half a dozen good shakes to arouse the blood to more vigorous action, and rubbing my eyes to dissipate the effect of lingering sleep, I commenced a search for camp once more. My first movement was to note where my footsteps had led me, and, after following them for an hour or more, found I had been wandering about in circles, which sometimes crossed each other, and had a general trend to the right.

I knew then that I was really lost, and had acted as nearly all persons do under the same circumstances; but as I had daylight to aid me I did not feel any great sense of alarm, and went about retracing my footsteps in the calmest manner. I first commenced to beat about in order to discover tracks that did not trend to the right, and, after a long search, I saw some that evidently led to the glade in which I first missed my bearings. This was a most welcome discovery, as I felt that I could not be far away from camp; so I commenced retracing them at a rapid rate. This was not a very difficult matter; for, by scanning the ground a little in advance with a quick glance, I could see, by the trampled grass and bushes, the lightness of the dew in some places, and an occasional distinctly marked footprint, the route I had taken.

While deeply engaged in this pleasant duty, I was startled by hearing a thundering crashing a short distance to my left, and, on looking in that direction, I saw the cause of my woe, the wounded bull, hopping away on three legs through the undergrowth. Forgetting everything but his presence in a moment, I started after him, and in less than twenty minutes headed him off by taking short cuts, and, as he passed by me within a distance of seventy yards, I fired at his head, and he fell on his antlers. When I approached him he was shaking his head violently, and roaring and grunting as if he were in the greatest agony. Supposing that I had hit him in some vital part, and not caring to fire another shot unless it was actually necessary, I advanced toward him heedlessly; but on reaching within a few yards of him I halted, as his tongue was out, and his eyes fairly blazed with rage and hate. While looking at him, he bounded suddenly on his legs, and charged me with the greatest impetuosity; but, though surprised, I did not wait the onslaught, but dodged behind a large tree, and, ere he could bear down on me, I had reloaded my rifle and given him its contents directly through one of his huge ears with a result most fatal to him, for he fell dead in his tracks. After enjoying my victory, and meditating for a short time on the law of compensation and the result of accidental circumstances, I started in search of camp once more.

Hoping that my companions were out looking for me, I commenced shouting as loudly as I could, but no responsive voice came back except the echoes of the forest. Seeing I could do nothing in that way, I tried firing the rifle; and though every tree and shrub seemed to carry its detonations afar, I listened in vain for the welcome answer. After travelling, shouting, and firing for three hours, and trying to retrace my footsteps—a feat which was beyond my power, owing to the various directions in which they led—I sat down near a small lake, as I was somewhat faint from hunger, and I wanted to think out, if possible, how I could extricate myself from the perilous situation in which I was placed. After a short rest, and a delightful drink of water, which revived me very much, I commenced exploring the lake to see if I could find a canoe upon it, or any indications that it was visited by man, even at a remote period. My explorations were futile, however, for I did not find a vestige of a human being in any direction. Thoroughly disheartened, I sat down once more to indulge in another painful meditation, and, while musing on my disagreeable situation, my heart gave a tremendous bound; for I heard afar off the call of the moose, and knowing it did not cry in the daytime, I felt it was the signal of my companions. Noting carefully whence the sound came—for woods, owing to their echoing character, are often deceptive—I started toward it at a brisk pace, and answered it occasionally by a loud halloo, and after walking about half an hour had the satisfaction of hearing it closer to me.

I then commenced firing my rifle as I advanced, and in a short time heard an answering shot. This was a most delightful sensation, and with an elastic step I strode through the forest, and in twenty minutes after, guided by shouts and rifle reports, I found myself shaking hands with my friends.

A short conversation informed me that I had wandered over ten miles from camp, and that, if I had not moved in a circle, I would probably have been irretrievably lost in the unknown forest, unless I met, by the merest chance, some hunting-party. They had been out searching for me since morning, and had tracked me up to the place where I turned to the right the previous night, while chasing the moose. When they reached that point they saw trails of blood, and followed them up for some distance, thinking I had followed the animal directly; but not finding my footsteps, they concluded that I had halted there and awaited daylight to return to camp. When I did not return, however, they sallied out again, presuming I had been lost; and knowing how men will act in such a situation, they quartered the woods, and used the moose-call, as it could be heard a long distance off. Were they not provided with that simple instrument, it is doubtful if they could have found me, and I might now be in another world. Returning to camp, about three miles distant, I made a hearty breakfast of the moufle of a moose and some cakes baked before the fire, and soon felt as jovial as if I had never strayed from it.

After bringing in the animals that were first killed, we started in quest of the cause of my woe, and had little difficulty in tracking him by his slots and the drops of blood, until we reached the spot where he had laid down. From that point we followed him easily, and were soon beside him. A hungry panther had been feasting off him, however, while I had been away, for a large portion of the throat and shoulder were eaten off, and scarcely a drop of blood remained in the body. As he was too far from camp to be hauled there, he was skinned, and the carcass left for the use of carnivorous birds and quadrupeds. I learned, on my way back, that my hunting companion had also been charged by an infuriated wounded bull the previous night, and only escaped by having the Indian come to his aid just in time. We had, therefore, killed four moose on that occasion; no bad result for one night's work.

"Calling" moose is certainly exciting sport, and is full of incidents, some of which may not, as in my own case, be very pleasant for the time being, yet they are interesting to recall in after-years. To still-hunt the moose successfully, a person must resort to the same means employed in stalking any other wary animal; but if he does not know their habits, he will in the majority of cases, or at least in a large percentage of them, get only his pains for his labor, unless he has unusual good-luck, or is favored by accident.

Running them down is practised only in winter, when the snow is deep on the ground; and this requires endurance and perseverance on the part of the hunter rather than skill. It is resorted to principally by Indians who want meat, or by white men who want the skin; and as they can travel on snow-shoes at a rapid pace while the poor moose are constantly sinking into the drifts, if the crust is not strong enough to support them, the latter are of course soon exhausted, and bleeding from wounds in the legs. To kill them in this way is only butchery, as they can neither resist nor escape. Hunting the animal with hounds in winter is a more spirited sport; but in this case, also, it is brought to bay through exhaustion, and is slaughtered as easily as a cow; for while its attention is engaged with the dogs, all the hunter has to do is to knock it on the head with an axe, or blow its brains out with a rifle or revolver. The Indians, and some white men, frequently follow it for two or three days at a time on snow-shoes, and finally run it down, as the deep snow through which it must flounder fatigues it speedily, and each day's chase only renders it more easy of capture the next.

During one of my days of idleness I accompanied a snow-shoe party who were going out on a moose-hunt.

We had several dogs of all breeds, from terriers to fox-hounds, with us, and one mongrel that was a combination of bull-dog and greyhound. This individual would not only run down but boldly attack a moose; hence his fame was

SNOW-SHOE.

great, and many were the laudations he received. Our route led through a heavy forest, where the ground was deeply covered with snow having a hard but rather light crust. When we reached a favorable situation we scattered out and commenced searching for "signs," and quartered in every direction to the windward. After beating a tract of four or five square miles, we struck a large yard that was surrounded by a wall of snow three or four feet deep, and was traversed in every direction by well-beaten paths. This must have had an area of two or three square miles, as the trails led into a dense thicket of foliaceous trees, which we subsequently found to be three miles from where we first met the yard. On reaching this most welcome spot, the dogs, which had been kept to heel before, were now set to work, and in a few moments we heard a tremendous howl in many keys directly in front. We knew then that the game was started, and away we sped in pursuit at our best pace. As I was not very proficient in the use of snow-shoes, I found the run exceedingly laborious, and often sent myself sprawling on the hard snow by my awkwardness. I also collided against trees occasionally, and brought their white covering in showers over my person. These might be pleasant enough if a portion did not go down my neck and back, and make me shiver as if I had been dipped in ice-water. The suddenness of the showers also took my breath away sometimes, but the effect of the shock was soon dissipated by streams of perspiration.

The baying was rapidly waning in the distance, and my companions had all vanished, when I concluded to halt to tighten one of my shoes which had become loose. While engaged in that endeavor I saw a splendid young bull approaching, evidently on his way back to the yard, and the only dog in pursuit was an active, wire-haired terrier that was too busily engaged in snipping at his heels to have time to give tongue. The bull went right through the deep snow at every plunge, and the result was that he was almost pumped, while his legs were bleeding from the wounds inflicted by the crust. The terrier, on seeing me, began to wag its tail, and to bark and gambol around the unwieldy creature that could not resent its annoyance; but when it placed itself in front, and commenced to growl and show its teeth and snip at him, the maddened moose made several dashes at it with his horns. This pestering prevented him from seeing where he was going; so he floundered into a large drift nearly deep enough to swallow him up, and, while he was struggling to extricate himself from that position, I approached and shot him through the head; but after I had done it I did not feel very proud of my exploit, as it resembled too closely the shooting of a bound bull. He was so deeply mired that, even when dead, he did not fall over, but stuck in his position, an inanimate statue.

Before I had decided what next to do, one of the party, who had been following his tracks, arrived, and with his aid, and a sturdy bough, we prised him out on the crusted surface. Some of the others were equally successful, and our day's sport—if sport it could be called—netted us eight cows, calves, and young bulls out of probably fifteen or twenty that were in the yard. This is a specimen of nearly all runs in the snow, so one may see how much real hunting there is in it.

A moose-drive as conducted by the Indians is a veritable slaughter, and is about on a par with a pheasant battue,

but with this exception, that those taking part in it must
exert themselves to a certain extent, and display a knowledge of the haunts and habits of the animal. Previous to
commencing the drive, a grand moose-dance is held, in
which all the so-called braves join; and, when this is ended,
they, accompanied by their families, dogs, and horses, and
all the paraphernalia of an encampment, start for the forest
in September or October, when the moose have left their
woodland recesses, and are running boldly about in search
of mates. Selecting a locality where the animals are numerous, they form a large cordon, and, by beating and
shouting, drive them toward a common centre, where they
are slaughtered indiscriminately, and not only them, but all
four-footed game they meet. In this manner they hunt the
forest for miles, and sweep it almost clean of all edible
quadrupeds; and if they can manage to bag a grizzly, great
is their joy thereat.

At other times they place men in concealment in a mountain pass, or one that leads to water or connects two lakes,
and the remainder drive the moose toward them. When
the animals enter this gorge or pass of death, they cannot
well advance or retreat without running past a line of fire,
and the result is that hundreds fall in a week. The moose
are skinned by the squaws after the drive is over, and their
flesh is made into pemmican, or eaten fresh, *viscera* and all.
The meat is generally excellent, but is sometimes tough;
the fat part is delicious, however, at all times. The nose or
moufle is very good, and is much like the tail of the beaver
in flavor. Many persons consider this the best part, and
are extravagant in its praise; but I would always prefer a
good sirloin off a two-year-old cow in good condition.

The moose of the North-west, unlike their congeners in
the eastern portion of the United States and Canada, do
not yard, as a rule, but travel in pairs, or, at most, four or
six together. They are more abundant, however, and less
cautious, owing to their immunity from the rifles of skin-
hunters; hence a good shot ought to be able to make a
good bag in the wooded mountainous regions of Idaho,

MOOSE-HUNTING.

Montana, Manitoba, British Columbia, and Alaska. They are very common on the Yukon River in the latter Territory, and are useful to the Indians, as their bones supply them with arrows, needles, spear-points, and knives; their skins are used for clothing and for making wigwams; and the flesh is eaten fresh, or made into pemmican.

The Western species is larger than the Eastern, I fancy; at least I have seen some there that in height, and in the width, length, and massiveness of their antlers, excelled any of their kindred I saw in the forests of Maine or Canada. One of the largest pair probably ever brought to London had the following dimensions: outside measure of horns, sixty-two inches; across the blade, points not included, twenty inches; circumference above burr, seven and a quarter inches; length of the blade, thirty-nine inches.

To hunt moose successfully requires the display of the highest qualities of an Indian Nimrod; for cautiousness, patience, perseverance, endurance, acuteness of vision, and a knowledge of woodcraft and the habits of animals, are far more requisite than bravery and expertness with the rifle. Whoever, therefore, is a good moose-stalker may claim to have reached the highest pinnacle of the venatic art, and may safely compete with any man as a forest-hunter.

CHAPTER IX.

THE ELK, OR WAPITI.

The Wapiti.—Its Range, Haunts, Habits, and Gait.—Fierce Contests between the Males.—How they may be detected by the "Shaking."—Courage of the Elk.—Two Men charged by a Couple in Oregon.—The Escape.—Novel Mode of killing it in the North-west.—Thousands never saw Man.—When started, said not to stop until it crosses Water. —How Herds run when in Flight.—Their Speed and Endurance.—The Elk as a Roadster and Saddle Animal.—Hide-hunters.—Great Slaughter of the Animal.—Why Hinds lead the Columns.—How to Hunt it successfully in the Forest and on the Plains.—Dr. Carver's Great Feat. —The best Weapons.—How to Shoot on Horseback.—The most Exciting Run I ever had after it.—Bagging a Stag.—Pursuit of a Hind, and why she was Captured.—Escape of a Fawn.—Surprised by Indians. —The Assembly.—Our Plans and Stratagems.—A Running Fight.— Loss of the Indians.—Find Refuge in a Chasm.—Death of one of our Men.—He is mutilated, and burned to Death.—Our Retreat.—Suffer from Hunger.—Loss of our Camp, and Escape of the Camp Guard.— Where we found Safety.—A Scalp Dance.—Unusual Abundance of large Game.—We kill sixty Elks in Colorado.—Lassoing Fawns.— Visions of the Sport.

THE so-called elk, or wapiti (*Cervus canadensis*), is found in every grand division of the region west of the Rocky Mountains, its range extending from California in the south to British America in the north; but it is most numerous between the parallels of thirty-eight and fifty-two, where, in many instances, it was formerly seen in herds numbering from fifty to five thousand. It is more abundant in the Coast Range, where it passes through Oregon and Washington Territory, than in any other section, so far as I could learn; yet it is also common in the wooded portions of Northern California, Idaho, Montana, Utah, Wyoming, Dakota, British Columbia, and in the beautiful and extensive natural parks of Colorado. Being exceedingly gregarious in habit, where one is found there are sure to

WAPITI DEER.

be others; and in many places they spread over the country like small herds of domestic cattle. This antlered monarch of the forest stands about as high as a horse, and often attains a weight of eight hundred pounds. Having strong though lithe limbs, a full body, large dark eyes, and a splendid head, which is adorned with magnificent branching antlers five or six feet in length, and bearing from five to seven prongs each, it is, in my estimation, the finest specimen of its family on the continent. It has a proud, defiant, yet graceful mien, which makes it one of the most superb adjuncts to a landscape, and its very gait is enough to arouse the ardor of the most unimpressible sportsman, it being the acme of easy yet vigorous motion. Its antlers, which are highly prized for adorning dining-rooms, frequently weigh from fifty to sixty pounds, so that they are fit trophies to grace the proudest baronial halls. They sometimes assume eccentric shapes; for it is no very unusual sight to see a burly stag with one of his antlers largely palmated, and the other curving downward, instead of upward, so that it resembles the bend of the horns so marked in the mountain sheep. Such antlers are deemed to be unusually valuable, as their eccentricity is highly prized by collectors and ardent lovers of the chase.

During the summer the color of the wapiti is a reddish-chestnut, but it becomes darker in the autumn, and in winter the hairs are tipped with a pale brown. The male has long hairs on the neck and breast at all seasons, except the summer, but these the female never possesses. The former has a bell of hairs on the throat that frequently attains a length of five or six inches, but it seems to be longest on the largest species.

The sexes differ considerably in size, the female being much the smaller, and, unlike the antelope, she is devoid of antlers; yet one has been known occasionally to possess these useful appendages—a thing by no means uncommon in the deer family. The animal ruts in September; but the season being short, the sportsman will find the stags in good condition about the latter end of November, and ready to test to the fullest his powers and endurance. Many of them are shot during the running season by red and white hunters; as their melodious whistles, when calling for the females, readily indicate their presence, and lead the hunters to their quarters, when the slaughter is commenced. Their whistle is most peculiar, and differs widely from that of all other deer; indeed, so strongly marked is it that a person having heard it once would recognize it among the voices of a thousand animals. I never knew a person who could imitate it well, and this has prevented hunters from calling them as they do the moose and other deer. The difficulty in imitating the call is due to its varied character, it being composed of several parts. The first part consists of a shrill and prolonged whistle, which sometimes sounds afar off, although the animal uttering it may be very near a person, and this is followed by four or five deep brays or grunts, which end in a low, soft, and musical bellow, not displeasing to the ear, no matter how acutely it may have been attuned to harmony and melody. I have noticed, as a fact that struck me as being peculiar, that the bravest and largest wild animals always had deep voices, and that they were generally melodious—full of music, as it were—while the small fry, which would run from a common cur, had high, sharp voices. I have hunted with some of the bravest men, the best scouts, and the most famous hunters in the West, and I found that they also had deep, heavy tones, as a rule; and I deduced from this that the highest order of animals, those that were brave and daring, were always deep in voice, and that their intonations never jarred on the ear. When I saw that the heroes in an opera were the tenors, it struck me as an odd idea that thin-voiced animals were seldom so courageous in actual life as their deeper-voiced congeners, and this has caused me to express it here to see if it is in any way founded on fact, or whether it is a mere artificial system of display.

If the males meet during these whistling tournaments, long and severe is the battle they wage, and the weaker often gives his life to the stronger for his presumption in rival gallantry. The hinds bring forth their young in May or June, but their families are confined to one at a time, twins being unknown. The calf, which is spotted like the fawn of a deer, is a beautiful creature, and so active that it is able to run about with its dam in the course of a few days after its birth. The mother is very much attached to it, and fights bravely in its defence, if necessary, with head and feet; but the best protectors are the males.

The latter wander away from the herd during the spring and early summer, and secrete themselves in the thickest underbrush while they are growing their antlers; and their presence is then readily detected by the shaking of the undergrowth, against which they are almost constantly rubbing their irritated frontal appendages. They may be easily approached from the leeward during that time, as the swaying of the shrubbery produces noise enough to drown the hunter's footsteps, and the animals are lost to everything but the alleviation of their irritation. Many skin-hunters — that is, those who hunt them for the hide alone — kill numbers of them while engaged in the "shaking," as hunters call it, and leave the meat to rot on the ground, or to furnish food to carnivorous birds and quadrupeds.

The production of the horns makes a heavy drain on the strength of the stag, and the result is that he is thinner and weaker in July than the hind, which has been nursing her young one for perhaps two months. By the latter end of August he is in splendid condition, however; and his magnificent antlers being then full grown, he roams through the forest and over the plain in all his majesty, ever ready, like the knight of old, to woo the gentle sex or to measure his strength against every rival for the love of the deer-ladies. How proudly he struts! how defiantly he stares at all foes except man! and how grandly he shows his strength and speed as he takes his long and measured paces over hill and dale, and through the light coppice or dense forest! During the running season he seems ready to meet all enemies, not excepting man himself, if pushed to it; and he generally comes off first best with any quadruped of less importance than a grizzly. I saw a proud fellow on one occasion engaged in mortal combat with a black bear that must have weighed at least three hundred pounds; but before the latter could use its great strength and powerful claws to any advantage, the former pierced it with his magnificent antlers, and after two or three charges left it dead on the ground. Stamping upon it two or three times with one of his forelegs, he gave a snort and a defiant look around, as if seeking for new foes, and, finding none, he gazed once more on the slain, then trotted off into the damp, dense forest. I was close enough to have shot him easily; but I refrained from injuring such a noble, spirited creature, for the sake of the pluck he had displayed.

That he will boldly face man when brought to bay, I have received the most authentic accounts. Two men in Oregon, who were employed to carry the mail to a small settlement with which there was no communication except by an Indian trail that led over a high and thickly wooded mountain, or by following the sea-shore when the tide was out, were arrested on one of their trips by the presence of two elks, a male and a female, that boldly barred the path in front of them, and manifested no inclination to leave it. This path was bounded on the upper side by huge crags which no four-footed animal could leap or clamber over, and the lower by high, wooded cliffs that rose perpendicularly upward from the boiling sea, so that neither party could very well advance or retreat, or move to the right or left, without suffering a serious inconvenience or endangering their lives. The men, being unarmed, dared not advance, and the elks being placed between the two horns of the dilemma of which would be best, either to face their most dreaded enemy, or meet death by hurling themselves off the cliff, hesitated about what to do. The men, seeing that they were undecided in their purpose, yelled loudly at them, and this startled them so much that they wheeled about suddenly, broke over a rise of the mountain, and disappeared from view. One of the men, remembering that the tide was full, and that the animals could not cross a small bay that divided two cliffs in the sea then raging, predicted they would return and charge them rather than face the surf; and the words were scarcely uttered before they reappeared over the rise, the male in advance. Lowering his horns almost to the ground, he charged upon them at his best pace; but they evaded him by swinging themselves out of his course by means of two young firs, and, when the hind passed, they resumed their march, thoroughly thankful for their escape from an ignominious death. They took excellent care after that to go armed, and this resolution saved their lives several times from the attacks of wild animals. Under ordinary circumstances, however, the elk is as timid as any member of its family, and a cur will keep a herd in motion all day.

The usual method of killing it in the forests of the North-west is by stalking; and where it is little hunted it may be approached from the leeward to within easy rifle range, and a herd almost destroyed before the survivors become alarmed enough to seek safety in flight. I have killed five out of a herd of twenty in the Coast Mountains before the remainder got out of range, and I could have killed as many more if I wished, by following them up; for they showed no fear of me, and seemed to look upon me more as a strange than a dangerous creature, if I should judge from their stupid stare, and their indifference to the reports of the rifle. Thousands of them in Oregon, Washington Territory, Wyoming, Colorado, and Montana never saw man, and have no fear of him if he is to their leeward; but let them once sniff him to the windward, and they would be off like a shot, nor would they stop until they had placed many a mile between him and themselves. If they are once started in an alarmed condition, hunters say they will not halt until they have crossed a stream or lake; but while this is true in many cases, especially in the open or in sparsely wooded valleys, it does not hold good in the dense forest, for I have routed the same herd three times in one day; and that it was the same, I inferred from the presence of two wounded animals, and the fact that it was led by a splendid hind.

When a herd is started, the males throw their cumbrous antlers far back on the neck, so that the nose is high in the air. One might imagine that they could not see the ground very well under these circumstances; but whether they do or do not, they trot through dense shrubbery and over fallen trees with the greatest ease, and never falter or break their gait, no matter what ordinary obstacles they may have to surmount. Their pace is a long, measured trot, which carries them over the ground at a rapid rate. They can, I fancy, trot a mile several seconds under four minutes, and, if pushed, might do it in three minutes. On open or rocky ground they can put a good horse to his mettle to overtake them, if they have a fair start, nor must he lag on closing with them, if he would keep them company. They seem to be able to move at the same pace over all kinds of ground, and it appears to be a matter of indifference to them whether it is one mass of stones, ruts, and hillocks, or a level prairie. This is where they have the advantage over horses, and why it is so difficult to run them down in a rough country. I have done it, however; but in nearly all cases I broke their trot first, and this fatigued them so promptly that I was able to pull along-side and give them the contents of a revolver or rifle. They can go twenty or thirty miles easily without showing signs of weariness or flagging, and, if forced to it, I am inclined to think they could go a hundred miles over a good country.

The size, strength, and speed of the elk ought to fit it for some useful domestic purpose. It could be trained to be a valuable beast of burden; and its speed is so great, and it has so much power of endurance, that it could be used either for drawing a carriage or to carry couriers who have to ride long distances at a rapid rate. By treating it as geldings are, the pugnacity and ill-temper it displays during the rutting season could be readily overcome, and it would be rendered as docile as a donkey. A friend of mine once owned a pair treated in this manner, and he found that very little training was required to fit them for drawing a carriage. When it came to road driving, he saw that no steeds he met could even keep in sight of his antlered Pegasuses for any length of time. Their long, trotting gait, which never seems to falter either in measure or speed, makes them the perfection of carriage roadsters; but they have this one great drawback, that if they hear the cry of hounds they will bolt immediately, and probably leave carriage and driver behind them. The pair which I refer to were startled suddenly one day, while enjoying their exercise, by the baying of a pack of mongrels, and no sooner did they hear the cry than they jumped over a high bank—carriage, driver, and all—and landed in a deep pool in a river. Making for the land with all possible haste, they soon battered the vehicle into small pieces, while the unfortunate owner had some difficulty in reaching shore. By offering a large reward, he recovered his runaways the next day; and, being a man of determination as well as resources, he concluded to get rid of their penchant for bolting at once. With this purpose in view, he put them into a field having very high fences, and kept hounds yelling about it all day long. The elks were at first thoroughly scared; but after running themselves nearly to death, and finding no means of escape nor any result from their great alarm, they gradually became indifferent, and settled down to feeding. This experiment being repeated a few times, their idle fears were allayed, and the owner suffered no more mishaps from their impetuosity. How far they could be made useful for carrying light couriers I cannot surmise, but the probability is that they would be found unequalled for such purposes in the wooded regions of the Far West.

It does certainly seem a pity that this animal cannot be domesticated, and made into something more useful and permanent than a means of affording the pleasure of shooting to a few sportsmen or hungry hunters, or enriching "skin-scalpers," whose sole idea of sport is to slaughter even the pregnant hinds for the sake of the pitiful sum they obtain for the hides. It is estimated that over ten thousand elks were slaughtered last year for their skins alone, and of these about four thousand were killed in Montana, principally in the Yellowstone region, where the animal is, or rather was, exceedingly numerous.

A skin realizes from two dollars and a half to four dollars, according to the character of the coating; and for this pittance many men devote themselves to destroying indiscriminately the most stately animal in the country; yet nothing is done to them, owing to the indifference of the legislators to framing a law that would punish such Vandals. At the present rate of destruction, the wapiti will not be known in Montana, Colorado, and Wyoming in a short time, and persons must hie to the dense forests of portions of Idaho, Oregon, Washington Territory, and other distant regions to enjoy a legitimate hunt after it.

I have said that the animals were more numerous in the two latter countries than in any other portion of the continent; and this I believe to be a positive fact, for I have seen them, during the autumnal migrations when they were fleeing from the icy breezes of the mountains to the warmth and shelter of the coast, pass a run-way in herds nearly all day long; and had I remained I might, perhaps, have seen the same sight for a week. They moved in long columns and in single file, and each column was led by a sturdy stag or a matronly hind, but the rear was always occupied by old males. When startled, they would move at a tremendous rate through the thick woods and matted undergrowth, but they seemed to have no special leaders; for in some cases a young stag, and in others an old hind, headed the fugitives, the young being in the centre. The cause of this lack of a regular commander in a stampede would seem to be that the males are often too heavy to lead the van, and that, as with the buffalo, the lighter-footed females are compelled to do it on account of their superior activity.

To hunt them successfully in the forest, I have found a breech-loading shot-gun, well charged with buckshot, the best weapon, but, for open shooting, I prefer a fifty-calibre double Express that is accurate up to three hundred yards; and for running them down on horseback, few weapons are more convenient than a heavy self-cocking revolver, that carries a bone-smashing bullet and a large charge of powder, so that one shot at close range may be able to disable or kill a fugitive. A good breech-loading rifle, provided one has a trained horse, is preferable to a revolver, however, owing to its longer range, greater accuracy, and more destructive power.

Dr. Carver, the celebrated rifleman, who has performed the unparalleled feat of killing thirty-three elks in one straight run, and two hundred and thirty in two weeks by running and stalking, considers that any rifle less than fifty calibre is rather light for hunting such heavy game, unless it carries a large charge of powder and a long bullet; and he deems a revolver to be of comparatively little use for general work, owing to its want of accuracy, and its dangerous character in the hands of novices. I have seen some splendid work done with it, however, by troopers, officers, regular hunters, and even novices, especially when they had inexperienced horses that would not follow an elk without the use of the reins.

If a man has a trained steed that will chase an elk or a herd without any guidance from the hand, a rifle is by far the best weapon. This should be lifted promptly to the shoulder, and fired the moment it covers the object; for any attempt to take deliberate aim when a horse is at full speed is an impossibility, as the gun falls up and down with the strides. A slight glance along the barrel is generally sufficient, and a person will find, after a little experience, that he can shoot as well that way as if he rested half a minute on the sight.

The most effective and the surest shot is made quartering, so that the bullet may pass through the ribs and lungs, and possibly break the fore-shoulder. Another good one is to strike the animal in the back, so that the spinal column may be broken. This is not so easily made as the previous one, however, as the target is not so large. A capital weapon for general shooting on horseback is the latest model of the Winchester or Sharp rifle, the former being especially convenient, owing to its magazine, and the rapidity with which it can be fired. Few sights are more stirring than to behold a herd of elks, numbering from five hundred to a thousand, with their branching antlers, looking like a brush-thicket at a distance, and their graceful forms, scouring over the plains in wild confusion. When startled, they bound away in a body, and keep so close that they soon become enveloped in clouds of dust, through which is heard the clashing of antlers, and the heavy, measured tread of many hoofs. When hard pressed, they break up into small groups and run in every direction; and to prevent this, persons ought to keep about twenty or thirty feet behind them, and rake them from the flanks. To get within this distance and stay there for any length of time, fast and vigorous horses are required; for an elk can outrun any ordinary horse if the ground is at all rough, and can keep up its pace for a distance of seventy miles or more with apparent ease. It is no unusual incident, therefore, for a spirited steed to fall dead after a long chase; and to be knocked up for life is quite a common occurrence.

If the animals are driven toward a canyon, a person may tumble over half a dozen as they emerge on the opposite side; but the most effective means of making a large bag is to bound suddenly into the midst of a herd and open a rapid fire at once. This demoralizes them so much that they jump wildly about or stare stupidly at their foe, yet do not attempt to flee; but when once they get it into their heads that something is wrong, they wheel about, and soon disappear in the horizon. This interval is sufficient, however, to enable a good shot to kill from four to a dozen of them, and, if he is well mounted, he may claim as many more in a run of seven or eight miles. This chase is most exciting; and he who has once taken part in it will say that few sports can equal it, as it brings into action both equestrian power and surety of aim. Having stalked the animal, pursued it with hounds, and run it down on horseback, I prefer the latter to any other method of hunting it, as it gives both the hunter and the hunted an opportunity of displaying their best qualities.

The most stirring gallop that I have had after it was in the Wind River country in Wyoming. There were at the time to which I refer no settlers in the region where the chase came off, and I doubt if there are any now, as it was occupied three or four years ago only by wild animals and wilder Indians. I entered it with a party of miners who were going there on a "prospecting" expedition, it being reported that some of the hills there contained large deposits of gold and silver, and several small lakes of soda, besides other valuable mineral treasures. The leader of our party was a veteran scout and Indian fighter who had lived in the country for many years, and when he was the only white man to be found there, if I except an occasional visit from a few trappers employed by the fur companies. He had had so many contests with the Indians that he was known by name or person to every tribe in the Territory, and great was his fame among them; so great, in fact, that few of them would care to meet him in combat, or attack any bodies of men led by him, whether they were soldiers or civilians. He had also some influence with them on account of his being married to two squaws, and this induced us to hope that they would not molest us. In order to be prepared for all contingencies, however, we armed ourselves with the best bowie-knives, rifles, and revolvers we could procure; and being provided with two good American horses each, and a small pack train of mules to carry our baggage, we started from the Laramie Plains for the unknown Eldorado, about one hundred and thirty miles distant, just as the sun was about setting. We chose this time so as to prevent persons from knowing where we were going, and also to get well on our way before any prowling Indians could guess at our destination and lay a trap for us; for few red men can withstand the temptation of lifting a lot of fine horses and some attractive scalps at the same time. We marched principally at night, and rested during the day, generally in a chasm or piece of woods where we could find shelter and concealment, for we did not want to run any risks. We were even careful not to build any fires, except what was sufficient to boil some tea or coffee and broil a piece of bacon, as we feared the smoke would betray our presence.

After marching for five nights over treeless plains and pine-clad mountains, we reached our destination, and pitched our camp on the top of a wooded hill that both concealed us and gave us a commanding view of the surrounding country. The day after our arrival it was resolved to lay in a stock of fresh meat, as we had none, and we desired to provision the camp, so that all our time could be devoted to the object of the expedition. This did not seem to be a very difficult matter, for the tracks of deer were numerous everywhere, and the woods fairly swarmed with hares and several species of grouse. The latter were not deemed worthy of the powder to be wasted upon them, however, so we made preparations for an onslaught on the large game. Having saddled our horses and armed ourselves in the most careful manner, we sallied from our forest home and marched toward an extensive valley to our right, which was hemmed in on all sides by high, wooded mountains, and contained several coppices of cotton-woods, alders, and willows, which skirted the borders of streams. It was covered with a luxuriant growth of herbage and wild flowers, and looked as beautiful in the morning sun as any spot could possibly be. It was the ideal of repose; yet its surroundings were full of activity and motion, and gentle picturesqueness was contrasted with sublime grandeur.

Always careful and cautious, the scout, who had gained his experience by many a hard and dangerous lesson, would allow no one to enter it until he had carefully reconnoitred it from two or three directions, for fear any Indians might be lurking there. While he and two others were out scouting, I surveyed the valley with a field-glass from a commanding eminence, and saw that large throngs of antelopes and numerous herds of elks and deer were grazing over it, or playfully running about. When the leader returned, he stated that he could find no indications anywhere of the presence of the red men, and that it would therefore be safe to enter the place. As we wished to get as much meat as we could in as short time as possible, we concluded to run the elks, as they would afford us the best sport and meat, and our chances of success were greater with them than if we went after the smaller deer or the prong-horns.

Moving forward slowly, we were soon to the leeward of two herds of elks which were grazing on the outskirts of a coppice, and, when we got near enough to them to undertake a dash with some assurances of success, we charged them boldly. That seemed to be the first time they had any suspicion of our dangerous character; but, when once assured of it, they broke away singly or in groups, and headed directly up wind and across the valley. Each man singled out his quarry, and in a short time the hills and mountains were echoing with the reports of rifles and revolvers. I selected a burly stag that had magnificent antlers, and in a run of less than half a mile was near enough to cause him to break his trot, and fall into a fast, ungainly gallop. Knowing that he could not keep that pace very long, I urged my horse forward at his best speed, and kept him at it until the quarry resumed the long and rapid trot for which its family is noted. The ground being good, I had every advantage over the fugitive, as my horse was both fast and enduring. After a run of two miles or more, I drew along-side his flank, and, placing my revolver close enough to his back to burn the hair, I fired, and broke his spinal column. He fell headlong on his antlers, but, before he reached the ground, I got in another shot in the head, and he tumbled over dead. As he lay outstretched before me, I fairly gloated over him, for he was one of the largest and handsomest stags I ever saw. On looking around for my companions, I saw several of them pursuing the animals in every direction, while others were dismounted, having evidently been successful in the run. Having marked the position of my victim, I was returning to join a group of two or three of my comrades, when I met a hind and her fawn coming toward me in the most unsuspicious manner. I dashed at them, but, instead of running up wind, they cut across it, and headed for a coppice of cotton-woods three or four miles distant. I pursued them at a rattling pace; but, my horse being quite pumped, I could not get them to break their trot, so the chase continued for a couple of miles, when the hind fell forward suddenly on her head as if shot; but before I could overtake her she was off again. I noticed in a short time that she was running in a peculiar manner, as if one of her legs were injured, yet I could not close the distance between us. After awhile she showed signs of faltering; her pace was becoming unsteady; and the fawn which had kept by her side all the way shot ahead of her. Feeling assured that she was injured, I did not press my horse very hard, as I was hoarding his strength for a final dash. As every step she took seemed to weaken her more, I finally made a spurt, and was beside her in less than ten minutes, and, putting my revolver to her head, I shot her dead. The fawn broke away in an opposite direction, on seeing me close on it, and by this means escaped. On looking at the hind, I saw that one of her forelegs was broken near the fetlock, the result of stepping into a prairie-dog hole, yet she must have run at least two or three miles more after that accident.

Having extracted the *viscera*, I marked her position, and started back to where two men were left with our extra horses, as the animal I rode was quite done up, and covered with foam. While returning, I noticed that the elks and antelopes which we had driven toward the mountains were scurrying back, as if they were being pursued; and this caused me to halt and closely scan the landscape. I fortunately carried my field-glass slung over my shoulder, and, taking it out, I made a survey of all that portion of the valley which the animals were leaving. After a careful scrutiny, I could see a column of mounted men moving along the edge of a heavy copse; and when it passed the wood, it seemed to open out like a telescope, and dark dots could be seen moving rapidly to the right and left and suddenly disappearing, as if the ground had swallowed them. "Indians, by Jove!" thought I; so I hastened at once to find our veteran commander, to see what could be done to escape the serious danger that threatened us. After going at full gallop for about a mile, I was startled by hearing my name called out of a tree, and, on looking up, saw the leader perched on the branches of a fir, and his horse tied to its base. Reining up abruptly, I was going to tell him what I had seen; but he anticipated me by coolly remarking, "Seen 'em, didn't you? I knowed it as soon as I saw you stoppin'; but I saw 'em long afore you did. That aire machine o' yourn isn't as good as my eyes, after all. I reckon I can tell an Injun as far off as any telescope." This statement, which was yelled at me as if the whole thing was a joke, was followed by the rapid descent of the speaker; but on reaching the ground he changed his tone of voice, and said that we were in for another sort of hunt, and that he feared we should have to play the part of the elk. "There's more'n a hundred Injuns in that crowd near the mountains," said he, "and there's more'n fifty in the woods toward which you were running after that last elk; so we've got one hundred and fifty against twelve. Mighty lively times we'll have of it afore long, I tell you; and if any of us can scratch our head to-night we'll be mighty lucky, you bet your boots."

Asking him what he thought ought to be done, he replied that there was nothing to be done just then except to collect our forces, mount fresh horses, and fight for a passage through the mountains in front. To attempt to reach camp, which was left in charge of two men, he considered to be a piece of folly, inasmuch as the Indians must have seen whence we emerged into the valley, and made their preparations to check us in that direction; for the first principle with a warrior is, that a white man retreats on the same line that he advanced; so his first move is to block that route, and depend on a surround, and the demoralizing effect of yells and charges, to win a victory. Most of our men had little fear of our foes in anything like equal numbers, for they were used to a rough-and-ready life among a fighting people with whom a word too often meant death.

While we were conversing together, another member of the expedition rode up; and he being made acquainted with the condition of affairs, we resolved to summon our party together at once, and fight the Indians in the copse, and, if we defeated them, to dash for the mountains and reach the settlements if possible. The Indians felt so sure of us that they were in no hurry to open the battle; and we wished them to infer that their presence was not known, for fear of forcing the issue before we were ready. We decided, accordingly, that we should chase an antelope in the direction where our spare horses were held, and there hold a council of war. Acting on this idea, we tore away from the copse at our best pace; and meeting hundreds, I might say thousands, of antelopes on our way, we pretended to pursue them, but we took excellent care that those we followed went in the direction we wished to go. A run of two miles brought us to where our extra horses were held; and pretending that we had done something extraordinary, which pretension we made manifest by firing our rifles and revolvers, we shouted in our most stentorian tones "hoo-oo-hoo-oo-oo-ah-oo-ah," as if we were overjoyed at an unusual piece of success.

I was sent out on the plain to fire my revolver in rapid succession, in order to attract the attention of the remainder of our company, while our veteran leader rode in another direction to watch the manœuvres of the Indians. Our signal was successful, and in less than ten minutes the whole of our party was assembled. I had, in the mean time, saddled a fresh and my best horse, and felt so thoroughly confident of outrunning any Indian that I was almost anxious to race with any one of them. When the position of affairs was explained to the men, they were all animation at once; and though the news was exceedingly disagreeable, not one showed the least sign of fear. All displayed in their features the seriousness of the coming contest; but though their faces might have been a little blanched, yet there was an expression of a thorough determination to fight to death if necessary.

Some—and myself among them—put a revolver into their boot-legs, intending to kill themselves with it if they were captured, or so seriously wounded as to be unable to keep with the remainder of the party. After a brief consultation, our plan of operations was decided upon. This was, that it would be worse than madness to retreat to camp; and, having no other recourse left, we concluded to make for the only passage in the mountains in front, and resort to every stratagem we could think of to lead the foe away from that. All were to obey the leader's motions, or take the consequence; and no person was to leave a wounded comrade until it was evident that he could not escape the red demons, and he was then to be shot in case he could not do it himself. That matter being understood, all mounted fresh horses; and deploying into a long line, so as to prevent the effect of a fusillade, we moved forward as if we were going on a grand drive. The Indians in the coppice in front, on seeing us advancing, sallied out promptly to meet us, and we, feigning to be surprised, faced about at the command of our leader and retreated in the direction whence we came. They dashed after us at once; and when they got within rifle range we let them have a volley, which tumbled over some men and horses. Our fire was answered by a fierce yell of defiance and a fusillade that looked dangerous enough, but all the bullets fell short. After a halt of five minutes, we galloped in an oblique direction to the right, in order to lead them away from the route we intended to take; and this ruse was successful; for, instead of closing on us, the larger number rode as rapidly as they could to head us off from camp, while the others spread out so as to completely surround us. A ride of a mile or two showed us that we had drawn nearly all the screaming braves from the rear, and that we might therefore be able to break through the thin line that covered the mountain pass we were anxious to reach. We decided, accordingly, to face about, and put our horses to their best pace, and make it a veritable race for life; but, before we could act on this idea, a line of mounted warriors rose out of the ground about five hundred yards ahead, and gave us a rattling but harmless volley. We returned the fire hotly for a few moments, and saw several men fall. Not caring to do more to them than show that they could not attack us with impunity, we wheeled about suddenly, and, moving obliquely to the left, where our foes were least numerous, we gave our horses a free though firm rein, and sped over the ground at a pace that was soon carrying us away from the fire of the main column. It was not until we dispersed the Indians in front that the others had any idea of what we were about; but, on divining our purpose, their yells of defiance turned into yells of rage, and they commenced firing aimlessly, and trying to surround us; but this they found a difficult matter, as they were too widely scattered. The race continued at a slashing rate for five or six miles, without any injury to us, when we suddenly met another group of warriors, and a fight then commenced that lasted for three miles. We did not waste a moment in halts to take aim; we merely placed the rifle to the shoulder and banged away.

To shoot at distant objects with any degree of accuracy when a horse is at a full gallop is an impossibility; hence we did not expect to do much harm. We did, nevertheless, have the satisfaction occasionally of seeing a warrior fall, but he would scarcely touch the ground before two of his comrades would run on each side of him and lift him on his horse, or drag him out of the range of our fire.

As we approached the pass in the mountains, the Indians redoubled their efforts to head us off; but we had the inner line, and intended to keep it. Seeing that they could not check us in that direction, they opened on us from every quarter, and bullets went whizzing or droning past us, while the fierce screams of the prairie braves were fairly demoniacal in their intensity. Had they been less careful of their persons they could have annihilated us in a few moments, but, Indian-like, they wished to destroy us without any injury to themselves; hence they kept beyond the range of our rifles except for a few minutes at a time, when they tried their useless system of charging. The stirring combat was kept up uninterruptedly, however, until we saw the gap that yawned in the mountain and offered us our only refuge. This caused a thrill of joy to pass through both body and mind, and we, for the first time, answered the screams of our foes by hearty shouts. A few of the more daring and best mounted warriors made a bold and determined attempt to charge us, but they were glad to relinquish that system of fighting in a very short time. A little later, and we were dashing into the rocky pass or chasm, and, once inside, we halted, and climbing promptly to an eminence, gave our pursuers as defiant a shout as ever issued from human throats. We were horror-struck, however, to see a group of the fiends dancing and yelling about some object; and on inquiring if any of the party were missing, found that a man named Evans was not seen after the head of our column entered the pass, he being the last in the line. This loss affected us very much, and we were almost enraged when we saw the way in which he was being tortured; for the cowards were evidently wreaking their revenge and losses on him. Much as we felt inclined to save him or his remains from the mutilating hands of his captors, we felt that we were powerless to do so, and that we might be risking our own lives to no purpose. The Indians did not, of course, dare to follow us into the pass, so we pursued our journey unmolested. We subsequently learned from friendly Indians that our foes were some of Red Cloud's renegade band, and that we had killed and wounded fifteen of them. They captured our camp, however, but the men in charge escaped by leaving it where it stood, and fleeing toward the settlements when they observed us retreating.

After resting a short time in the chasm, we resumed our retrograde movement, and continued it for three nights, when we reached an army post, where we were kindly treated and hospitably entertained by the officers. We suffered a good deal from hunger and thirst during our retreat, as water was scarce, and the only food we had was the flesh of the sage hare and sage cock; and that, though tender, is anything but pleasing even to the palate of a hungry man, as it tastes as if it had been steeped in a decoction of quinine, gall, and bitter-almonds. We were so thankful at escaping a terrible death, however, that we grumbled but little at our diet; yet we were very glad when we exchanged it for something more palatable.

Several months after this affair I happened to be at the Sioux reservation, and there learned the full particulars of the horrible death of poor Evans. The murderers who had been out devastating the country during the spring and summer, and slaying men, women, and children in the most merciless manner, returned to the reservation to rest during the winter, and grow fat on the generous rations supplied them by the Government, in order that they might be in good condition to resume the slaughter of innocent whites the following spring. Having nothing to do except to eat, time became rather heavy on their hands, and, to escape this dulness, they instituted a round of their various dances, some of which were kept up for a fortnight at a time, night and day. I witnessed their hideous scalp-dance, in which the scalps were placed on long wands, which were held by women in the centre of a large circle, while the sanguinary braves yelled and jumped around them like so many lunatics, and each related in the most boasting manner imaginable how many scalps he had taken; how he secured them; and went through horrifying pantomimic gestures with hands and face and body to show how he acted in the terrible contest that had made him such a famous warrior, and furnished him with so many gory trophies. When one assassin finished relating his tale, all present uttered a guttural " wach " of approbation, as a certificate of his truthfulness; and after some more stamping, yelling, and hideous grimaces, another leaped into the circle and told his exploits; and so it was continued until all had proclaimed their martial deeds, and elevated themselves into the greatest of heroes. I noticed that one scalp aroused two of them into the greatest state of frenzy, for they screamed and roared, barked, yelped, stamped with their feet, snapped their teeth, distorted their facial muscles, and hissed as they pointed at it, and brandished their arms and weapons in the most frantic manner, to show how hard its owner had struggled to keep it on his head. When they had finished their wild harangue, an unusually loud and prolonged " wach " from all announced that it was a great feat indeed; and, when the braves left the ring, an old chief told the audience how many men they had lost in trying to get that scalp.

I did not understand a word of what they said, but I could readily comprehend their gestures, and deduced from them that one of the greatest deeds ever performed by the tribe was to secure that scalp. Turning to the French half-breed who was with me, I asked him to translate their speeches for me, and he said that the scalp was that of a white man which they had taken in the Wind River region a few months previously. The party of whites of which he was a member had killed or wounded fifteen of their men, and then escaped in the great chasm; but that he, being the last in the line, had his horse shot under him, and he fell to the ground. He mounted another, however, in a moment; but, before he could escape, one of the two braves stunned him with a shot in the head, and then pulled him off his horse, while the second shot him through the right arm with an arrow. On recovering consciousness, the white man drew his revolver, and shot three warriors as they were crowding around him; but, before he could inflict any further injury, he was seized by the two Terpsichoreans, unarmed, bound, and tied to a tree, where he was burned alive, after being terribly mutilated and having his body filled with arrows. He bore his fate with Indian stoicism; and this and his bravery had induced his captors to consider him a great warrior, and his scalp to be therefore unusually important. When I heard the tale, I felt as if I should like to see the whole murderous, boasting throng shot like dogs; and so anxious was I that they should be punished, that I left the savage scene, with its ghastly accessories, and hastened at once to the house of the agent or sub-agent, and told him of the incident, and asked him to see that the murderers were punished.

He, however, treated the matter rather indifferently, saying that it would be difficult to bring those engaged in the brutal deed to justice, as none of their own people would testify against them, and a scalp could not be identified or produced in evidence to prove their guilt. When I told him that those present had told the tale themselves, he said that was nothing, as they would deny it all in a body if questioned about it; and he thought it was better to let the matter rest, as the dead could not be called to life, and any attempt at punishing his murderers would only create a useless disturbance, and probably send a portion of the tribe on the war-path.

Seeing that nothing could be done, I relinquished my efforts at having them punished, and the next week I went to see another dance of the braves. This was like the preceding, except that the scalps were not held up by the women; but I noticed that several were employed to fringe the garments of the warriors, and that they pointed to their dress instead of to wands when they were relating their great deeds and the number of scalps they had taken. I tried to buy some of these garments, but found they were deemed invaluable, and that neither money nor ammunition could induce their owners to part with them. I have been in that country since I was so unceremoniously hunted out of it, but I never think of it without recalling the horrible fate of Evans, and feeling thankful for my own escape from an ignominious death.

The abundance of the elk in some of the unpopulated regions beyond the Rocky Mountains is almost incredible. I have seen in a valley in Colorado, near the Ute reservation, at least four thousand in one herd, and I have frequently seen them in throngs numbering from fifty to five hundred in various sections extending from Oregon to British America. I once formed one of a party in Colorado who were exploring a region that contained few settlers, and they were often far apart; hence game was as plentiful as if the entire country were a park, and was as closely preserved as a Scotch deer forest. Elks, deer, and antelopes were scattered over the plain as far as the eye could see, and they were so unused to the presence of man that they seldom fled before us when we approached them from the leeward until we were quite close to them. During the two months that we spent there, we captured about sixty elks by running them down with horses; and we could have slain five times the number, I believe, if we cared to do so, or preferred wanton slaughter to sport. We also lassoed some calves, but the greater number were let loose after we picked out the best for the larder. Lassoing them is a very interesting amusement, especially if a person is well mounted, as they run well, and twist and turn rapidly when being overhauled; and a young buck will sometimes, especially if much blown, charge the horse, and try to pierce him with his tiny antlers. Visions of those scenes arouse the most buoyant feelings of one's nature, but with them comes the sad thought that in a few years one of the finest game animals on the continent will have disappeared before the advance of civilization, and the knife and rifle of the skin-hunter.

CHAPTER X.

THE MULE DEER.

The Mule Deer.—Its Haunts and Habits.—General Characteristics.—Origin of Name.—Weight, Size, and Appearance.—Why it is called the Jumping Deer.—Fire-hunting.—Herding of Bucks.—Hunting with Hounds.—Stalking.—Migrations of the Animal.—Large Numbers killed by Hunters.—A Hunt in the Bitter Root Mountains.—Wailing of Squaws.—A Visit to an Indian Cemetery.—Disappearance of the Mourners.—A Retreat.—Wolves.—Sit up all Night.—Fear of Indians. —A Visit from them in the Morning.—Our Preparations for their Reception.—Mutual Recognition.—The Trapper's Story.—Visit the Indian Camp.—The Pipe of Peace.—Speeches.—A Buffalo Dance.—Revisit the Burial-ground.—Mode of Burying the Dead.—Mourning Songs of Squaws.—Change Camp.—Number of Deer captured, and how we Bagged them.—Wolves attacking a Stag.—Death of Five of them.— Change Quarters.—Hunting Does and Fawns.—Why these keep to the Foot-hills.—Our Success with them.—Another Visit to the Indian Camp.—An Aged Couple deserted.—How Indians treat Old People.— Their Fate.

THE mule deer (*Cariacus macrotis:* Gray) is a denizen of the vast area lying between the bad lands of Dakota and Nebraska, and the Sierra Nevada and Cascade Ranges. It is virtually the deer of the mountains and plateaux, as its congeners are of the forest and lowlands; for it is seldom found on the plains, unless they are closely surrounded by rugged hills or steep mountains, and even then only rarely; for the lowest points to which it seems to descend voluntarily are the foot-hills that jut out from the main ranges. Its favorite haunts are near the summits of mountains having an altitude of from one to five thousand feet; and there, free from many foes, it leads a life of comparative ease and security. It always seeks shelter in the timber during the day; but in the morning and evening it frequents the more open grounds near the mountain crests to graze on the tender and dainty grass that is nurtured during the spring and summer by the melting snow on the higher pinnacles. In these retreats, notwithstanding the fact that wolves and cougars are comparatively scarce, it exercises the most scrutinizing vigilance, and the hunter that would approach it undetected must have the caution, cunning, and patience of an Indian. Like all mountain an-

THE AMERICAN DEER.

imals, it is very keen of scent, and easily alarmed; yet when it is not hunted much, and persons approach it from the leeward at a snail's pace and halt frequently, they may get a shot at it; for, like all its family, its vision seems to be so defective that it is able to distinguish objects only when they are in motion. Those who would be successful in stalking it should, therefore, move slowly, tread lightly, and use their eyes instead of their feet. The great point is to see the quarry before it sees you; and as its coating closely resembles the grass and leaves, and it is generally concealed in dense shrubbery during the day, the only way in which this can be done is to peer sharply in every direction, and let the gaze rest steadily for a few moments on spots where it is supposed to lurk. One should work to the windward under all circumstances; for the keen nostrils of a deer will detect the presence of a hunter several hundred yards away, and it would be off in the most noiseless manner before he even knew that it was about. Its hearing being also excellent, the breaking of a branch, the rustle of the shrubbery, or the crackling of a rotten bough underfoot, would send it scampering away in a hurry; hence the general advice may be summarized in a sentence: keep your eyes open, walk very slowly and lightly, and work to windward. If a deer passes a person's front while he is out stalking, he may cause it to halt long enough to get a shot by giving a sharp whistle or call, as its curiosity is so strong that it wants to know the meaning of every unusual sound and the character of every strange object, even when the hounds are in full pursuit. I have shot several that would have dashed past me in full flight but for this ruse, and I remember few cases in which I failed to cause a halt by its means. The stop might be only for a second or two, yet it was long enough to give a good opportunity for firing. Cautious as the mule deer is, it will halt on hearing the signal, even in the open, and with the hunter in plain view; for if it is one of the most vigilant, it is also one of the most inquisitive of its family.

This fine animal, which seems to be the connecting link between the wapiti and the smaller deer, derives its name from the length of its ears and the form of its tail. The former, which are eight or nine inches long, are well bent 'forward, and are constantly in motion, as if trying to catch every sound; and the latter, which is about the same length, is rendered conspicuously prominent by the fact that it is thin and rat-like, bare of all hair beneath, but well covered with white hair above, while the outer tip is decorated with a tuft of black hairs two or three inches long. This deer attains a height of from three and a half to four feet, and weighs from one hundred and eighty to about three hundred pounds. The body is round, and generally full in outline, and the legs are so long, slender, and graceful that they seem scarcely strong enough to carry the heavy body which they support; and one would certainly never give them credit for the power they display in making the stupendous bounds which have made the animal famous as the "jumping deer." I have seen it leap over matted trees and branches which must have been all of twelve or fourteen feet in height; and on one occasion it bounded over a fallen monarch of the forest, a gigantic pine, which we found by measurement to have a circumference of twenty-four feet at the base, and to be elevated four or five feet from the ground, by the quantity of soil attached to its roots. Its ability to leap is a favorite theme with old hunters, and some of the tales told by them approach closely on the marvellous.

Another distinguishing feature in its appearance is the magnificent antlers the stag bears. The lower beams in these are well set back, and the prongs jut straight upward. The number of points frequently amounts to fifteen or sixteen, but the usual number in an adult is ten; and if it exceeds this, they appear clumsy, and are irregular in position. When seen from a front view, they look very striking and stately, and cause a person to sigh for them and their owner. During the rutting season, which commences about the last of October or the first of November, they are used to good advantage in the combats between erotic males, and they sometimes become so entangled that they cannot be separated, and both animals, as a consequence, die of hunger.

The sirens whose voices lead the gallants to destruction bring forth their young in June. These number one or two at a birth; and while they are in their infancy the mother keeps them concealed in the most inaccessible thickets, in order to protect them from hungry foes. She remains with them until the commencement of the next rutting season, then leaves them to shift for themselves, while she goes careering and whistling through the woods in search of lovers. The cry of the females and the defiant snorts of the males may then be heard in the usually silent forest; and these sounds give it an air of life and animation most pleasing to the lurking hunter. Should he then be engaged in "fire-hunting" during the night, he may feel assured of bagging many a stately stag and graceful doe, as their whistling makes their position known; and they are attracted so much by the blazing torches or gleaming jack-lamp that they may be approached from the leeward to within a few feet, and killed as easily as cows in a farm-yard. Aim is always taken between the large, soft, and glistening eyes; and as the bullet goes crashing into the brain, death is the immediate result.

The mule deer is seldom, so far as I could learn, hunted with hounds in the Far West, owing to the rugged character of its haunts, and its habit of dashing for the mountain peaks and concealing itself, if possible, in rocky ravines or steep precipices. It always selects the most stony and difficult ground it can find, and where the scent cannot lie well; hence it escapes in the majority of cases. When the bucks isolate themselves to grow their horns, they assemble in small groups occasionally, and frequently use the same bed several nights in succession, especially if they are not hunted much. Thinking I could avail myself of this characteristic to bag some, I tried to run them with hounds on one occasion, but soon found I could do nothing, as they separated at the first signal of the dogs, and ran in different directions toward the summit. Presuming some would return on what I supposed to be a regular run-way, I posted myself there, but I waited in vain, for none came near me; as they kept a straight course, and led the pursuers a merry race among rocky pinnacles, where the line was soon lost. I heard the hounds giving tongue at intervals among the peaks; but as they seemed to remain in one spot, I sounded the recall, and they came back with an evident air of being nicely outwitted that time.

Thinking I might be able to capture one after all, I made a cast on a new line; but before the dogs had run what I should imagine to be a mile, they became silent. I followed their tracks as well as I could for three or four miles, and found them pottering about in the most indecisive manner amidst ledges of trap-rock and a grassless soil that would scarcely retain the odor of a polecat. I then learned that their apparent proximity was due to the resonant echoes of the mountain and forest, and that I had had a hard tramp for nothing. On looking for the slot or seal of the deer they had been pursuing, I saw that it led into a ravine, and, on entering this, I detected the wily character of the animal immediately; for when it entered the rivulet it did not emerge on the other side, but waded downward with the current. Not caring to go on a wild-goose chase, I retraced my footsteps, and went back to town without a trophy. That was my first and last attempt at hunting the macrotian creature with hounds; though I would not presume to infer from this failure that it cannot be pursued to good advantage with dogs in a less difficult region than the one I was in.

The best time for hunting it is when the early snows of winter force it to descend to the foot-hills in order to secure food and shelter. One may stalk it then rather easily, if it has not been hunted much, as it seems loath to leave its coverts, and is not so liable to head for the steep summits on the first alarm. If one can secure a good position in a frequented run-way during this annual migration, he may reap a large deer harvest, for the animals come trooping down rapidly in single file, and seem more anxious to reach their destination than to avoid danger. If the hunter should have a rifle that carries a small charge of powder and a heavy ball, he is more likely to be successful than if he were armed with the usual hunting weapons; as the report is not so great as that of the latter, nor are the woods so prompt in echoing it. It sounds more like the crash of a branch than an indication of danger; hence the deer are not so readily alarmed by it. I heard of a man who killed over a hundred on one stand in a mountain pass in Colorado; and he would have probably slain as many more had he not been injured seriously by the charge of a furious buck he had wounded, and disdained to avoid until it was too late to escape a thrust.

It is nothing unusual for an experienced hunter to bag from two to five deer in a day, if they are at all numerous; and I heard of a hunter who killed ten between sunrise and sunset; and I knew a French half-breed to claim the death of fifteen after an absence of fifty-six hours.

The number killed in a week by those who supply the market, or hunt for others under contract, is almost incredible to persons whose greatest exploit has been to bag a stag in a week, perhaps, or who do not know how abundant deer are in portions of the West. Were they told that a man has killed two hundred and thirty wapitis, eighty deer, and several buffaloes in two weeks, they would be likely to consider the matter for awhile at least before giving it credence; yet it has been done, I understand, by Dr. Carver; and I knew a stock-raiser who was said to have killed thirty mule deer from Monday to Saturday in Idaho County, Idaho Territory; but there the animals were numerous indeed, and, according to his statement, "were almost as thick as flies in June." This is one of the best game regions in the West, as nearly every large quadruped peculiar to the country may be found there.

One of the most interesting week's sport that I had in the West was in that section of country. The party was limited to two, as our purpose was to devote our attention specially to the mule deer, which was said to be very abundant, and little hunted. My companion was a veteran Nimrod who had, in former years, lived by trapping, but who, when the country began to get settled up, and gold and silver were discovered there, turned miner, only to change after awhile to a stock-raiser and rancher. His career had been one of arduous toil and bold adventure, and he had had more than one contest with Indians and wild animals; yet, notwithstanding his hard and unsympathetic life, his heart was as tender as a woman's, and he had a species of chivalry which, though rude, was founded on as high principles of honor as those which governed the conduct of the most famous knights of old.

Bold and daring, and ready to meet any man with deadly weapons in a moment should he give him cause therefor, yet he would be the first to help him afterward if he were worthy of it. Strong in friendship, generous in character, tender and true, he was a fine type of those men who formerly lived on the wild frontier, but who are now passing away, owing to the settling up of the country, and the cessation, comparatively speaking, of the fur trade in regions where no other business was once known. Hunter, trapper, and Indian fighter, it could be well said of him, as it was of one of his prototypes:

> "And the happy, careless rover,
> Through the wilds he wandered over,
> Told his deeds by glade and cover
> All along the wild frontier.
> Oft the squirrel, listening near,
> When long-parted comrades greeted,
> Heard the wondrous tales repeated;
> Heard that when the game was started,
> Sped their fortunes well or not,
> He was still the lightest-hearted,
> And the surest rifle-shot."

Under his guidance I wended my way to the Bitter Root Mountains; and as I have cause to long remember the scene of our hunt, I have entered into unusual details to show what manner of men are often met with in the West.

We took with us a small tent, a generous supply of food and tobacco, a full equipment of arms, and a large mastiff to act as camp guard. Each rode a hardy mustang, and we had two mules which acted as pack animals. A march of twenty miles brought us to the hunting-ground late in the evening, and there we pitched our camp, near a rivulet, and in a dense thicket of firs, pines, and larches.

When supper was finished, my companion fell to relating reminiscences of his life; and so interesting were they to me that it was past one o'clock before we retired to our humble couch on the ground. We had been asleep half an hour, perhaps, when I was awakened by the loud wailing of a woman; and this sounded so strange in that wild region that I jumped to my feet at once, and listened attentively for a few moments in order to find out the direction whence the crying emanated. I supposed at first that the moaning was that of somebody in distress; but before I had decided what to do, my comrade, whom I supposed to be asleep, said, "That's nothing; only a squaw crying about some of her dead relations."

"How came the squaw here?" said I.

"I don't know," was the laconic reply, "unless there's a camp somewhere near us."

As I was rather anxious to know positively the cause of the wailing, he arose, and both of us having armed ourselves, we started in the direction whence we heard it, I for one feeling somewhat alarmed, as I feared something was amiss. A walk of five minutes in the dense forest, through which the moonbeams could scarcely penetrate, led us into a small glade in which several trees grew in a clump; and on reaching this place we halted, as the wailing seemed to issue from that thicket.

As I could see no camp there, nor any signs of one, I was rather dubious about the correctness of my friend's surmises, and told him so; but he cleared my doubts in a moment by saying that the coppice was a burial-ground of a band or tribe of Indians, who often camped there during the summer when they were out gathering roots and berries, or on the march for the buffalo-grounds of Montana or British America.

As the moon was then shining brightly, I expressed a strong desire to visit the cemetery to see what it looked like. He objected at first, saying that Indians did not like to have white men intrude on such sacred ground; yet when he saw how anxious I was about the matter, he complied with my wishes, and we entered the copse together. We had scarcely done so, however, than the crying ceased, and a moment later we saw a squaw gliding through the trees like a shadow, and before we could assure her of our friendly character, she disappeared as suddenly as if the ground had swallowed her up.

When he beheld this, he said, in the most laconic manner possible, "That means trouble for us, I fear."

"Why?" said I.

"Because she'll tell her people, who can't be far off, that there are white strangers here; and as they are naturally of a suspicious disposition, they may think we have some designs against them; and if they do not attack us, they may try to steal our animals."

"What ought to be done, then?" said I.

"Get out of here as quickly as possible," said he, "and go to camp and put out the fire, so that they cannot find us by its light. They won't attempt to harm us now, as they have a superstitious fear of making a night attack; and if they try to hunt us up in the morning we know that they mean mischief, and we also know what we ought to do."

This state of affairs was not pleasant to contemplate, and I chided myself for my stubborn curiosity; but when I saw that my companion displayed no change in his looks or demeanor, I felt reassured, and hoped I had not placed him in any serious predicament.

On reaching camp, we found it surrounded with gray wolves; but they were too cautious to make a raid on our edibles or animals, owing to their fear of the mastiff, which was tied near the tent, and barking loudly. The mules seemed to be in the greatest state of alarm, for they strained at their pickets, and plunged and neighed with fright. Fearing that our steeds would break away, and that we might be left to the mercies of all foes if we did not drive off the wolves, we were compelled, much as we disliked to make any noise, to open fire on them; and after the second volley from our shot-guns they disappeared in the gloom like magic, leaving three dead and two mortally wounded behind them. The latter two were finished with our hunting-knives; and, throwing their carcasses on a tree, we put out the blazing fire by scattering it, and covering it with wet leaves and branches.

We then loaded our arms and waited patiently for daylight; for it was our intention to be the first to make a movement if the Indians came to hunt us up, or make any hostile demonstration.

We could not have slept, even if we desired to do so, as the wolves were howling fearfully all night long; and their cries, which sounded more weird and dismal than even those of the squaw, were kept up so uninterruptedly that they would seemingly awake the Seven Sleepers.

About five o'clock the first streaks of dawn appeared, and, as soon as it was light enough to move about, we emerged from the tent, and, taking the dog with us, concealed ourselves in a dense thicket about two hundred yards away, so that we could watch the movements of the Indians should they approach the camp. We adopted this measure instead of retreating, for the reason that we did not know how they would treat us. If they intended to do us any injury, we surmised that they could readily overtake us; if they did not, we thought it unnecessary to change our quarters until we desired to do so; neither did we wish to show them we feared them—a most dangerous thing to do; but besides this was the fact that we knew we could escape from them more readily on foot than on horseback in that region of woods and chasms.

In the course of half an hour we heard the mules kicking and plunging and neighing with fright, and guessed, from their actions, that our anticipated visitors were near the camp, for a mule can wind an Indian when no other quadruped would be aware of his presence; and as it has the greatest fear of him, it is by far the best sentinel known to announce his coming. Peering from amidst our foliaceous retreat, we saw ten armed braves boldly advancing toward our mustangs as if about to seize them. My companion, who was as cool in his demeanor as if he were in his own house, said he would be hanged if some of them would not pay dearly before he left them if they touched his animals.

"We can wipe 'em out in two minutes with our Winchesters," said he; "and if there are any more of 'em, we can mount and make a run for it, as I don't feel inclined to try my legs in running over these mountains from a pack of redskins; but if there ain't any more, we have the field to ourselves."

Before they reached the horses, however, another figure appeared on the scene, not twenty yards away from us. He was a stout, medium-sized man, about fifty years of age, and was dressed in a glaring scarlet blanket, leggings of the same material, and a hare-skin cap covered his head. He was evidently a personage of importance, for he walked with a certain air that indicated he was a chief, or at least a sub-chief. My companion, who was waiting for some overt act to be done before commencing the battle, scanned him closely, and, after a scrutiny of a few seconds, said, "Why, I know that old buck well; that's Bannock Jem; and I think he ought to know me. I've made a fool of myself this time, anyway. Let's get out of here at once; but we mustn't go the front way, as they might think we were afraid, and were hiding from them; and we don't want any Injuns to think that."

We therefore retreated for some distance, then struck to the right, and approached the camp in a roundabout way, to lead our visitors to infer that we had been out hunting, yet we took excellent care to have our rifles ready for instant use. When we reached our head-quarters, we saw some of the Indians unloosening our packs of provisions, and helping themselves to some of them; but, on seeing us, they stopped their work immediately, and looked at us with an air in which there was not a little fear and suspicion.

When my companion saw the chief, for such he proved to be, he advanced toward him, held out his hand, and said, "How!" and the salutation was promptly and, for an Indian, earnestly returned. Both then conversed together for ten minutes or more in the Indian language, the remainder of the party being wondering spectators; and when it was over, my comrade gave the chief some tobacco, buckshot, tea, coffee, and sugar. The others received a present of tobacco, but nothing else, as the donor said he had not food enough to last while we intended to be out. This seemed to satisfy them, for, on going away, all said "How!" to both of us, and a few moments later vanished in the forest.

I asked my companion who the Indians were, and how he happened to know them so well; and he, in response, told me the following story:

"'Bout twenty years ago I was trapping in the Blackfeet country 'way north-east; and, as I wasn't doing much, I concluded to go into the buffalo country and try my hand a bit at shooting, in order to get food for the winter, and a few hides to provide myself with tobacco and powder and shot. While on my way there, I met the band of Injuns commanded by this Jem you've seen; but he had some other name then which I don't now recollect. He isn't a real Bannock; and his band was then, and is now, made up of renegades from several tribes; and they never count for much, as they won't stop on the reservation, and they acknowledge no law but their own. Well, when I struck their camp, I was so mighty hungry that I didn't care what I did, and I'd have fought the whole of the tribe for a piece of meat; for I tell you a man doesn't care much for bullets when he is starving and food is near. So I entered their camp boldly. They were as surprised as Injuns can be when they saw me riding down between their tepees, but they made no effort to injure me, for Injuns always like sand in a man, even if he is their foe; and none of the Injuns were then overfond of the whites.

"When I saw the chief's tent, which I knew by its size,

I jumped off my mule and walked in. I found this Jem and his whole family—wives, children, and dogs—inside. The women, children, and dogs were all eating together, so I knew he had finished his grub; for the braves never eat with the squaws and youngsters, and the only company these have are their flea-eaten curs. When they saw me they looked kind afraid, but they never said anything, nor did I; and walking toward a big iron pot, which they must have stolen from the whites, I looked into it, and, finding it full of meat, helped myself to some; and after I had stuffed myself full—for every person can help himself in an Injun camp to any grub he sees there—I lit my pipe and offered a smoke to this ere Jem, who was lying down on a buffalo-hide near the fire; and he took it mighty quick, I tell you, for I think he was out of tobacco. When he finished he gave it back; and knowing by his looks that he wished he could have a few more puffs, I took out my pouch and gave him half I had, and he grabbed it as quickly as a starving man would a piece of venison.

"Well, I stopped in camp that night, but not in any tepee, as I had plenty of blankets of my own; so I slept under a tree. Next day I traded some powder and ball for a large chunk of elk, and slinging this on my saddle, I marched out of camp without saying a word to anybody. I travelled about five miles that day, and, seeing beaver signs plenty, I concluded to try my luck there. I made a nice *wickiup* in a thicket of cotton-woods, and, after that was built, I placed my traps in the creek until I got within two miles, maybe, of the Injun camp; for I saw the Injuns weren't working it, because, perhaps, they were after scalps, not beavers."

"Were you not afraid of being so near them when alone?" said I.

"No," was the answer, "because I knew they wouldn't hurt me so long as I had made a friend of the chief; and that he was a friend I guessed from the way in which he took some matches from me. He didn't know what they were, except that they would light when struck; and as this seemed to be great medicine to him, I knew he would put them in his medicine-bag and worship them ever after, and I, of course, would always be respected by him for giving him the medicine.

"Well, I stayed in camp there two days, but I wasn't idle, for I killed four deer, in order to have plenty of meat for a week or two. On the third day I visited my traps, and when I got to those near the Injun village I heard a tremendous yelling, and, on looking about, saw a dozen of the redskins running out of a piece of woods not seventy yards away from me, and about fifty more legging it after them and shooting arrows at them in a lively style. ·

"I knew at once that it was a surprise by the Blackfeet; and as I did not care to be jumped by them, I dodged into the sage-brush and threw myself flat on the ground. Very soon after I saw three Injuns running across my front, and, on sitting up a little, found that the first was this Jem, and that the other two were big Blackfeet, who were screaming like the steam-whistle of a cotton-mill. Now, Jem having been good to me, I didn't care to see him double-banked; and as I had no great love for the thieving Blackfeet, I drew a bead on them and tumbled them both over in two shots as dead as a sardine-box.

"When Jem heard the report of the firing he turned round; and seeing that the Blackfeet had somehow disappeared, he guessed what had become of them. I jumped up at the same time and beckoned to him to stop, which he did, and we both ran for camp together. I told him by the sign language what I had done, and, though he said nothing, I knew he was mighty thankful; for it was more than likely that if I hadn't been round there his scalp would have gone to the Blackfeet nation, and he knew it.

"Well, when we got to camp all the braves had turned out to fight the Blackfeet; but, before they were driven off, I had a chance of trying my old 'Long Tom' on them, and I reckon I plunked four or five of them badly, if not for good.

"After the old thieves had dusted out of sight, I learned

how they had surprised the Bannocks; and a nice trick it was, I tell you. Two of them dressed in the skins of the black bear came out on a knoll in sight of the camp, and began to act as Cuffey does, by raising themselves on their hind-legs, hanging down their paws, and tossing their head as that coon does when he is playing. The Bannocks saw them, and about twenty went out to capture them, intending to have lots of fun; but before they had gone a mile from the village they ran into a pile of Blackfeet, who were in ambush in a ravine, and these bounced 'em at once and killed seven of them.

"When the Bannocks learned of their loss, the squaws and children set up the most tremendous piece of howling and crying I ever heard, and kept it going for two or three days; while the boasting skunks, who had run away like scared antelopes, told of the great deeds of those who were scalped, though I doubt if they did anything more than scoot for camp as fast as they could.

"When the wild howling was over, the village moved north, and I went with them, trapping and hunting wherever I had a chance. I learned their language in a short time; but as I wasn't dead in love with their company, I left them as soon as I had a load of peltries, and went back to the settlements for three months.

"I saw Jem again during the Snake War, as I was a Government scout, and did him a good turn when the Injuns were whipped. I have also met him several times since then, and always treated him kindly, so that he ought to remember me; and if he didn't do me a kindness I should consider he was meaner than a rattlesnake, or a tarantula and a skunk put together."

While telling this tale he was preparing breakfast, and, when we finished that, he proposed that we should visit the Indian camp and cemetery on our way back.

A walk of twenty minutes brought us to their village, which was picturesquely situated on the banks of the rivulet, and on the edge of the forest. When we entered, the chief met us and led us to his wigwam, and we were soon re-enforced by several others, who had come in to meet the friendly strangers. As soon as all were seated, the chief drew a long and large black-slate pipe out of a dirty bag, and filled it with tobacco; and while he was doing this my companion told me it was intended as a sign of welcome, and that when it was passing around I should not speak a word, as even a whisper was considered to be bad medicine, and sure to bring them ill luck; and to break its spell the pipe would have to be refilled, and the same ceremony gone through with *ab initio*. "I know you don't want to keep that pipe long in your mouth," said he, naïvely, "for it's old, foul, and dirty." I promised compliance with his request, and the ceremony commenced. The chief first took a few whiffs in the most grave and formal manner, then handed the pipe to my friend, and, when he had taken two or three pulls, it was handed to me, and so it went all round the squatters. When all had taken a puff, the chief told them in short, broken sentences, which were vigorous though solemn, how kind a friend my companion had been; and, when he finished his oration, there was a unanimous "uch" of approbation, which proved how thoroughly the friendship was appreciated.

The guest answered them sententiously, and explained to them his purpose in coming into that region, and another "uch" followed, to prove that his statements were deemed correct and everything *comme il faut*. A young brave then arose, and said they were very sorry for disturbing our camp; that they would not have done so had they known who we were; but that, though friendly to the palefaces, some bad whites frequently stole their horses, and they did not know but we might be some of these bad people, as none of the regular settlers ever visited that section. More grunts followed this vigorous explanation; then all dispersed, as they were anxious to recommence the buffalo-dance which they had been indulging in for several days, in order that they might have good medicine or luck in their buffalo-hunts; for they were then preparing to go on their annual chase in Montana or British America.

We witnessed this dance, but it differed in no way from their ordinary rude jumping and stamping in a circle, except that the warriors wore masks made of buffalo-heads, or the skins of the animal thrown over their shoulders, while they sung, or rather yelled, some rude refrain, the leading part being taken by the medicine-man.

All carried their rifles, or bows and arrows, in their hands, and went through the ceremony of shooting and cutting up imaginary buffaloes, and offering the best pieces to the Great Spirit. When a warrior became fatigued he retired, and his place was taken by another; and so the ceremony was continued, perhaps, for days at a time.

After looking at it as long as we wished, we left the camp and moved toward the burial-ground, and, on approaching it, we heard loud wailing again. This cemetery was certainly novel, if not interesting, to look at; for several mummy-like bodies, which were tightly wrapped in old clothes or buffalo-hides, were placed on poles or trees, and a number of skulls and bones were strewn over the ground. The feet of all pointed toward the rising sun; and beside them were placed bows and arrows, old rifles, camp utensils, and such other articles as they were supposed to need in the happy hunting-grounds. The skins of mustangs and dogs were placed on tall poles in some places, these useful companions being intended to accompany the braves in their wanderings through the unknown land.

They do not always get rid of their dead in this manner, however; for if they are on the march they stick the body into any hole they meet, covering it lightly with stones, branches, and dirt; and a squaw or unimportant personage does not even receive this rude sepulture, very often, but is left to rot on the ground, or is tumbled into a precipice, to be devoured by wild animals. A chief or famous brave is always buried with much barbaric pomp, and food is carried to him for several days, so that he may not want for pabulum on his long journey to his everlasting abode. The squaws often visit the remains of their kindred in the regular cemetery, and moan and wail by the hour beside them, calling them endearing names, and asking their forgiveness for any wrongs done them in life. Such a scene certainly appeals to a person's sympathy; but, from what I could learn, I should fancy that the ceremony was one of formality rather than of feeling.

We found two squaws in the burial-ground who were alternately crying loudly, or crooning a mournful chant, in which, according to my companion, they were calling upon their departed husbands to look with pity and kindness upon them, as they had ever tried to be good and dutiful wives. They also bemoaned their loss, as they had no person then to supply them with food, to kill the shaggy buffalo, or to speak kind words to them.

It is a custom, it seems, among some of the tribes, that a widow has no standing; and unless her own kindred provide her with food and shelter, she might starve for what the majority cared. When we left the Golgotha the women were still wailing; and so intense was it that it rung in my ears for several days afterward.

When we returned to camp we decided to pack up and move some miles farther, as we did not expect to be able to find much game in that quarter, owing to the presence of the Indians. By five o'clock we reached a splendid camping-ground in a thicket of graceful, black pines, and convenient to water. After supper we retired to rest in security, and awoke the next morning before daylight, and after breakfast started toward the summit of the mountain, intending to beat downward—always the best plan to be followed in stalking the mule deer. In the course of half an hour we entered a most picturesque glade, which was clad with the greenest of grasses, and dainty, bright-hued sub-alpine flowers, and there saw two stags grazing as serenely as if they did not have a foe on earth. After a brief consultation we concluded to separate, and, while my friend worked to the windward, I crawled tediously downward from the leeward, taking care not to even tread on a decayed branchlet. When I reached to within what I deemed to be sixty yards of them, I raised my head and peered cautiously forward; and when I saw they were still there my heart gave a throb of joy, for I felt almost sure of one at least; but, before I could raise my rifle, they were off like a flash, and running past me up the mountain. I fired at random, and almost simultaneously with my report came another from the left. Rushing into the glade to see what the result of the fire was, I met my companion, and we both commenced searching for some signs of blood; and though we followed up the slots, which were readily discernible in the grass for half a mile, in the most careful manner, we concluded that both had missed, and we blessed ourselves accordingly.

As the characteristic of a true hunter is to never get disheartened under any circumstances, we resumed our journey, and began crawling and peering as before. We had not proceeded far before we saw four or five in a group near a ravine, and these we tried to stalk at once. I went up the mountain to head them off; and on reaching a favorable position for a running shot, I gave a long but not loud whistle, as a signal to my companion that he might open the ball. He answered promptly with his rifle, and, on hearing it, I jumped behind a tree and placed my gun to my shoulder. In a few seconds I heard a crashing through the bushes, and, on looking out, saw a splendid stag come bounding toward me at an easy gait. I waited until he came to within a few yards of me, then gave a sharp whistle. He halted at once to learn its import, and gazed in the direction whence the sound emanated; but before he could decide what it was, I planted a bullet right between the eyes, and he fell forward on his face stone dead. "Hoopee!" yelled I, in the most joyous manner, and, a little later, I heard a voice issuing from the forest, and calling out, "Have you got him?" "Yes," said I; "come and see what a fine fellow he is." The owner of the voice was soon beside me, and using complimentary terms for bagging "such a fine critter." He was evidently full grown; for his antlers, which were large and wide-spreading, boasted of sixteen points, and his body was as plump as that of a stuffed pheasant. We drew his *viscera* at once, and tried to suspend him head downward on the bough of a large fir; but as he was too heavy to be pushed up conveniently, I was compelled to climb the tree, and help to haul him up on the stub of a huge branch by means of a stout piece of twine that was fastened to the hind-legs.

That matter being finished satisfactorily, I descended, and asked my companion what success he had met' with, and he replied, in the dryest manner possible, that he reckoned his deer was making fun of him on the other side of the ravine, but he hoped to be able to laugh at it in a short time. "I'll make that there critter pay for wagging his tail and kicking up his heels at me," said he, "and treating me with as much contempt as a horse-thief would a justice of the peace."

Further inquiry revealed the fact that he had fired and missed, although he thought he had made a hit, and that the animal had been making fun of him by wagging its tail violently as it disappeared down a canyon.

As he presumed that the group had not moved far off, we returned to where they had been started, and followed their slots into the chasm, thence across it and up on the other side. We had scarcely emerged from its depths, before we saw the animals trotting quietly away; but they did not move more than a hundred yards ere they stopped to gaze at us. The range was a long one — all of three hundred yards — but my companion concluded to try a shot, nevertheless; so he picked out a large stag that presented a three-quarter view, and, taking deliberate aim, he fired at the heart; and when the smoke cleared away we beheld the herd scampering off at full speed. When he saw his quarry going as fast as the others, he burst into a vigorous expletive, and said he was sure the buck must be an enchanted one, or he would not have missed him twice in succession.

As every hunter knows a stag that nothing can kill, and defies every stratagem planned for his destruction, I was rather amused at his apparent sincerity of expression, and asked him if he had ever known or heard of an enchanted stag; and he replied that, while he did not believe in enchantment except when exercised by woman's eyes, he was positively sure that there was an occasional buck that no person could hit with an ordinary rifle, and he felt certain that this was one of that class. While this conversation was taking place we were moving rapidly after the runaways; but before we had proceeded five hundred yards he gave an exclamation of surprise, slapped his right thigh vehemently, and said, in the most emphatic manner, "By Jerusalem! I've got him; he ain't enchanted after all." On looking at the ground, I saw several large drops of blood, and, following them up, we came upon the stag in a clump of bushes. He was perfectly dead, and by the manner in which he lay we presumed he had received a wound in the heart. An examination revealed this fact, and also that a rifle-ball had struck the under portion of his tail; as it was cut, though not deeply, from the tip to nearly the root.

After my friend had exhausted his joy at having killed such a tough customer, he said he would pardon him now for waving his tail at him, for almost any "critter" would hoist his flag when it was stung like that. We treated this one as we had the last, but, instead of hanging it, we *cached* it on a huge bowlder, to keep it safe from wolves and bears.

Our next move was to clamber toward the summit of the mountain, but always beating to the windward, as we did not want to lose any chances, and the deer were apparently so plentiful, and so little hunted, that we were anxious to secure venison enough to last for some time. We trudged along for an hour or more, but saw none, though their slots were visible in many places. On reaching a small basin-like tarn, we scanned its banks closely, and descried on the opposite side a group of half a dozen or more stags, which were slaking their thirst in its bluish water.

While we were standing in the shade of a tree, we noticed that they took only one long draught before raising their heads to survey their surroundings, and that some one of them was always peering about. While watching them with keen interest, they made a sudden plunge into the water, and swam rapidly toward us; and, on looking for the cause of their unexpected alarm, we saw a young stag struggling bravely against a dozen or more wolves; but as his hamstring was evidently cut by the cunning prowlers, he could do nothing more than use his horns vigorously, while they harassed him on every side.

The poor fellow was snorting and plunging and scattering the leaves and fallen branches about, in his mad efforts to escape; but, before we could learn his fate, our attention was attracted to the animals approaching us. When they reached to within a few yards of the bank, we fired at them in rapid succession; but we killed only two, the remainder escaping by swimming toward another portion of the bank. I have found it rather a difficult matter to shoot deer in the water when they were moving from me, as only a small portion of the skull is seen; hence, though we fired at them several times, I doubt if we hit one severely enough to cripple it. The two in the lake were pulled ashore by my friend, who dragged them after him one by one until they were in water so shallow that we could both pull them on *terra firma* together.

When they were landed, which required no small effort to accomplish, we turned our attention to the wolves, and ran as fast as we could around the lake in their direction. When we reached to within one or two hundred yards of them we halted to watch their actions, and to get a shot at them if possible. A momentary glance revealed to us the fact that they were fighting and snarling over the slain animal; but we could see nothing of it, so closely were they grouped about it. We therefore concluded that we might bag one or two, owing to their heedlessness to all things but the feast they were enjoying; so we advanced toward them as stealthily as possible, and got to within fifty yards of them before we were detected.

They showed little fear of us, however, for they did not

attempt to escape; and as we intended to make hay while the sun shone, we opened a rapid fire on them, and kept it up for several seconds. When we ceased the majority of the pack were gone, but they left five of their comrades, dead and wounded, behind them. Two were killed outright; and the other three were so badly crippled that they could not escape; and these we soon finished with our revolvers. They made no effort to show fight, and we could have kicked them without, apparently, eliciting any more display of feeling from them than a howl of pain.

Having had a most unexpected and unusual, if not extraordinary, morning's sport, we decided to place all our game together in a secure *cache*, and to take home only one buck for fresh meat. It took us four hours of hard walking and steady toil to accomplish this; and, when we finished, we were as weary a pair of hunters as the country could produce that day. When we returned to camp we found its faithful guardian dozing near the fire, and received from him a joyous greeting.

While my comrade attended to the preparations for supper I went for water to the rivulet; and there I found a splendid yearling doe lying dead, her throat being cut open and torn from the jowl to near the chest. I supposed at first it was the work of a cougar, but, on tilting up the legs, I saw the blood run out; and knowing the habit that animal has of drinking up the life fluid before it touches anything else, and then dragging the body away to a place of concealment, I concluded I had guessed wrongly that time; yet I knew it could not have been wolves that had killed her, or they would have eaten her in the twinkling of an eye. I was sorely puzzled to account for her death, and, when I returned to camp, I told my companion of the fact. "It must be Dick's work," said he; "and, if it is, we'll soon know it." Calling the dog, we returned to the rivulet, and when we approached it that intelligent fellow ran forward and commenced worrying the animal—a proof that he had seen it before; so we decided that he was the hero of the occasion.

When we carried it back we cut it up, and cooked a portion of it for dinner; and I must say it was the tenderest and most succulent venison I had ever tasted. We hung what we did not use on a tree; but its smell brought so many wolves about the camp during the night that they annoyed us sorely, and we had to use our rifles and shotguns occasionally on them, always taking aim at the shining eyes, which were illumined so brightly by the fire that they seemed to glow. We killed seven of them before eleven o'clock, and after that time they gave us a rest, though their melancholy howling rung in our ears all night long.

My companion told me during the evening that he had never seen a deer so easily captured by wolves as the one in the morning, and he attributed it to its being surprised. Deer always head for the water, it seems, when pursued by these animals; but he never knew the latter to follow them through it, though he had seen them head one off in a lake, and finally capture it by keeping it swimming until it was so exhausted that it could make no defence against them.

We hunted in this section for two days with splendid success, then descended to the foot-hills, in order to bag some does and fawns; for the latter rarely go as high up on the mountains as the males, as they think they enjoy greater security by hiding in the thickets than in bounding over the rocky pinnacles. Another reason advanced by hunters for this characteristic is, that when the fawns are young they have not the sense of smell, so that they are more likely to escape their many foes when concealed in thickets than if they had the sense fully developed, and kept to open ground. Dams also prefer such places to secrete their youngsters while they are out grazing; so that it is evidently a wise choice on their part to keep to the foothills. The ground being wet, we decided to make a bed for ourselves that would lift us out of the reach of rheumatism; and this we did by driving four crotches, sharpened at one end, into the ground, and placing stout boughs upon them. We then put branches across the main supports in the same manner as slats are in the ordinary wooden bedstead, and these we covered with a generous supply of the branchlets of pine, fir, and larch, until we had completed a fragrant couch fit for the gods. Over this we spread our blankets; and after pressing it once or twice to see that it was soft, we were perfectly contented with it, and enjoyed, in anticipation, a stretch upon it after the toils of a day's hunting. Having partaken of a hearty dinner, we set out in quest of deer; but after a tramp of two hours we saw nothing at which to fire, except some coveys of blue grouse; but as we did not care to waste ammunition on them just then, we allowed them to rest in peace. While loitering along on our way back to camp, my friend called my attention to the outline of a deer's head, which was visible through the shrubbery about thirty or forty yards away. The animal was evidently looking at us with the greatest curiosity, and trying to decide to what species we belonged. As we were at a halt, and to the leeward, it did not become alarmed; and I do not know how long it would have remained staring at us, had not my companion asked me to fire at it. Taking deliberate aim, I pulled the trigger slowly, and, when the report ceased, I heard a heavy crashing in the undergrowth. On reaching the spot, we found a handsome doe lying dead, the ball having entered the skull near the top, and coming out at the back part. She was such a handsome creature that I felt almost sorry for killing her, and actually wished her alive again. On looking at her, I could not help noting the ridiculous contrast which her huge, awkward-looking ears and rat-like tail presented to her fine body and graceful limbs; and this caused me to think that Nature must have some special purpose in view in combining the graceful and the ludicrous in the same animal or thing.

Leaving her where she fell, we commenced beating down and across the wind, and soon espied two does and their fawns a short distance ahead; but, before we could fire at them, they went scurrying to the right up the hill. Still onward we toiled; but though we saw several fawns and their dams, they were off like a flash the moment they espied us. I always found it an exceedingly difficult matter to approach does when their fawns were with them, as they fled immediately on beholding any strange object; and the crackling of boughs or the brushing of leaves caused them to stampede even before the hunter appeared in sight. Their long ears catch sounds a great distance off, and their sight is also fairly sharp; so that one has to move in the most circumspect manner, and halt frequently, if he would bag them. We found it a much easier matter to stalk the stags than the does, so we concluded that we had not improved our prospects much by a change of camp. We kept up our hope, however, and toiled away until near sunset, when we came suddenly upon a group of does and fawns as they were drinking in a ravine a few feet below us. We approached them so cautiously that they did not hear us, and it was not until we stood over them that they detected our presence. On recognizing us, however, they were off like a shot, and, as they dashed up the opposite side, we let drive at them. Following in rapid pursuit, we found one dead within a distance of three hundred yards, the ball having entered the spinal column at the root of the tail, and from traces of blood seen farther on, we deduced that another was wounded. We followed the trail at a rapid run for a mile or more; but not seeing anything of the injured animal, we returned to the slain one, and carried it to camp by slinging it on a pole by the hind-legs, and placing the pole on our shoulders. The first doe killed was brought in a little later, and all our trophies were then placed together after the *viscera* were drawn.

We hunted in these mountains seven days, and killed twenty deer, a few wolves, and several brace of pine hens; but we could have done much better if we had kept to the peaks instead of the foot-hills; for the stags, cautious as they may be, cannot be compared in this characteristic with does having fawns by their sides. Our departure homeward was hastened by having a polecat invade our camp— an intrusion which the dog resented, so he killed it; but not before he received such a shower of perfume as made him the bane of every person he came in contact with for a week or two afterward.

Our stock of venison was so large that we had to transport it in detail on the backs of the mules and mustangs to the valley, and this required two days to accomplish; for some of the deer were so heavy that one was an ample load over rough ground. When all were together we *cached* them in a ravine; and while my friend went home after two wagons to take our trophies back, I remained behind to keep guard over them, and to spend a day by myself in the mountains.

Mounting my mustang early in the morning, I rode toward the Indian camp, and reached it in three hours; but where all had been barbaric revelry a few days before, nothing was now to be seen except old poles and piles of bones and offal. While wandering carelessly through it, I was startled to see two creatures, which bore a strong resemblance to revivified mummies, seated under a *wickiup* made of a few fir-branches; and, on drawing near them, I found they were a squaw and a buck, who were so aged that their skin was one mass of flabby wrinkles, and so decayed that their features looked like old and crumpled parchment. They were so blind that they could not see me, though only a few feet distant; and it was only when I spoke that they recognized my presence, and gave me to understand by the sign language they knew I was a white man.

The only food they had was a few pieces of dog-meat, which were hung from a pole near them, while a feeble fire of wet boughs was the only heat they had to warm their stagnant blood. Though I could not speak to them, I knew what their fate was; for it is a common custom among the Indians to leave the aged and decrepit behind them when they go on a long march or on a hunt; because they are considered to be too much of a burden to be taken along, and are deemed to be of no greater use than to feed wild animals, which they sometimes do, or to eat up the substance of the young, which they are not often allowed to do. They expect to meet this fate, and do not grumble at it; as they say they acted toward their forefathers in the same manner, and they cannot, expect any different treatment.

On seeing their condition, I built a rousing fire for them, left wood within their reach, and soon brought them in a young wolf, which I cut up and left near them, so that they might not be compelled to make any efforts to obtain it. After this I returned to camp; and I had scarcely done so ere a violent storm, accompanied by thunder and lightning, burst forth with the greatest fury. The rain seemed to come down in black lines through a yellowish atmosphere; the lightning darted like flashes of electric light across the sky; and the mountains seemed to fairly vibrate beneath the shocks of thunder that growled, spluttered, and roared without much intermission nearly all night long. When I awoke the next morning, the air was so clear and bracing that I concluded to have a walk before breakfast; but, on emerging from my tent, I was surprised to see volumes of dense smoke hanging over a portion of the mountain in the direction of the Indian camp, and to note the occasional appearance of a tongue of lurid light, as it shot skyward.

I realized the situation at once; and as the flames appeared to be approaching my position, I struck tent in the promptest manner, and then awaited the arrival of my companion most anxiously, for I was very much afraid that, if he did not hasten, the trophies of the week would be lost to us. He did not disappoint me, as he arrived at an early hour; and after placing the teams and venison in a place of safety, we tried to enter the forest in the direction of the Indian camp, to see if we could rescue the poor creatures who had been left there; but we found all our efforts unavailing, owing to the density of the smoke, which blinded and partially suffocated us, and the terror of our horses, which nothing could induce to charge through the black clouds. Finding we could do nothing further, we wheeled about and rode back to our *cache*, but not a moment too soon, as the fire had broken out so closely behind us that we were just able to flank it without being compelled to get any nearer the crackling flames than to barely feel their heat, though the smoke was thick and choking enough to make us gag a little, and to bring the tears in streams to our eyes. Had we been a little later in getting away, we should have been forced to leave our horses to their fate, as we could not have ridden them across a chasm that approached our position closely on the left, and which would have obstructed our passage had we not been able to flank it by our timely retreat.

On reaching the teams, we started for home at our best pace, and arrived there in good time, much to the delight of the housewife. While discussing the events of the morning and our narrow escape, my host said that the fire was undoubtedly caused by a thunder-bolt striking an old tree, and that this soon communicated the flames to the grass and shrubbery, so that a large section of country was in a blaze in a short time. As the Indian camp was evidently one of the first places to catch fire, it was an easy matter to guess at the horrible fate of the two poor wretches who were left there; and this led the host to indulge in the most vigorous denunciation of the inhumanity of the red race. The fire raged for a week or more before its fierceness began to wane, and when I left that section of country a large portion of the forest was still enveloped in clinging clouds of smoke.

The mule deer, which is known as the *burro*, or jackass deer, among the Spaniards and Mexicans of California, was formerly so abundant in Montana that out of fifteen hundred deer killed by three men in the Judith Basin in less than six weeks, the larger number was supposed to belong to this species. These were destroyed for their hides alone; and as each hide did not probably realize more than a dollar, one can understand how many valuable animals were slaughtered for a paltry sum. This ruthless destruction is producing the most disastrous results; for where mule deer were so plentiful in 1868 that they could be seen by the hundred in a march of twenty-four hours, scarcely a dozen could be seen in the same region in 1877.

The reckless skin-hunters are mainly responsible for this waste of life, for the Indians, much as they live by the fruits of the chase, are careful to utilize the meat; whereas the others allow it to rot in the sun or be devoured by predatory animals. Where these men have not commenced their nefarious work the mule deer is still plentiful; and of these regions I do not know any that are better than portions of Montana and Idaho, the eastern division of Oregon, and Washington Territory, especially in the wooded mountainous parts, and the Coast Mountains in California. To these might be added some of the more sparsely settled sections of Colorado and the hilly sections of Manitoba.

CHAPTER XI.

THE BLACK-TAILED AND VIRGINIA DEER, AND THEIR VARIETIES.

The Black-tailed and Virginia Deer, and their Varieties.—Range of the Black-tail.—Misapplication of Names.—Size, Speed, and Jumping Power.—Character of its Flesh.—Its Abundance.—Great Numbers slaughtered Annually.—Objection of Pot-hunters to Hounds.—Best Kind of Dogs for hunting it in the Forests.—Packs in the North-west.—Use of Deer-hounds.—Where to find the Black-tail.—The White-tailed Deer.—Its Haunts and Habits.—Difference between it and the Black-tail when running before Hounds.—Its Intrusive Character and Abundance.—How Farmers keep it away from their Crops.—Antipathy between Sheep and Deer.—Fondness for Salt and Sulphur Springs.—Best Weapon for hunting it.—The Spotted and White Deer.—The Former a Great Pet.—The Latter supposed to be a Wandering Spirit by the Indians.—Where found.—The Virginia Deer.—Its Feeding-grounds.—Best Time for stalking it.—How to stalk it.—The Dwarf Deer.—Its Haunts, Habits, and Numbers.—Different Methods of hunting Deer.—A Day's Hunting in the Woods with Hounds.—Number Captured.—A Fortnight in the Forests of Washington Territory.—Our Camp and Hunting Experience.—Extraordinary Abundance of Fur, Fin, and Feather.—Incidents of Sport and Camp Life.—Merry Times.—Attacked by a Buck.—Lost in the Forest.—Actions of a Man when lost.—How I reached Camp.—Excursions after Fin and Feather.—Homeward bound.—A Grand Huntball.—The Ball-room and the People.—An Original Band.—The Terpsichoreans, and how they were put through their Figures.—Ball-room Scenes and Repasts.—A Hunt-dinner.—Rambling once more.—A Pleasant Reminiscence.

THE black-tailed deer (*Cariacus columbianus:* Gray) is confined to the region lying between the Sierra Nevada and Cascade Ranges and the Pacific Ocean. Its range extends from Alaska and British Columbia to Mexico; hence it is found in Washington Territory, Oregon, and California, and large numbers frequent the dense forests of these regions. I never heard of it or saw it in the interior plateaux lying between the above chains and the Rocky Mountains, the so-called black-tail of that vast area being the mule deer. This indiscriminate application of names causes much confusion to persons seeking a knowledge of the distribution of deer, unless they kill and examine the animals themselves, or receive their information from some competent authority; but as there is no work thus far that describes the mammals of the United States, they must, if they have had no experience, depend on a local naturalist for their facts.

Having made the acquaintance of the true black-tail on the shores of the Pacific, and having never seen it east of the Sierra Nevada and Cascade Ranges, in California, Oregon, or Washington Territory, I was rather surprised to hear of it in Utah, Wyoming, Montana, and Colorado; but, on killing the species called by that name, I found it to be the true *C. macrotis*.

The black-tailed deer receives its technical name from the Columbia River, and very justly, I should infer, for it is found in greater numbers along the wooded portions of that stream than in any other part of the Pacific Coast. It is a true denizen of the woods, its favorite haunts being amidst the deepest and dampest recesses of those gigantic forests of firs and spruces which extend for hundreds of miles along the shores of the Northern Pacific Ocean.

It ranks next to the mule deer in size, being much larger, fleeter, and heavier in frame than its Eastern congener, the Virginia deer. I have known some full-grown stags to attain a weight of over two hundred and fifty pounds, but the does are, of course, much lighter. I would also feel inclined to assert that it has few among its kindred that can excel it in running and jumping, for I have seen it clear a corral wall ten or twelve feet high, and I have often been astonished at the ease with which it bounded over fallen trees and their high, bare branches. I made some notes of leaps which I have seen it make; but as they have been lost, I can only speak from memory; and, depending on that alone, I would say that it can clear a fourteen-feet wall or fence.

It is not so highly prized, from a gastronomic point of

VIRGINIAN DEER.

view, in the Far West as the mule deer, as its flesh is less succulent and more fibry. It is, however, in my estimation, equal to any of its European congeners, and, when it is not injured by hard running, any epicure might gloat over a haunch of its flesh, and have few criticisms to make on its daintiness. Some persons consider the meat dry and somewhat leathery; but that has not been my experience, and I doubt if any one could find fault with a buck or doe in good condition. Fawns are not fit for the table before the October or November after their birth, that is, when they are about six months old; for previous to that time their flesh is insipid and devoid of much fat.

The black-tail is found from the wooded plains to nearly the snow-line on mountains in some portions of the West, and in California it frequents thickets of undergrowth; hence it is also known as the mountain and the brush deer, besides its ordinary appellation, according to the character of the country which it inhabits. It is so abundant in certain portions of the Pacific Coast that I have heard of market hunters who killed five and six hundred in a season by stalking alone; and it was reported to me in 1874 that over three thousand were slaughtered within a period of five months in a region having an area of less than two hundred miles, and that most of them were sent to market and sold at four cents, or twopence per pound. The retail sellers charged from ten to twelve cents per pound for the venison, so that they realized more than a hundred per cent. profit on their investment.

Great as the slaughter is, the animal is still very abundant, especially in the densely wooded regions north of California; and for years to come it will probably be looked upon as a nuisance by some pioneers in that country, as it frequently injures or devours young crops of growing cereals, and tramples down strawberry and vegetable beds. Its profusion may be judged from the fact that a person need not go three miles from any town in Oregon or Washington Territory to meet one, and perhaps a dozen. It is, I believe, the most numerous species of deer in California, for thousands are slaughtered there annually by market hunters, pot-hunters, and sportsmen. This is specially true of the more northern region of the State, where the forests are still heavy and extensive, and settlements are scarce compared to the more southern parts.

Many of the ranchers depend largely on wild game for their fresh meat, and of this the flesh of the black-tail forms the most prominent portion.

A person can seldom visit a cabin hidden in the forest without finding a deer or two suspended outside the door, while he may see dozens of splendid mountain trout, a barrel of fresh salmon, or the white-fish of the Pacific inside. The consequence is, that some persons live there in almost Oriental idleness; for many might say, as one said to me, "Why, what's the use of working? I can kill all the meat I want in the woods, and catch all the fish I want with a grasshopper, and grow all the wine I want in my back garden, and all the fruit and vegetables I want in that patch behind the house, and I can kill deer and bears enough to supply me with clothing and whiskey. Now, why should I work hard, when I can get everything I want without it?"

I learned from this man that he had earned over a hundred dollars by selling deer-skins alone in one winter; but as he could not realize more than fifty cents or a dollar for each skin, he must have slain one or two hundred of the animals to obtain that amount. I asked him how he managed to kill so many, and he replied that he never allowed a hound to run a deer in his district; and if he found one doing so, he either poisoned or shot it. These pot-hunters never allow hounds in what they call their own country, if possible, as they say that the deer are driven off by the baying and running, and, if pursued much, that they desert the region for good.

In Oregon and Washington Territory, however, the animals are largely hunted with hounds of all grades, from the half-bred mongrels to harriers, fox-hounds, curs, and Indian dogs.

The best dogs, and those most prized for the general purposes of hunting in that country, are those that are rather small, keen of nose, and have a rich musical voice.

Large hounds would be of little use in many parts of that densely wooded region, as they cannot well force their way through the matted shrubbery and heavy fern brakes without much severe labor; whereas small ones can easily pass under the entwining branches, or scramble through the tangled mass. They are not so liable either to get footsore or leg-weary as the others; hence one can hunt with the same pack day after day by dividing it into detachments.

When a grand hunt is organized in a neighborhood, the farmers who are on friendly terms with each other unite into one company, each bringing his own dogs with him; and in this manner an excellent working pack is soon assembled—though in looks, voice, and breeding its members might not bear the criticisms of judges of canine excellence. If the hunt is to last for a week or two, the hounds are divided into groups, and those that run one day are left in camp the next; and when rested in this manner they are able to work uninterruptedly for three or four weeks at a time, and to run from five to twenty deer in a day. Those persons who relish the cry of the hounds as much as the haunch of venison, keep seven or eight couples of good dogs and run them together, and their "sweet voice" causes the forests to ring with melodious strains from morning till night. There are few more pleasing sounds than the cry of a clear-voiced pack amidst the woods and mountains of the country, as every note is echoed and re-echoed in stentorian tones over an area several miles square; and this gives one an idea that thousands of dogs are giving tongue at the same time. Another advantage that a slow-going pack has over a swift one is, that the deer are not driven at such a pace as to injure their flesh, and that the hunter has a better chance of killing them as they move past his stand.

One of the greatest annoyances attending deer-hunting

in the dense forests of the North-west is the number that escape after being mortally wounded, as they seek shelter in the heaviest shrubbery, where it is almost impossible to find them, let one be even Argus-eyed. This is specially true in stalking or still-hunting, for a deer will often carry away a large quantity of lead before it falls. I have known one to be shot in the heart and run a long distance ere it fell, and another to escape for good although its fore-shoulder was broken. This was killed a year later, and when skinned it was found that the leg was as stiff as a bone, while the flesh had become as hard as leather, owing to the paralysis of the muscles. Shots in the abdomen and ribs are not likely to bring it down promptly, and I knew one to receive a load of buckshot in the neck and escape. I have, on the contrary, seen one tumbled over with a buckshot that struck it in the root of the tail, or in the forehead, and I have killed one myself with a charge of No. 6 shot.

To hunt the black-tail with any degree of success, persons must resort to a dense part of the forest; and if the country is hilly, so much the better is the opportunity for sport, for the animal seems partial to a somewhat rugged habitat. It roams to an altitude of three or four thousand feet in summer, but late in the autumn it descends to the lowlands; and in the Far North-west it is fond of frequenting the regions near the Pacific Ocean, to enjoy the thermal currents of air that flow toward the interior from the Sea of Japan. Hundreds of deer and wapitis may then be found close to the shore, and if a person is any kind of a shot he may kill many of them by exercising ordinary precautions.

The white-tailed deer (*Cariacus leucurus:* Gray) is not so much attached to the forest depths as the preceding, for its favorite habitat seems to be glades or the coppices which skirt the borders of small prairies. It is not so large or so swift as its black-tailed congener, and many persons consider it to be inferior in flesh. This animal, which seems to be a variety of the Virginia deer—the difference between them being very slight—is known as the long-tailed, the white-tailed, and the valley deer. Its range on the Pacific slope extends from the Rocky Mountains to the ocean. In the interior basins lying between the Cascade and Sierra Nevada Ranges and the above mountains, it is distributed geographically over the same area as the mule deer; but west of the Sierra Nevadas the latter is comparatively scarce, while the other is abundant. It has, in fact, the same range over the Far West that the Virginia deer has in the East, and the habits of both are almost identical.

When pursued with hounds, it does not head for the hills, and double and twist, as its black-tailed congener does, but dashes straight for rivers or lakes, let them be even several miles distant. It always follows one of the numerous trails which leads to its watering-places; and should it be checked on its route, it will sometimes turn back and run until it is caught by the hounds. Its jumps are shorter and quicker than those of the black-tail, and it also seems to tire more readily, for I have known it to be captured by rather slow dogs in a run of three or four hours.

This species is so abundant in many parts of the Northwest as to be also considered a nuisance, and ranchers are often compelled to scatter poison over a portion of their young crops to keep it away, especially if their farm is situated in the dense woods, and the animals are not hunted much. During the rutting season the male becomes very bold, and does not hesitate a moment to leap over a fence to lead his chosen mate to the dainty young cereals that the pioneer has planted near his house. It destroys these very frequently; hence those persons who live close to forests have to keep dogs to drive the intruders away. I knew a man in Washington Territory to kill several one evening with a rifle from his bedroom window, and I have shot three myself in a garden within an hour on a moonlight night.

When its numbers become less, some pioneers in that country will be glad of it, for at present many consider it too numerous, and to do more harm than good. "If I had my way," said a pioneer to me, "I'd pizen the whole pesky lot of 'em in this deestrict, for my heart is broke tryin' to keep 'em away from my young crops of wheat and vegetables. It's no use tryin' to kill 'em off, for them thar women deer have two or three kids at a time, and the youngsters are jest as bad as their mothers in a couple o' months after they're born; and as for them bucks, I think they're the most tarnal impident critters that ever lived. Why, one of 'em charged my little gal when she went to drive him and his mate away; and but for the dog runnin' up to her, he might a hurt her."

This man did not have any feelings about the enthusiasm of the chase, and he looked upon a deer more as a nuisance than as a game animal. He thought a sheep was of far more use than the antlered beauty, and that its flesh was also more palatable; and he supposed that one deer would eat as much as two sheep. He had discovered that the former would not graze wherever the droppings of the latter were found, and that it would assuredly leave any region over which sheep roamed; so he drove his flock through the woods in various directions, and made a circuit with them for several hundred yards about his small farm; and he found after awhile that the deer, much to his satisfaction, deserted the immediate neighborhood, and let his crops grow without attempting to molest them. I have heard of other forest ranchers who adopted the same method of protecting their gardens, and they found it successful. This antipathy between deer and sheep is so strong that the former will even avoid salt licks and sulphur springs, of which they seem madly fond, if the latter graze about them or leave their droppings near them.

Hunters who are in the vicinity of these springs or "licks" kill more deer than they could elsewhere, as the animals frequent them both morning and evening, and revel in the dainties they afford. If a person is well concealed, and to the leeward, he may slay many a fine buck or graceful doe during the evening or early morning near these places, for they do not readily take alarm at the report of a rifle or shot-gun. The latter is by far the most effective weapon for forest shooting, as the woods are so dense, and the shrubbery so matted, that a rifle-ball is readily deflected from a straight course by intervening bushes, whereas some of the buckshot is almost sure of reaching its destination. A ten-bore, weighing about ten pounds, would prove a capital arm for deer-shooting, as it is good up to a range of ninety or one hundred yards; and it is seldom that one can see an animal beyond that distance in the forest, or fire at it with any degree of success.

I have tried both rifle and shot-gun in these North-western woods, and found that I made my best bags with the latter, and where I made two misses with one, I made none with the other. For shooting in the open, however, the rifle is much the better, as the deer, if hunted much, are shy and vigilant, and, unless surprised, rarely allow a person to approach them to less than two or three hundred yards, except by the most careful stalking.

The white-tail, which is largely pursued with hounds in the Far North-west, affords many a splendid run to both dogs and hunters, for the latter must not allow the grass to grow under their feet if they would get a shot at it as it dashes through the woods. Its numbers enable nearly all persons, even in a large party, to bag some; and if one has his wits about him he may score three or four in a day sometimes.

Two other varieties of deer are found in Oregon and Washington Territory, but they are most numerous on Whidby Island, in the latter region. These are undoubtedly hybrids; but they are nevertheless the prettiest specimens of their family, and are great favorites with the inhabitants, who frequently keep them as pets about the house. Even the unromantic skippers of the small trading-vessels that ply on Puget Sound have one aboard very often, and its bright and prominent colors contrast strongly with the woods or vegetables that cover the deck of the craft.

The most abundant variety boasts many different hues, and this fact has given it the name of the spotted deer. Some that I saw had reddish cheeks and a white face; the sides were sprinkled over with large patches of brownish-red and white; the under parts and tail were white; the legs below the knees were of a chestnut color tipped with white, and the muzzle was very black. The fact that nearly all had white tails caused me to think it was an albino of the white-tailed species; hence I classified it as *C. leucurus*, variety *variatus;* and this classification was adopted by the Museum of Natural History in Portland. I learned from a very competent authority that these animals were the prevailing type on Whidby Island; that they associated together and produced their young spotted like themselves; and from this I deduced, though perhaps without sufficient authority, that the variety was permanent, and therefore worthy of being distinguished from its kindred by a varietal name.

I saw several cases of albinoism in the country, but the specimens differed from the preceding in their markings. One captured on a range of hills in Oregon had the front part of the face near the antlers of a pure white, while that near the nose was a dark chestnut tipped with gray. The cheeks were white; the ears were white inside, and a reddish-brown outside; the sides were a dark chestnut mixed with grayish-white; the belly and flanks, and the legs as far as the knees, were a pure white; the lower portions of the limbs were rufous; and a broad, white dorsal band extended from the ears to the tail. This seemed to belong to the black-tailed species, as the cauda was black above, and white and black beneath.

A snow-white deer is also found on Whidby Island, and high up on several of the mountain ranges. This is also said to keep its hue permanently, and to herd together in groups varying from five to a dozen or more. A man in Washington Territory had four of them about his house for three or four years; and he reports that they never changed their color, except that the white seemed to brighten in winter. This variety is said to be new to the country, and Indians report that it was not known until a short time previous to the advent of the white man. When first discovered by the Indian hunters they were astonished, and refused to kill it, thinking it was the wandering spirit of some man or woman transformed into a deer for transgressions committed while on earth; and many of them even now hold the same opinion, and would not injure it on any account. When the medicine-men and prophets heard of the new animal they began their incantations to learn what it signified; and some of them deduced therefrom that a white race of men would soon appear, and that, like the white deer, they would be cautious, vigilant, and hard to kill, and would finally prevail by numerical superiority. This legend is distributed among several tribes in the North-west, so it would seem that it has been in existence for many years. The creature, for all that, is rather scarce, and has by no means kept pace with the increase of the race of men to whom the red prophets have allied it. It is more abundant in the Siskiyou Mountains, which separate Oregon and California, and in the Cascade Range, than in any other portions of the country, its favorite haunts being the higher plateaux of these chains. Very little is known of its habits, but they, apparently, do not differ from those of the other deer.

The Virginia deer, the typical species of the Atlantic States, is abundant in some portions of the West and South-west, and large numbers are killed annually by Indians, market and pot-hunters, and sportsmen. These are stalked, hunted with hounds, or shot from stages erected near the trails they make during their migrations from one section of the country to another. Some naturalists consider this and the white-tail to be the same species, the difference between them not being sufficient to entitle them to particular distinction; hence the latter is considered to be only a variety of the former, if it is not the same animal changed a little by climate and the character of country it frequents. The difference is so slight, certainly, that it would be best to keep them in the same species, for zoology is already rendered too cumbersome by elevating varieties into the dignity of species; and this causes a confusion which it would seem well to avoid.

The antlers of both animals are almost alike in form, and in the number of prongs or points they display. When these are shed the stags retire from the herds and seek the closest thickets, venturing abroad in search of food only at night; yet in regions where they are little hunted they may be seen browsing during the day. They are very active on moonlight nights in summer, and one may then kill them without much trouble if he will only work cautiously, and move to the windward; and if on elevated ground, he should in all cases work down, not up, as the animals seem somewhat afraid of open ground and the regions below.

The best time for stalking them is in the morning or evening, as they are out feeding at those times. They may be found on the sunny side of a hill in the morning, and near water in the evening, as they then go to drink enough to last them for the night. In an open and level country they conceal themselves in the coppices skirting streams or lakes during the day, and remain there until near sunset, when they move out to allay their thirst and hunger. When started by hounds, they head for the water at once, by following a well-known and well-worn run-way; and if a hunter is posted there he may tumble one over easily with his double-barrel gun loaded with buckshot.

Another variety of this animal, and probably the smallest of its family in the United States, is found in Arizona. This is designated as *C. virginianus*, variety *Couesii*, in honor of Dr. Coues, of the Smithsonian Institution at Washington. It is a dwarf compared to the others, for the bucks seldom weigh over seventy pounds, while the does range between forty and sixty pounds. It has small ears; the hoofs and false hoofs are black; the tail has a total length, hair at tip included, of eight inches; the largest antler is about seven inches long; and the general color of the body is a pale fawn. It is light and graceful in movement, and rather proud in aspect when gazing at an object.

It is very abundant in Southern Arizona, where it frequents the coniferous forests of the mountains. The bucks often wander as high as three or four thousand feet, as they obtain plenty of food at that altitude in the bunch-grass and tender shrubbery. The does keep to the thickets while their young are with them, but during the running season they scamper about in every direction. These dwarfs are so little hunted, and so numerous, that they show no fear of man unless they scent him to the windward; hence they may be approached to within fifty or sixty yards, and a group shot down, before they become alarmed enough to flee.

As they feed abroad during the daytime, owing to their immunity from foes, they may be readily found at all times; and this gives the hunter an opportunity of making a larger bag than he could probably boast of in any other part of the world.

By summarizing the various species of the deer family found in the West and South-west, we find, excluding the caribou, which rarely comes south of the fifty-fourth parallel, that there are five distinct species, and five varieties, allowing that the white-tail is a variety of the Virginia deer. The species are the moose, wapiti, mule deer, black-tail, and Virginia deer; and the varieties are the *burro*, or jackass deer, of California, the dwarf deer of Sonora and Arizona, the white-tail, and the spotted and the white deer. It is evident, therefore, that the *Cervidæ* are well represented in the country; and as for numbers, they cannot be equalled in any portion of the continent.

The methods employed in the West for hunting deer are confined to three; and these are stalking, driving, and still-hunting at night with a lamp or a torch. The two first are considered legitimate sport; but the latter is tabooed by all true lovers of the gun, as it does not give the animals any chance for their life, and they are shot as easily as a cow tied up in a barn. When the poor creatures see the light they stare at it in stupid amazement, if the person carrying it is to the leeward, and keep staring until a bullet, fired at a distance of a few feet or yards, goes crashing through their brains. This is, literally speaking, cold-blooded assassination, and is only fit for hungry men or starving Indians: it is certainly unworthy of sportsmen; yet I am sorry to say that many persons who call themselves by that name resort to it, and actually boast of the number they have slain in a night.

I heard of a band of Indians in Washington Territory who killed forty in one night by using torches of pines, and I knew two market hunters who said they had averaged eight a night for several nights in succession. The deer were of course very abundant, to permit such slaughter; but as they are considered too numerous to be agreeable in some of the wooded portions of that country, no persons objected to this seemingly wanton destruction.

In still-hunting, patience and perseverance are two essential qualities to insure success. It is tedious work, though, and one which galls on a restless, sanguine nature. Practice dispels the ennui, however, and the most impulsive person may become the most skilful hunter after awhile. One thing every person ought to practice, and that is, to keep the eyes on the alert, and to step high when walking, so that the foot, when it comes to the earth, should not make much noise, and that the ball might touch it first.

Novices, as a rule, walk too rapidly, cover too much ground, and use their legs instead of their eyes; so the result is too often a failure, and they return home comparatively dispirited. Experience corrects such mistakes; and they soon learn that the less they walk in a country where deer abound the more successful they will be. The stalker would find a deer-hound of great use in the forests of the West to bring wounded animals to bay; otherwise he is liable to lose several, or to tramp after them for miles when he is so weary that he can hardly move. If ever there was a country where that noble animal would be of use, it is out there; in fact his services would be invaluable to those who hunt much, and nearly everybody there seems addicted to the sport.

Stalkers should also remember that, when a deer is startled from its retreat, it bounds away as silently and rapidly as possible, keeping the head very low, as if it would utilize the undergrowth to protect it from being seen by the hunter; hence his gaze should be directed some distance in advance, and he should turn the head from side to side slowly, so as to sweep the ground in front of him. He should also scan the ground for signs, and note where the grass or leaves are trampled, or the dew brushed away from the shrubbery. If his dress is of a neutral tint, and he walks slowly, he may approach a deer to close range from the leeward, as its sight is somewhat defective, and it seems to recognize objects only when they are in motion.

It may be stalked to good advantage on moonlight nights, as it is then out grazing; but one may be sure that he will not see many during the day after such expeditions, as they keep concealed in the densest thickets.

Driving deer is a favorite sport with those who have good horses. This is a very sociable affair, and is participated in by, probably, all the farmers in a neighborhood. After the meet they take their dogs into a piece of woods which the deer are known to frequent, and the pack is left there under the care of an improvised huntsman who knows where to look for the game, while the company seek the run-ways, and wait until the canine chorus announces that the quarry is afoot. Those whose steeds will stand fire remain in their saddles; but those whose animals are not so well trained, dismount, and tie them to trees, while they keep watch on foot. The former have the best chances of getting a shot, as they can dash about and head off the game sometimes; whereas the latter have to depend on its passing their stand, with the probabilities strongly against them, too often, owing to the number of mounted men present.

When the deer is started, if a black-tail, it heads for

the hills, generally keeping to the roughest and stoniest ground, and following the course of ravines as much as possible; it does not dash boldly upward, however, but swings around the hill, generally moving from right to left, and doubling when necessary, and, if hard pressed, it makes for some convenient river or lake. Then it is that the hunters have an opportunity of firing at it; and, if they are at all expert with the shot-gun, they may tumble it over with a dozen buckshot as it flees past them, or they may cause it to halt by a whistle, and kill it while it is trying to analyze the import of the strange sound. If it reaches open ground, some persons pursue it on horseback; and if their steeds have any speed worth mentioning they are sure to get within shooting range of it, for a deer is by no means the ideal of swiftness which it is often assumed to be. Even when fresh, a good horse will push it hard on fair running ground; but in a rugged country it has all the advantages in its favor, as it seems to run as well on one kind as on the other.

When the quarry is killed, a joyous shout or a blast on the mellow horn announces the event, and dogs and men assemble to gaze on the trophy. The successful Nimrod is congratulated; a dose of something stronger than tea is generally partaken of in honor of the event; and the pack is sent out to make another cast, when the same hurrying and scurrying to and fro is indulged in until the quarry is either slain or escapes to the water. If it takes to a river, it floats down with the current for a short distance, and scrambles out on the opposite bank; but if it has been driven hard, it frequently stays in the water under the shelter of friendly branches, even if the hounds are giving tongue within a few feet of it. Its head is all that is visible on such occasions; so he who would detect its hiding-place must carefully scan the water. If the wind is blowing from its direction, experienced hounds will follow it in the river almost as well as they would on land, and they frequently kill it there. On such occasions the stags fight bravely for their lives, and often kill some of their assailants, and escape; but when they are overpowered by numbers they soon become exhausted, and are killed, or dragged helplessly ashore by the hunters, when they are finished at once.

The favorite method of hunting the antlered beauty in the North-west is to organize a party, and take tents, cooking utensils, commissary supplies, and teams into the forest, and encamp there for a week or two, changing quarters according as the deer are hunted out of a district by the dogs. It is not often necessary to change camp, however, for the animals expelled from a region one day may return to it the next, if they have not been alarmed in the interval; hence, as long as they are not all killed off, persons may find good sport in any place they are known to frequent if they get a rest for a short time.

Five of us bagged forty deer in less than four days in a section of Southern Oregon, although there were several hunters and their packs in the field at the time, and eight of us killed sixty in a week in Western Washington.

I have sometimes shot two and three in a day in Idaho, Wyoming, Montana, and other fresh fields, although the pursuing pack seldom consisted of more than two or three couples of slow hounds. As a specimen of what deer-hunting in the forest is, I may cite two hunts which came off in the North-west, as they will be sufficient to show the excitement of the sport, the manner in which the deer run, and the jolly life one can lead in the woods away from all the trammels of society and civilization.

I was at one time visiting an army post, and, while there, the officers decided to go on a deer-hunt—a proposition with which I felt much pleased, as I had not used rifle or shot-gun for six months, and I longed to roam in the woods once more.

After spending the night among congenial companions, whose hospitality is proverbial, I retired to the simple couch in use among bachelor officers, and slept soundly until the boom of the cannon aroused me in the morning. A hasty breakfast was soon despatched, and we were ready for the sport which promised so much buoyant, virile pleasure. Our party was composed of five persons, including an orderly, who had charge of half a dozen hounds, and a French half-breed, who acted as guide. In the course of half an hour after leaving camp we were in the midst of a dense forest of those gigantic firs for which the Northwest is famous, and a few moments later the dogs were set to work on a fresh trail. They soon gave tongue, and their melodious tones rang through the silent woods with a clearness I had never before heard equalled. This was the signal for a scurrying race to get to some convenient points in order to have a shot. The guide placed me on a promising run-way, and I had scarcely taken my position ere a magnificent black-tailed stag (*C. columbianus*) broke cover not twenty paces from me. His head was high in the air, and his antlers were thrown back, so that he appeared in his most majestic mien. I gave him a low whistle; he halted to learn its import, and ere he could decide upon moving I planted a load of buckshot in his neck and shoulders. Before I could give him the second barrel he was bounding through the shrubbery with those long, high jumps for which he is noted, and the last I saw of him was an erect cauda clearing the branches of a fallen tree. I was of course much piqued at my bad shooting, and still more so when I was rejoined by my companions, who commenced chaffing me most unmercifully, and predicted that we should have no luck that day, as I had missed the first deer. The feeling of chagrin was bad enough; but to be taunted good-naturedly with spoiling the day's amusement was the acme of depressing pride. I insisted that I had wounded the animal so seriously that it could not run very far; but this only elicited a sarcastic laugh, and the query if I did not think I ought to challenge certain redoubted hunters to engage in a week's contest to test superiority. My victory soon came, however; for the guide, who was sounding a mellow cow's horn to recall the pack, reported that they must have overtaken the quarry, or they would have returned in answer to his peremptory summons. This induced two of us to follow the trail, which we did quite readily by noting the condition of the fallen leaves; and we had not proceeded half a mile ere we came to a brook, and on its bank we found the animal lifeless as a stone, and the hounds grouped about it. A joyous halloo from our party soon brought the others, and I was the recipient of theatrical congratulations, which were given demonstratively, as an antidote to the previous wounds. We dressed the stag in a few moments, gave the entrails to the hounds, placed the carcass on the limb of a tree, and then resumed our sport.

The dogs were next sent into a dense fern-brake that reached nearly to our necks. They were there about a minute, when a simultaneous cry from all startled us, and, ere we could recover our wits, two does of the white-tailed deer species (*C. leucurus*) bounded into our midst with such suddenness that before any one thought of shooting them they were twenty yards away. It was then too late, as the shrubbery was so dense that no shot could penetrate it, except by mere accident; and as each person seemed anxious to have some excuse, we contented ourselves by expressing our surprise at the unexpected appearance of such visitors.

"We can get them yet, sir," said the half-breed, "for they are white-tailed deer; and after running a short time they will make for the river, and we can get there before them."

To the river we accordingly ran at our best speed; but that was slow enough, owing to the quantity of fallen timber that strewed the ground, and the tropical luxuriance of the salmon and whortleberries which were entwined together in thick, tangled masses. We were there, however, and had taken up our posts, before the musical chorus of the pack began to approach us. Every eye then peered vigilantly into the gloomy, silent woods, as if they would penetrate the leafy coverts, and all assumed an air that indicated a thorough determination not to be caught napping again. The cry now became loud and clamorous, and so close, that every weapon was held near the shoulder. Bang went a gun in the glades, and bang went another to my right. These were followed by a joyous "hoopee," which indicated that the Nimrods were successful. On arriving on the ground, we found both animals dead, and their slayers proudly gazing upon them. Congratulations of all grades, from the cynical to the serio-comic and tragical, were bestowed on them, and these they received as a matter of course, and in a modestly becoming manner. One curious incident about the run was that both animals kept together from the start, for nothing of the sort had ever before come under the notice of our experienced guide. The only way in which he could account for it was that they were pressed so closely by the hounds, which were famous for their fleetness, that their wits were scattered, and they were therefore unable to employ their usual stratagems. They were, besides, rather young; so that their inexperience, as much as any other circumstance, was the means of leading them to death. One fact in connection with the running of the two species of deer, common in Western Oregon and Washington Territory, is that the black-tail heads for the hills and ravines the moment it is started, and makes for the water only when all other stratagems have failed; while the white-tail prefers to run on the lowlands and in the forest, and resorts to a brook or river as soon as it can get the opportunity. Hunters avail themselves of these characteristics, and act accordingly; and so quick are they in detecting which species is started, that the pack will not be in motion perhaps five minutes ere they hie either to the hills or the stream. The white-tailed deer also runs in a more direct line than its congener, as if it would outstrip the dogs by its fleetness; but the other doubles like a hare, and chooses the most rocky and difficult ground, as if it knew that the scent would be lost more readily in such places, and that its means of escape would therefore be better. The former has also the greater speed, but lacks the endurance of the black-tail, which is a splendid type of cervidean strength and power, and, in my opinion, one of the best of its family for giving the dogs a run that will test their pace and staying power.

Having cleansed the last animals, we suspended them from trees and left that section, as we presumed that the dogs had scared away all the deer in the immediate vicinity. We had not proceeded half a mile, however, before a fine buck leaped out of a glade in front of us, but the guide brought him down before he had gone thirty paces. A little farther, and another full-grown stag bounded from his foliaceous retreat and dashed away, with the hounds in full cry behind him.

"No use running after him," said the guide; "he'll go for the hills; so we had better wait here until the dogs lose him, and then go for another."

We sat down accordingly, like men who were powerless, and devoted half an hour of our time to discussing the points of each dog, according as we distinguished its rich notes echoing through the soughing forest, and the merits of cigars that would not burn. In a short time we heard new canine Richmonds in the field, and, as they were approaching us, we jumped to our feet and eagerly ran for cover, for we expected the quarry at any moment. We waited about five minutes, when a buck dashed past; but ere he could disappear, four barrels had sent their contents into his palpitating sides, and he fell, crying piteously. Before we could reach him the hounds had throttled him, and were fighting for a mouthful of his tender flesh. We soon appeased their hunger, however, by giving them the entrails, and they threw their wearied bodies on the ground beside their prey, while we prepared it for transportation.

As the day was declining, we concluded to return home; for we were well content with our day's amusement, which enabled us to enjoy some fine runs, and at the same time to reap the reward of vigilance. As soon as our own dogs were assembled, we hired a farmer's wagon to take the trophies to town; and in the evening, over a dish of savory venison, washed down with some Veuve Clicquot, we discussed the events of the day, and brought from the perspective of memory recollections of former hunts which had long laid dormant.

I spent a fortnight at one time in the forests with a party of genuine hunters, and jovial, hospitable fellows, and never, to me, did two weeks pass more rapidly and pleasantly. Each man furnished his own bedclothes and a proportionate share of the food, but a large tent sufficed to hold all; and though our bed was lowly, and composed solely of straw, no king on his couch of state ever slept more soundly or contentedly than we did. We had three wagons with us, and one of these contained a generous supply of fodder for the horses, so that we should not be compelled to employ any person to herd them during the day.

After marching fifteen or twenty miles into the forest, we reached a low chain of hills which had an altitude of four or five hundred feet, and on the summit of one of these we pitched our camp, under the shade of an old and wide-spreading fir, and close to an abundance of water; for a beautiful tarn and a crystalline river were only a few paces from us. When the tent was erected, each man devoted himself to some special object; thus, while one cut up wood, another brought it in; some laid in a supply of water, and others attended to preparing the dinner; while still another party went after grouse in the woods, or to catch trout in the lake, and these soon returned with more than enough to last for twenty-four hours. I was among the anglers, and was fortunate enough to catch two dozen splendid fish, that averaged about four pounds each, in less than three hours, with no better bait than a grasshopper.

Our dinner-party that evening was a merry one, although our repast was anything but epicurean in character, as it consisted of cold beef, fried bacon, grouse, fish, potatoes, and bread and butter, and these were eaten off tin plates. Our dessert was confined to rosy apples and a cup of coffee, and after that came the rude loving-cup, composed of punch that was hot, strong, and sweet. When this was finished, we devoted ourselves to puffing pipes or cigars and relating hunting reminiscences, until we retired to our pallet of straw, where each man rolled himself up in his blanket. The pillows were not very soft, as they were composed of our boots overlaid with coats, waistcoats, and other articles of attire. If not downy they were not very uncomfortable, and were appreciated accordingly.

We were awake by three o'clock; and after partaking of a hearty breakfast—a feat which was rendered possible by the glare of the fire—we started off in a body toward the lake, while a half-breed took the hounds to the left, so as to run the deer down toward a large stream that brawled through the woods half a mile below. He had not proceeded twenty yards from camp before the pack started a splendid stag, which came bounding toward us as if he had no fear of man; and before he could detect our dangerous character the contents of two shot-guns were planted in his sides, and he fell headlong on his antlers. "Good-luck for this day, anyhow," yelled the enthusiast of the party; and, to see that his prophecy was carried out, he commenced a series of mock incantations and an Indian dance about the slain, and wound up with a loud and piercing yell that would have done credit to a Sioux brave in a charge. His ludicrous antics elicited roars of laughter from the spectators; and several were shaking so violently from their cachinnatory exercise that they could not shoot a buck ten paces away at the time.

After the ceremony of a mock baptism of the stag, and feeding the hungry hounds with the *viscera*, we started toward the river, as run-ways were exceedingly numerous, and all showed that the deer had used them the previous night, judging by the freshness and direction of the slots. Long before we had taken our stations, which were several yards apart, the musical chorus of the hounds was heard amidst the forest depths, now here, now there, until it finally burst into a full and thrilling cry, which the trees and rocks and hills, and even the lowliest shrub, seemed to take up, and to echo and re-echo in such stentorian tones that the whole country in front appeared to be occupied by enchanted packs numbering many thousands. The dogs coursed about the hills for some time, until the quarry became weary, when it headed for the river. This brought the pack toward us; but we could not tell in what particular direction it was running, owing to the sonorous echoes that resounded from every quarter.

While anxiously waiting on a well-worn run-way, I espied a splendid doe come bounding through the forest. I intended at first to fire at her before she got too near, but I thought my chances would be better if I allowed her to come so close that I could get a shot at her sides; and acting impulsively on this idea, I reserved my fire until she came within a few paces of me on my left. I then pulled the trigger, but before the shot reached her she was a stride away, and when I turned round to give her the second barrel, she was screened by a net-work of fallen trees and bushes, which she had cleared with a tremendous bound. I was so incensed at myself for missing such an easy shot that I was fairly crestfallen; but before I had much time to think over my chagrin, a report to the right attracted my attention, and this was soon followed by a joyous shout —a proof that somebody had been more successful than myself.

As the baying of the pack still sounded in the distance, instead of answering the summons for aid, I concluded I had better keep my post, in hopes of being able to retrieve my lost luck. I waited an hour in vain; and though the time seemed long, yet I was not uneasy, for newts and salamanders crossed the trail with their slow pace, the little pewee intoned its soft, musical notes amidst the towering firs, woodpeckers drummed on the trees in every direction, and coveys of grouse went whirring by in a state of great alarm, while numerous small birds whistled and chirped or sang in the heavy shrubbery. The forest was sometimes as silent and gloomy as it could well be, and the only sound that disturbed its brooding stillness was the occasional echoing melody of the dogs, which sounded afar off, and was wafted toward me by tree and zephyr.

While sitting listlessly on a fallen fir, and paying much more attention, even though it was mechanical, to the sights and sounds about me than to the purpose for which I was there, I heard a tremendous crashing in the shrubbery a short distance to my left. This caused me to jump promptly to my feet, and to grasp the gun firmly in my hands, and when I saw the bushes swaying I put it near my shoulder, ready to fire at once. When the undergrowth parted, however, instead of seeing a deer emerge, out bolted the French half-breed who acted as guide, in a state of trepidation. On seeing me he rushed forward impetuously, and said that he had been pursued by a cougar for a short distance, and that he had met a bear so suddenly that it had scared all his wits away. I asked him what brought him from that direction, and he replied that the hills were full of deer, that the dogs had divided on a dozen or more of them, and that they were now making for the river. After telling me to keep my stand, and not to leave it on any account, he dashed away through the woods, intending to take up a position on my run-way near the river. He had scarcely been gone ten minutes before a full-grown stag bounded out of the very track he had been following; but before the noble-looking creature could cross the road I shot him dead. Hearing another crashing to my right, I looked in that direction, and saw a doe leap clear across the track; but before she could disappear I gave her the contents of the second barrel. I knew I had hit her, yet she did not fall; so after her I went at my best pace, now clambering over fallen trees, anon stumbling through matted shrubbery, or tearing, with eyes half closed, through dense fern-brakes. I travelled in this manner for two miles as rapidly as I could, the only halt I made being a short one to load my gun, and finally emerged on a splendid wild meadow that skirted the stream. While heedlessly passing over this, for I saw no deer tracks, the doe I had wounded started up about twenty yards to my right; but before she could get as many feet away I planted a load of buckshot in her heart, and she toppled over after running a short distance. I gralloched her there and then, and started off toward my old stand; but, as I could hear firing in every direction, I decided to halt to learn its import. Shots were heard detonating through the forest for several seconds, like explosions of fire-crackers, and, as soon as they ceased, the long mellow tones of three or four cow's horns, which are there used for hunting-horns, were heard ringing through the woodlands, as a signal for an assembly.

Before I started to answer the summons, the half-breed was at my side, and so noiseless was his approach that I did not know he was near me until he spoke. He, the best hunter of the party, had killed nothing, owing to his desire to do too much, and deserting his stand; so he helped me to carry the doe to where the other victim lay, and we placed both together. The guide then sounded his horn; and as his blast was well known, and it was supposed he had some new project in view, the party began to straggle in from every direction, some emerging suddenly from the undergrowth, while others strolled down the run-ways. When all were assembled I learned that twelve deer had been killed inside of three hours, and that the hounds must have driven twenty more at least toward the river, judging from the number that passed on either side of the men on the stands.

Knowing from this that the animals were very abundant, we concluded to hunt that section all day, and to place some of the party on the run-ways that led up toward the hills. All the slain were then collected together and placed under the care of the oldest member of the company, who found the exercise of the morning too severe for even his hardy frame, as he had been compelled to run a good deal. While moving toward the hills the hounds started two deer; but instead of running upward they broke for the river at once, and the dogs soon lost them there, at least we presumed they did; but the guide attributed the cause of their speedy return to the fact that they had been fed too much on the *viscera* of those captured, and they therefore did not feel much in the mood for running. On resuming our march, two fawns were started, and the hounds went in full cry after one; but the second, having scented us, dashed for a fern-brake close by and concealed itself there. We beat it up in a short time, however, and it was tumbled over by one of the party with his first barrel.

The dogs having run their quarry to water, rejoined us, and they were given over to another huntsman, who was requested to go as high up on the wooded hills as he could and beat downward, so that the deer might be driven to the river at once; and as soon as he started for his destination the party deployed in various directions, and each took position on a promising run-way.

We had scarcely taken our stands, however, before the rain began to pour down in torrents; and this necessitated our taking shelter under some of the huge firs whose soughing tones and gloomy hues accorded so well with the bluish-black rain and heavy, murky sky. All living objects in nature seemed hushed into silence except the trees; for even the chattering squirrels sought their cosy retreats, and remained there in mute repose. I waited an hour or more in my shelter without hearing any sound save the melancholy sighing of the accrose foliage and the loud patter of the downpour, and was becoming moody myself out of sympathy with the gloom that reigned all round, when I was fairly startled into an excited condition by hearing a loud snort or whistle a few feet away. On looking for its cause, I noticed a proud black-tail stag gazing intently at me with the greatest curiosity, and expanding his wide nostrils as if trying to judge by those sensitive organs to what species of the animal world I belonged, and whether I was friend or foe. I permitted him to stare for a few moments, then brought the gun to my shoulder; but I had scarcely moved my arm before he was off. I fired at him as he was disappearing in the undergrowth, giving him both barrels in rapid succession; and when I went to seek him, I found him lying dead within one or two hundred yards of where he had vanished from sight. He was hit with only one buckshot; but that reached a vulnerable part, the end of the spinal column. He would have fallen at once, in all probability, were it not for the pace at which he was running, and that momentum carried him to where he fell. I gralloched him in a few seconds, and dragged him after me to my original stand, where I resumed my weary sentinel duty.

After being there half an hour longer, I heard the stirring cry of the hounds far in the distance; and this produced a most welcome feeling of animation, for I knew by the clamor that the game was afoot. The chorus sounded exceedingly musical; for the echoing hills and forests modulated every tone to a soft, silvery strain, and wafted it in so many directions that phantom canine voices seemed to issue from every tree, shrub, and rock. The cries were heard all over the hills, apparently far away; but they soon began to approach, and I became on the alert immediately. In what seemed to be only a period of ten minutes, the chorus swelled into a grand volume that echoed through the forest from end to end, as if hundreds of dogs were giving tongue at the same moment. Onward it rolled like the peals of some organ in a massive cathedral; now far, now near; now here, now there. While listening to it in the most interested and anxious manner, I was surprised to hear it cease suddenly, and was wondering what could have caused it, when the detonations of several rifles and shot-guns, which came crackling through the forest, gave me the explanation. A few moments later, and the hounds emerged on my run-way, weary and bedraggled; and I could see by this that they must have chased more than one deer during their long absence.

Several of them were missing; and thinking they would soon come up, I waited half an hour or more for them, notwithstanding the many horn-blasts that came echoing toward me, as a signal for a rally. Finding there was no immediate prospect that they would appear, I started to rejoin my comrades; but I had not proceeded half a mile before a full-grown doe started out of a clump of hazel and dog-wood bushes not ten yards in front of me. She made for the river at once, with the hounds in full cry behind her; and I started after them, taking every advantage of crosscuts to try and head her off. When I reached the stream I could hear the hounds baying a short distance below, and, on drawing near, I saw them grouped around the quarry in the water, and worrying her. Having a forty-one calibre pocket revolver in my belt, I put it in my mouth, undressed myself, and swam toward the growling hounds, which were fastened to the poor bleating creature in every available part; and, placing my weapon near her ear, I killed her with the first shot. With the aid of the dogs, which still held on to her, I pushed her ashore with one hand, while I used the other for swimming; and on landing, I dressed in a hurry and ran as fast as I could for several hundred yards in order to warm myself and take away the chill, for the water was very cold. I left the animal where it lay on the bank, and started to join the remainder of the party; and these I soon found, as they were following the cries of the dogs, not so much in hopes of getting a shot at a deer as to keep the choristers from straying too far. With their aid the doe was taken back to where the buck was lying, and the two were carried to a central position, where others were placed with them. I then learned that the cause of the sudden silence of the dogs was due to the death of the animal they were pursuing, and that four others had been started out of a fern-brake, and all killed.

As we had had plenty sport for the day, having bagged fourteen deer, we returned to camp; and while some attended to cooking dinner, others took two wagons to bring in the slain. We feasted that evening on venison, fresh trout, grouse, and our own edibles; but the chief dish was a stag's head roasted whole in the ashes.

Notwithstanding our hard day's work, all were in excellent condition; and as soon as the punch was finished, the enthusiast of the company took a large accordion out of a box, and began to play all the jigs and reels he knew with such spirit that he made some of the more impulsive jump from their outstretched position before the fire, and go tripping the light fantastic toe for dear life, amidst the numerous branchlets and leaves that strewed the ground. They went bounding about like rubber-balls or Terpsichoreans at a country fair, and yelled and swung each other about, in their joyous excitement and enthusiasm. It was certainly a scene of good-natured jollity, and one could readily understand from it how Robin Hood's merry men could make life tolerable amidst the depths of Sherwood Forest. The music was followed by singing, and this was kept up so long that it was past midnight before we retired to rest.

We were awake before daylight the next morning, and had breakfast finished by five o'clock, when we resumed our day's sport as fresh as if we had not been out of camp for a week. We found the deer as numerous as they were the previous day, by going two miles farther on, and scored many a kill; but the number bagged was only a fraction of what escaped to the hills or sought safety in the river.

We had magnificent weather—some splendid runs; and mingled with the soul-stirring music of the hounds were the songs of birds, the screams of the wild-cat and puma, the growl of the bear, the lively chatter of squirrels, the startled whistling of the deer, and the gentle monotone of the soughing trees, as their tops and leaves swung to and fro in response to the cooling zephyrs. The forest was full of life and animation, and its varied sounds made one forget that there was such a thing in existence as trouble and tribulation.

The whole day long was one scene of good-luck in hunting; hence, when the party returned to camp at night, nearly everybody was in the best of humor. Two incidents occurred during the day, however, to prove that there is no bliss without alloy, no success without its consequence; no rose without a thorn; nothing, in fact, whether for good or evil, that does not seem to have its correspondence on the opposite side, to either check or alleviate its full significance. The first was, that one of the most courageous and experienced of the party wounded a stag so severely that he was overtaken by the hounds in a short time, and forced to fight bravely for life for fifteen minutes or more. While engaged in a contest with his canine foes, the hunter approached to give him a finishing shot; but he broke away from the dogs so suddenly, and charged his human adversary so vigorously, that the latter was taken by surprise, and before he knew what to do he was knocked down and seriously injured in the chest and abdomen by the antlers of the infuriated beast. Fortunately for him, succor arrived promptly, and he and his assailant were taken to camp together. This is no uncommon thing for stags to do; hence persons should be cautious in approaching them when they are wounded. The hunter was sent home to receive medical assistance, and was soon himself again.

An incident which occurred to myself the same day is one I shall not readily forget, as it taught me a useful lesson. Having heard what I supposed to be hounds belonging to some other hunters a short distance away from my post, I started toward them in hopes I should get a shot at the quarry; but, after travelling two miles or more through the dense forest, I could see nothing of them, though their voices were audible among the hills. As the evening was getting late, I decided to go no farther, so I returned toward where I supposed the camp stood. I wandered about until dusk in various directions, but I could find no traces of it, nor could I see any footsteps of men or dogs—a proof positive that they had not been in that direction. Feeling that I was lost, I commenced an examination of the branches of the trees to see on which side they were longest, and where the moss grew; but as I had not taken any notice of the situation of the camp, my knowledge of woodcraft was of little use. I then climbed a tree to note the appearance of smoke anywhere, but the lateness of the evening prevented me from seeing it. Not knowing what else to do, I commenced blowing the cow's horn which I carried slung over my shoulder, and kept it up until my lips were sore. I was moving all the time, but I did not know where I was going, for I sometimes found myself back at a point from which I had started half an hour before. I finally reached the bank of a precipice, through which a turbulent stream loudly brawled, and there I heard the welcome notes of an answering horn seemingly to my left. This joyous sound nerved me amazingly, and gave me the strength of a giant, apparently, for I blew a blast that caused the forest and chasm to resound with it for miles. I then stumbled through the canyon, crossed the stream in some manner that I cannot now recall, for it was deep and swift in places, and, emerging on the other side, I commenced running at my best speed, halting only long enough to give a loud halloo or to sound the horn. I received answering shouts and blasts at intervals, but they sometimes sounded afar off, and at other times very near. After travelling for an hour I reached a morass, and a small, deep stream; and these I crossed on fallen slippery trees with a dexterity I could not again equal.

While passing through a part of the forest so deep and gloomy that even the stars were not visible, owing to the density of the shrubbery, I started a bear from its lair, and it went growling and tearing through the bushes ahead of me. Nervous and excited as I was, I could notice everything passing about me in the keenest manner possible. The weird hoot of the owl, the whistle of the startled deer, the howl of the wolf, and the loud whirr of alarmed coveys of grouse impressed me at once; and, though uneasy in mind, through fear of getting lost in the untrodden forest, yet I felt a sort of pleasure in the dark and strange scenes, and the wild animals that surrounded me.

Another hour's travelling led me through three chasms, and these I crossed in hot haste; but finding I was getting no nearer the answering shouts and horn-blasts, I commenced firing my shot-gun. This was responded to by a rattling volley, and then for the first time did I get the true bearings of the sounds of succor. I hastened rapidly toward them, firing as I advanced, to show my position, and finally came to a steep cliff, up which I clambered with the nimbleness of a goat. When I reached the summit, I heard human voices approaching me, and, a few moments later, I was amidst five of my companions who were out searching for me. I learned from them that I had been travelling in a circle, and that instead of crossing four or five chasms and two streams, as I supposed, I had only crossed one, my movements having led me to the same chasm and stream every time.

This chasm had taken up the shouts and the blasts of the horns, and echoed them in so many directions that I was deceived, and led hither and thither, and forced into a veritable will-o'-the-wisp chase for which there was no necessity. The sharp detonations of the shot-gun not being so well adapted to produce an echo as the other sounds, I was enabled to hear them distinctly in the direction from which they issued; and were it not for these, I would undoubtedly have been compelled to sleep that night without shelter in the damp forest. I have slept there alone since then, but under different circumstances, and after experience had taught me what to do; hence I felt no alarm about my safety.

When we reached camp, I was hailed as the prodigal, and many a witty joke was cracked at my expense as a woodsman; but the *persiflage* was atoned for by a thoughtful, considerate kindness that would have done credit to tender-hearted women.

We spent a fortnight in the woods in the most pleasant manner possible, and were almost sorry to leave our wild, free life for the labor and conventionalism of civilization. All our days were not devoted to hunting the lordly stag, however, for we made excursions to interesting scenes in our neighborhood, explored lakes not even known to local geographers, and spent many a pleasant hour angling for the delicious trout of the streams and tarns, and in shooting wild-fowl, or searching for grouse among their leafy coverts.

When we turned our faces homeward we had three wagon-loads of venison, a bear, two otters, and three beavers, the two latter species of animals having been shot during moonlight nights while they were out enjoying themselves. The abundance of trout in these streams and lakes is something wonderful, it being nothing unusual for one rod to capture a hundred pounds in weight in a day. Winged game was so abundant in the region in which we were encamped that one gun brought down a hundred ducks or geese on morning and evening flight shooting alone; and I heard of a hunter there who killed over two thousand ducks in eleven days with a muzzle-loader. I have brought in twelve brace of grouse for a morning's work myself, and when out after hares I did not find much difficulty in bagging from twenty to twenty-five in a day.

Game animals were so abundant, in fact, that the whole country seemed one preserve, and a person might shoot there day after day for months without seeming to affect their numbers. One cause for the profusion of small game, whether fur or feather, is the absence of foxes in the wooded districts; so that, having few enemies except wild-cats or wolves, and having a mild climate and plenty of food at all seasons, they multiply in the most rapid manner. We had our choice of all of them, and if ever men feasted on the best of wild game, we did.

When we returned home, the venison was distributed equally among all the party, my share being given to the gentleman in whose house I was temporarily residing. To cap the climax of our fortnight's fun, the musical member of the expedition decided to give what he humorously called "a grand hunt ball," and to this all the neighbors were invited.

A large wooden barn, which was used as a store-room for wheat and other grain, was emptied of its bins, and turned into a sightly and capacious ball-room by entwining the roof with evergreens, and hanging garlands of the same from side to side, and decorating them with rosettes made of vari-colored paper. The seats were made of barrels on which wooden planks were placed; but those who preferred softer material were requested to bring chairs with them. The ball was an important event in that quiet neighborhood, and caused much pleasurable excitement among the young people—it even proved a pleasant topic of conversation among the old; hence, when it came off, it was attended by the beauty and chivalry of Blank Prairie. The former were perfect specimens of rustic life, and the latter were typical representatives of the ideal pioneers who cared little for "biled" shirts, and tripped it away gayly without coat or waistcoat, while some of them had their trousers tucked inside their heavy cowhide boots. The gentle sex evidently never paid much attention to the fashions, for the dresses of the majority consisted of simple calicoes, which clung to their forms with the tightness of a porous plaster.

The band consisted of one fiddler, who was perched on a chair that rested on two planks surmounting some barrels; and though his position looked precarious, he seemed to pay no attention to it, and to think of no such thing as a backward tumble. When the company were assembled, the band scratched his fiddle violently a few times, caused it to give several excruciating screams, and after producing several cat-like flourishes, he ordered all who wished to dance to form on the floor for a "country" dance. When the lines were in position, he shouted out something like the following: "Now, any of you who don't know how to dance Monymusk had better get off the floor and sit on the planks, because I don't want you to spile the fun of all the rest."

As nobody seemed inclined to move, he turned to a young man near him, and said, "Jem Coffee-pot, do you know how to dance this?"

Jem replied that he did.

"I don't bleeve that," said the band, "'cause I've seen you try it on before, and you couldn't dance worth a cent. But never mind; drive ahead now, as I see Susan Bumpas is your partner."

" All ready?"

"Yes," shouted several voices; and with this he commenced scratching away for dear life, while the Terpsichoreans went rushing up and down the floor and bumping against each other so vigorously that the weaker were frequently sent reeling against the wall.

Everything was done in the greatest hurry; hence what the dance lacked in grace was atoned for in strength, and boisterous, laughing confusion. Half of those on the floor did not know the first principles of the figure, so they went rushing wildly about, while a dozen others were calling off the movements. The more stupid couples were frequently seized bodily by some man near them and pushed through certain parts of the figure, but no amount of impromptu instruction could teach them what to do, and the result was that all were soon mingled up in the most perplexed manner. This seemed to make the self-sufficient band angry, for he yelled out authoritatively,

"Stop! stop! Not one of you knows any more about dancing than a coyote! Now, do as I tell you; and those who don't like to do it can find a seat on the boards, where they belong.

"Jem Coffee-pot, no foolin'; and you, Hezekiah Sheepshank, needn't spile the set by knowin' more'n you do. You weren't made for a dancin'-master. I could get a herrin' knows more about it 'n you do.

"You ladies needn't keep swingin' so long; a ball-room ain't no place for showin' your feelins'.

"Now; all ready?"

"Yes," shouted several.

"Fire away, then," was the answer.

"Now, Tom Fryin'pan, take Susan Fish by the hand and bow to her politely. Bow all. Up and down the centre, Tom, and swing. Lead off, and make it lively. Scoot to the 'ind agen and back here. Come, make it lively; none o' your waltzin' airs here. Swing opposite couples until you get to the 'ind. Make it lively; one might think you were goin' to a funeral. Now balance all and swing partners. That's the way to do it. Tildy Fatt, take Dandy

Tim through the same manœuvres the others did. Hefty, isn't she, Dandy? Your biled shirt 'll be wet if you swing her much. Now swing opposite sides. You'll knock the dust out o' the floor, Tildy, if you peg it away like that. It'll do you good, though. All balance and swing partners. That's life for you; that's dancin'. Even the barrels under me are dancin' so lively that I'll soon be off. Nothin' like good music. All promenade. Jerusalem! what a dust! I'm nearly choked. Fire away, though; never mind me if any of you have anything like 'stone fence' about you."

With such comments as these, many of which were so ludicrous that the Terpsichoreans were roaring with laughter, he sent all through the figure; and, when it was over, they were panting loudly, while their faces were steaming and covered with perspiration.

The dances consisted principally of quadrilles, but an occasional polka or varsovienne was introduced, much to the delight of those who knew how to "show off with them," as the band expressed it.

These exhibitions of strength were kept up almost uninterruptedly until morning, the only interval of any consequence being that devoted to refreshments at midnight. These refreshments were as solid and hearty as the Terpsichoreans themselves; for they consisted largely of boiled beef, pork, or mutton, bread-and-butter, and, for dessert, sweet-cakes, cold tea and coffee, and rosy apples. Each family party brought its own provisions, and ate them off improvised tables made of knees. The only seats the majority had were the planks of the floor, so that they lolled in various attitudes, several of which were so ludicrous that they would make the fortune of a pantomimist who knew them.

The hunting-party had an excellent dinner, however, in the host's house, the *pièce de resistance* being venison cooked in many styles, while the fluids were confined to home-made currant-wine and "stone fence," the latter being composed of old cider and whiskey. It is a drink that soon produces a strong effect, and leaves a person the next morning with a splitting headache, should he exceed the most moderate bounds.

When the dancing-party dispersed in the morning, few there were who did not look thoroughly fagged out, yet all were delighted with their night of pleasure.

I left the neighborhood shortly afterward; and though it is many a day since I was there, few trips that I have made in the West are so distinctly marked in my memory as the fortnight I spent in the forests of Washington Territory and my tarry among its hospitable inhabitants.

CHAPTER XII.

THE ANTELOPE, OR PRONG-HORN.

The Prong-horn.—Its Haunts, Range, and Abundance.—Character of its Food.—Its fear of Woods.—Its Position in Natural History.—General Characteristics.—Strange Growth of its Horns.—Its Glandular System. —Is easily Tamed.—Sterility when Domesticated.—Its Speed.—Coursing it with Greyhounds.—Vigilance of the Animal.—A Herd on Guard. —Best Means of stalking it.—Great Curiosity of Males.—Weeps when wounded.—Twenty-four killed by one Dog.—A Day's Coursing on the Laramie Plains.—Lassoing Fawns.—The best Dogs for the Chase.— How experienced Hounds hunt the Antelope.—Stalking and its Result.—Playful Fawns.—Stags and Wolves.—Fate of the Antelope.

THE American antelope, or prong-horn (*Antilocapra americana*), is found all over the open plains of the West, but is never seen in wooded regions, nor at any point east of the Missouri River. It was formerly very abundant, and thousands covered the plains as far as the eye could see; but it is fast disappearing now before the onslaughts, and the precise, long-range rifles of red and white hunters.

This very interesting animal was first made known to the scientific world by Lewis and Clarke, who found it on the Upper Missouri River in 1804, and met it in large numbers from that point westward as far as the Cascade Range. It does not cross west of that great chain in Oregon and Washington Territory, owing to the wooded character of the region, but it crosses the Sierra Nevada Range, in California, and small herds may now be met with in several parts of that State. It is still numerous in British America and the sections south of it on the Pacific slope, and is found extensively in all the Territories, as their population is very small at present.

Its favorite habitat is the open, undulating, and treeless plains which have a light gravelly soil, and produce such

364   SPORTING ADVENTURES IN THE FAR WEST.

FEEDING-GROUND OF THE ANTELOPE.

succulent vegetation as the buffalo and the bunch-grass. The cause of its limited range may be attributed to its cautiousness, extreme fear of forests, and its peculiar taste in food. Its aliment is entirely herbaceous, and, unlike some of its kindred, it cannot be induced to partake of arboreous food, even when suffering from hunger. The only time when it can be persuaded to enter timber is when the old bucks wish to seek seclusion from their associates during the growth of the horns;· but they will not seek refuge in it even then, if it is in any way dense, and is not surrounded by prairies. When startled there, instead of trying to conceal itself in the undergrowth, it breaks away at once for the plains, as if it depended more on speed than any other quality for safety. It is a fine specimen of grace and nimbleness, and, when in motion, is an ideal representative of a quadruped in flight.

It is interesting to naturalists from the position which it occupies in the animal world, it being the only species of its genus thus far discovered. It might really be called a combination of the deer, antelope, and goat, for it has some of the characteristics of all three. It differs from the true antelopes in having a branch or snag on its horns, in having no lachrymal sinus, and in being destitute of the posterior or accessory hoofs. It is smaller than the ordinary deer, an adult male seldom exceeding four feet four inches in length, and three feet in height at the shoulder, while the weight rarely exceeds seventy pounds. The head is rather short and broad; the ears are small and erect; the neck is short and erect; the body is short and round; the tail is so small as to be scarcely visible at any distance; and the legs are long, thin, and tapering. The horns, which are its most characteristic feature, and which cause it to differ widely from all other ruminants, are worn by both sexes; but they are little more than rudimentary in the female until she is full grown, and even then they seldom exceed three or four inches in length. I have known them to measure fourteen inches on the male, by following the curve; to have the snags five and a half inches from the base of the horns, and to be over twelve inches apart; whereas the horns, where they rise from the skull, are only from three to three and a half inches apart. The great peculiarity of these corneous appendages is, however, that while they are hollow, like those of the goat, the cow, and other ruminants, they are deciduous like those of the deer. This fact, which was acknowledged by the scientific world only after receiving overwhelming evidence of its truth, has given the animal a niche to itself, and it now seems to be accepted as the connecting link between the *Cervidœ* and the *Capridœ*—another proof that Nature abhors a vacuum.

The male, when born, has protuberances where the horns are to grow, and by the time he is six months old these are developed into sharp-pointed little stumps capable of doing injury in an assault. They grow about an inch the first year, and are cast in January; but all succeeding horns are cast a month or two earlier, until the creature reaches maturity, when they are cast after the rutting season. Thus we have the peculiar and interesting fact of an animal that sheds and produces perfect hollow horns in a few months; whereas, in all other ruminants that have the same style of horns, the growth is slow and gradual, and takes some years to complete. Here, then, we have the missing link between those animals that have hollow and persistent horns, and those which have solid and deciduous ones. In its dental formula it is also a link between the two families mentioned, for it has no canine teeth; but it has eight incisors in the lower jaw, and boasts twenty-four molars. In its glandular system and salacious disposition it resembles the goat, but it differs from it in the fact that, while the former is the most indiscriminate of feeders, the most active of climbers, and a lover of rocks and mountains, the latter is the most particular of creatures in its choice of food, one of the least able to clamber amidst crags and precipices, and is at home only on the broad, treeless plains, where all objects are distinctly visible. It has the coat of the deer, and the eye and foot of the antelope, but it has the habits of neither in any particular degree; so that it may say, like Shakspeare's personage,

"I have no brother;
I am myself alone."

The hair of the antelope also differs from that of nearly all ruminants, but it is most closely allied to that of the deer. It is coarse and tubular, and therefore fragile, except at the points, where it is solid, and, as a result, tenacious.

It differs in quality in various portions of the body, that on the face and abdomen being the toughest. The general color of the animal is a yellowish-tawny; but the lower part of the sides, the belly, and a large patch on each flank are white. The mane, which is quite conspicuous on the male, is composed of long, firm, and erect red hairs. An important feature in the animal is its glandular system, which closely allies it with the true deer. Ten of the glands, all of which are dermal, are in pairs, and emit a pungent odor, which is more marked in the adult males than in the females and young, and is stronger at certain seasons than at others, being most powerful during the running period.

If taken young, and treated kindly, this interesting creature is easily tamed, and being of an affectionate disposition, and intelligent withal, learns to follow a person about like a dog in a short time. It is a great pet in several parts of the West, and a dozen may be seen at a time running about some farm-yards. It does not breed in domestication, however, and I doubt if it lives long, as I did not see one older than a year or two anywhere. If it does not join its wild companions, some mysterious disease, not unlike a poisoning of the blood, carries it away suddenly; and when it is severely indisposed it weeps copiously, as if it were in deep affliction. Even in its natural condition, and amidst its favorite haunts, it is often attacked by a malady that destroys it in a few days; and this frequently becomes an epidemic, so sweeping that few are left alive in a large tract of country. The result is, that the animal is very abundant one year and exceedingly rare another; but in this it only follows some hidden law of nature relative to the deer family in general. The last great epidemic occurred, as near as I can remember, in 1873 or 1874, and that swept away so large a number that one section of the country was almost cleared of them.

The rutting season commences in September, and lasts until November, and during that time the males engage in severe contests, which are waged with horns and legs; yet I never saw any fatal results from them.

The females breed when a year old, the period of gestation being about eight months. The young are dropped in June, the number at a birth being one or two, and never more, so far as I could see or learn. They are able to move about briskly in a few days after being born, and at the end of a fortnight may be seen out grazing with their dams. Their worst foes are the wolves; and to protect them from these prowlers, the mothers often seek shelter in places which they could not be induced to frequent at other times.

When startled suddenly, an antelope makes several leaps or buck-jumps straight upward, and stares stupidly and wildly about for a short time before it attempts to flee; so, if a number are grouped together, that is the time for the sportsman to do his best work, for he may pour in half a dozen shots before the herd gets beyond range. Even after being fired at, antelopes will often run only a short distance before they halt, wheel about, and stare in a vacant, startled manner at the hunter, and this gives him another opportunity for planting a few bullets in their midst to good advantage. When they break away, however, there is no more "ringing up," for they will not stop, in all probability, until they have placed a goodly distance between themselves and the object of their suspicion; and this they do in a short time, for they scarcely seem to touch the ground when in full flight; so all the hunter sees are numerous legs bobbing up and down as rapidly as if they were worked by a ten-thousand-horse steampower. They present a graceful aspect in motion, and when a large herd runs together the scene is very spirited. Although the animals are very swift for a short time, and have fair staying powers, yet they are by no means so fleet of foot as some persons have given them credit for. I have seen good horses keep up with them long enough to enable hunters to empty their revolvers into a herd, and I have myself kept close enough to them, when mounted on a fleet American horse, to bring down a few with a rifle in a run of three or four miles. They have, however, a decided advantage over a horse in a rolling country, as their long hind-legs enable them to dash up a hillock with perhaps greater speed than they can show on the level; but where the undulations of a plain are not very marked, or hillocks are far apart, I am inclined to think that a fast horse can fairly compete with them for a short distance. A good deer-hound or greyhound would make short work of them if they did not get too much of a start; but if that exceeds one or two hundred yards, the dog must be fleet indeed that can pull down a full-grown stag in a dash of a mile or two. Coursing them with greyhounds is now the most popular means of capturing them in the West; and most exciting sport it is, as persons can follow the chase on horseback, and, if well mounted, they ought to see all its turnings. Several officers of the army, and even rough-and-ready farmers and stock-raisers, keep dogs specially for hunting them, as the old system of stalking them is rapidly dying out among true sportsmen.

To approach a herd undetected requires the most careful working, as sentinels are always on duty on elevated knolls; and as they command a broad view of the surrounding country, their eyes and noses are keen enough to discover the approach of any hunter, unless he is well concealed by bushes, hillocks, or ravines, and beats toward them from the leeward. Their hearing is also very acute; so the stalkers must be careful to make as little noise as possible. I have often thought them to be as defective in vision as the ordinary deer, and to be unable to identify objects unless they were in motion; for I have frequently sat on the prairie to the leeward of a group, and seen several approach me without any sense of fear, the only indication they gave of recognizing my presence being to stare at me at intervals. They have often come near enough to give me a shot at them while in that position; but the young were the most incautious and unsuspicious. If I made the least visible movement, however, they would scamper away at once, and circle around me at a distance, as if trying to solve what my designs were toward them.

When shot at, I have known them to make several jumps before leaving for safer quarters, they seeming to have no idea that the smoke, noise, and hissing of bullets about them referred in any way to themselves. I fired five times one day at a yearling without hitting it, owing to defective cartridges, or some other cause; and although the balls tore up the ground beside it, or whistled about its head, it made no effort to leave until I, displeased with my shooting, attempted to approach it, and then it vanished out of sight in a second, taking a large herd with it.

One of the surest means of stalking the animal successfully is to arouse its curiosity by waving gently, or allowing the wind to blow, a handkerchief or a piece of bright-colored cloth. On seeing this, it approaches cautiously, halts frequently, and stares in the most inquisitive manner; and having finally decided that the object is something worth knowing, advances boldly and by circling movements, until it comes within rifle range, when the hunter drops it. The male, in contradistinction to the usual rule, is far more vigilant and inquisitive than the female, and the first to be attracted by the deceptive lure; and if a herd is together, the largest stags take the lead in approaching, and they are followed by the females and the young, which are ranged at respectful distances behind them. It is amusing to see with what ludicrous gravity all go through the same movements almost at the same time, and the mingled expression of astonishment and caution they display. This propensity of the lords of the herd proves of use to the hunter, for he can pick out the best of them, and by one or two shots get more meat than he could by three times as many if he had to take the animals indiscriminately.

The sportsman cannot get many shots at them, however, unless he is well concealed, and in such a position that they cannot get his wind; for their curiosity would vanish in a moment did they sniff his dangerous character.

The most interesting mode of capturing them is to chase them with trained greyhounds or deer-hounds, and some exciting fun can be enjoyed by lassoing fawns; for if a person is mounted on a good horse he can run down the latter in a mile or two, and have a bucking youngster at the end of his lariat. I have killed both old and young from cover; I have shot them from horseback with a rifle, and tumbled one over occasionally with my revolver, by bounding suddenly into the midst of a herd; but I prefer coursing them with greyhounds to any other means. If a person is not accompanied by these interesting companions, however, he can have some pleasant sport, if mounted, by jumping suddenly from cover upon a herd and firing away until he has knocked over several; for they become so thoroughly frightened on seeing their human foe that they dash wildly about in circling movements, and do not attempt to flee until a dozen or more of them, perhaps, are stretched on the ground.

I have heard Dr. W. F. Carver, the famous rifle-shot, say that when he lived by hunting he frequently loaded a wagon with antelopes by surprising them in this manner, and that on one occasion he killed a small herd before they recovered their wits sufficiently to break away beyond range of his deadly rifle. Few men can boast such a feat, however; and it would, perhaps, be safe to say that the best scout or hunter in the West has never done anything to approach it.

It is rather disagreeable for a man of feeling to approach a wounded antelope, as the poor creature weeps copiously, and looks so appealingly toward him with its large and beautiful eyes, that he is fortunate if their glance does not affect him so much as to prevent him from putting it out of its misery. The same is somewhat true about lassoing fawns; for, when captured, their eyes are often overspread with tears, especially if they have been driven hard, as if they were suffering the greatest pain. In many cases they are, no doubt; for they cut their forelegs badly, when closely pressed, because, according to old hunters, they cannot, when tired, get them out of the way of the hinder fast enough; and the result is that the skin is worn away from above the knees to the hoofs, and this, of course, causes much suffering. To capture them without doing them any injury, they should be run down in as short a time as possible, and, when caught, be placed in a wagon, so as to prevent any necessity for dragging or forcing them along.

As a proof of how greyhounds can compare in speed with the fleet-footed antelope, I may say that General Stanley's dog, Gibbon, captured twenty-four unwounded pronghorns in 1873, and that a hunter near O'Fallons Bluffs, in Nebraska, owned a couple of hounds that allowed few to escape if they did not have too much of a start. I have seen a brace of greyhounds that could overtake the swiftest stag in a run of two or three miles, if he did not have a leading start of more than three or four hundred yards; but if it exceeded that distance they became discouraged sometimes, and gave up the chase.

One of the pleasantest days I ever spent among the prong-horns was on the Laramie Plains of Wyoming, which was then probably the best antelope grounds in the West. Our party consisted of half a dozen gentlemen, and a scout who acted in the double capacity of guide and cook—one of those men who are unknown in any other portion of the world, and who combine in themselves the qualities of hunter, naturalist, soldier, and Indian detecter.

Our first movement was to hire a wagon for the purpose of taking our tents, clothing, and provisions to the camping-ground; the next, to secure the best horses we could find in the hamlet of Laramie; and the third, to arm ourselves with heavy rifles, revolvers, and long lariats. When all preparations were completed, the cavalcade marched out on the plains just as twilight was appearing, and moved rapidly onward until midnight, when it halted on the bank of a small stream which the antelopes were known to frequent in large numbers in the morning. The night being fine, we did not pitch our tents, but rolled ourselves in heavy blankets, and slept until daylight. I may add that we were accompanied by three magnificent types of the

Irish greyhound, having some mastiff blood in them, as they were kept specially for antelope coursing; the latter blood being infused in their veins for the purpose of giving them that combativeness and tenacity of purpose necessary not only to chase, but also to throw the agile and timid creature. Some pure-bred animals of the race, if trained when young, will not only pursue, but also pull it to the ground; but, as a general rule, some cross-blood, either of the mastiff, deer-hound, or blood-hound, is considered an improvement, in order to give staying powers. I believe, however, that the unmixed race is thoroughly adapted for the work, provided it is educated at an early age; but that idea would be a rather difficult matter to impress upon those whose experience is entitled to the fullest consideration.

After three hours of fitful repose we arose from our hard couch, fed our horses, drank our dark coffee, partook of a slight breakfast of smoked beef and bread, then vaulted into the saddle. Our steeds were in excellent condition; so we felt that they would give us no cause to deplore our want of good-fortune. Moving from the streamlet to the high rolling plateaux back of it, we could distinguish by the dim morning light several groups of antelopes quietly grazing. Stealing to their lee to avoid being detected by their keen nostrils, and to seek the cover of some hillocks, we approached one herd to within fifty yards ere we were discovered. The dogs having been put in leash for the purpose of giving us an opportunity of trying to ride down a few animals, and tumbling them over with our rifles and revolvers, we put spurs to our horses as soon as we saw the creatures in motion, and were soon in full pursuit. Our steeds were given a free rein, and each person picked out his own quarry. I selected a dam which was accompanied by a brace of youngsters two or three months old, and pursued them only a short distance ere I came close enough to get a shot. This I delivered with my revolver at the fore-shoulder of the dam, and when the hazy smoke cleared away I had the satisfaction of seeing her tumble over on her side. Leaving her, I followed the youngsters, which were running wildly about, as if dazed with fear and the loss of their guardian, and in a few minutes had my lasso about the neck of one. Taking a quick turn of the lariat about the pommel of the Mexican saddle, I dismounted, and left the well-trained mustang to hold the quarry while I tied its legs. This done, I went in quest of its mate, and soon descried it on a knoll, gazing wistfully about for its lost companions. A run of two miles or more after this also placed it in the noose of my lasso; but it was more difficult to capture than the previous one, as it coursed and turned with the agility of a hare; and the morning breeze, which had just begun blowing, sent the lariat wide of its mark in several instances. I had to throw at least a dozen times before I was fortunate enough to accomplish my purpose. Tying a rope behind the fore-shoulders of this creature, I led it *nolens volens* to where I had left its comrades, and finishing the dam with a shot in the head, I gazed with pleasure on my spoils. I was so lost to everything but the excitement of the chase that I paid no heed to my companions; and it was only when I heard the hunter's call, "Hoo-oo pee-ee," delivered in a sharp, high falsetto tone, that I was reminded of their existence. I responded to the cry, and in a few moments more the party came dashing on, yelling, "Victory! victory! hoop-la!" A brief consultation was held, on meeting, and it was decided that, as our horses were too fatigued to run again for awhile, we should give the dogs their share of the amusement for the remainder of the day. That matter having been settled, the wagon was sent for, and we went around picking up the slain animals, which amounted to only four. I was the only person who was fortunate enough to lasso any of the numerous progeny that followed their guardians; so they were given to me to dispose of as I pleased.

Leaving that section, from which all the animals were driven by the reports of the firing, we marched five miles, and entered a small knoll-bound plain, along whose crests we could see several herds quietly grazing; but every few moments a sentinel would raise its head to survey the landscape, as if fearful of the approach of some enemy. In all my experience I never saw this animal feeding on any ground that did not allow a broad range of vision; and if by chance a herd should frequent a valley, several are always kept on the lookout on the summit of the highest pinnacles, and if the fears of these sentinels are aroused, they give a sharp warning note, and in a moment after the entire column is scampering at its best pace for the ridges, whence they can survey their adversary. On reaching the valley, we decided to drive a portion of the herd across it, in order to give the dogs a fair run, and to give ourselves an opportunity of witnessing the sport. With this purpose in view, four of the party made a détour of a mile around the vale, and then dashed in among the startled groups from different directions. The suddenness of the attack caused a dozen adults, and twice as many fawns, to bound into the valley not a hundred yards from where two of us were trying to conceal ourselves. As soon as they struck the lower ground the dogs were unleashed, and away they went in pursuit at their best speed. As soon as the frightened animals became aware of the presence of their enemies, they seemed to fairly fly over the ground; but the sturdy hounds, extending their noses and bending their bodies until the abdomens apparently touched the ground, gradually closed upon them. One burly stag, desiring to test his powers alone, broke to the right from the herd, and he was selected by the hounds. Running together, both dogs kept as close as if they were yoked; but when they reached to within twenty yards of the quarry they deployed, and ranged themselves one on each side of it. Finding itself outrun, it attempted a double, but, being checked, resumed its former course, then tried a sharp turn to the right. The experienced hound on that side was too swift for it, however, and with a bound he leaped at its throat, and, fastening his fangs deep in the flesh, brought it to the ground. The second dog, having quite a détour to make, was just in time to help to stifle the pitiful death-cries of the poor creature. While this run was taking place, the third and youngest dog was pursuing a fawn, which he captured in a few minutes, after some pretty turnings and good bursts of speed. When the hunters saw the stag overthrown they gave an enthusiastic cheer, as the chase displayed to good advantage the swiftness and tactics of both the pursuers and the pursued; so, heedless alike of prairie-dog villages and the opportunities presented for shooting some terrified fawns that ran wildly about in every direction, they dashed over the vale, and were in soon after the death of the quarry. The efficacy of the cross-blood in the dogs was proved by the fact that they killed the animal themselves, while their training was manifested by the mode in which they hunted; for none but experienced dogs would run in couples and select one quarry from the herd. Did they not adopt these means of pursuit, they would be apt to receive only pains for their labor; for if an antelope receives more than a few yards of a start it is likely to leave the hounds far in the rear, unless they possess unusual strength, fleetness, and staying powers. Some hunters in that region who live by the fruits of the chase have the finest antelope dogs I ever saw, they being long and strong of limb, lithe of body, and having heads both long and broad. They are not only useful in the field, but also about the house, as they are exceedingly vigilant and, apparently, fierce; for they rush at a stranger with flashing eyes and distended jaws. They are much handsomer than the pure-blooded varieties, as they display both strength and gracefulness of outline, while they are also taller and longer.

In many cases they scorn to chase a hare, and if trained specially for deer or antelope, will not do it at all; otherwise they would be of little comparative use to their owner. In running, they hug the ground closely, and keep the head rather low, as if they were prepared to leap at the throat at any moment.

After watering the dogs, we left the valley, and, moving to the north, trotted across a series of wave-like ridges, where we expected to meet some sturdy males that would test to the utmost the speed of the dogs. We had not proceeded half a mile, ere we encountered a solitary and burly old fellow grazing in a gully. As soon as he saw us, he gazed at the unusual apparition for a few moments, then broke away at a slashing gait. The young hound having strayed off a short distance, managed to get on his line of flight and to turn him to the left; and this movement enabled the larger dogs to get a short-cut, by which they closed rapidly upon him. Breaking away in a straight line, he made for the streamlet near which we encamped in the morning; but the hounds clung to him, and for a distance of two miles forced him to his best pace, so that they did not seem to gain an inch. Our party, who were quietly seated in their saddles, were preparing to follow the chase, as it was rapidly retreating from our range of vision, when it suddenly appeared on the right, the crafty stag having decided to seek safety among the higher ridges; but the determined pursuers had closed the distance so much that, ere he could seek his retreat, he was compelled to double and turn in every possible direction. This was the prettiest bit of a run I ever saw, for, quick as were the twists of the fugitive, those of the hounds were not less so, and they lost little ground in the doublings. Within an area of one mile the animal was turned twelve or fifteen times, perhaps; but overcome by fatigue, and the presence on every side of some one of its pursuers, which left it no means of escape except outrunning them, it began to slacken its pace, until it was finally dragged to the earth by its merciless foes. When we reached the quarry it was alive, the hounds being too weary to kill it; so a revolver was put to its head, as it was injured so much as to be unable to live any length of time. Were it not for its injuries, the gallant creature would have received its life for the sake of the amusement it afforded and the display of speed it manifested.

As the dogs were too fatigued to run any more for some time, we went in quest of fawns, and, meeting many, we spent the greater portion of the day in lassoing them; but we secured only three, as our party were not much used to that mode of hunting. We returned to camp about four o'clock in the afternoon and partook of a hearty dinner, of which antelope-steak was the most prominent portion. The meat was by no means pleasant to the taste, being both dry and leathery; but as we wanted sport and not pabulum, we cared little for that, and ate it only because it was a novel dish to some of us. After smoking our cigars, we again started out; but this time each carried a long staff, to which was attached a red piece of cloth, as well as our rifles. Riding about two miles from camp, we struck a herd, but, instead of chasing them, we dismounted, and, planting our pennants in the ground at a distance of several yards from each other, we tethered our horses and lay down near our gaudy banners. The antelopes, which were startled at our first appearance, began to circle around us while engaged in this preparation, as if trying to learn what in the world it meant. Finding that they were not molested, they commenced to draw closer gradually, until a dozen finally came within range of the rifles. A sharp series of reports followed, and four fine animals were tumbled over. This was as much as we expected to accomplish that evening, so we collected our spoils, and, throwing them across our horses, wended our way toward camp.

The system of still-hunting is the one most in vogue among the Indians and pioneers; but it lacks all the spirit and excitement of the chase, and is in reality only fit for pot-hunters. The sons of the forest were the first to make it known to the white hunters; for, with their usual sharpness of observation, they noticed that curiosity was one of the principal faculties in the *Cervidæ*, and, acting on this knowledge, they made that faculty the means of luring them to destruction. Were the pleasures of antelope-coursing more generally known, it would become what hare-coursing is in the British kingdom, and with this greater advantage, that it affords much keener amusement, and gives hounds, horses, quarry, and hunters a better opportunity of testing their speed, power, mettle, and endurance.

The Scotch deer-hound would, in my estimation, be an invaluable dog for chasing the antelope on the plains of the West; yet that splendid creature is scarcely known there, for I saw only three of the pure-blooded species in the entire region beyond the Rocky Mountains, though mongrels and crosses were not rare. Many of the best hunters in the country know little or nothing about the various breeds of dogs useful in the chase; hence they take no pains about procuring them, and seem to be content with anything in the canine form so long as it will chase an animal.

In stalking the antelope, I have sometimes killed three and four in a few hours, but I have on other occasions been out all day without getting more than a fawn. I have found that it will allow a person on horseback to approach it nearer, without taking alarm, than it will one afoot, and that it will often give a man a good opportunity for an excellent shot if he walks slowly and halts occasionally, provided he is to the leeward, as its curiosity, rather than its fears, are then aroused. A Sharp's rifle of forty-five calibre, and carrying one hundred grains of powder, is an excellent weapon to use in stalking it; and if a person is only careful in his movements, is not in too much of a hurry, does not walk too rapidly, and hunts to windward, he will find that the supposed great difficulty of killing the wary prong-horn will soon vanish, and that he may place it among his trophies of the chase without much difficulty.

It is an easy matter to get fawns at almost any time, as they are rather tame and unsuspicious, and so fond of playing, that, if they have none of their own companions to romp with, they make imaginary playfellows out of clumps of weeds or grass, and indulge in all sorts of gambols about them. Even the adults may be brought within rifle range if a person stands still or sits down, provided they do not wind him; as they become accustomed to the strangest objects which are stationary in a short time.

The males keep by themselves from spring until the running season commences in September, when they rejoin the females and the fawns. They may be found near water in the evening, but during the day they frequent the uplands, as they feel more secure there, owing to the extent of country they can survey at a glance.

A wounded stag—unlike his Cervidean kindred, the moose, wapiti, and mule deer—shows little combativeness; yet he will occasionally charge a hunter, and, if he can, use both horns and legs upon him. He will boldly face a wolf, however, when brought to bay; but his opportunities for such a display of courage are rather scarce, I fancy, as I never saw his lupine foe able to overtake him in a straight run, and a six months old fawn can get out of the way of a pack of prairie wolves before they could ask where it was going.

This interesting animal, like some others, is destined to disappear in a short time from the list of the American fauna; for it cannot live in a thickly inhabited country, and its favorite haunts are now being occupied so rapidly by stock-raisers that their herds and flocks are pushing it farther into wild and inhospitable regions, where it often falls a victim to cold and hunger, or the attacks of stronger foes.

CHAPTER XIII.

THE ROCKY MOUNTAIN GOAT.

The Rocky Mountain Goat.—Position in Natural History.—Its Classification.—Supposed to be a Goat-antelope.—Its Appearance, Haunts, and Habits.—Character of its Hair.—Vigilance of Sentinels.—Its Nimbleness.—Fear of the Lowlands.—Getting Scarce.—Flocks in Flight.— First Introduction to the Goat.—A March with Indians.—A Stalk in the Cascade Range.—Its Result.—Disappointment.—A Ram killed.— Skin spoiled by a Fall.—A Hunt in Montana.—Sharp Terriers.—Their use in stalking.—Trophies and Tramping.—Opinion of an old Hunter on Goat-shooting.—A successful Stalker's Faculties.—Charging Goats. —The use of Dogs in hunting them.

THE wild-goat indigenous to the United States is one of the most interesting animals on the continent to either naturalists or sportsmen; for, being the only species of its family found in the country, and making its home amidst the gloomy chasms and rocky fastnesses of the great mountain ranges that traverse the Pacific Coast in every direction, a certain air of mystery clung to it which made it doubly interesting as a trophy of the chase. Many skilled hunters were, therefore, anxious to bag it; but, considering its numbers, few have been slain, owing to the difficulty of reaching its retreats or surprising it. The Indians have thus far proven to be the most successful in its pursuit, as they have a knowledge of its haunts and habits, and are patient and persevering in stalking it.

Among some tribes in the Far West the skin has been largely used for making caps and other articles of wearing apparel, but it seems to be most popular as a lining for other garments.

This animal has received so many different technical appellations that it is difficult to know which to adopt, but I should suppose that *Aplocerus montanus* was quite appropriate, besides the fact that it is the one most generally used in its designation.

Being a member of the *Cavicornia*, or hollow-horned family, some naturalists assume that it is deficient in some of the characteristics of a true goat, and to be so closely allied to the antelope as to be in reality a goat-antelope or antelope-goat, or whichever is the true name to apply. Professor Gray, of the British Museum, has placed it, with the European chamois and the mountain goat of the Himalayas, in a particular group which he calls goat-like antelopes, and he has given it the specific name of *Mazama americana*, while he has classified the group under the generic name of *Mazame*. Unlike the American antelope, it does not, however, shed its horns; and it may, therefore, be assumed to be the connecting link between the antelope and the goat families. In looks and habits it is a true *caprus*—a fact which one may soon learn by teasing a tame youngster. The head and face are unmistakably those of a goat, but the body seems heavier, deeper, and less rounded than that of the common species. It is about the size of the domestic sheep; and, on account of its resemblance to the merino breed, it is often called the mountain sheep in portions of the West, while the true mountain sheep is known as the big-horn.

There is some excuse for this mistake on the part of those who have no knowledge of natural history, for its fleece, which is snowy white, hangs down on the sides like that of an ordinary sheep; yet it may be readily detected from wool by the fact that, though long, it is straight and coarse. It is, however, much finer and softer than the covering of the domestic goat. The inner hair, which is about one and a half inches long on the adult, is fine, soft, fleecy, and tenacious, and is not unlike that of the Angora goat. The outer covering is abundant on the neck, back, shoulders, chest, throat, and thighs, but rather thin on the lower part of the limbs. The tail is short, and, though generously clad with long hair, it is almost concealed by that which covers the flanks and contiguous parts. A long white and pointed beard adorns the chin, and completes its Capridian appearance. It is purely white throughout, except the hoofs, horns, lips, and the margins of the nostrils, which are black, so that it is a true denizen of the snow-peaks in hue.

Its nose is strongly ovine; the ears are pointed, and lined with long hair; the eyes are small, and are evidently intended more for length and intensity of vision than a broad range; and the limbs are thick, short, strong, and sinewy. It has no tear-bag or muffle, so that it bears no resemblance to the deer family in that characteristic. The horns, which are about six or eight inches long, and are "ringed" half-way upward from the base, are sharp pointed, somewhat recurved at the upper extremities, and of a darkish hue. The hoofs, which are full in outline and very hard, are of a deep black color, and are deeply grooved on the soles; and the small posterior hoofs do not touch the ground.

Its range, so far as my knowledge goes, extends from Southern California to Alaska, and from the Cascade and Sierra Nevada Ranges to the Rocky Mountains; these mighty chains seeming to check its habitat on the west and east. It is much more alpine in its character than the big-horn, and frequents regions which the latter seldom visits. It is a daring climber, a nimble leaper, and bounds over crags and dangerous places that nothing less than a bird could apparently attempt with safety. It loves the higher pinnacles, where the daintiest vegetation grows, and where nothing but the eagle, snowy ptarmigan, and a few small creatures are its companions.

It generally moves in flocks of from a dozen to fifty, but the former number is the most common, as one leader is sufficient; and therefore any combats to decide which is to be commander is prevented. The young, which generally number two at a birth, are brought forth early in June amidst the lower ranges, say from five to six thousand feet in height; and when they are old enough to leap about briskly, their faithful guardians lead them to the higher peaks, where they are safe from nearly all foes except man or the daring eagle. They seldom fall a prey to prowling bear or panther, owing to the facility with which the latter can procure food in the wooded regions below; hence they have few enemies to disturb the peaceful solitude of their lives. While grazing, a flock has a sentinel to stand guard and give notice of the approach of an enemy. The sentinel is always a male; and when he detects the presence of man or dangerous beast, he sounds an alarm in a few short peremptory calls. This brings his companions huddling to his side; and when all are assembled, the mothers and their offspring being in the centre, they dash for the most inaccessible peaks at their best pace, and never stop until they have placed a goodly distance between themselves and the object of their suspicion. Once on safe ground, they throw out vedettes again. These occupy some huge crag or elevated knoll that commands a view of the surrounding country—which is generally treeless—and this enables them to see all transpiring within range of vision.

Since the settlement of the Pacific Coast the animal has been driven to the very highest mountain ranges to find food and security, and it is only near snowy pinnacles that it may now be found. Judging from the conversations of an old Indian in the Walla Walla Valley, in Washington Territory, it formerly occupied the peaks of the Blue Mountains, a range having an altitude of only five thousand feet; but I doubt if a specimen can be found there now. The Indians, to whom it was known as the *wow*, state that it was very difficult of approach, owing to its vigilance, keenness of scent, and the extensive view which the sentinels, always on duty, had of the surrounding country. Their most successful mode of hunting it was to drive a flock toward a canyon, where a party was concealed, and to shoot them as they dashed up or down the bluffs. They succeeded sometimes in bagging one by means of pitfalls and traps; but they placed little dependence on such means of capture, owing to the caution of the leaders. In many places where it was formerly quite numerous, it has disappeared entirely, but not through the war waged upon it so much as its natural inclination to keep away from the haunts of man, and especially, according to Indian tales, of the white man, whom it seems to fear more than any other foe. An old chief, known among his tribe on Puget Sound as *Mowich*, or the " deer," from his success as a hunter, informed me that the goat was more abundant than ever along the snowy crests of the Cascade Range, especially in the vicinity of Mounts Baker, Rainer, and St. Helen's, owing to the cessation of peltry hunting, which was so vigorously prosecuted by the North-western Fur Company, and the gathering of all but a few vagrant Indians on the reservations. This would seem quite probable, not only in that region, but in every other section that it has been known to frequent; so that it would be quite safe to state that it is more numerous now than it has been for many years. From inquiries among hunters, both pale and red, I should deduce that it may now be found in the mountains of Manitoba, Wyoming, Idaho, Montana, Colorado, Oregon, and Washington Territory; but I should infer that it was more numerous in the latter than in any other section of the country. Some years ago a few were to be seen in a domesticated state at Deer Lodge, Montana; and I heard of an Indian family on the Lummi River, Washington Territory, having, what is most unusual for the red race, a brace of kids in their *tepee* so tame that they would follow the children around like the spoiled and playful members of the domestic species.

To hunt goats with any degree of success requires patience, perseverance, an unusual degree of caution, and a contempt for arduous toil; and he who is willing to display these qualities need not fear a failure. A white hunter informed me that a couple of active terriers trained to drive the animals from their lairs, or to keep them at bay until the arrival of the Nimrod, would be the surest means of bagging them; otherwise one could only hope to get a shot at them by accident, or unusual good-luck. They are not, in reality, any more difficult to hunt than the big-horns, except, perhaps, that they are scarcer, and frequent higher latitudes; and in some respects the bagging of a few would seem easier, as they lack the speed of the latter, and, as a rule, run obliquely to the right and upward, even if the wind is blowing in that direction.

A good idea for a hunting-party would be to send some men above a flock, keeping well to the leeward, and for those below, if they have no dogs, to move to the windward, and advance rapidly so as to surprise the quarry. This would send them scampering in the direction of those concealed above, and result in an opportunity for a few good shots, as they dash for crags or the mountains without any apprehension of danger from that direction. Should they be checked even, instead of turning back they would break to the right and left, and try to reach the highest pinnacles, owing to a blind instinct they have that all their danger lies in the regions beneath, which they so scrupulously avoid.

The best time for hunting the animal is the early morning or the dusk of the evening, when it is out feeding in some rocky vale; as it is then more readily seen, and the hunter is enabled to approach it with greater facility by keeping to the leeward, and in the shelter of crags, until an opportunity for a shot is presented. It is very difficult to find during the heat of the day, as it lies concealed amidst dangerous ledges or gloomy precipices, and any attempt to track it would lead to the detection of the hunter before the hunted, for its hearing is as acute as its nasal power. If pursued at all at this time, it should be with the aid of keen-nosed terriers, as they are sagacious enough to find any four-footed animal running wild, and to chase it too, whether it be bear, puma, goat, or weasel.

From many inquiries, and a limited experience, I am rather inclined to think that where it is little hunted it shows no great fear of man if he approaches it from the leeward, and does not alarm it by rapid movements. To stalk it successfully, he must therefore move slowly and cautiously, halt frequently if he thinks he is seen, make as little noise as possible, and use every available cover presented by rock or shrub. My first introduction to this mountain sprite was in Washington Territory, and that taught me that the tales related by hunters of the difficulty of killing it were little exaggerated.

I joined a party of Indians that were moving into the eastern division of the Territory, their chief having kindly, consented to let me accompany them, on the ground that I sympathized with the creed which they had been taught by a self-denying Christian missionary. Our route led us through those dense forests that cover an area of nearly seventy thousand square miles of Oregon and the region mentioned, and grand and gloomy they seemed in their silence and magnificence. We followed a trail known only, so far as I could learn, to the red men, and this led us away from all vestiges of civilization, for not a house or a white man did we see until we entered the great plains of Eastern Washington.

We moved onward by easy marches, halting for a day or two to enable the squaws to gather some of the innumerable berries of many species with which the woods teemed, and to give the men an opportunity of killing game. This, fortunately, was quite plentiful, and the hunting-parties returned each day with a stock of meat which embraced every variety, from the bear and deer to the hare, squirrel, and showtl.

As we approached the snowy summits of the Cascade Range the forest became less dense, and we caught glimpses of open mountain dells, as picturesque as any the mind could conceive, which were covered with a luxuriant growth of tender grass, green mosses, and dainty sub-alpine flowers, or we gazed on those stupendous bowlders—veritable mountains of bare rocks, which were the haunts of the mountain sheep and goat.

Having halted one day to have a hunt among these animals, I was allotted as a companion a handsome—for an Indian—young fellow, known to his tribe as *Itsoot*, or the

Bear, from the fact that he had once killed the plantigrade single-handed.

Leaving the others, we moved toward the snow-fields, and after trudging half a mile obliquely upward, we struck goat "signs," and these induced us to halt to reconnoitre. My companion, after glancing at them some moments, told me in classical Chinook that they were fresh, and that we should soon meet a colony of the *Capridæ*, if nothing unusual occurred. Advancing slowly and silently, and glancing cautiously about, we entered a deep ravine, and, to our surprise and disgust, found, ere we had been there many seconds, that the colony had detected us, and were hastening up the cliffs, some yards beyond, at a tremendous rate. Clambering up the steep bluffs the best way we could, now stumbling forward, then threatening to fall into the chasm below, we finally reached the upper world, only to see a small cloud of goats disappearing in the distance. I was angry at our ill-luck; but the red man was as stoical as a statue, and showed no signs of emotion; not even a word or facial thought escaped him. We toiled on once more until we got among some loose shelving and snow, and, after scanning our position, we saw three goats a short distance below us standing in an attitude of vigilance. They looked proud and enticing, and as we wanted them badly we attempted to stalk them. Bending low, at a signal from my cicerone we moved downward, now dodging behind rocks, now creeping almost on the ground, until my back seemed ready to break. We at length reached a convenient covert behind a huge crag, but, on peering out to get a peep at our quarries, we saw them moving up to the right. I was so disgusted that I fired; but the only result was to see one give a sudden bound as if wounded, and dart around rocks that hung over a precipice—and where a cat could hardly find a foothold—with remarkable ease and celerity. I followed it, but I dared not do more than attempt to peer toward its line of retreat for fear of having my head made dizzy by the depth and terrifying character of the chasm below.

Nothing daunted at this failure, we commenced beating again, and, after working two or three hours, came upon an old ram that was promenading on the edge of a deep canyon in which we were walking. The Indian fired, after taking deliberate aim; but instead of seeing the old fellow come tumbling down, he merely sent down a shower of loose stones, while he bounded away to less alarming quarters. The "Son of the Forest" got disgusted then himself, for he gave a grimace, and started for the summit as if he considered goats perfect nuisances, or wills-o'-the-wisp. After toiling all day, we came back to camp with only one poor marmot, known as the "whistler," from the quaint noise it makes, and I killed that as a specimen.

Our return was awaited with some interest by a few of the old men, who expected that my repeating rifle would accomplish wonders, and that it would be able to supply the encampment with goat's meat for several days; but when they saw us come back almost as empty-handed as when we started, some of them looked disappointed, but they said nothing. One of the party killed a full-grown ram by stealing upon him; but before delivering up the ghost he tumbled into a chasm, and that fall broke the horns, and mashed the body so much that the skin presented a sorry appearance. I took the measurements of the animal, but, having lost my note-book, I cannot now recall them. I ate some of its flesh during the evening, but I could not consider it to possess high gastronomic qualities, it being rather dry, and goaty in flavor.

The most successful hunt among the goats that I ever enjoyed was in Montana. During one of my excursions in that fine game region I was fortunate enough to meet a pioneer who, in the early days of the country, before it was overrun with gold-seekers, procured his meat by hunting, and in his company I spent two days in one of the mountain chains that trend to the north and west from the town of Deer Lodge. Our only companions, besides the pack animals that carried our camp equipage, were two rough-coated terriers that were trained specially for driving goats and mountain sheep from retreats where the hunter could not well follow them. The first morning after our arrival at the scene of operations we were awake before daylight; and ere the earliest rays of the sun topped the highest pinnacles we were clambering amidst crags that reduced us to the most dwarfish human dimensions. Keeping well to the lee of a spot which the animals were generally known to frequent, we struggled upward for a couple of hours, but not a sound, except our heavy breathing, escaped us. We kept our eyes steadily engaged, however, if we did not our tongues, in order that the expedition should not prove barren of results through any want of vigilance on our part.

A short time after daylight we reached a small plateau that enabled us to survey the horizon on every side; and here I brought my glass to bear, but no goats loomed within its range. "There must be some on 'em here, though," said my companion, "for I never yet knowed this place to fail me; so I'll bet my boots we'll get a crack at one in less than twenty minutes." The words, which sounded unusually strange at such an altitude, owing to the rarity of the atmosphere, had scarcely passed his lips ere a group of about a dozen, the greater number of which were kids and their dams, broke from the cover of a huge crag not fifty paces from us, they having been routed by the active little terriers. "Fire quickly," shouted the ready scout; and, without waiting to take more than the most cursory aim, I fired at the fleeing flock thrice in rapid succession, while my comrade sent four bullets whizzing in the same direction. Before I could get another shot, the terrified animals had vanished in a precipice at, apparently, one bound. Following their line of retreat to see what the result of our fire had been, we were gratified to find within an area of fifty yards a dam, and two kids about six weeks old. "Fust-rate shootin' that," said the reticent guide; "so it seems to me we'll have good-luck to-day, and make a reg'lar haul; but we needn't expect to git such good shots again, as they never allow one to get so close as that to 'em." I asked him at what range he generally shot them, and he replied that it averaged at least from two to three hundred yards, and that he considered himself very lucky if he killed one in motion, owing to the difficulty of shooting any object that bounds in an irregular manner. "I'd rather bet on killing five deer than one goat," said he, with the cold tone of an experienced hunter; "for I know how the deer will go, but nobody knows which way a goat will jump; and, besides that, he generally covers himself with rocks when he can." Experience has proved the correctness of his assertions, for I have found that one who would slay the animal must steal upon it unawares—a difficult feat to perform—and fire at the first opportunity, or the nimble creature may flee beyond reach.

After "drawing" those we had slain, we placed them on a crag, which we marked by bearings, and went in quest of more; but after trudging through deep gullies and over rock-bound plateaux until noon, we were compelled to return to camp, the guide having concluded that we could do nothing in the heat of the day, as the animals concealed themselves after the morning repast until evening again. After reaching our primitive quarters, we cut off a portion of the kid and roasted it, but it did not prove as palatable as one would infer; for, though tender, it was dry and insipid. I did not try the flesh of the adults, being willing to accept the judgment of the guide, who stated that it was tougher than Leavenworth boarding-house steak. Throwing ourselves on the bunch of boughs and leaves which answered for a couch, we dozed until 5 P.M., when we again sallied forth. Taking a direction opposite to that which we had followed in the morning, a walk of half a mile brought us to a perfect little paradise of a valley, which was covered with green, luxuriant herbage, and watered by a pretty stream that took its rise in a granitoid formation, and was therefore never dry. Being surrounded by stupendous crags of igneous formation, the guide felt assured that we should meet some goats; so we prepared for the event by filling up the magazine of our Winchester rifles and half-cocking them. After a careful scanning of the bowlders, we espied a group of half a dozen animals in a niche far above us. Making a détour to the right, where a chasm yawned, we got to within a quarter of a mile of them; but finding ourselves to the windward, and in a spot where we could get only one shot ere they might disappear, the guide took up one of the dogs and showed him where the goats were browsing. Wagging his tail to indicate that he understood his mission, he started off at his best speed, followed by his companion, while we hastened back to an isolated mass of rock that skirted the vale on the north-east. The dogs having a wide détour to make in order to get above the goats, we were concealed before their sharp bark announced that they had found the quarry. As soon as the animals were started, they came bounding down into the valley, in contradistinction to their usual manner, closely followed by the active pursuers, which kept up an incessant yelping. I was so interested in watching the daring leaps and nimble clambering of the flock that I forgot all about my purpose of tumbling one over; and it was only when the guide stated that we would have "to run for a shot" that I was recalled to it. Running at our best speed toward a series of bowlders that marked the line of a canyon, we reached there in time to see the flock bounding upward again; but, ere they disappeared, we managed to get a rather indifferent shot at a couple in the rear at a distance of about one hundred yards. We did not expect to claim any prizes from that effort; but we concluded to search, nevertheless, in hopes that we might have wounded one at least. Great, therefore, was our satisfaction to find a handsome kid stretched dead on the ground, and a trail of blood a little farther on —a proof that another had been seriously wounded. Following this gory pathway for a distance of several hundred yards, we reached a clump of dwarf pines, and there found a yearling ram in the last throes of dissolution. An examination revealed the fact that he was shot through the heart, so we were not a little surprised at his tenacity of life. Shouldering the slain, we returned to camp, and feasted that night on tender kid. Having satisfied to the fullest an ambition of mine, we broke up our quarters, and four days after were back in Deer Lodge, I, for one, being highly pleased with our good fortune.

To hunt the mountain goat successfully one must be cautious, patient, and persevering; and he who can exercise these faculties need have little fear of not placing a few among his trophies of the chase. He may have to dare crags and chasms; but as sport means exercising a person's mental and physical qualities against those of wild animals, few care for dangers and annoyances in comparison to the success achieved. This goat will, it is said by old hunters, charge its human foe if it thinks it cannot escape otherwise, and display its butting power to as good advantage as the domestic species. It prefers to seek safety in flight if it can, however, and does not hesitate a moment to plunge into a precipice to escape threatened danger. Fabulous tales are told about its immunity from injury in these terrific leaps; yet it is no more daring than the ibex or chamois, nor is it superior to them in passing over pendent crags, vaulting gloomy precipices, or clambering up the most stupendous ascents. Hunting it is much the same in character as pursuing these animals, except, perhaps, that it is less cautious where it is not hunted much. He who would follow it, however, must learn to be patient and daring, and care little for disappointments, for he is likely to have many of these unless he is more than ordinarily fortunate. It might, I think, be hunted to good advantage with sharp terriers or sheep dogs, as they would keep it at bay until the sportsman arrived on the scene, when he could easily finish the work, and then boast of something more tangible for his day's labor than a view of majestic mountain scenery.

CHAPTER XIV.

THE BIG-HORN, OR MOUNTAIN SHEEP.

The Big-horn, or Mountain Sheep.—Its Haunts and Habits.—Characteristics required to Hunt it successfully.—Its Caution and Vigilance.—Order of a Flock in Flight.—Hunters' Tales of its Nimbleness.—Pugnacity of the Males.—Contest between a Wolf and a Big-horn.—Size of Rams.—Measurement of Horns.—The Rutting Season.—Flocks of Old Rams.—Best Time for Hunting them.—Stalking Exercise.—A good Rifle.—Usefulness of a Field-glass.—Indian "Sheep-eaters."—Pemmican.—My First Hunt.—A Kill.—Stalk a Flock.—Detected.—The Assembly.—Result of a Fusillade.—Tedious Chase after an Old Ram.—I get Butted over.—A tardy Capture.—Flavor of wild Mutton Cutlets.—Dogs for Sheep-hunting.—A Hunt in the War Eagle Mountains.—Our Success.—A Cougar scared. —"Dancing" Sheep.—Big-horns waiting for their Leader.—Adventure of the Guide with a War-party of Indians.—Defeat of the Latter.

THE only species of the *Ovidæ* found wild in the United States is the so-called big-horn, or mountain sheep (*Ovis montana*), which is confined geographically to the mountainous regions of the Far West. It is closely allied to the *Ovis ammon* of the Himalaya Mountains, and differs from it mainly in size, being about one-third smaller, and the corrugations of the horns are also somewhat different. Amidst the many-shaped crests of the Western mountains this nimble creature loves to dwell, for there it finds an abundance of dainty food in the tender alpine and subalpine vegetation, and is free from nearly all foes except an occasional red or white hunter. A rather active warfare has been waged upon it lately, however, in certain portions of the Territories, especially in Colorado, Wyoming, and Utah; hence it is getting rather wild and scarce in these regions; but in Montana, Idaho, Oregon, Washington Territory, and portions of British America it is almost as abundant as ever, and in some places more so, as the

Indians can now procure pabulum in an easier manner than by laboriously following it amidst the snow-enshrouded mountains which it selects for a home. The amateur hunter who would, therefore, slay a large number must move to the distant regions of the North-west, and there he will find little cause to complain of ill-luck. Few creatures are

THE BIG-HORN.

more difficult of approach than the big-horn, for, like all mountain animals, it is exceedingly keen of scent, unusually vigilant, and so cautious that it carefully reconnoitres a country from an elevated stand-point ere it presumes to advance toward it. The Nimrod who would, therefore, place the heads of many.among his trophies of the chase, must be not only of an active and vigorous form to bear steep mountain climbing and a rarified atmosphere, but he must also possess the qualities of patience, perseverance, and hardihood; for its pursuit may lead him through deep and gloomy precipices, over ground so stony and rough as to seem impassable, and amidst pinnacles whose towering altitudes and craggy sides make their ascent almost as difficult as many of the famous peaks of the Alps. In early summer, however, it may be found at elevations of only four or five thousand feet above the level of the sea; but from May to September, or as soon as the lambkins are able to travel, it moves higher up, for the greater safety of the young, and to secure the dainty vegetation that grows in every available spot as soon as the snow disappears.

Though the favorite habitats of this animal are rugged hills and mountains, yet it will also thrive in a rough and broken country where the herbage is not only coarse but scanty, provided there are rocky steeps and dark chasms within convenient distance to which it can retreat when alarmed, or when it is pursued by foes. When a flock is migrating to pastures new, the sentinels, or leaders, carefully scrutinize the country before them from every commanding position, and when they are satisfied with its appearance, the whole party advance boldly, and, having made it their head-quarters, throw out vedettes, generally males, which mount guard on elevated crags or hillocks, and vigilantly survey their surroundings until their companions have dined, when all seek shelter amidst crags, small pine or fir coppices, and inaccessible shelves of rock or sombre canyons, where no ordinary enemy can follow them without making its presence known.

When a sentinel detects the approach of a suspicious object, he sounds an alarm at once by a few loud and peremptory hissing snorts; this brings the flock huddling together, the ewes and lambs being in the centre; and when the column is formed, all dash for the highest ridges at their best pace, and never stop until they have sought a safe refuge among crags or chasms. The advance is always led by a sturdy ram, one that is generally looked upon as the leader, and the rear and flanks are carefully guarded by the young males. When flocks of old rams congregate together, which they always do after the running season is over in December, the first one in an alarm that moves off is the leader, and all the rest, like the domestic sheep, follow him heedlessly, in a bunch, until a halt is made, when sentinels are again posted, and the source whence danger is expected is carefully watched.

In regions even where they are little disturbed, they raise their heads every few minutes while feeding, and survey their surroundings; and as they are both sharp of eye and keen of scent, it requires the most careful stalking to approach them within shooting range without being detected. They will get the scent of a hunter to the windward seemingly half a mile away; and when that terrifying odor is made known to the flock they display the greatest symptoms of terror, and dash wildly for the highest pinnacles, now leaping nimbly from crag to crag, or vaulting dark and narrow chasms with the greatest ease, anon plunging head foremost into precipices apparently deep enough to shatter them into fragments should they strike the ground; nor do they stop until they have placed a goodly distance between themselves and their most dreaded foe. They hurl themselves from giddy heights into the depths below with such readiness that one is liable to give some credence to those tales related by red and white hunters, which specify that they would prefer death to an encounter with man; and that their horns are so strong and elastic that they can fall upon them on a crag several feet below, and rebound to their feet none the worse for the concussion. The latter statement may be taken with a large grain of salt; for though I have seen them make some terrific plunges, and some which I thought would result in their instantaneous destruction, yet they escaped uninjured, not, however, because they alighted on their horns, but on their feet; and these being enveloped in a corneous and elastic covering, capable of bearing a severe shock, they were able to scamper away as easily after their bounds as if they had never made them. The broken tips of the horns, and the often scaled or split character of portions of their outer rind, are supposed by old hunters to be the result of falling on them constantly; but this is evidently a mistake, and is due to the habit the animals have of using their appendages to aid them in climbing steep and stony places. The rams also use them freely enough in combats, and this undoubtedly causes the scaling or splitting; for they must be hard, indeed, if they can resist uninjured the terrific force with which two warriors, weighing from one to over two hundred pounds each, strike each other. These combats are waged according to the rules in existence among the domestic species, but, owing to the closeness of the horns and their forward projection, the animals do not suffer so much from headache after the contests as the latter, nor do they seem to be so fond of causeless warfare.

Both sexes are adorned with head appendages, but they are rather light on the females, those of a veteran great-grandmother not being larger than those of a two-year-old male. They are also less recurved, being more like those of a goat; yet they are most effective weapons in an assault, as prowling foxes, wolves, and wild-cats have learned to their sorrow. I once saw a wolf trying to make a delicious repast off a lamb three or four months old, which it caught in a bit of wood during the temporary absence of the mother; but, ere it could kill it the latter arrived, most unexpectedly, on the scene, and, charging the bandit with the greatest vehemence, gave it such a crushing blow on the ribs that it was glad to beat as rapid a retreat as its stomach-ache would permit, while mother and lamb trotted off up the mountain.

The skulking brute, which looked thoroughly disappointed, sore, and heart-sick, was not through with its troubles, however; for in its hungry meditation, it paid no heed to surrounding objects, so found itself unexpectedly among a small flock of rams which had just emerged from a ravine, where they had been drinking. When it saw these new foes it looked thoroughly scared and crestfallen, and attempted to flee from the threatening eyes and heads; but, before it could decide upon its line of retreat the flock charged it from various directions in a body, and one burly fellow, having horns on him like a gnarled oak, struck it in the ribs with such terrific force that he doubled it up, and sent it flying two or three yards away with a velocity that must have scattered its wits, and caused it to deplore the day that its love of mutton had induced it to try and feast on lamb.

Before any of the others could assail it in the flank it managed to collect its sore and sadly dispersed faculties, and, placing its tail between its legs, it got up and dusted down that mountain-side at a higher rate of speed than ever it did before; and right glad it seemed, when it found itself beyond the reach of those powerful battering-rams. I was so much interested in the scene, and laughed so heartily at the discomfiture and terror of the runaway, that the flock got beyond the reach of my shot-gun before I recovered myself sufficiently to think of attempting to shoot one. Had I tried it, however, it is doubtful if I would have been successful, as I did not expect to meet them in that quarter, and they were so vigilant that it would have been only by the merest chance that I could have approached them near enough to get a shot. Although these animals are exceedingly timid in the presence of man, and wildly flee before him, yet they will not hesitate a moment to face any ordinary foe, and to render a good account of themselves in a combat. In their usual haunts they are, however, free from nearly all enemies except man; and what few they have they can easily elude by their vigilance and caution, and the inaccessible character of their country.

The big-horn bears very little resemblance to the domestic species; but it is almost a perfect copy, except in size, of the Asiatic wild sheep (*Ovis ammon*), and it is also like it in character. It is, in the first place, more like a deer in outline and color of body than a sheep, its ovine face, taste of flesh, and habits being the qualities that ally it to its domestic congener. It is much taller, fuller, and more spirited in action than the latter, and all its movements are characterized by a lithe grace, a rapidity of movement, and a prompt agility that the farm-yard variety never possessed. The height of a full-grown male varies from thirty-four to forty-one inches; length, from forty-four to sixty inches; length of caudal vertebræ, from one and a half to three inches; and length of face, from base of horns to tip of nose, from ten to twelve inches. The heavy recurved horns which adorn both sexes also make a marked difference between it and the domestic species; and in place of long, fine, and soft wool, it is covered with coarse tubular hair of a yellowish brown color, which changes to a dull line of white on the posterior side of the fore and hind legs, and to a white patch on the flanks and abdomen. The outer hair, which resembles somewhat that of the caribou and antelope in character, is not very coarse to the touch, and the inner is fine and soft. The coat changes according to the seasons, being lighter in the winter and spring than in the summer. Some old males are almost hoary in early spring, owing to the rubbing away of the black tips of the hair; and when in that condition they looked like grizzled veterans. The horns of the latter are magnificent appendages, and well worthy to adorn the finest dining-halls. They measure along the curve from thirty to thirty-eight inches, and, in rare instances, even forty-two inches; their circumference at the base varies from ten to fifteen inches; and the width between the tip of one to that of its fellow ranges from sixteen to twenty-seven inches. I have found the measurement of several horns examined to vary much, but it was generally in their length and distance apart; the difference in their circumference at the base, when full grown, seldom exceeding three inches. The hollow part of the horn of a large ram will hold two gallons of fluid; but it is so inconvenient and awkward that even the Indians rarely use it as a water vessel.

The males sometimes attain a weight of three hundred and fifty pounds, but the average lies between two and three hundred pounds. The females are somewhat smaller than the rams; and their appendages, though lacking in massiveness, are well formed and graceful, and do not give the head the stunted appearance of the males. The face, which is narrow, is thoroughly ovine in appearance; the eyes are large and full, and are intended for breadth as much as intensity of vision; the legs, which are long and tapering, yet sinewy, are evidently intended for both leaping and running; and the body, when in good condition, is round rather than deep; and this gives the animal a graceful, active, and vigorous aspect.

The running season, which commences in the early part of December, does not last very long; and though contests between the males are often waged then, yet they seldom prove serious, for one, on finding that it is worsted, yields the field at once to the sturdier rival, and seeks elsewhere for a mate. The selection of companions is not so easy a matter as it is among the domestic species, and the weaker members have often to pay dearly for the affection they have won. When the running season is over the old rams congregate together in bands of from eight to thirty, while the younger keep with the lambs and females, and act as their escorts and guardians.

The lambs are dropped in May or early in June, according to the climate of the country, among the lower foothills; but as soon as they are able to travel, which is generally at the end of two weeks, the mothers commence working gradually upward, according as the atmosphere becomes warmer and the vegetation more abundant, until they reach the snow-line; and there they remain for some time, feasting on the small and succulent herbage that sprouts wherever it can raise its head. They tarry there until the lambs are able to move briskly about and take care of themselves, if necessary; then they scour the hills in every direction, going wherever fancy leads them, and revelling in the fredom and delights of their mountain home. The lambs are old enough to make delicious mutton, and to furnish excellent hunting at the end of three months; and as their dams and sires are also in the best of condition at that time, say about the middle of August, he who would feast on wild cutlets should then seek them amidst the crags and chasms of their exalted retreats.

The best time to hunt them is early in the morning or late in the evening, as they are then out feeding and playing, or searching for water; and as they are prominent objects in a landscape, they may be seen by the contrast they present to their surroundings, or they may be tracked by their "signs" or droppings. There is only one way in which they can be hunted with any degree of success, and that is to stalk or "still-hunt" them up wind, taking care to use every rock and shrub for shelter; to move as noiselessly as possible, as their ears are as sharp as their eyes, and they are very suspicious of the least disturbance of the mountain stillness; and not to be too anxious for a shot, as impatience is apt to lead to many disappointing and weary tramps. They should be stalked from above, if possible, as they do not expect any danger from that direction, all foes being supposed to come from below. If alarmed from above, instead of running down, they scamper obliquely upward and against the wind, and this habit often leads them to death, as hunters conceal themselves behind bowlders, and, as the terror-stricken flocks rush past, they present an excellent opportunity for close shooting. The best weapon that I ever used against them was a Winchester magazine rifle, as it enabled me to fire in rapid succession; and its charge of powder, which might be considered too small for larger game, was strong enough to send a bullet crashing through the body of a big-horn at a distance of three or more hundred yards. As they are rarely stalked under one hundred yards, except by unusual fair fortune or accident, a good and accurate rifle is an indispensable necessity to success in hunting them. The novice would find a field-glass an excellent aid in discovering them among ledges; and should he be accompanied by a guide, he may, through its advantages, get several shots to the other's one, as it is seldom that two hunt close together;

and he who has the best range of vision is the person most likely to see them first, and to be the first among them. As they are quite numerous in Montana, Idaho, and in Klamath Basin in Oregon, any amateur may class them among his trophies of the chase, provided he is willing to bear the toil and expense of visiting their haunts. They are common also in Wyoming; and one peak is called Sheep Mountain, from the numbers which formerly frequented it. A small remnant or band of Indians who dwell in its vicinity are known as Sheep-eaters, from the fact that they lived principally on the flesh of the big-horn, and that they are more partial to it even now, though they have partaken of the foods used by the white man, than to any other class of meat. Several Western tribes make the flesh into pemmican, and consider it superior to that made from the buffalo, while they use the fat for making candles. These give a bright flame, and burn like a wax-candle. The whites, even, consider wild cutlets a rare delicacy, for the flesh of a big-horn in good condition brings fifteen cents a pound, whereas venison sells for five cents, and often for less.

I first became acquainted with mountain sheep in Oregon, in which State they are still quite numerous along the eastern slope of the Cascade Range, and especially in that vast zoological garden known as the Klamath Basin; and I felt prouder of the first one I killed than I did of all that has since fallen to my lot. The friend in whose company I hunted on that occasion lived in Eastern Oregon, and cultivated a fertile farm at the base of a high and long spur of the above Range. Starting out from his house by half-past 3 A.M., one fine morning in autumn, a long and toilsome climb led us to the summit of a mountain spur; and working our way slowly to the windward along this, and peering about everywhere for "signs," an hour's tramping carried us into a small and green vale, which was buried deep down in the mountain-side. It was covered with the greenest and most luxuriant of grasses, and was hemmed in by dark basaltic crags, sloping terraces, and func-

real pines and firs that soughed in the morning breeze. A fairy-like tarn nestled in the centre, and reflected the shrubbery that margined its banks with mirror-like fidelity. Passing through this vale, we reached the steep ascents on the farther side just as the blood-red morning sun began to peer above the mountain; and this revealed to us in a weird light the vast panorama of hill and plain, which stretched out before us in all its grandeur. Magnificent as the scene looked, and much as we should have liked to have gazed long and earnestly upon it, time forbade us such pleasure, so we were compelled to commence clambering once more, and to strain our eyes in quest of "signs."

After beating about for an hour we came suddenly upon them, and they were so fresh that we knew the sheep must be somewhere in our immediate vicinity. Moving as noiselessly as we could, taking advantage of every shelter furnished by shrub or rock, and peering about us with the greatest cautiousness, as if we feared that the movements of the head would startle the quarry, we advanced very slowly; so slowly, in fact, that it was painful to me, as my heart seemed heavy with suppressed excitement, and my breathing was short and labored.

After crawling to the windward in this manner for half an hour, I approached several huge bowlders that towered upward from the ground to a height of thirty or forty feet, and, on rounding one of these, I came suddenly upon five sheep which had evidently only commenced their matutinal meal, as one of them was just arising from its couch when I arrived on the scene. Their sudden and unexpected appearance was as great a shock to me as my presence was to them; and for a second or two we both stood still and mute, when they, with a loud snort, dashed for the summit at a rate of speed I would not have credited them with. Their movement aroused me also, and, taking a hurried aim, I fired at them when passing in a bunch through a rocky gate-way in the dell; but I did not have the satisfaction of seeing any fall. Deeply chagrined at my bad shooting, I hurried after them as rapidly as I could, and was soon rejoined by my companion, who felt as keenly about my want of success as I did myself, as he feared we should not be able to get another shot during the morning, and perhaps not during the day, owing to the noise created by the firing, which would send them all scampering toward the highest pinnacles, where it would be difficult to pursue them. After pursuing them for about two hundred yards, we came upon spots of blood, and this brought us the joyous assurance that one at least was wounded.

Following up this trail until it led to a large piece of shelving formed of loose stones, which overhung a deep but very narrow chasm, I commenced scouting over it, while my companion worked to the right among some young firs and large crags that skirted a ravine. I lost it suddenly, however, and though I quartered in every direction I could find no trace of it. Returning to where I first lost it, I saw that some of the small stones were overturned very recently, evidently by the stamping of an animal in pain; and this caused me to look at their under side, and that I found freely sprinkled with blood. Turning up those that were disarranged, I followed their course for a few feet until I came to a small wall or terrace, which was scarcely two feet high, and ran along the outer end of the shelf.

Not daring to advance to that treacherous foothold, I, gave a lusty shout to arouse any game that might be concealed there, and the mountains had scarcely taken up the echo before a splendid ram bounded from the shelter of the wall and attempted to leap the chasm; but I was ready for him that time, and he had scarcely risen in the air before a ball went crashing through his sides, and sent him headlong into the canyon; but, very fortunately, instead of being dashed to pieces on the rocks below, he fell into a fir that grew on a most convenient ledge, whence I was able to drag him to a more eligible locality, where I could gloat over him in comfort. My companion joined me half an hour later, he also having succeeded in killing one by coming suddenly upon several that were grazing among huge bowlders; and, much to my satisfaction, as I wished to secure the heads of both sexes, I heard it was a female about two years old. By cutting two stout branches off a pine-tree, we made a litter, and placing the ram upon it, carried him to where the ewe was concealed. Both were then despoiled of the *viscera*, and a long pole was placed under their hind-legs, which were tied, and they were pushed high up against a tree, to prevent them from being devoured by any prowling quadrupeds.

Continuing our course upward, and still against the wind, we scrambled and stumbled about for about an hour, and finally reached a small plateau which gave us a commanding view over a large area of the mountains. Sweeping it in every direction with a glass, I could see no traces of sheep there; but not so my companion, for he called my attention to some irregular specks that loomed against the horizon far to the north. After watching them carefully for several minutes, I discovered they were groups of sheep that were migrating to pastures new; so we made preparations to intercept them. Running toward them with all possible haste, we got so near in less than an hour that we commenced stalking them. Moving toward the summit, we gained a position a little above them at a distance of perhaps two hundred yards, before our haste caused us to be detected by a vigilant old ram, whose eyes seemed to be ubiquitous; for we were often compelled to throw ourselves flat on the sharp stones to avoid his piercing gaze, when we supposed he was interested in his food.

As soon as he announced our presence by a hissing snort, the animals, which were widely scattered, ran together in a bunch; but before they decided upon moving, we fired at them four times in rapid succession, and, when the smoke cleared away, we saw two young rams and a lambkin on the ground; but we inferred that we had wounded others, as we found drops of blood on their line of flight. Being too well satisfied with our good-luck to follow the fugitives, we turned our attention to preparing our captures for transportation homeward.

It seems to be a characteristic of the big-horns that when they are first startled they rush together and remain bunched up for a short time previous to their flight, as if they were dazed; and that is the best time to shoot at them, as one shot then is worth half a dozen when they are fleeing. While moving down the mountain we espied a sturdy ram stalking about, as if he were monarch of all he surveyed; and his stately mien and vigorous action caused me to long so much for his horns that I resolved to capture him if possible. Leaving my companion with the "drag" of mutton, I crawled carefully toward a clump of pines, where I expected to be within range; but, on reaching that point, I saw the object of my ambition quietly strolling over a hillock several hundred yards away. I felt severely disappointed at this unexpected movement; but as I was still anxious to procure the horns, I concluded to have them, if I tramped after him all day. Moving up the mountain once more, and taking every advantage afforded by bowlders, declivities, and trees—and where these were not to be found bending low to the ground—I crawled along as if my back were built on the right-angle principle, and my legs were intended to make an obtuse angle from the knees downward; while my forehead was a mass of wrinkles, and one eye was constantly turned skyward, as if the quarry were up in that direction.

After half an hour's tedious running and crawling, I halted, and craned my neck slowly from behind a small crag to see if I could detect the ram. Yes, there he was, not two hundred yards away, gazing proudly about him, and surveying the noble landscape, visible in every direction, with a critical eye, and in an attitude of vigilance. I crouched behind my shelter when I saw his glances bent in my direction; but when he turned them away I lifted my head carefully and gradually above the rock, then pulled up my rifle as slowly as if its movement through the air could be heard, and, taking deliberate aim at the body, I fired, and felt a great sense of relief on hearing the detonation. When the smoke cleared away I saw him bounding away to the north at a tremendous rate, and evidently thoroughly scared, if not hurt. I was almost sure I had hit him; but his pace seemed to give a contradiction to my thoughts, and I felt anything but pleased with myself. After gazing mechanically at his retreating form for a few moments, I saw him lie down on a treeless plateau several hundred yards away, and I then inferred that he was wounded. I therefore concluded to try another stalk, and commenced that tedious operation once more. By crawling carefully on my hands and knees, and halting occasionally, I got within one hundred and fifty yards of him; and seeing his horns peering above some rocks, I aimed and fired at his head, or, rather, where I supposed it to be. The report was followed by a violent scrambling, which led me to believe he was breaking away; but he had scarcely emerged from his place of concealment before he pitched forward on his horns as if he were dead. On seeing this, I advanced toward him, and laid my rifle on the ground within twenty feet of him, as I intended to use my knife for cutting his throat; but what was my surprise to see him bound suddenly to his feet when I drew near him, and break away for a mass of crags that rose abruptly upward from the mountain a few yards away! I was taken aback so much at this unlooked-for movement that I merely gazed at his retreating form in blank amazement until it disappeared amidst the rocks. The meditation that I indulged in after he had vanished would never take me among the angels, for I was actually disgusted at my own bad shooting and stupidity; but I became calmer after awhile, and then resolved to have that ram if I followed him for a year and a day.

Starting out again, I crawled through the grass, wriggled past rocks, and craned my neck until it ached, and finally reached a shelter from which I could see the horns once more. Taking a most deliberate aim at the lowest portion of them visible, I fired; and not hearing any noise after the report, I concluded I was successful that time, and felt delighted accordingly. Advancing boldly, I saw my tough old brave lying on the ground, and, seizing him joyously by the horns, I turned the head round to have a look at his grizzled features; but I had no sooner done so, than he scrambled to his feet, and giving me a dig in the stomach that doubled me up, and sent me sitting, in the most violent manner, on some of the sharpest stones I ever remember resting upon, scampered away, and vanished behind a huge bowlder like a spectre.

I sat on the ground for a short time after the bump, in order to practise a few wry faces; then arose calmly and deliberately; and after indulging in a few orisons! for the welfare of the *ovus*, and rubbing myself vigorously, I seized my rifle, and strode forward with the most determined idea of making that ram pay dearly for so unceremoniously offering me such a seat, and causing me to practise shampooing when there was no necessity for it. I was fully resolved to have him at the next shot, even if he bore an enchanted life; so I put my teeth together and grasped the rifle firmly in my hand. On rounding the bowlder behind which he had disappeared, I scanned the rocks around me, but I could see nothing of him. This was another surprise and disappointment; for I knew he was so severely wounded that he could not run very far without being compelled to lie down and rest. Supposing he had headed for the mountain, I moved forward; but I had not gone twenty paces before I saw him lying, face downward, behind a few shrubs, and as dead as a door nail. My work was over then; all disappointments had vanished like magic; and the memory of the stomach-ache and the rocky seat only remained; but these were atoned for by making a chair of the ram for a time. After a short rest, I made a drag of a bough, and hauled my victim down the mountain-side as proudly as if I had captured several hundred. This feeling was the result of youthful exuberance and inexperience, and was probably natural; so I only refer to it now to merely say that one hard-won success is

18

more highly prized than many won with ease. It is no easy matter at any time to bag a big-horn, unless circumstances are unusually favorable; but I never saw one which gave me as much trouble to capture as this one, so it remains indelibly marked in my memory.

When I reached my companion I found he had *cached* all the animals, as he did not know when I would return, and he feared to leave them to the mercies of bears or wolves. As we did not expect to be able to find any more sheep until evening, when they would come out to graze, we decided upon returning home; as we had been more successful than the most sanguine could have anticipated, and we cared more for sport than the pot. It is always a difficult matter to make a big bag of sheep, owing to their inaccessible haunts, and their timidity and vigilance, especially in regions where they are hunted much; so we were not a little pleased with our good-fortune. We attributed it, however, to the abundance of the animals, the excellence of the ground for stalking them, and the fact that they were not hunted much, rather than to any excellence on our own part; for I have known some of the best hunters to tramp hard all day and not kill one, although numbers might be roaming over the snow-fields or the rocky crests.

We dined that evening off wild-mutton cutlets; but excepting that they had a somewhat gamey flavor, and were by no means succulent, they tasted like flesh of the domestic species. In hunting over that region afterward we used mongrel dogs, and found them excellent adjuncts in the chase; as they would not only run, but attack, the big-horns, or hold them at bay until we got within shooting range. They were not strong enough to kill the animals alone, and they had a wholesome fear of the head appendages, but they were very useful in more ways than one. I should fancy that trained dogs would be found of great advantage in sheep-hunting, but my experience is not extensive enough to form an opinion on the matter.

One of the most interesting and successful excursions

after sheep that I ever enjoyed came off in the snow-capped War Eagle Mountains, in Idaho. Being full of small circular valleys that teem with graminaceous verdure, and are watered by numerous streams, this chain affords an ideal residence for the lordly big-horn; and that its advantages are appreciated is evident from the large number that frequent it at all seasons. The party which I accompanied consisted of three sturdy miners, a sporting merchant, and a captain in the cavalry who was enjoying a short vacation. The miners were experienced tramps and veteran Nimrods, having often been compelled to depend on their rifles for food while out on prospecting tours; so we left the provisioning of the detachment and the selection of the route entirely to them.

Starting out from a mining hamlet early in the morning, the evening of the same day found us encamped at the base of the mountains; and, as we had to be astir before dawn, we retired to our hard couch on the ground quite early in the evening. Long before the sun began to appear above the eastern peaks the next morning, we were laboriously clambering up steep ascents or picking our way through cavernous precipices, whose gloomy walls recalled most forcibly the Plutonic regions.

By five o'clock we had reached an altitude of four thousand feet, according to the aneroid; and there the principal guide informed us we were to remain while he went in search of "signs." He returned in about half an hour, and stated that he had discovered a flock of a dozen or more a furlong above us, but that we should be compelled to make a wide détour to get to their lee, in order to approach them undetected. Our hearts beat wildly at this piece of good news—at least mine did; so we examined our rifles carefully and saw that they were perfectly clean and properly loaded. I was armed with a Winchester rifle, which carried several bullets in the magazine, and I was resolved to shoot them all at one animal rather than permit it to escape. At the command we moved forward, and, after an hour's severe struggling, approached the flock to within three hundred yards, under shelter of some gigantic bowlders of basalt, without being discovered.

To shoot from that distance would be risking too much, yet we could get no closer without revealing ourselves to the sentinels, who lifted their heads every few moments to survey the landscape. As they were feeding toward us, we concluded to wait their nearer approach; but the minutes dragged heavily, and each moment seemed a torture. After waiting patiently for about half an hour, though it seemed treble that time, four sheep and three rams advanced about a hundred yards farther, and, as our impatience was becoming unbearable, the guide allowed us to fire. This was a joyous moment, and we resolved to profit by it. Each selected his quarry, and at a signal all fired simultaneously. When the smoke cleared away, great was our joy to behold three males and one ewe stretched upon the ground, and two sheep leaping wildly about as if badly wounded. Rushing from our place of concealment, we delivered several shots in rapid succession at the now thoroughly alarmed flock, which were making for the rocky summit at a breakneck pace; but the excitement having somewhat unstrung our nerves, the fusillade brought us only one yearling, which seemed too dazed to break away with the others.

We followed the retreating flock up the steep mountain-side, but found in a short time that the old proverb of a stern chase being a long one was especially true in this case, so we relinquished it in about half an hour. Knowing that two sheep were severely wounded, by the manner in which they acted, and having failed to discover them among those that escaped, we deployed and commenced searching in every direction for some trails of blood. It being a characteristic of this species to head for the mountains under all possible circumstances, we moved toward the summit, but, after working for an hour, we could find no trace of them. We then returned to our slain quarries, and, cutting them open, made a *cache* in a small fir-tree and placed them upon it, to prevent their being unceremoniously appropriated by some prowling bear or cougar. This important duty finished, we resumed our exploration for the wounded animals, and in less than a minute came upon a trail that plainly indicated the severity of their injuries, as the blood formed a miniature stream in some places.

Following that for half a mile, we came to a deep, broad chasm, and down this we clambered, or rather stumbled, for we were sliding more frequently than walking. Reaching the bottom, we found that one of the sheep had followed its course upward and the other down, so a party went in each direction. I was with the latter, and was fortunate enough to get a shot at a cougar that was quietly preparing to make a meal off one of the wounded animals, which it had captured and slain. I don't know whether I hit it or not; but I am thoroughly sure I scared it a little, from the way in which it dashed through the canyon. It certainly acted as if it had forgotten something lower down, and was in the greatest possible hurry to get it. The sheep on which it was preparing to feast was little injured, it having had only time to cut the throat before it had orders to leave. Making a litter of two fallen boughs, we placed the slain creature upon it, and in this way managed to get it to the upper world. The other party were unsuccessful in their search; but as we could claim one animal for each member of the expedition, we did not repine much at their ill-luck. Leaving this spot, we moved obliquely to the left and upward in quest of more game, and, after travelling two or three miles, came suddenly upon a flock of twenty or thirty; but before we could recover from our surprise they were dashing away. We fired at random, little expecting any result from it; but we were fortunate enough to get a splendid male, which was hit right on the skull, and one ewe. This piece of good-fortune we attributed more to the numbers of the flock rather than to any marksmanship; so we felt little pride in our achievement, for no one could tell who killed the animals.

Our experience of the morning having taught us the folly of a direct pursuit, we stored the game, and moved on along the original line of route. We had not proceeded more than a mile before we met another flock; but, as they were on the opposite side of a precipice, we could not approach them undetected. They were at least five hundred yards away; and knowing we could have little chance of killing any at that distance, we concluded to test the range and accuracy of our rifles upon them. Selecting a huge crag for a shelter, one of the miners fired, but his bullet passed over them. Another tried it, and he planted the ball directly in their midst. This seemed to arouse them; as they all jumped from the ground at the unusual apparition, then stared wildly about. Several more bullets were then sent among them; but, instead of attempting to run away, they only began to stare and jump, and dance a queer sort of jig as the balls whistled over, or tore up the ground beside them. One at length got struck somewhere near the flank, and that caused it to think the locality disagreeable, if not dangerous; so it gave a startled jump and dashed away, closely followed by the others. As they were moving off, we saw a sturdy ram hastily run up the precipice and bound after them. We could not understand why the flock waited to be shot at several times, but the unexpected presence of this veteran soon gave the proper explanation. It was his privilege, apparently, to lead all movements; and being absent in the canyon, perhaps for the purpose of allaying his thirst, his charge did not know what to do without him; but, like all sheep, when one moved the remainder followed, without thinking of the ceremony of waiting for the commands of the chief. If we did not reap much profit from this bit of shooting, we enjoyed a good share of quiet amusement; for it was quite ludicrous to see the heavy-horned creatures give a startled bound, then gaze stupidly about in search of the cause of their annoyance. Having been more successful than the most sanguine could have expected, we concluded to return to camp with our spoils, as the hot August sun was becoming disagreeably intense, and it was so late in the morning that we could scarcely hope to meet any more sheep until the cool breeze of the evening appeared.

On reaching our *caches*, we made a drag of the heaviest fir and pine boughs we could break off by our united weight, and, placing the game on this, we hauled it down the mountain without any very laborious efforts.

Arrived at camp, those unused to the heavy climbing of the day were soon so stiff as to be scarcely able to move; but the rugged miners seemed to consider it a mere nothing, and laughed heartily at the "drawing-room hunters." The success of the expedition had been so great, however, that they condescended to say that the "drawing-room hunters" were not bad shots. I have been out among bighorns frequently since then, but never did I see such goodluck attend a large party the first day.

That evening, while discussing the merits of wild-mutton cutlets and the contents of a couple of bottles of "Chateau Lafitte," the principal guide related an adventure which befell him on the first occasion that he had hunted big-horns on the scene of our morning's exploits. He and a companion, who were "chums," in prospecting for gold, being out of meat, concluded to kill some mountain sheep, not having any other means of procuring it, as there were no settlers in that section of the country at the time except a few miners. The Indians, who had been very troublesome in other quarters of the territory, had let them alone, and from this they supposed that there were none anywhere near them. In an hour after starting they came upon a flock of bighorns, and killed two fine ewes; and while engaged in preparing them, another flock suddenly appeared on the opposite side of a chasm near which they were standing, and were preparing to cross it, when they were arrested by the foe in front. As they stood still for a few moments, the hunters threw themselves on the ground and fired; but simultaneously with the reports of their own rifles came others directly behind them, and several bullets passed over their heads. Alarmed by this unexpected fusillade, they jumped to their feet and leaped behind a crag just in time to escape another shower. Looking up, they saw, a short distance above them, a party of Indians, in all the hideousness of war-paint, preparing to fire at them a second time. Without waiting to see any more, they discharged their rifles at the group and fled at their utmost speed down the mountain-side. The Indians followed in hot pursuit, yelling like panthers, and sending either a bullet or an arrow after them whenever a good opportunity presented itself. The fugitives rarely gave them the chance, however, as they dodged among the crags, and bowed low when they scur-

RIVER SCENE, MONTANA.

ried through or past any sheltering bushes. The chase lasted for a distance of four miles, when they fortunately struck a canyon, and into this they plunged with a suddenness that nearly carried them to the bottom at one bound. Along this they ran with renewed energy, and, in fifteen minutes after entering it, were delighted to find that the Indians had lost their trail or had been outrun. They reached their cabin late in the evening, but, instead of resting, they mounted their mustangs and went around among the miners, arousing them to the danger that threatened them. Being always prepared for warfare, those daring fellows were soon armed, and assembled at a common rendezvous under the command of our guide. They advanced against their foes the next morning, and, meeting them at the base of the mountain, dispersed them after a few volleys, which placed one-sixth of their number *hors de combat*, while they escaped scathless themselves. This summary defeat kept the treacherous red men away from that region ever after.

Thanking the *raconteur* for his story, we retired to our pallet of hay, and early the next morning returned to the mining hamlet, where we were received with many congratulations on our good-fortune. I have had some adventures among the big-horns since then in nearly all sections of the North-west, but none which equalled in pleasurable excitement my introduction to them among the rugged pinnacles of the War Eagle Mountains.

CHAPTER XV.

FOXES.

Foxes very Numerous in the West.—Hunting-clubs.—Various Species and Varieties of Foxes.—Difference between the American and the European Red Fox.—Size, Color, Characteristics, and Value of Fur of the Prairie, Cross, Black, Silver, Swift, and Arctic Foxes.—Difference between the Red and the Gray Fox.—The Latter trees, but rarely runs to Earth.—A true Woodland Animal.—Its Food.—Is being superseded by the Red Species.—The Dwarf or Island Fox.—Lives on Insects.—Fearlessness and Numbers.—Cause of its Diminutive Size.—Value of Fox-skins in Commerce.

FOXES are very numerous throughout the West, as many a farmer and stock-raiser knows to his sorrow; but instead of utilizing them as objects of the chase, and getting madly enthusiastic over the runs they afford, they destroy them in a more practical manner by spreading strychnine over meat and placing it where it will do most good—by capturing them in traps made of steel, and by shooting them as they take to their familiar run-ways when roused by the baying of many mongrels.

Grand battues are sometimes held, and a section of country is then almost cleared of them; for few can escape the circle of hunters that drive them toward a centre, and shoot them down as they run about in a bewildered manner, or catch them by the neck or tail and knock their heads against a tree or a rock. These people have no time to waste on sentimental dashes and the music of the hounds, and a fox is to them only a midnight assassin that preys on their poultry. "Gone away" is not a pleasant sentence to them; as it means that they have lost four or five dollars' worth of fur, and that their farm-yard will soon be in mourning for defunct fowls, which are considered of more value than all the living foxes in the neighborhood.

Fox-hunting as carried on in Europe was a favorite amusement with the Southern planters before the war, and many a genial assemblage followed Reynard all day to the music of hounds and horns; but the loss of their wealth in that great struggle has forced them to devote their attention to business of late, so that fox-hunting, according to the old style, has become almost a memory in some places.

The establishment of fox-hunting clubs and packs of hounds in New York and a few other places may have

THE FOX.

some effect on the remainder of the country, and cause kennels to be established in various cities; but this does not seem very probable at present, at least to any extent, as the people are too much absorbed in commercial pursuits to have much time to devote to following Reynard. The sport as carried on in Great Britain can hardly become general under present conditions, owing to the wooded character of the country, and the high and crooked wooden fences, which are even more dangerous than the stone walls of Galway and Roscommon.

Although there are several varieties of foxes in the country, there are really only two distinct species; and these are the common red fox (*V. vulgaris*), and the gray or Virginia fox (the *Urocyon cinereo-argentatus* of Coues). The former is larger than the European species; it has a shorter and more pointed nose; the ears are shorter; the legs are not so robust; the eyes are nearer together; the feet and toes are more densely furred; the brush is larger; and the fur is softer, finer, and of a brighter hue. It is equally as swift and cunning, and bears out in the most marked manner the traditional character of its family.

One of the principal varieties of this species is the long-tailed or prairie fox (*V. macrourus*), which has a beautiful fur and brush, the latter being very hairy; and the pads of the feet are concealed by hairs. This animal has a length of from thirty-three to thirty-five inches, while its brush often exceeds twenty-two inches. The next is the cross fox, variety *Decussatus*, which is readily recognized by its having a dark band along the back, which is crossed by another on the shoulder. This has a heavy, long, and bushy tail, which gives it a very pleasing aspect. Its skin is valued at five dollars in the market. The black fox and the silver fox are highly prized for their fur, the peltries being worth from twenty-five to fifty dollars.

The Kitt, or swift fox (*V. velox*), which is not found west of the Sierra Nevada and Cascade Ranges, is smaller than the red or gray; its limbs are short and robust, and its inner fur is full and close. Its pads are covered with hair to such an extent that they are concealed from view. Its head is shorter and broader than its specific red congener, and its ears are also smaller. It has a length of two feet or more, and its tail is from nine to eleven inches long. It does not, it seems to me, deserve the name it bears for speed; for it cannot, so far as I can judge, excel its larger kindred in pace and endurance, and a good fox-hound can run it down, with a fair start, as easily as it can its European congener. It is very prolific, and brings forth from four to eight young in its burrow, about the latter end of March.

The arctic or stone fox (*V. lagopus*) is very common in Alaska and the northern parts of British America. It is considered to be the most valuable member of its family when attired in its winter coating of white, its skin being valued all the way from fifty to two hundred dollars, and sometimes more.

The most common colors of this specimen in summer are blue, gray, and white, the former predominating. This handsome creature is one of the most prolific of its family, its litter often numbering from ten to fourteen youngsters. It has been introduced on several of the large islands on the Alaska Coast by the Russian American Fur Company, and they take excellent care that it is not destroyed without their consent. Its striking and strange hue seems to be a slate color tinged with darkish purple, and this is one reason why its fur is so highly prized; but, besides that, is the fact that it is also very fine, soft, and dense, and therefore makes excellent lining for cloaks or beautiful carriage robes. In its island home this creature lives on sea-birds and their eggs, and the carcasses of seals or fish washed ashore by the waves.

A fox that differs in many ways from its kindred, the red species, is the gray or mane-tailed fox. It differs from it, in fact, more than the latter does from the wolf.

The common red fox has a thoroughly canine skull, a long muzzle, and a tail uniformly haired: but the gray has a comparatively short muzzle, a short and broad head, and the brush has a hidden mane of stiff hairs along the upper side. While it is as large as the common species, it is more stoutly built, and its tail is not so cylindrical. It may be readily known by its grayish color, even if a person did not notice its peculiarity in form, physiognomy, and its rounded skull. It is literally a woodland animal, for it carefully shuns open ground. Its favorite haunts are in the Southern States, but it is very common in California,

Oregon, and other Northern wooded regions. It has a length of from twenty-seven to thirty inches; its brush varies from thirteen to eighteen inches in length; its ears project about two and a half inches above the skull; and it has a height of from twelve to fifteen inches.

It does not burrow like the red fox; but if it does go to earth at all, its den has only one entrance, so that it is easily driven out. Its favorite places of concealment are in thickets or the hollow of fallen trees; and, if started from these, it seeks safety in rank herbage, or in the densest part of the forest. I have hunted it sometimes, but I never saw it run to earth, its usual means of escape being to leap on an inclined tree and jump from branch to branch. Though having no retractile claws, yet it can climb small trunks by hugging them much as a bear would, and it can get to the topmost branches almost as quickly as a raccoon.

When pressed by the hounds, it is treed as surely as the red fox is run to earth, and is generally brought down from its lofty pinnacle with a rifle or shot-gun, as its skin is valued at five dollars. The old fable about the fox that had a thousand tricks with which to baffle its pursuers, while the cat had only one, and that to climb a tree, would not hold good on the Pacific slope, for the gray is not much behind the *felis* in its power to get among the branches. They tell of a Californian youth who was sent to a university in the Atlantic States to complete his education, and who corrected his teacher (a native of Europe) in natural history about the ability of the fox to climb. "What!" said the irritated tutor; "do you mean to tell me an untruth, and say that a fox can climb a tree?" "It ain't an untruth," said the other, "because I've seen him do it." The teacher appealed to the class to know if any of them had seen such a phenomenon, and they all replied in the negative. The daring student was then escorted to the president to learn what should be done with him for his impertinence, and making the statement he did; but that worthy individual, turning to the tutor, said, "I think, Mr. P——, that in future this young man might help you to teach natural history to the class, as he observes for himself; while you accept every statement because it is uttered by a professor, who probably never saw the animal. Now, I have seen gray foxes climb trees myself; so that he is right, and you owe him an apology." The crestfallen birch-wielder returned to his duties with a much less exalted opinion of himself, but he solaced his pride after awhile by telling a friend that he was not supposed to know how animals acted in America, being a stranger there; but he was positive that students, presidents of colleges, and foxes at least differed from their congeners in any other part of the world.

The creature which caused this dispute is disappearing before the advance of population, for, as the forest is cleared away, it has to seek other quarters to find food and shelter. It lives almost entirely on birds and small quadrupeds, and seems indifferent whether it feasts on a grouse, hare, squirrel, wood-rat, or field-mouse. As it recedes from settlements, its place is taken by the red fox, which finds shelter convenient to the farm-yard in a deep and tortuous burrow, whence it can make its nightly raids on the poultry. It is, therefore, a much greater enemy to the farmer than the other; hence every effort is made to exterminate it with rifle, trap, and strychnine.

One of the most curious specimens of the *Vulpidæ* to be found on the continent is a variety of the gray fox, called the coast, island, and short-tailed fox, and known to science as the *Urocyon littoralis*. It is the smallest member of its genus, a full-grown male not being larger than a house cat. It resembles the gray or woodland fox in every characteristic except size; but it would seem to have been formerly as large as that species, and to have been reduced to its dwarfish proportions through many generations of half-starved ancestors. It is found only on the islands of San Miguel, Santa Cruz, and Santa Rosa, off the coast of Southern California. It lives almost entirely on insects, grasshoppers forming the largest portion of its food; yet it sometimes manages to catch a sea-bird, and to enjoy an unusual feast of meat. It also makes a raid on the nests of gulls, cormorants, guillemots, and kindred birds, but they are generally too cautious to place their eggs within its reach, so make their domiciles amidst the most inaccessible crags.

This fox is supposed to have been isolated from the main-land by the advancing sea, which covered a large area of country, and placed a strait sixteen miles wide between its home and the region where pabulum was plentiful. Being unable to find any bone-making, nourishing food, its remote ancestors began to dwindle gradually in size, until, in successive generations, the present limit was reached. Were these insect-eating dwarfs transferred to the main-land, where food is abundant, their posterity would probably regain the original size in the course of years.

They may now be seen loitering about all day long, turning over stones and plants in search of insects, and, when found, devouring them with the greatest avidity. Several have been dissected, but nothing was found in their stomachs except grasshoppers and kindred insects. Their habits have been even changed by isolation, for, instead of prowling about at night and fleeing from man, they roam abroad at all hours, and have no more fear of their human foe than they have of a shrub. They will scarcely move out of his way in many instances, and they may look up into his face with a gaze that expresses curiosity more than fear. The reason for this simplicity of nature is that man has long been a stranger to them, though he is more familiar now, as some persons have occupied the islands as sheep-ranges.

These say that the creatures are perfectly harmless even to lambs; but that would seem to be an open question, as it does not look probable that they could have lost all their carnivorous propensities by even an insect diet. They are so numerous on the islands that a person may meet twenty of them in an hour's walk; and on Santa Cruz Island, which has an area of one hundred and fifty square miles, they are very abundant. The skins of the adults are often lined inside with cactus spines, which enter through the fur and become arranged in layers; and so thick are they frequently that a knife-blade cannot be inserted between them. Some become soft and flexible from age, but others are as stiff and hard as if they were in full vigor on the plants.

This species whelps in early summer, and brings forth its young in a rocky crevice or a simple burrow, the family being generally large. The males range from thirteen to seventeen inches in length, and the tail and legs are equally small, the latter being very weak.

While the foxes of the West do not afford sport as their European kindred do, yet they form no small part of the wealth of the country, as their skins bring good prices, and many thousands are sold annually by the trappers and hunters. If their total value was placed at $1,000,000 per year, it would not, I think, be overstating the matter.

CHAPTER XVI.

HARES.

Hares.—Their Abundance.—The "Jack Rabbit."—Mark Twain's Opinion of its Speed.—Marvellous Tales of Pioneers.—What constitutes an Oregon Mule.—Coursing-clubs.—California Greyhounds.—Characteristics of the Water-hare.—Swims like a Retriever.—How it escapes its Pursuers.—The Swamp-hare.—Its Peculiar Appearance.—Measurements.—The Washington, Prairie, California, Wood, and Sage Hares, and the Smaller Varieties.—Peculiar Character of Baird's Rabbit.—The Males suckle the Young.—Dissection by a Surgeon.—How Indians and Whites capture Hares.

HARES are so abundant in the Far West and South-west that they are considered nuisances in many sections of the country. Their numbers are actually incalculable in several places, and any ordinary shot can easily kill from twenty to fifty in a day without much trouble, and in many cases he may bag one hundred without travelling more than two or three miles. No person who has not been in the country can possibly comprehend how profuse they are, or how little fear they have of man. I have hunted them with a shot-gun; but I found that after awhile to be mere butchery, and was compelled, for the sake of sport, to use a rifle, and to try and shoot every one in the head, or not consider it a fair kill. When the creatures stand within twenty feet or less of you, and look at you as though you were no more dangerous than a shrub, it is proof positive that man is a stranger to them; yet this I have seen frequently.

The great hare, and the species most characteristic of the Far West, is the *Lepus callotis*, known as the mule and the jackass rabbit; yet it is no more a rabbit than any of the European hares, for it does not burrow as the *L. cuniculus* of Europe does, nor is it so prolific, neither is it cannibalistic in character. It has its "form" amidst long grass or thickets, or in the crevices of rocks, and produces its young above-ground. Mark Twain, in his "Roughing It," has credited this species with unusual speed, and describes one as bowling along easily at the rate of a mile per minute; but, when startled, to scud away at such a pace that it could be heard whizzing through the air long after it was out of sight. Strangers to the Pacific slope frequently indulge in exclamations of surprise on seeing it the first time; but if they give vent to their feelings in the presence of veteran pioneers, they

THE HARE.

are sure to be stuffed with a lot of marvellous tales about its size, fleetness, and the length of its legs and ears.

An immigrant to Oregon could not find adjectives enough, without indulging in expletives, to express his surprise at the ungainly aspect of such a hare, but he was soon shocked to hear an old hunter assail greenhorns in the most vigorous terms for not knowing the difference between a hare and a mule. "Why, isn't that a hare?" asked the immigrant. "Certainly not," was the response; "that's a mule, and any one but a fool from the States ought to know it." "But no mule can run like that," said the other. "Oregon mules can," was the answer, "for they are sprung from coyotes and Indian mustangs." The immigrant looked at the speaker in blank amazement; but when his assertion was gravely backed by other settlers present, he could only yield, and say that the Pacific Coast did indeed contain many wonders. He wrote a description of the new "mule" to an Eastern newspaper under the dictation of the pioneer; but, unfortunately for him, the journal published it with comments so pointed that he was afterward known as the Oregon mule.

This long-eared creature affords much sport to those army officers on the frontier who keep greyhounds, and many a pleasant day have I had with it myself both with dog and gun. When started it heads for the highest ground at once, and manages to lead the hounds a jolly run ere it is caught. Notwithstanding its long hind-legs and light body, I doubt if it is as swift as the English hare; at least I have seen few escape a good brace of greyhounds on open ground; but I should fancy it had more endurance.

In California, that land of keen sportsmen, its representative there is hunted regularly with greyhounds, that being the only portion of the United States where a coursing-club exists. It is governed by the same rules as similar clubs in Great Britain, and its meets are reported with as much detail as those held at Altcar. The victorious dogs are also made much of, and their progeny commands a high price in the market. It is said that dogs imported into the country increase in size, speed, and staying power; and if that is the case, it would be worth while to match its best representatives against those of Great Britain at some important meeting, such as the Waterloo.

I have heard it stated that English dogs, when first imported, are beaten, in the majority of cases, by the native-bred, but that they improve so rapidly under the influences of the invigorating climate, that they are able to render a good account of themselves in a short time.

Notwithstanding its apparently large size, the mule rabbit is smaller than the European hare, especially in the body. Its enormous ears, often six inches in length, which have given it the name it bears, are long and broad, and are nearly one-third longer than the head. It has a length sometimes, when full grown, of thirty-three inches or more, and its hind-legs are very long. Its general color above is a yellowish-gray, blotched, and lined with black. The upper surface of the tail is black, and, beneath, grayish-white; the legs are ashy, and the tip of the posterior surface of the ear is black. There is much variation in hue, according to age and season, yet no one who has ever seen it would mistake it at any time for another species. While this creature is seen in almost every character of land between the Rocky Mountains and the Cascade Range, yet it seems to prefer a rolling country, where hill and vale alternate. It is fair eating, and I have often found it a most useful addition to a camp larder.

The opposite to this in every way is the *L. aquaticus*, called in some places the swamp and the water rabbit. The latter is the more appropriate name, for it is almost amphibious in its habits, and is remarkable for the size of its head, compared to its body, and the shortness of its ears. The head is very large; the ears are scarcely half the length of the head; the hind-feet, which are shorter than the head, are pointed, and the claws are uncovered. The tail is about the same length as the ears; the hind-feet look slender, owing to the depth of the pads, and they are pointed at the toes, instead of being blunt. The shortness of the ears and the size of the head give it a peculiar appearance, especially as the former are broad and round at the apex, and are heavily covered with long hairs. The color above is a yellowish-brown, closely lined with black; the sides are grayer; the tail and legs are a rusty brown; the tail beneath and the abdomen are very white; and a black spot is found on the forehead. The fur is coarse, bristly, and harsh, and is of little use in commerce.

This creature is found principally in the South-western States, and is one of their most peculiar fauna. It is rarely seen on high grounds or prairies, but is always found near streams or lakes. It takes to the water as readily as a retriever, and may often be seen swimming about in search of the water-plants which it loves. When startled by men or dogs, it goes for the water at once, and generally escapes, as its scent is lost immediately. It is not considered edible by hunters, as it is very often attacked by a red bug which produces sores, and these soon breed maggots that fairly eat it up alive. The male attains a length of twenty inches; the tail is nearly three inches long; and the hind-feet are from three to over four inches in length.

The next species allied to this is the true swamp hare (*L. palustris*), whose head and incisors are disproportionately large. The ears are not more than two-thirds the length of the head: the hind-feet are shorter than the head; the toes are pointed, and the nails are visible. This, also, is one of the most peculiar of American hares, owing to its short and thinly-furred feet, its wide head, and small, weak legs, especially the hinder. The tail is short, being scarcely half the length of the ear, and the fur is coarse and bristly. It changes much in color at various periods, but its usual summer coating is a grayish yellow-brown above, and a grayish beneath.

One striking peculiarity between the Western hares is, that while the skull of the mule and the large California hare is narrow, the width being less than one-half the length, that of the others is broad, the width being about half the length. The European rabbit (*L. cuniculus*) would seem to be the connecting link between these two classes, so far as the form of the skull is concerned, as it occupies the medium position.

One of the largest, if not the largest, hares in the Northwest is the polar hare (*L. glacialus*), which is very abundant in Alaska and portions of British America. Its ears are four-fifths the length of the head, and its tail is proportionately long. It turns completely white in winter; but in summer it is a yellowish-brown and gray above, varied with black; and the ears are a glossy black outside.

The *L. washingtonii* takes the place of the common American hare, of which it is a variety, west of the Rocky Mountains, and is there very abundant. The ears are shorter than the head, but the hind-feet are longer, while the tail is very short. The back, sides, and throat are a reddish-brown; the abdomen is pure white; and the tail is a lead color above, and a rusty white beneath. It is a handsome specimen of its family, and occupies a position between the *Lepus americanus* and the wood hare, *L. sylvaticus*; but it is readily distinguished from the latter by its smaller size and shorter ears, which are reddish externally. It turns white in winter.

The *Lepus campestris*, or prairie hare, is one of the largest of the American *Leporidæ*, and is the only species of the long-eared hares that turns white in winter. Its ears are about one-fifth longer than the head; the tail is as long as the head, and the hind-feet are longer. Its summer color is a pale yellowish-gray above, a white beneath, and the tail is all white. It attains various degrees of weight and length, according to its habitat; but it is no unusual event to find one over two feet long, and having a tail exceeding five inches, while its weight reaches from ten to twelve pounds.

The California hare (*L. californicus*), which is hunted a great deal with greyhounds, is also very large, the ears and the hind-feet being longer than the head, while the tail is as long. Its color varies much, but in summer it may be said to be a bright cinnamon red, mixed with some black, the under parts being a pale cinnamon. The tail is black above, and of a light cinnamon hue below. It attains a length of twenty-five inches, and its hind-foot is over five inches long.

The ubiquitous cotton-tail, or gray rabbit (*L. sylvaticus*), has ears two-thirds the length of the head. It is the largest of the short-eared hares, its length often reaching eighteen inches, and its weight varying from two to three pounds. The coating is of a lead color, the extreme tips being a blackish-brown, and the under part of the tail a cottony white.

The sage rabbit (*L. artemisia*) is one of the most abundant species in the West and North-west, and is found in immense numbers amidst the so-called sage plains, where the artemisia (*A. tridentata*) prevails; it may, in fact, be counted by the thousands in many places. Indians, wolves, foxes, badgers, and other carnivorous animals live on it largely in the regions bordering the Columbia River and its tributaries, and the former eat it with apparent relish, notwithstanding the fact that its flesh has a rank taste, owing to the chåracter of its food, which is composed almost entirely of the wild sage, purshia, or greasewood, linosyris, and kindred shrubs. This disagreeable flavor may be obliterated, however, by "drawing" it the moment it is killed, and placing an onion and a piece of lemon in the abdominal cavity when it is about to be cooked. The man who could not eat it then must be fastidious, and anything but hungry.

This creature, which is among the smallest of the hares, has ears as long as the head, and its feet are heavily clad with fur. Its general color above is a mixed black and brownish white; but the hue changes so much in different sections that this color cannot be called permanent. It is readily known from its haunts, and the way in which its feet are furred; it also turns white in winter.

Audubon's hare (*L. audubonii*), which is confined to the Pacific Coast, is smaller than the wood hare. It has long ears and short legs, and the tail is from two to three inches in length. It is very common in California, but is not much thought of as an animal for sport, owing to its size and lack of fleetness. The fur is close, and marked with black and grayish tips.

The *L. trowbridgii*, another California species, has a small head, and a tail that is almost rudimentary. The ears are as long as the head; but the hind-legs are unusually short, so that its gait resembles a series of jumps more than running. In color it is a dark brown above, and a plumbeous gray beneath; it may be readily distinguished from Audubon's hare by having no black edging on the tip of the

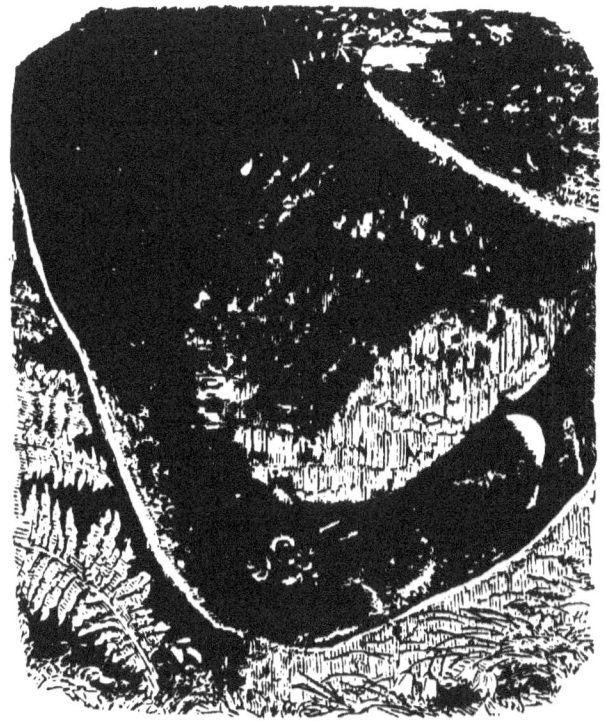

THE RABBIT WARREN.

ear, in being less of a pure white beneath, and in having a shorter tail and hind-feet. It attains a length of from twelve to fifteen inches, and a weight of one and a half pounds or more.

One of the most curious species of the *Leporidæ* found in the Far West is the little rabbit or hare known as *L. bairdii*, which is a Rocky Mountain variety of the *L. americanus*. This seems to be the result of a new departure in Nature, or at least a desire to prove that her general laws are mutable. The first specimen of this extraordinary creature was caught by Dr. Hayden in the Wind River Mountains, in June, 1860, but it has since been found from Wyoming to nearly the head-waters of the Yellowstone River. Five specimens were captured in 1872 by the surveying party under the professor's charge, and it is from these that the remarkable traits of the creature have been discovered. These are, primarily, that all the males have teats, and help to suckle the young. This has been assumed from the fact that four out of the five specimens captured were adult males, that all had large teats full of milk, and that the hair around the nipples was wet, and stuck to it, showing conclusively that they were nursing the leverets. As the party found no females, they thought their captures might be a hermaphrodite form; and to judge for themselves the truth of their suspicions, they got Dr. Curtis, one of the company, to dissect a large one. He found it to be a perfect male in every way; but, to be sure that it was not exceptional, he dissected others, and this assured him that he was right. Having seen no females, he could only say that he supposed both sexes took part in suckling the young. The doctor certified this report publicly in Washington, by stating that he had carefully examined the specimens in the field, and found they were males, yet gave external signs of being suckled. To satisfy himself, he carefully dissected one which was unmistakably marked, and found conclusive evidence that it had been suckled for some time previous to its death. The milk was abundant in the teats, but, excepting this, it had no other characteristics of the female sex, all the male organs being perfect.

Those mentioned are, so far as I know, the various species of true hares in the Far West and the South-west, if I exclude the common hare (*L. americanus*), which is abundant in portions of the country adjoining the Missouri River, and the Texan variety of the jack rabbit. All resemble their European congeners in habits; for they feed at night principally, have about the same number of young at a litter, and, like them, do not burrow. There is not, in fact, a specimen of the true rabbit in the country, if I except the descendants of the European species that may have become wild.

The hares are so profuse that they are shipped by the tons to the markets of the Atlantic States, and sold at prices so cheap that they could not, apparently, pay for the ammunition wasted on them. They are hunted in various ways in the West. One method is to run them out of covert with slow-hounds, and shoot them as they flee past a stand; another is to course them with greyhounds, but this affords little sport except with the mule rabbit; and the next is to trap or snare them. The latter is the favorite means of capturing them with market hunters and Indians, for by it thousands are caught in a day sometimes.

The grand drives of the Piute Indians of Nevada have often yielded them from three to ten thousand heads in a week; and had their traps and nets been more perfect they could have probably doubled the number. I have shot twenty in a day on the sage plains of Idaho, without walking two miles, and I could have shot many more if I wished to. Hares, or rabbits, as they are called, are in fact so abundant that they are nuisances in some places, so that the sportsman need have no compunctions of conscience about killing them.

CHAPTER XVII.

THE RACCOON, OPOSSUM, AND SQUIRREL FAMILIES.

The Raccoon, Opossum, and Squirrel Families.—Number of Species.—How Hunted.—Two Negroes and a Coon Stew.—Best Way of Shooting Squirrels.

AMONG the smaller game which often afford pleasant sport to the lovers of the gun are the above animals, especially when pursued with dogs; as they frequently give one an exciting run, and the coon struggles bravely against its canine foes when captured. The first two are hunted

THE RACCOON.

principally at night, as they are nocturnal in habits, and are generally killed amidst the leafy retreats of trees and shrubbery, where they take refuge. I have seen coon-hunts which were scenes of excitement and laughter, and which produced more ludicrous situations and mirth-provoking incidents than any other sort of sport I ever witnessed.

There are two species of raccoon in the West, the *Procyon lotor* and the Mexican or black-footed raccoon (*Pro-*

cyon hernandezii), which is found in the regions bordering the Pacific Ocean, from British Columbia to Mexico. Both are alike in general character, being cunning thieves, nimble tree-climbers, and one of the most inquisitive, restless, and mischievous of pets when domesticated. Nothing is safe from them if they break loose in a house, and they try to devour everything they can find, from stale bread to hair-oil. They are as bad as monkeys; but they differ from the latter in the fact that they will obey no order unless it is accompanied by force.

Adult males weigh from fifteen to twenty pounds, and, when cornered, they not only fight bravely, but often wound several of their assailants; for their jaws are large and powerful, and their claws are sharp and curved.

This species brings forth from four to eight young at a time, in the hollow of a tree; and while the mother remains with them she is a terror to bull-frogs, fish, and even birds and their eggs. She has also the fondness of the bear for honey, and will even risk an encounter with a dog to obtain it. Both sexes pay much attention to cornfields and orchards, and revel in the milky kernels, or the juicy apples and pears. I have frequently hunted a brace of them out of an apple-tree, and, when they reached the ground, the dogs and themselves generally had it out, unless they gave indications of being able to get away, when a shot-gun brought them down. Bull-terriers or large Irish terriers would be capital dogs for hunting them, as these have the combativeness and strength necessary to engage in a fair fight with them. For trailing them in the woods, the latter would be the better, owing to its keenness of nose and endurance, and the readiness with which it learns the habits of the creatures it pursues.

The raccoon is hunted principally on moonlight nights; and pleasant sport it is if one is with a jolly party, and the dogs are large and brave enough to relish a struggle. When the animal is treed, the tree in which it has sought refuge is generally cut down; and should it attempt to escape it is shot, or is killed by the dogs.

The negroes of the South are the greatest coon-hunters, and they spend many an hour of the night in the woods with dogs and guns to obtain the animal, whose flesh is considered by them to be unexcelled in delicacy of flavor. Coon-stew is a favorite dish with them; and so highly is it prized that I heard a negro preacher say that "Heaven is sweeter dan a coon-stew, or cabbage biled wid a hog's backbone."

As a specimen of how fond they are of it, the whites relate an anecdote about two of them who were out until morning in search of their beloved game, but captured only one. When they returned to the house they were very sleepy; but Jem told Sam that if he would sleep for awhile and then relieve him, both could have a nice nap before the coon, which was in the pot, could be cooked. Sam complied with this, and was soon fast asleep and snoring loudly. As the flesh of the coon began to get digestible, the pot-watcher commenced tasting it and drinking the soup; and so interested was he in his work that he forgot all about the sleeper, and devoured every bit of the animal. When that was done, the fear of the consequences caused him a great deal of tribulation, as he did not know how to escape from his difficulty. Finally, a bright idea struck him, and he carried it into effect at once. He rubbed Sam's lips with some fat, placed all the bones and the pot in front of him, taking care that a bone was also put into his hand, and then retired to rest, conscious of the efficacy of his stratagem. When Sam woke up, he was amazed at the condition of affairs, and his huge eyeballs rolled in astonishment as he gazed first at the bones, and then at his sleeping companion. He, at length, became both bewildered and angry, and laying his hand heavily on the shoulder of the sleeper, yelled out, "Come, Jem, none ob you foolin' wid dis chile; what's you done wid de coon?"

Jem stared at him with a look of blank surprise, and said, "Why, Sam, is you crazy? Dat coon? why you eat it all up in you sleep, and you wouldn't gi' me a moufful when I axed it, 'cause you said you was asleep."

"Go way now, Jem, none ob you foolin' wid me; I want my shac ob dat coon."

"Why," said the other, "dere's all de bones and de pot befo' you, and dere's you mouf all smead wid de fat, and now you say how I eat it!"

Sam felt his mouth, and finding that it was besmeared, he became calm, and begged pardon for his suspicions; but, placing his hand on his very empty stomach, he said, "I say, Jem, I s'pose I did eat dat coon; but it was the smallest and worsest one I eber seed, for I don't feel him here a bit." Jem was so delighted with his stratagem that he told it to his friends, and the result was that he and Sam soon dissolved partnership in coon-stews.

The opossum, which is the only member of the marsupials indigenous to North America, is found all over the South and South-western States, and extends into Southern California and Arizona. It has a total length of about three feet, and of this the tail takes up fifteen or sixteen inches. Its hair being white, with brownish tips, gives it a pale grayish color. It has rather a rat-like appearance —a resemblance which is increased by its long, round, and prehensile cauda.

The darkies are the great enemies of this little creature, also, and hunt it through woods, brakes, and briers, with mongrel dogs that have been trained to the chase. Persimmon thickets are favorite places for a meet, as the animal is very fond of this acrid fruit, and frequents its vicinity during the night. When the dogs have started the wily 'possum they run it up a tree or sapling, and there they remain and yelp until the colored Nimrods arrive on the scene in a state of breathless excitement. When the 'possum's position is known, some one climbs to its retreat and knocks or shakes it down, when the dogs finish it in a few moments. Its flesh is highly prized by the negroes, and they would travel far to obtain it. There is much fun to be gleaned from one of their hunts, as they get wild over the baying of the dogs, and indulge in the most grotesque remarks about their capture.

Squirrels may be counted by the millions in the West and South-west, there being some twelve or fourteen species of the *Sciurus*, about the same number of the *Spermophiles*, or ground-squirrels, four of the *Pteromys*, or flying squirrels, four of the *Tamias*, or striped squirrels, and two species of prairie-dogs—the common and the short-tailed. Add to these the *Arctomys*, or ground-hog, and the showtl (*Aplodontia leporina*), and it will be seen that small game is abundant enough.

Although these creatures seem to be created for the special purpose of feeding the larger carnivora, yet they form no small portion of the food of the wandering Indians. I have spent some pleasant hours in shooting them with arrows, and my captures were eagerly sought by hungry war-

THE SQUIRREL.

riors, or by chiefs with fierce-sounding names. The red men coax the little animals out of their burrows by chirping with the lips; and as soon as they appear at the entrance, to learn what the strange sound signifies, an arrow is sent twanging into their skull with a force that sends it through from side to side.

To hunt wood-squirrels successfully, small curs or terriers ought to be used; for the moment they tree one of the nimble creatures they announce it by sharp yelps, and if a person is any sort of a shot he may then bring it down from its leafy covert. If the squirrels are any way plentiful, one may bag a large number by quietly sitting on a tree-stump and shooting them as they scurry past, for they take little notice of a man if he is not moving about. They are used for food in some portions of the West by the whites, and are seldom absent from the bill of fare of game dinners given by sporting-clubs, and even by private persons. I have eaten squirrels frequently, and I can say that they are much better eating than persons give them credit for. The ground-squirrels are such nuisances in some places that the farmers have been compelled to resort to every means to get rid of them; but now, fortunately, some enterprising men have discovered a poison so subtle and cheap that it only costs ten cents to clear them off an acre of land, while the poisoners realize a handsome sum from the skins, these being their perquisites.

CHAPTER XVIII.

FUR ANIMALS.

Haunts, Habits, and Mode of capturing the Wolverene, Mink, Fisher, Marten, Ermine, Musk-rat, Skunk, Badger, Land and Sea Otter, Fur-seal, Beaver, and Showtl.—An Unpleasant Adventure while after Fur-seals.—Enormous Destruction of Fur Animals.—Latest Statistics.

ALTHOUGH the greater number of the animals known by this name in the West are not game, in the ordinary sense of the word, yet they form so important an article in the commercial world, and are sought after so much by some sportsmen, that I have assumed that a little information about them might be acceptable to those who wished to trap them, or to shoot a few for the purpose of making a robe or a mat. Another reason for introducing them is, that some of them are comparatively little known to the general reader, and that they possess characteristics which make them interesting to those who have a taste for natural history.

As all the *Mustelidæ* are known as fur animals, I mention them first, and place at their head the wolverene (*Gulo*

THE WOLVERENE.

luscus), whose mythical qualities have made it famous among hunters and trappers, and even caused grave naturalists to endow it with characteristics it never possessed.

This fabulously gifted creature receives its technical name from its supposed gluttonous qualities; and while it is true that its appetite is worthy of a gourmand, it is by no means so great as some persons have asserted.

The statements of old naturalists that it generally ate so much that its abdomen became swollen to such an extent that it passed between two trees, close together, to reduce its dimensions into something like decent proportions, is on a par with their assertions that it killed a deer by climbing a tree and dropping a piece of moss before it, and when the latter stopped to eat the tempting morsel, pounced quickly on its back and destroyed it in a moment; or those uttered by old trappers that no bullets could kill it, as it spat them out the moment they entered the body, and that no man could approach it unless he had the medicine bag of a great Indian chief about his person. The tales told about its courage, cunning, daring, and nonchalance are indeed numerous in the North-west; but it is hardly necessary to state that while some of them are founded on a substratum of fact, the greater number have no stronger basis than the imagination of superstitious and often ignorant trappers, and their congeners, the half-breeds and Indians.

The animal whose fabulous characteristics have made it so famous looks like a small and clumsy bear-cub, though its gait is not so plantigrade as that of Bruin. It has strength without activity, courage without caution, and energy without apparent motive; but it has so many other excellent qualities that these seem to be only the negative sides. It is certainly ungainly in appearance: the body being thick and rather long; the legs thick and short; the back arched, and higher than the head or rump; the eyes very small and wide apart; the ears low; the head broad, with a short, pointed muzzle; and the tail being drooping, of medium length, and very bushy. The feet are large for its size, and unusually furry, but the balls of the digits are naked. In color it is a dusky brown, with a perceptible band of yellowish-brown along the sides. The under parts, tail, and legs are blackish; and the claws are white, curved, sharp, and strong. It has an average length, excluding the tail, of about twenty-six inches, while the tail ranges from twelve to fourteen inches.

Like its family in general, it is not very odorous when aroused by anger, as it secretes a fluid in the anal glands which is very disagreeable when discharged. It is an arrant thief in character, and neither traps nor *caches* are safe from its depredations; it will even steal the most useless articles, and hide them with the cunning of a professional burglar. Camps and cabins are rifled in the most careful manner by this kleptomaniac during the absence of the proprietors, and what it cannot eat it destroys or conceals. It is caught very frequently in steel-traps or in dead-falls made of large logs, the bait being generally a piece of meat or some small animal, such as a rat or a squirrel, which has been sprinkled with castoreum. It is one of the greatest enemies the trapper has, as it will follow a line of marten traps for fifty miles, should they extend that distance, and devour all the captives. The young, which generally number four or five at a time, are brought forth in burrows, and while these are sucking the mother is seldom seen; but should she be encountered, she would fight as courageously as any animal living in defence of her cubs.

The fur of this creature is so highly prized for carriage robes that professional trappers consider themselves fortunate if they can get a few peltries, as they bring good prices, generally from four to ten dollars each. These men say that it will scatter its excretions over all food it may have concealed, to prevent other animals from touching it; and so fetid are these in scent that even a starving wolf will not approach any object under their protection.

The wolverene is probably one of the most ferocious animals known, when attacked or wounded, and, for its size, it is also one of the strongest—a fact which may be inferred from the ease with which it will pull down a disabled deer. It is not only brave but daring; for it will boldly enter a cabin when hungry, and fight, if forced to it, for anything edible in the house. It has been known to ransack cabins while the inmates were absent, and to steal everything in them that was at all portable, and to bury it deep in the ground. Such *caches* are often found by the odor of the excretions, as these are strong enough to be smelled several feet away.

The many tales told of its boldness, courage, and cunning prove that it is one of the shrewdest animals on the continent, and one of the most difficult to capture; for, if old trappers are to be relied on, it steals the bait from behind out of the traps, so that it avoids all danger. In order to catch it, the traps have to be covered with boughs, so as to make them resemble a *cache* as much as possible, and the natural propensity of the creature then induces it to steal whatever that contains. No clumsy contrivance will do to catch it, however, and if the trap be of steel, and it is not well fastened, the wolverene will probably walk away with it.

The animal will, it is said, shade its eyes with its paws on seeing a man approaching it from the leeward, and gaze at him intently until he draws quite near; and it will then either retreat or show fight, according to its disposition. It does not climb trees or hibernate, and its ordinary food is small animals, or such offal as it may find. It is, on the whole, one of the most interesting creatures in the country, and possesses an individuality of character which none of its allies can boast. It is probably the greatest enemy the fox has; as it will open up the burrows of the latter and devour the cubs, and their parents, if convenient, in the most ravenous manner. It is as destructive to Reynard and all his offspring as the latter is to the denizens of the farm-yard, and the result is that it destroys many young foxes in the course of the year.

Its allies of the *Mustelinæ* are very numerous in some portions of the North-west—a fact that is evident from the large number of peltries sold annually in Europe. The greater portion of these are purchased for the French, German, and Russian markets, where furs are largely worn, the finest quality being generally shipped to the latter country. Of these the mink, marten, and fisher are the most important, and they are followed by the musk-rat, polecat, and badger. These animals are nearly all caught in steel traps, or in garrotes or wooden dead-falls; and it is anything but pleasant to approach some of them, especially the mink (*Putorius vison*), as it emits an effluvium which is only exceeded in foulness by that of the skunk. This has its use, however, for trappers employ the fluid to scent baits, in order to make them more efficacious. The mink is very abundant where rivers are few, as it then keeps in colonies, and is not so widely dispersed as when the streams are common. I have seen dozens of these creatures within a distance of two miles in some portions of the North-west, but I found it of little use to try and shoot them in the water, as they dived on seeing the flash of the gun, and even when hit they sunk; so that I could not secure them without more trouble than they were worth.

The best means of capturing them is to build a small enclosure of stones in shallow, rippling water, and place the trap near its entrance, the bait being farther in, and well saturated with mink odor; and the animals, in trying to get that, are almost sure of putting their leg or head in the trap. If they are only caught by the leg they often gnaw that away above the jaws of the trap and escape, as they have strong vital power, and the pluck and furious temper of their family.

They are as aquatic as the beaver, and spend most of their time in the water, being to that element what the weasel is to the land. They feed on rats, mice, the marsh hare, birds, fish, crustaceans, and other denizens of the swamps and streams, and they seem to excel all other animals in their attachment to frog dinners. The mink, when tamed, is a pleasant pet about the house, and is a far better ratter than the domestic cat, but its odor is somewhat against it as a companion.

The fisher, or black cat (*M. pennantii*), is found in nearly all the mountain ranges of the West, and is quite common in many places. Though called a fisher, it is not aquatic in habits, but is thoroughly arboreous, its favorite haunts being the dense and damp woods adjoining water, and in this it differs from the marten, which prefers the driest parts of the forests of evergreens. It receives its name from the fact that it destroys fish found in traps, but it never angles for itself, as the mink does, and it seems to prefer meat to fish. It travels much at night in search of its prey, which includes everything from field-mice to squirrels; and as it fights fiercely, it is often able to kill animals larger than itself. Its length varies from twenty-four to forty inches, excluding the tail, which ranges from twelve to twenty inches, and its weight sometimes reaches from fourteen to eighteen pounds, so that it ranks next to the glutton in size. It is very destructive to marten traps, being almost as bad as the wolverene, and this causes hunters to execrate its presence, unless it gets trapped itself—an event which does not occur as often as they wish; for, being strong and plucky, it can tumble down dead-falls, and even get away with a steel-trap unless it is well fastened with an iron chain. Its skin is valued at from one to two dollars in the West, but it brings much more than that sum in the market. It is highly prized by some of the Indian tribes for making arrow quivers, as it is showy, long, and durable. The fisher has from two to four young ones at a time, and they are brought forth in the hollow part of a tree.

The American sable, or pine marten (*Mustela americana*), is abundant where settlements are scarce, as it is very prolific, its family generally numbering six or eight at a time. It is well able to live in its forest home, for, though not so insatiably blood-thirsty as the weasel, yet it is exceedingly destructive to birds and small mammals, so that it manages to secure plenty of pabulum at all times.

An adult male has a length of about eighteen inches, excluding the bushy tail, which is about ten or twelve. Its fur, which is in the best condition from November to April, is often over an inch in depth; but it differs in quality, some portions of it being finer and longer than others. Large numbers of this animal are captured annually in steel-traps and wooden dead-falls, the traps sometimes extending for a distance of forty or fifty miles in a certain direction, and numbering several to the mile. The bait consists simply of a bit of meat, a bird's head, or even a field-mouse; for it seems to have an appetite for all things edible, from insects to eggs and rats.

Like its congeners, it emits a strong effluvium at will, but it is not so strong as that of the skunk or mink. This creature is thoroughly arboreous in its habitat; hence it is seldom found in clearings or near settlements, so that it does little harm to the poultry-yard. It is an expert climber, most active worker, and a shrewd little creature in many ways; and, were it not for its odor, it would make an amusing house-pet. Its fur is in such active demand that it meets a ready sale; and this causes trappers to capture it in large numbers during the winter.

THE ERMINE.

The stoat, or ermine (*Putorius erminea*), is very common in Alaska and British America. This graceful, untiring, brave, and destructive creature has four or five young ones at a time, their birthplace being generally the hollow of a log, a tree, or a rocky cavity. The stoat certainly deserves its technical name, for, when aroused by anger or sexual passion, it emits a vile odor which is almost unbearable; so that it is no wonder that rats and ground-squirrels flee before it in terror, as, omitting its fierce and destructive nature, which induces it to kill even when there is no necessity for it, the stench alone which it exhales is enough to make its superiors in physical strength scamper away from it. It roams abroad principally at night, but it is also often out in the daytime.

This creature has a total length of about fourteen inches; and its fur, which is soft, thick, and fine in the Northern latitudes, becomes white in winter, when it is in the best condition for the market. This is a favorite fur on the Continent for several purposes; hence it is nearly always in active demand. There are two or three other species of the weasel in the country, but they amount to little in the fur market.

MUSQUASH, OR AMERICAN MUSK-RATS.

Of the musk-rat, polecat, and badger little need be said, as they are well known. The former is amphibious; the second is famous for its destructive character, courage, and perfume bag; and the third is notorious for its combativeness and its nocturnal habits. The skin of the skunk is now becoming so popular that thousands of this animal are killed annually, to supply the increasing demand. The sooner they are all made into robes the better will the Western pioneers like it; for not only is the creature offensive to the nose and the farm-yard, but its bite is often attended with fatal results, the symptoms it produces being similar to those attending an attack of hydrophobia.

THE BADGER.

The badger is so common in some portions of the West that its burrows cover a large area of country; and it is so numerous that it is dangerous to gallop a horse in some places. As this animal seldom travels abroad in the daytime, it is a rare thing to see one; but should a person meet it accidentally, and try to head it off from its burrow, it would probably pay no heed to his presence, and attempt to enter, *nolens volens*, though he might keep kicking it.

I have routed it out sometimes with terriers, and sometimes by pouring water into its burrow; but as a game or a fur animal I could not see much in it to make its pursuit pleasant; though it may be profitable to trap, as its fur is in active demand for making the cheaper class of goods. It is usually caught with a No. 3 trap. This animal roams to a high altitude on the mountains, often to a height of seven or eight thousand feet, but its favorite habitat is the treeless plains, where ground-squirrels are abundant.

The land-otter is increasing in numbers in some of the regions bordering the Pacific Ocean, owing to the cessation there of trapping, at least to any extent; but it is rapidly decreasing in other sections of the country, especially where the fur companies have depots. The system of capturing it varies in different quarters; but, as a rule, the idea is to conceal a steel-trap in or near the water in places which it is known to frequent, and these are readily detected by the slides which it makes down an embankment to a stream or a lake.

The American otter differs from the European in a few minor details. It is larger, has a shorter tail, and the fur of the abdomen is as glossy as that of the back. The fur is very fine, and somewhat waved, and in summer it is short and nearly black, but in winter it turns to a handsome reddish-brown. It resembles that of the beaver in character, but seems shorter. The length of an adult is about five feet, and the tail about eight inches. It is seldom seen during the day, yet I have had a shot at one early in the morning and toward sunset. Shooting it is of little use, however; for, unless it is on land, the probability is that it will sink in the water and be lost. Trapping it is therefore the only reliable method of capturing it, to make its skin useful in commerce. This animal has one litter of young in a year, and they are brought forth in a burrow

THE OTTER.

close to the water about the month of April. Were it hunted with otter hounds it would afford capital sport, as it is almost as common as the beaver in many places.

The connecting link between the preceding animal and the seal family seems to be the sea-otter (*Enhydra marina*), whose habitat extends from Alaska to California. This lover of boisterous waves is probably the most valuable fur animal known, its skin being worth from forty to ninety pounds sterling in the London market, according to its size and condition. The latter price is paid only for the largest size and the finest quality—those which show the whitish or silvery hairs scattered through the denser black or blackish-brown.

This beautiful creature resembles its congener of the rivers and lakes in outline, but differs from it in some particulars. Its forepaws are larger and stronger, and the webbed hind-feet are covered with a thick coarse hair, so that its web is not like that of the beaver. It possesses most formidable teeth, the grinders being round, broad, and thick, to enable it to crush bivalves and other hard substances with facility. It lives entirely on the marine denizens of the sea, but its favorite food seems to be the larger species of fish.

Though rarely found on land, except when it visits some wild and wave-lashed rocky islet to produce its young, yet it is sometimes seen near the shore in salt-water inlets, and is then readily caught by cutting off its retreat to the sea by means of boats or canoes, and forcing it shoreward. Being exceedingly timid, it is readily alarmed, and dives immediately on seeing any strange object approaching it in the water; hence it is rather difficult to capture.

It sleeps in the water, generally on its back; and if the female has her cubs with her, she may, on awaking from her slumber, play with them in the most affectionate manner, now holding them aloft in her paws, then rolling over and under the waves with them in the most sportive way imaginable. This animal generally travels in families, it being rare to see large shoals together, yet groups are met at intervals, though they, apparently, have no common purpose in their migrations. They are hunted regularly by the Indians when the opportunity presents itself, but it is an unusual occurrence to see the whites devote much attention to the business, as it is too uncertain to please them. Some of the Pacific tribes go far out of sight of land, probably fifty miles or more, in their pursuit, but that is generally when they are known to be seeking the rocky islands for the purpose of cubbing. If the hunters are successful in making a good haul, a feast and a dance is the result; but if not, they think that the spirit of ill-luck has worked against them, and, to appease that, they frequently indulge in barbaric ceremonies and incantations to allay its anger.

The animal was formerly shot with bows and arrows, but since the introduction of fire-arms many of the red men have discarded their own primitive weapons for the latter; yet it is doubtful if they are any more successful, as they are apt to fire at too great a distance, so that if they even kill the otter it is liable to sink and be lost before they can reach it.

Some are recovered, however, by diving for them, as they do not go down like a stone as the seal does. Rifles are also likely to frighten the animals by their noise, and thus make them scatter more quickly than if the silent spear or arrow were used. Several of the more Northern tribes are skilful otter-hunters; and it is really an inspiriting sight to behold a fleet of their canoes riding the boisterous waves, as they ply spear and arrow, or use the more destructive fire-arms in pursuit of their game.

The Makahs of Washington Territory are the best otter-hunters that I saw on the northern coast south of Alaska; but in the latter country the Aleuts, who make capital sailors, were acknowledged to be the chiefs. I accompanied the former a few times on a hunt after the otter and fur-seals, but our luck, on the whole, was only moderate, as the sea was often very rough; hence we could not land on some of the islets in Fuca Straits. Their mode of capturing their quarries was to spread out in every direction and beat about; and whenever a seal or otter was discovered it was chased immediately, and was kept diving and swimming until its lungs became so full of air that it could not dive again; it was then promptly speared or shot. The otter sometimes rose to the surface very near a canoe, and the moment its head appeared, a spear, to which was attached a large bladder, was driven into its body; and if it was not then killed, and attempted to dive, the spear-point and bladder came off the handle, and the creature had to try and bear the pain of the one, and overcome the difficulty of sinking the other. When it had been planted with two large bladders it could not go far beneath the surface, owing to their buoyancy, so was made a prisoner in a short time. This is the method generally applied by this tribe in hunting all marine animals; and that it is successful is evident by the amount they earn during the hunting season—that being often from twenty to one hundred dollars a day per man, if the weather and luck are at all favorable.

When the Indians intend to surprise a rookery of otters, they generally select a tempestuous day for their enterprise, as their chances of success are then the greater. Placing provisions and short heavy clubs in their canoes, they land on the islets as silently as possible, and, when they find the animals, the clubs are plied with such vigor that they frequently kill from thirty to one hundred before the remainder can seek refuge in the seething ocean. Such enterprises are frequently attended with danger, for many a red man finds a watery grave where he went to find a treasure.

The peltries secured are, when dried, sold to the fur companies for sums ranging from thirty to one hundred dollars. A good skin is about six feet by four, exclusive of the tail, as that is always sold separately, it being generally given as a *douceur* to the wife. Some otters attain a length of seven feet, however, but they are the giants of their family.

Large numbers of these animals were killed formerly; but they have become so scarce of late, owing to the war waged against them, that it would seem as if they must soon become unknown. Behring's sailors were most indefatigable in pursuing them, as it seemed to open up an inexhaustible source of wealth; and the result was that nearly 115,000 skins were taken in the eleven years from 1786 to 1797, so that many of the men realized in this pursuit what was a fortune to them in Russia. Not more than a fraction of this number can now be taken in the same time, as they have been almost decimated in some places.

Another fur animal that is hunted extensively by nearly all the littoral Indians of the North Pacific Ocean is the fur-seal; and some of them, at least, find it a profitable business, judging from the number of peltries to be seen in the markets of San Francisco. The Russian-American Fur Company have the monopoly of the trade in Alaska; hence the red men dwelling south of that region do much

FUR-SEALS AT ENGLISH BAY, ST. PAUL'S ISLAND.

better with the animal than their Northern kindred, as they can kill it wherever they find it; whereas the latter cannot.

An adult male seal has a length of about seven feet, and the female of five feet. The former is polygamous, his harem usually consisting of eight or ten of the opposite sex, and more, if he can get them; and for these he will fight desperately against all rivals.

The lords of the harems and their spouses go ashore on

the islands in November to produce their young, and remain there, as a rule, until the following May. When the pups are born they are blind, and remain so for some time; but when they are a month old they are taken into the water by their mothers and taught to swim, and after that they spend most of their time in it. If caught when young they are easily tamed, and soon learn to know a person's voice and to expect his caresses. They are very active in the water; and as they move through it with great velocity, it is a most interesting sight to watch them. Their gambols are very pleasing, especially when they are leaping, as they can bound seven or eight feet into the air with apparent ease.

They sleep on their sides while in the sea, and when they go ashore they scramble and tumble over the rocks, until sometimes an island is fairly black with them; while their gruff barking is heard above the roar of the tempest and the screaming of the surging waves, especially if the males are fighting, as the females of their harems seem to encourage them to the combat by persistent cries.

When the Indians intend to attack these they drive them inland slowly, allowing them to rest at intervals; and when

THE SEAL.

they have reached a good position some of the herd are separated from the others, and the red men commence plying their sharp-edged clubs. One blow on the back of the head is generally sufficient to produce death, owing to the thinness of the skull.

When the hunters have killed all they want, or opportunity permits, the carcasses are skinned, the hides are dried, and the remains are made into oil, or boiled and eaten, so that no portion is wasted.

This valuable creature, whose hearing is very sharp, is readily distinguished from the hair-seal by having flippers destitute of hair, external ears, and only three nails, whereas the other has five nails on the hind flippers. It is, in fact, more closely allied to the sea-lion than to the hair-seal; hence is classed with it in the genus *Otariidæ*, instead of being placed in the *Phocidæ*. The allied kindred do not seem to care much for each other's society, however, for the sea-lion scrupulously avoids places occupied by the other, and very properly, if it has a sense of smell, for the rookeries of the fur-seal have anything but a pleasant odor.

I had an adventure once, while out on a short cruise after this animal, that I shall not readily forget, as it came near sending me over to join the great majority. I was in a large canoe in Fuca Straits with a party of Indians who were out on a sealing expedition, and our course led us to one of the small islands which dot that splendid body of water in many places. When we started from the reservation the day was fine, but after being out a short time the wind freshened into a stiff breeze, and the billows reared up into foam-crested hills that presented anything but a pleasant sight to us; and before we reached our destination they were so huge that our frail craft threatened to be ingulfed every moment in the vale of waters.

By pushing the paddles deep into the sea on the starboard side, and running across the waves, to avoid their following us and coming aboard, we managed to make slow headway—very slow indeed, as we had to watch the seas carefully and to steer right into the teeth of a land-breeze, while another coming from the ocean quartered us.

After a most tedious voyage of four or five hours we were compelled to land on the first islet we met, and were only able to do that through the immense force of a surge that carried us far up on the sloping beach and left us there high and dry. Finding ourselves safe, we pulled the canoe shoreward in a hurry, and had it beyond the reach of the waves before the next one arrived. The islet on which we were stranded was small, and contained scarcely anything interesting except a few breeze-torn firs, a meagre grass, and some humble flowers; yet it was land, and it was therefore very important then. In wandering about it, I noticed several caverns through which the seething waves dashed in masses of foam, and roared and rumbled as if they were in the greatest distress. Mingled with this thundering were the screaming of the wind and the cries of many seals—sounds which seemed to be in harmony with the boisterous elements of air and sea; and on looking down through an opening in the basaltic crags I saw a number of the animals lying on the rocks below, but they were beyond the heavy blows of the billows. Pointing this out to one of the men, I told him he had evidently come to a good place; but he only gravely shook his head, and walked away without uttering a word.

Toward evening the storm abated somewhat, but the violence of the wind was followed by a heavy rain that caused the sky to look like a black pall. To avoid this, we sought shelter in a cavern; yet that was not rain-proof enough to keep us from getting a drenching. Our position was made more uncomfortable by the want of food; for though the Indians had some dried clams, which they ate with avidity, I had nothing, as I expected to return to the reservation the same day. I envied my dusky companions their stomachs and appetites just then, and wished I had them for a short time, as I was very hungry, and I kept wishing it so much that I finally tried to eat some of their loathsome food; but I had not eaten the second mouthful before I was seized with nausea and its consequence. This made me so faint that I could scarcely move; and when I thought of my situation and dripping garments, I wished myself back on the main-land.

The storm having decreased in violence by midnight, it was decided to re-embark, if possible; so the canoe was launched on a receding wave by two Indians, who were stripped to the buff.

I stepped in first, but I had scarcely entered before a large wave struck the craft, and, lifting it high up, carried it and the two men holding it shoreward with a rush; and as I had not sat down I was pitched into the sea backward,

THE BEAVER TRAP.

and made to drink a large quantity of salt-water. I remember distinctly making some blind efforts to find a footing and attempting to swim; but I do not know how I got ashore, except to suppose that my struggles aided me somewhat, and that the wave did the remainder. I scrambled to my feet on the beach as rapidly as I could, and made a dash for the interior as fast as my soaking garments would permit, and was soon beyond the reach of the treacherous combers.

Not knowing what had become of the remainder of the party, I commenced shouting, and in a moment after a lusty voice could be heard above the roar of the storm telling me to come on. The darkness was intense, yet I soon found the Stentor; and on inquiring of him what had become of the canoe and those who held it, he said they were all right, except that one of the men had received a hard knock in the stomach from the craft, and was temporarily laid up for repairs. On rejoining the others a few moments after, I learned that the Indians had saved themselves by clinging tenaciously to the boat, and that when the wave receded, their weight kept it from going to sea, it being cast high up on the beach.

After a short consultation, it was decided to remain on the island that night and attempt to reach the main-land in the morning, the sea then running being deemed too heavy to give us much of a chance for our lives in the darkness. That night was a most wretched one to me, and I gladly hailed the return of the morning; as it enabled us to launch our canoe and reach the main-land in safety. When we arrived there, I learned that the Indians considered the

THE BEAVER.

island to be the resort of evil spirits; that it was their wailing we had heard in the caverns; and that it was because we had intruded on their ground that we met with the accident, as a warning not to go there again, or take the consequences. I accepted their interpretation of our ill-luck, for that was the last time I visited the place, as my duties carried me elsewhere; yet I do not now regret my experience on that lonely isle, which is sacred alone to water-fowl and seals, the heavy clashing of waves and crags, and the moaning or the screaming of the wind.

The beaver is becoming abundant in some portions of the country, especially in the wooded regions bordering the Pacific Ocean, as very little trapping is done there, owing to the cheapness of the fur, and the fact that people have a more settled business; but it is decreasing in British America, owing to the numbers captured annually in traps.

Another little creature found in the North-west, though not strictly a fur animal, deserves mention, owing to its unique position in the animal world. This species, which is known to the Indians of the North-west coast by the names of sewellel and show'tl, is one of the most unique specimens of the animal kingdom. It is certainly one of the least known of the mammals of America, owing to its scarcity, peculiar habits, and the want of opportunities to study its characteristics; as its habitat is confined to a few isolated and barren sections of the North-west, little frequented by the wandering tourist, and rarely indeed by the scientific naturalist.

Its geographical range is limited, being bounded on the south by Oregon, and on the north by British Columbia, an area embracing probably some eight degrees of latitude; while its eastward wandering is checked by the high, rolling plateaux that lie directly east of the Cascade Range. Unlike most of the quadrupeds of the North-west, it crosses this towering range; and here it differs widely from other mammals, for that chain is the most arbitrary on the continent in its separation of animal life; and in this feature is, in all probability, equalled by no other mountains on the globe except the Himalayas. It has not yet been found in the Rocky Mountains, nor, so far as I can learn, east of the Blue Ridge, which runs in a general south-westerly direction through Eastern Oregon and Washington Territory. The probability of its being an inhabitant of any other section of the continent except where it has been already discovered is strongly in the negative, as the soil and climate elsewhere do not seem adapted to its comfortable existence. Its favorite haunts are the small sandy prairies adjacent to the rivers that run through the dense forests of Western Oregon and Washington Territory, for it can obtain an abundance of food and water in such localities at all seasons of the year; and it is comparatively safe from enemies, especially those which are the most untiring in its pursuit and destruction—the badger and the coyote, or prairie wolf, whose habitat is the Eastern plateaux. The showtl being an inveterate miner, the soft sandy soil enables it to dig a home for itself in a very short time; and this, and the profusion of vegetation, combined with the equable climate of the Western divisions, are the very excellent motives that decide it in selecting the prairies for its home.

Being the only species of its genus yet discovered, it possesses much interest for the scientific naturalist, and not a little for the amateur who speculates on Nature's laws. In its isolation it stands as an example in the animal kingdom; so the question now to be settled is, what purpose is it intended to fulfil in the economy of Nature? It was at one time supposed to be a member of the *Spermophiles;* but Sir John Richardson, after a careful anatomical investigation, proved it to be not only a new species, but also a new genus, of the sub-family *Castorinœ*, and to differ widely from the squirrel family, especially in its dental formation. The molar teeth being devoid of roots, he named it generically and specifically *Aplodontia leporina*, from *aplos*, simple, and *odons*, a tooth. Its special purpose, therefore, so far as may be conjectured, seems to be to unite the squirrel and beaver families; for while it is distinct from both in many particulars, yet it greatly resembles one of the *Spermophiles*—the prairie-dog—in its range of food, domiciliary architecture, and social relations.

Like the latter, it is a strict vegetarian, a ceaseless miner, and a provident commissary; for it is always careful to lay by something for a rainy day. Unlike the prairie-dog, however, it does not seem to care for the sunlight, is as grave as an owl, and seldom resorts to playfulness—at least above-ground. Nature seems to have fitted it specially for dwelling in comparative darkness, judging from the smallness of the eyes and the form of the ears; and that it loves its gloomy abode would be evident by the care it takes to avoid the daylight, for it is rarely ever seen outside its burrow before the approach of twilight. I have seen it during fine days in March pottering around among its stores, which were spread over the burrows to dry in the sun; but the moment it detected the presence of any unusual object, it immediately darted inside.

In general appearance, the showtl is not unlike a muskrat, but with this important difference, that the latter flourishes a handsome tail, while the former is devoid of it—it has at least none worth mentioning; for the little fleshy protuberance that terminates the spinal column can scarcely be called one, the vertebra not being an inch long. A full-grown male averages about fourteen inches in length and six in height; but it looks taller than it actually is, owing to its general hump-backed attitude. The muzzle is large and round; the head full and well developed; the ears are short, quite rounded, and covered on both sides with fine, soft hair; the eyes are very small, and of a dark-brown color, and are situated midway between the nose and the ears. The incisor teeth are exceedingly sharp, and well adapted for cutting the roots, bark, and fibrous vegetables on which the animal subsists. Like those of all the rodentia, the longer they are in use the more efficient do they become; for Nature has wisely made them of such material that time and work only increase their effectiveness. The legs are short and stout; the feet broad and strong; and the nails, which are long, thick, and curved, are powerful mining implements.

I am not acquainted with any animal that can burrow a

home for itself in so short a time as the showtl; and it is well for it that it possesses this quality, else its life would be of short duration; for it has numerous foes, and no means of defending itself against their attacks except retreating to its subterranean domicile. Its powers of locomotion are exceedingly limited, owing to the peculiar conformation of the feet; and this great disadvantage leaves it completely at the mercy of its enemies when once outside its burrow. Its usual gait is an awkward, shambling run; and that is so slow that any animal of greater speed than the porcupine could readily overtake it, even when pressed to its best pace by fear.

Its fur is thick, and tolerably fine. Its outer tinge is a reddish-brown, but the inner approaches a bluish-gray at the base. The density of its coating made it at one time an object of pursuit by the Indians; but since the introduction of civilization and cotton goods they capture it mainly for its flesh, which they consider to possess high gastronomic qualities. The robe made of its fur gave the animal the name by which it is now known to the majority of the hunters and the coast Indians of the North-west. Lewis and Clarke, who were sent out by the American Government in 1804 to explore the country between the Rocky Mountains and the Pacific Ocean, heard of it from the Clatsop Indians, and in their work they mentioned that "it could burrow in the ground, and climb a tree like a squirrel." As they had not seen it, in all probability, they took their statements from the Chinooks; and Indian assertions in matters appertaining to natural history are not always famous for their correctness. This tribe used a robe made of its fur, which they called "she-wel-el;" and the explorers applied this name to the animal itself, although it was not the one used by the red man. The Nisqually Indians of Washington Territory call it the "showtl;" hence the application of both names in its denomination. The male and female are exact copies of each other, except that the latter is a little the smaller. She produces two litters a year, the first appearing in spring, the other in autumn, and the number of young at a birth is usually from four to six. The nest in which they are nurtured resembles that of the rabbit in form, and is usually placed in the darkest part of the burrow. The first family is cared for by the parents until the second appears; but, according to Indian tales, the members are expected to set up house-keeping for themselves after that time.

The showtl is quite social in character; and though not so gregarious as the prairie-dog, yet it seems very much attached to its kindred in the colony. This colony generally consists of from a dozen to a hundred families, and they, apparently, live together in the most perfect harmony. They seem moved by one common impulse, and that, as a rule, is to dig up the ground as rapidly as possible. The result is that the region adjoining their village is honeycombed in every direction, and is covered with a mass of dead vegetation; for they do not spare the root or bark of anything green that they can devour or destroy. They are persistent seekers after food, and such articles as they do not immediately dispose of they store away in their labyrinthine cellars. This acquisitive talent causes them to uproot a large tract of country in a short time, and when they exhaust the resources of one section they move to another. According to Indian tales, they migrate only at night, and, in a few minutes after having chosen an encampment, they have their houses ready for occupation. They first dig a shallow passage, then come to the surface, and work down again. This system of mining is evidently intended to relieve them of the necessity of forcing or carrying the excavated dirt out of the burrow, so that they seem to have a good idea of the economy of labor. All their movements being, as a rule, performed underground, a study of their habits is rather difficult, unless a large amount of time and patience is wasted. They are so cautious about moving out of their burrows, that it is only after they have carefully reconnoitred their surroundings that they even presume to drink from the rivulet near their village.

Their mode of felling shrubs and trees is to cut away at

the roots; and when the object of their attention is prostrate, all work with a keen activity, as the share of each is only limited by its power to carry it away. The camass (*Camassia esculenta*), which grows extensively on the prairies, and is used as an article of food by the Indians, seems to possess great attractions for the showtl, and it is consequently looked on by the red men as an impertinent rival. The result of this enmity or rivalry is apt to be prejudicial to the longevity of the rodent; for the Indian considers a dinner of roast camass bulbs and showtl meat a feast fit for a Cæsar, and he takes every opportunity of enjoying it.

This little animal seems to be indifferent to the topographical conformation of a country, judging by my own experience, as I have found it from the table-like prairies of the forest to the snow-line of the rugged Cascade Range. It must, I infer, partially hibernate during the winter on the higher mountains; but in the valleys, where frosts even are not severe, it remains in an active condition throughout the year. It may be seen out on the Cascade Range as early as March, especially if the weather is fine; but murky days cause it to keep close to its burrow, no matter whether its habitat is on hill, plain, or plateau. Its fiercest enemy east of the Cascade Range is the pugnacious badger, which pursues it with the greatest pertinacity, notwithstanding the fact that ground-squirrels are exceedingly numerous, and much more easily obtained. The *Taxidea*, like the red man, is, however, an epicure in its own way, and both these products of the American continent evidently consider the flesh of the showtl superior to that of any other animal. The meat is certainly tender, and much less rank in taste than that of the wood hare, while it is more succulent than that of the squirrel.

Whenever a badger gets among a colony, it plays sad havoc with its members, and destroys them in the very wantonness of its fury, much the same as a terrier would a lot of rats. The result is, that it soon deprives itself of a most savory *bonne bouche*, and it has then to content itself with spermophiles and field-mice. The coyotes, or prairie-wolves, also prey on the defenceless rodent; but it frequently eludes them in its labyrinthine burrows, into which nothing can follow it but the badger. This latter animal being unknown west of the Cascade Range, the showtl lives in comparative security in that division of the Pacific slope; for its greatest foe there, the red man, does not slay it wantonly.

The Indians of Washington Territory have a tradition that it was the first animal endowed with life, and the

BULLS QUARRELLING.

source whence sprung the human race—the red portion, at least—and on this account they pretend to entertain a sort of reverence for it; but that, like several other sentiments which they profess, extends no farther than mere expediency, for they kill it whenever they get the opportunity, and devour it with the greatest avidity. This barbaric bit of the Darwinian philosophy I once turned to account to test the extent of an Indian's reasoning power; but I found that he checked all attempts at argument by steadfastly adhering to the red man's sole code of ethics—expediency. I wanted to prove to him that he was a cannibal if he ate his remote ancestor, and he answered me promptly by stating that his ancestor was good eating, and should therefore be utilized in the only way in which it was practicable to do so; but, besides that fact, he reminded me that the human race had progressed so far from their original source that both could not now be considered kindred by any system of logic, and he therefore could not be considered a cannibal. I yielded the point at once, much to his satisfaction, as soon as I had proved to myself the mainspring of Indian action.

The showtl furnishes good sport to those who wish for exercise with the bow and arrow. It may be brought out of its hole by chirping for a little while, and the moment it appears it affords an excellent target for a shaft. Even when running toward its burrow, it moves so slowly that it can be easily killed or wounded with an arrow, if one is at all an adept in the use of the bow. I have shot some in that way, and found it interesting sport, besides enjoying a pleasant *bonne bouche* when hungry.

I examined several specimens captured in this manner, with the aid of a surgical friend, and found that they differed from their kindred, the ground-squirrels, in many particulars, but especially in being devoid of the post-orbital process, and having rootless molars. This latter characteristic allied them to the beaver; so the inference would seem to be that the showtl is the connecting link between the squirrels and the beavers. But why Nature should have produced, in opposition to all her general rules, only one genus and one species of this interesting creature—should have rendered it so defenceless, made it so scarce, and confined its range to such narrow limits—is a question to puzzle the minds of those unacquainted with her great arcana.

The number of fur animals shot or trapped in America each year seems almost incredible; yet, by glancing at the list of fur skins sold in London and Leipsic during parts of 1878–'79, we find that the enormous quantity of nearly 9,500,000 were disposed of by auction; but that does not by any means represent the total amount, as several minor dealers also got rid of their stock during that time.

The large sales of American furs in London during the months of January, March, and September, 1878, and January, March, May, and July, 1879, and during the months of May and September, 1878, and May, 1879, in Leipsic, amounted to the above figures, and were divided as follows; but it should be understood the list does not include all peltries sold, such as those of hares and other animals:

Musk-rat	5,462,720	Blue Fox	5,898
Raccoon	1,086,927	Opossum	658,040
Skunk	782,955	Lynx	46,563
Mink	419,338	Bay Lynx	7,890
Fisher	13,729	Badger	14,037
Marten	128,817	Bear	27,540
Beaver	347,203	Squirrel	61,655
Red Fox	141,408	Wolf	9,555
Gray Fox	52,235	Wolverene	2,124
Kitt Fox	15,783	Land-otter	32,312
White Fox	12,133	Sea-otter	6,912
Cross Fox	8,591	Fur-seal	140,478
Silver Fox	2,333	Total	9,497,176

During the months of March and September, 1873, the following furs were imported into London alone:

Musk-rat	2,942,845	Opossum	240,505
Raccoon	465,762	Lynx	7,785
Skunk	263,343	Badger	5,197
Mink	97,458	Black Bear	13,736
Fisher	7,155	Grizzly Bear	857
Marten	97,808	Gray Wolf	7,006
Beaver	211,897	Dusky Wolf	2,118
Red Fox	64,052	Wolverene	2,136
Gray Fox	26,750	Land-otter	19,242
Kitt Fox	9,205	Sea-otter	5,471
White Fox	9,290	Fur-seal	130,590
Cross Fox	5,879	Hare	10,029
Silver Fox	1,648	Total	4,649,562
Blue Fox	1,798		

THE END.

VALUABLE AND INTERESTING WORKS

FOR

PUBLIC & PRIVATE LIBRARIES,

PUBLISHED BY HARPER & BROTHERS, NEW YORK.

☞ *For a full List of Books suitable for Libraries published by* HARPER & BROTHERS, *see* HARPERS' CATALOGUE, *which may be had gratuitously on application to the Publishers personally, or by letter enclosing Nine Cents in Postage stamps.*

☞ HARPER & BROTHERS *will send their publications by mail, postage prepaid, on receipt of the price.*

MACAULAY'S ENGLAND. The History of England from the Accession of James II. By THOMAS BABINGTON MACAULAY. New Edition, from new Electrotype Plates. 8vo, Cloth, with Paper Labels, Uncut Edges and Gilt Tops, 5 vols. in a Box, $10 00 per set. Sold only in sets. Cheap Edition, 5 vols. in a Box, 12mo, Cloth, $4 00; Sheep, $6 00.

MACAULAY'S LIFE AND LETTERS. The Life and Letters of Lord Macaulay. By his Nephew, G. OTTO TREVELYAN, M.P. With Portrait on Steel. Complete in 2 vols., 8vo, Cloth, Uncut Edges and Gilt Tops, $5 00; Sheep, $6 00; Half Calf, $9 50. Popular Edition, two vols. in one, 12mo, Cloth, $1 75.

HUME'S ENGLAND. The History of England, from the Invasion of Julius Cæsar to the Abdication of James II., 1688. By DAVID HUME. New and Elegant Library Edition, from new Electrotype Plates. 6 vols. in a Box, 8vo, Cloth, with Paper Labels, Uncut Edges and Gilt Tops, $12 00. Sold only in sets. Popular Edition, 6 vols. in a Box, 12mo, Cloth, $4 80; Sheep, $7 20. -

GIBBON'S ROME. The History of the Decline and Fall of the Roman Empire. By EDWARD GIBBON. With Notes by Rev. H. H. MILMAN and M. GUIZOT. With Index. 6 vols. in a Box, 12mo, Cloth, $4 80; Sheep, $7 20. *New Edition, from new Electrotype Plates, in Press.*

HILDRETH'S UNITED STATES. History of the United States. FIRST SERIES: From the Discovery of the Continent to the Organization of the Government under the Federal Constitution. SECOND SERIES: From the Adoption of the Federal Constitution to the End of the Sixteenth Congress. By RICHARD HILDRETH. Popular Edition, 6 vols. in a Box, 8vo, Cloth, with Paper Labels, Uncut Edges and Gilt Tops, $12 00. Sold only in sets. (*In Press.*)

MOTLEY'S DUTCH REPUBLIC. The Rise of the Dutch Republic. A History. By JOHN LOTHROP MOTLEY, LL.D., D.C.L. With a Portrait of William of Orange. Cheap Edition, 3 vols. in a Box, 8vo, Cloth, with Paper Labels, Uncut Edges and Gilt Tops, $6 00. Sold only in sets. Original Library Edition, 3 vols., 8vo, Cloth, $10 50; Sheep, $12 00; Half Calf, $17 25.

MOTLEY'S UNITED NETHERLANDS. History of the United Netherlands: from the Death of William the Silent to the Twelve Years' Truce—1609. With a full View of the English-Dutch Struggle against Spain, and of the Origin and Destruction of the Spanish Armada. By JOHN LOTHROP MOTLEY, LL.D., D.C.L. Portraits. Cheap Edition, 4 vols. in a Box, 8vo, Cloth, with Paper Labels, Uncut Edges and Gilt Tops, $8 00. Sold only in sets. Original Library Edition, 4 vols., 8vo, Cloth, $14 00; Sheep, $16 00; Half Calf, $23 00.

MOTLEY'S LIFE AND DEATH OF JOHN OF BARNEVELD. The Life and Death of John of Barneveld, Advocate of Holland: with a View of the Primary Causes and Movements of "The Thirty-years' War." By JOHN LOTHROP MOTLEY, LL.D., D.C.L. Illustrated. Cheap Edition, 2 vols. in a Box, 8vo, Cloth, with Paper Labels, Uncut Edges and Gilt Tops, $4 00. Sold only in sets. Original Library Edition, 2 vols., 8vo, Cloth, $7 00; Sheep, $8 00; Half Calf, $11 50.

BENJAMIN'S CONTEMPORARY ART. Contemporary Art in Europe. By S. G. W. BENJAMIN. Illustrated. 8vo, Cloth, $3 50.

BENJAMIN'S ART IN AMERICA. Art in America. By S. G. W. BENJAMIN. Illustrated. 8vo, Cloth, $4 00.

THE FIRST CENTURY OF THE REPUBLIC. A Review of American Progress. 8vo, Cloth, $5 00.

HUDSON'S HISTORY OF JOURNALISM. Journalism in the United States, from 1690 to 1872. By FREDERIC HUDSON. 8vo, Cloth, $5 00; Half Calf, $7 25.

JEFFERSON'S LIFE. The Domestic Life of Thomas Jefferson: Compiled from Family Letters and Reminiscences, by his Great-granddaughter, SARAH N. RANDOLPH. Illustrated. Crown 8vo, Cloth, $2 50.

SQUIER'S PERU. Peru: Incidents of Travel and Exploration in the Land of the Incas. By E. GEORGE SQUIER, M.A., F.S.A., late U. S. Commissioner to Peru. With Illustrations. 8vo, Cloth, $5 00.

MYERS'S LOST EMPIRES. Remains of Lost Empires: Sketches of the Ruins of Palmyra, Nineveh, Babylon, and Persepolis. By P. V. N. MYERS. Illustrated. 8vo, Cloth, $3 50.

Valuable Works for Public and Private Libraries. 3

KINGLAKE'S CRIMEAN WAR. The Invasion of the Crimea: its Origin, and an Account of its Progress down to the Death of Lord Raglan. By ALEXANDER WILLIAM KINGLAKE. With Maps and Plans. Three Volumes now ready. 12mo, Cloth, $2 00 per vol.

LAMB'S COMPLETE WORKS. The Works of Charles Lamb. Comprising his Letters, Poems, Essays of Elia, Essays upon Shakspeare, Hogarth, etc., and a Sketch of his Life, with the Final Memorials, by T. NOON TALFOURD. With Portrait. 2 vols., 12mo, Cloth, $3 00.

LAWRENCE'S HISTORICAL STUDIES. Historical Studies. By EUGENE LAWRENCE. Containing the following Essays: The Bishops of Rome.—Leo and Luther.—Loyola and the Jesuits.—Ecumenical Councils.—The Vaudois.—The Huguenots.—The Church of Jerusalem.—Dominic and the Inquisition.—The Conquest of Ireland.—The Greek Church. 8vo, Cloth, Uncut Edges and Gilt Tops, $3 00.

LOSSING'S FIELD-BOOK OF THE REVOLUTION. Pictorial Field-Book of the Revolution: or, Illustrations by Pen and Pencil of the History, Biography, Scenery, Relics, and Traditions of the War for Independence. By BENSON J. LOSSING. 2 vols., 8vo, Cloth, $14 00; Sheep or Roan, $15 00; Half Calf, $18 00.

LOSSING'S FIELD-BOOK OF THE WAR OF 1812. Pictorial Field-Book of the War of 1812: or, Illustrations by Pen and Pencil of the History, Biography, Scenery, Relics, and Traditions of the last War for American Independence. By BENSON J. LOSSING. With several hundred Engravings on Wood by Lossing and Barritt, chiefly from Original Sketches by the Author. 1088 pages, 8vo, Cloth, $7 00; Sheep, $8 50; Roan, $9 00; Half Calf, $10 00.

FORSTER'S LIFE OF DEAN SWIFT. The Early Life of Jonathan Swift (1667-1711). By JOHN FORSTER. With Portrait. 8vo, Cloth, Uncut Edges and Gilt Tops, $2 50.

HALLAM'S MIDDLE AGES. View of the State of Europe during the Middle Ages. By HENRY HALLAM. 8vo, Cloth, $2 00; Sheep, $2 50.

HALLAM'S CONSTITUTIONAL HISTORY OF ENGLAND. The Constitutional History of England, from the Accession of Henry VII. to the Death of George II. By HENRY HALLAM. 8vo, Cloth, $2 00; Sheep, $2 50.

HALLAM'S LITERATURE. Introduction to the Literature of Europe during the Fifteenth, Sixteenth, and Seventeenth Centuries. By HENRY HALLAM. 2 vols., 8vo, Cloth, $4 00; Sheep, $5 00.

GREEN'S ENGLISH PEOPLE. History of the English People. By JOHN RICHARD GREEN, M.A. 3 volumes ready. 8vo, Cloth, $2 50 per volume.

4 *Valuable Works for Public and Private Libraries.*

SCHWEINFURTH'S HEART OF AFRICA. The Heart of Africa. Three Years' Travels and Adventures in the Unexplored Regions of the Centre of Africa—from 1868 to 1871. By Dr. GEORG SCHWEINFURTH. Translated by ELLEN E. FREWER. With an Introduction by WINWOOD READE. Illustrated by about 130 Wood-cuts from Drawings made by the Author, and with two Maps. 2 vols., 8vo, Cloth, $8 00.

M'CLINTOCK & STRONG'S CYCLOPÆDIA. Cyclopædia of Biblical, Theological, and Ecclesiastical Literature. Prepared by the Rev. JOHN M'CLINTOCK, D.D., and JAMES STRONG, S.T.D. 8 vols. *now ready.* Royal 8vo. Price per vol., Cloth, $5 00; Sheep, $6 00; Half Morocco, $8 00. (*Sold by Subscription.*)

MOHAMMED AND MOHAMMEDANISM: Lectures Delivered at the Royal Institution of Great Britain in February and March, 1874. By R. BOSWORTH SMITH, M.A., Assistant Master in Harrow School; late Fellow of Trinity College, Oxford. With an Appendix containing Emanuel Deutsch's Article on "Islam." 12mo, Cloth, $1 50.

MOSHEIM'S ECCLESIASTICAL HISTORY, Ancient and Modern; in which the Rise, Progress, and Variation of Church Power are considered in their Connection with the State of Learning and Philosophy, and the Political History of Europe during that Period. Translated, with Notes, etc., by A. MACLAINE, D.D. Continued to 1826, by C. COOTE, LL.D. 2 vols., 8vo, Cloth, $4 00; Sheep, $5 00.

HARPER'S NEW CLASSICAL LIBRARY. Literal Translations. The following volumes are now ready. 12mo, Cloth, $1 50 each.

CÆSAR.—VIRGIL.—SALLUST.—HORACE.—CICERO'S ORATIONS.—CICERO'S OFFICES, etc.—CICERO ON ORATORY AND ORATORS.—TACITUS (2 vols.).—TERENCE.—SOPHOCLES.—JUVENAL.—XENOPHON.—HOMER'S ILIAD.—HOMER'S ODYSSEY.—HERODOTUS.—DEMOSTHENES (2 vols.).—THUCYDIDES.—ÆSCHYLUS.—EURIPIDES (2 vols.).—LIVY (2 vols.).—PLATO [Select Dialogues].

PARTON'S CARICATURE. Caricature and Other Comic Art, in All Times and Many Lands. By JAMES PARTON. With 203 Illustrations. 8vo, Cloth, Uncut Edges and Gilt Tops, $5 00; Half Calf, $7 25.

NICHOLS'S ART EDUCATION. Art Education applied to Industry. By GEORGE WARD NICHOLS. Illustrated. 8vo, Cloth, $4 00; Half Calf, $6 25.

VINCENT'S LAND OF THE WHITE ELEPHANT. The Land of the White Elephant: Sights and Scenes in Southeastern Asia. A Personal Narrative of Travel and Adventure in Farther India, embracing the Countries of Burma, Siam, Cambodia, and Cochin-China (1871-2). By FRANK VINCENT, Jr. Illustrated with Maps, Plans, and Wood-cuts. Crown 8vo, Cloth, $3 50.

Valuable Works for Public and Private Libraries. 5

LIVINGSTONE'S SOUTH AFRICA. Missionary Travels and Researches in South Africa: including a Sketch of Sixteen Years' Residence in the Interior of Africa, and a Journey from the Cape of Good Hope to Loanda on the West Coast; thence across the Continent, down the River Zambesi, to the Eastern Ocean. By DAVID LIVINGSTONE, LL.D., D.C.L. With Portrait, Maps, and Illustrations. 8vo, Cloth, $4 50; Sheep, $5 00; Half Calf, $6 75.

LIVINGSTONES' ZAMBESI. Narrative of an Expedition to the Zambesi and its Tributaries, and of the Discovery of the Lakes Shirwa and Nyassa, 1858–1864. By DAVID and CHARLES LIVINGSTONE. Map and Illustrations. 8vo, Cloth, $5 00; Sheep, $5 50; Half Calf, $7 25.

LIVINGSTONE'S LAST JOURNALS. The Last Journals of David Livingstone, in Central Africa, from 1865 to his Death. Continued by a Narrative of his Last Moments and Sufferings, obtained from his Faithful Servants Chuma and Susi. By HORACE WALLER, F.R.G.S., Rector of Twywell, Northampton. With Portrait, Maps, and Illustrations. 8vo, Cloth, $5 00; Sheep, $5 50; Half Calf, $7 25. Cheap Popular Edition, 8vo, Cloth, with Map and Illustrations, $2 50.

GROTE'S HISTORY OF GREECE. 12 vols., 12mo, Cloth, $18 00; Sheep, $22 80; Half Calf, $39 00.

RECLUS'S EARTH. The Earth: a Descriptive History of the Phenomena of the Life of the Globe. By ÉLISÉE RECLUS. With 234 Maps and Illustrations, and 23 Page Maps printed in Colors. 8vo, Cloth, $5 00.

RECLUS'S OCEAN. The Ocean, Atmosphere, and Life. Being the Second Series of a Descriptive History of the Life of the Globe. By ÉLISÉE RECLUS. Profusely Illustrated with 250 Maps or Figures, and 27 Maps printed in Colors. 8vo, Cloth, $6 00.

NORDHOFF'S COMMUNISTIC SOCIETIES OF THE UNITED STATES. The Communistic Societies of the United States, from Personal Visit and Observation; including Detailed Accounts of the Economists, Zoarites, Shakers, the Amana, Oneida, Bethel, Aurora, Icarian, and other existing Societies. With Particulars of their Religious Creeds and Practices, their Social Theories and Life, Numbers, Industries, and Present Condition. By CHARLES NORDHOFF. Illustrations. 8vo, Cloth, $4 00.

NORDHOFF'S CALIFORNIA. California: for Health, Pleasure, and Residence. A Book for Travellers and Settlers. Illustrated. 8vo, Cloth, $2 50.

NORDHOFF'S NORTHERN CALIFORNIA AND THE SANDWICH ISLANDS. Northern California, Oregon, and the Sandwich Islands. By CHARLES NORDHOFF. Illustrated. 8vo, Cloth, $2 50.

6 Valuable Works for Public and Private Libraries.

VAN-LENNEP'S BIBLE LANDS. Bible Lands: their Modern Customs and Manners Illustrative of Scripture. By the Rev. HENRY J. VAN-LENNEP, D.D. With upward of 350 Wood Engravings and two Colored Maps. 838 pp., 8vo, Cloth, $5 00; Sheep, $6 00; Half Morocco or Half Calf, $8 00.

SHAKSPEARE. The Dramatic Works of William Shakspeare. With Corrections and Notes. Engravings. 6 vols., 12mo, Cloth, $9 00. 2 vols., 8vo, Cloth, $4 00; Sheep, $5 00. In one vol., 8vo, Sheep, $4 00.

STRICKLAND'S (MISS) QUEENS OF SCOTLAND. Lives of the Queens of Scotland and English Princesses connected with the Regal Succession of Great Britain. By AGNES STRICKLAND. 8 vols., 12mo, Cloth, $12 00; Half Calf, $26 00.

BAKER'S ISMAILÏA. Ismailïa: a Narrative of the Expedition to Central Africa for the Suppression of the Slave-trade, organized by Ismail, Khedive of Egypt. By Sir SAMUEL WHITE BAKER, PASHA, F.R.S., F.R.G.S. With Maps, Portraits, and Illustrations. 8vo, Cloth, $5 00; Half Calf, $7 25.

BOSWELL'S JOHNSON. The Life of Samuel Johnson, LL.D., including a Journal of a Tour to the Hebrides. By JAMES BOSWELL, Esq. Edited by JOHN WILSON CROKER, LL.D., F.R.S. With a Portrait of Boswell. 2 vols., 8vo, Cloth, $4 00; Sheep, $5 00; Half Calf, $8 50.

SAMUEL JOHNSON: HIS WORDS AND HIS WAYS; what he Said, what he Did, and what Men Thought and Spoke Concerning him. Edited by E. T. MASON. 12mo, Cloth, $1 50.

JOHNSON'S COMPLETE WORKS. The Works of Samuel Johnson, LL.D. With an Essay on his Life and Genius, by ARTHUR MURPHY, Esq. 2 vols., 8vo, Cloth, $4 00; Sheep, $5 00; Half Calf, $8 50.

SMILES'S HISTORY OF THE HUGUENOTS. The Huguenots: their Settlements, Churches, and Industries in England and Ireland. By SAMUEL SMILES. With an Appendix relating to the Huguenots in America. Crown 8vo, Cloth, $2 00.

SMILES'S HUGUENOTS AFTER THE REVOCATION. The Huguenots in France after the Revocation of the Edict of Nantes; with a Visit to the Country of the Vaudois. By SAMUEL SMILES. Crown 8vo, Cloth, $2 00.

SMILES'S LIFE OF THE STEPHENSONS. The Life of George Stephenson, and of his Son, Robert Stephenson; comprising, also, a History of the Invention and Introduction of the Railway Locomotive. By SAMUEL SMILES. With Steel Portraits and numerous Illustrations. 8vo, Cloth, $3 00.

Valuable Works for Public and Private Libraries. 7

RAWLINSON'S MANUAL OF ANCIENT HISTORY. A Manual of Ancient History, from the Earliest Times to the Fall of the Western Empire. Comprising the History of Chaldæa, Assyria, Media, Babylonia, Lydia, Phœnicia, Syria, Judæa, Egypt, Carthage, Persia, Greece, Macedonia, Parthia, and Rome. By GEORGE RAWLINSON, M.A., Camden Professor of Ancient History in the University of Oxford. 12mo, Cloth, $1 46.

THE VOYAGE OF THE "CHALLENGER." The Atlantic: an Account of the General Results of the Voyage during 1873, and the Early Part of 1876. By Sir WYVILLE THOMSON, K.C.B., F.R.S. With numerous Illustrations, Colored Maps, and Charts, from Drawings by J. J. Wyld, engraved by J. D. Cooper, and Portrait of the Author, engraved by C. H. Jeens. 2 vols., 8vo, Cloth, $12 00.

ALISON'S HISTORY OF EUROPE. FIRST SERIES: From the Commencement of the French Revolution, in 1789, to the Restoration of the Bourbons in 1815. [In addition to the Notes on Chapter LXXVI., which correct the errors of the original work concerning the United States, a copious Analytical Index has been appended to this American Edition.] SECOND SERIES: From the Fall of Napoleon, in 1815, to the Accession of Louis Napoleon, in 1852. 8 vols., 8vo, Cloth, $16 00; Sheep, $20 00; Half Calf, $34 00.

WALLACE'S GEOGRAPHICAL DISTRIBUTION OF ANIMALS. The Geographical Distribution of Animals. With a Study of the Relations of Living and Extinct Faunas, as Elucidating the Past Changes of the Earth's Surface. By ALFRED RUSSEL WALLACE. With Maps and Illustrations. In 2 vols., 8vo, Cloth, $10 00.

WALLACE'S MALAY ARCHIPELAGO. The Malay Archipelago: The Land of the Orang-Utan and the Bird of Paradise. A Narrative of Travel, 1854-1862. With Studies of Man and Nature. By A. R. WALLACE. Maps and Illustrations. Crown 8vo, Cloth, $2 50.

BOURNE'S LIFE OF LOCKE. The Life of John Locke. By H. R. Fox BOURNE. 2 vols., 8vo, Cloth, Uncut Edges and Gilt Tops, $5 00.

BLUNT'S BEDOUIN TRIBES OF THE EUPHRATES. Bedouin Tribes of the Euphrates. By LADY ANNE BLUNT. Edited, with a Preface and some Account of the Arabs and their Horses, by W. S. B. Map and Sketches by the Author. 8vo, Cloth, $2 50.

GRIFFIS'S JAPAN. The Mikado's Empire: Book I. History of Japan, from 660 B.C. to 1872 A.D. Book II. Personal Experiences, Observations, and Studies in Japan, 1870-1874. By WILLIAM ELLIOT GRIFFIS, A.M., late of the Imperial University of Tōkiō, Japan. Copiously Illustrated. 8vo, Cloth, $4 00 ; Half Calf, $6 25.

BROUGHAM'S AUTOBIOGRAPHY. Life and Times of Henry, Lord Brougham. Written by Himself. 3 vols., 12mo, Cloth, $6 00.

8 Valuable Works for Public and Private Libraries.

THOMPSON'S PAPACY AND THE CIVIL POWER. The Papacy and the Civil Power. By the Hon. R. W. THOMPSON, Secretary of the U. S. Navy. Crown 8vo, Cloth, $3 00.

THE POETS AND POETRY OF SCOTLAND: From the Earliest to the Present Time. Comprising Characteristic Selections from the Works of the more Noteworthy Scottish Poets, with Biographical and Critical Notices. By JAMES GRANT WILSON. With Portraits on Steel. 2 vols., 8vo, Cloth, $10 00; Sheep, $12 00; Half Calf, $14 50; Full Morocco, $18 00.

THE STUDENT'S SERIES. With Maps and Illustrations. 12mo, Cloth.

FRANCE.—GIBBON.—GREECE.—HUME.—ROME (by LIDDELL).—OLD TESTAMENT HISTORY.—NEW TESTAMENT HISTORY.—STRICKLAND'S QUEENS OF ENGLAND (Abridged).—ANCIENT HISTORY OF THE EAST.—HALLAM'S MIDDLE AGES.—HALLAM'S CONSTITUTIONAL HISTORY OF ENGLAND.—LYELL'S ELEMENTS OF GEOLOGY.—MERIVALE'S GENERAL HISTORY OF ROME.—COX'S GENERAL HISTORY OF GREECE.—CLASSICAL DICTIONARY. Price $1 46 per volume.

LEWIS'S HISTORY OF GERMANY.—ECCLESIASTICAL HISTORY. Price $1 75 per volume.

CAMERON'S ACROSS AFRICA. Across Africa. By VERNEY LOVETT CAMERON, C.B., D.C.L., Commander Royal Navy, Gold Medalist Royal Geographical Society, etc. With a Map and numerous Illustrations. 8vo, Cloth, $5 00.

BARTH'S NORTH AND CENTRAL AFRICA. Travels and Discoveries in North and Central Africa: being a Journal of an Expedition undertaken under the Auspices of H.B.M.'s Government, in the Years 1849–1855. By HENRY BARTH, Ph.D., D.C.L. Illustrated. 3 vols., 8vo, Cloth, $12 00; Sheep, $13 50; Half Calf, $18 75.

THE REVISION OF THE ENGLISH VERSION OF THE NEW TESTAMENT. With an Introduction by the Rev. P. SCHAFF, D.D. 618 pp., Crown 8vo, Cloth, $3 00.

This work embraces in one volume:

I. ON A FRESH REVISION OF THE ENGLISH NEW TESTAMENT. By J. B. LIGHTFOOT, D.D., Canon of St. Paul's, and Hulsean Professor of Divinity, Cambridge. Second Edition, Revised. 196 pp.

II. ON THE AUTHORIZED VERSION OF THE NEW TESTAMENT in Connection with some Recent Proposals for its Revision. By R. C. TRENCH, D.D., Archbishop of Dublin. 194 pp.

III. CONSIDERATIONS ON THE REVISION OF THE ENGLISH VERSION OF THE NEW TESTAMENT. By C. J. ELLICOTT, D.D., Bishop of Gloucester and Bristol. ' 178 pp.

Valuable Works for Public and Private Libraries. 9

ADDISON'S COMPLETE WORKS. The Works of Joseph Addison, embracing the whole of the *Spectator*. 3 vols., 8vo, Cloth, $6 00; Sheep, $7 50; Half Calf, $12 75.

ANNUAL RECORD OF SCIENCE AND INDUSTRY. The Annual Record of Science and Industry. Edited by Professor SPENCER F. BAIRD, of the Smithsonian Institution, with the Assistance of Eminent Men of Science. The Yearly Volumes for 1871, 1872, 1873, 1874, 1875, 1876, 1877, 1878 are ready. 12mo, Cloth, $2 00 per vol.; $15 00 per set of 8 vols.

BULWER'S HORACE. The Odes and Epodes of Horace. A Metrical Translation into English. With Introduction and Commentaries. By LORD LYTTON. With Latin Text from the Editions of Orelli, Macleane, and Yonge. 12mo, Cloth, $1 75.

BULWER'S KING ARTHUR. King Arthur. A Poem. By LORD LYTTON. 12mo, Cloth, $1 75.

BULWER'S MISCELLANEOUS PROSE WORKS. The Miscellaneous Prose Works of Edward Bulwer, Lord Lytton. 2 vols., 12mo, Cloth, $3 50. Also, in uniform style, *Caxtoniana*. 12mo, Cloth, $1 75.

DAVIS'S CARTHAGE. Carthage and her Remains: being an Account of the Excavations and Researches on the Site of the Phœnician Metropolis in Africa and other Adjacent Places. Conducted under the Auspices of Her Majesty's Government. By Dr. N. DAVIS, F.R.G.S. Profusely Illustrated with Maps, Wood-cuts, Chromo-Lithographs, etc. 8vo, Cloth, $4 00; Half Calf, $6 25.

CARLYLE'S FREDERICK THE GREAT. History of Friedrich II., called Frederick the Great. By THOMAS CARLYLE. Portraits, Maps, Plans, etc. 6 vols., 12mo, Cloth, $12 00; Sheep, $14 40; Half Calf, $22 50.

CARLYLE'S FRENCH REVOLUTION. The French Revolution: a History. By THOMAS CARLYLE. 2 vols., 12mo, Cloth, $3 50; Sheep, $4 30; Half Calf, $7 00.

CARLYLE'S OLIVER CROMWELL. Oliver Cromwell's Letters and Speeches, including the Supplement to the First Edition. With Elucidations. By THOMAS CARLYLE. 2 vols., 12mo, Cloth, $3 50; Sheep, $4 30; Half Calf, $7 00.

TENNYSON'S COMPLETE POEMS. The Poetical Works of Alfred Tennyson, Poet-Laureate. With numerous Illustrations by Eminent Artists, and Three Characteristic Portraits. 8vo, Paper, $1 00; Cloth, $1 50.

CRUISE OF THE "CHALLENGER." Voyages over many Seas, Scenes in many Lands. By W. J. J. SPRY, R.N. With Map and Illustrations. Crown 8vo, Cloth, $2 00.

10 *Valuable Works for Public and Private Libraries.*

DU CHAILLU'S LAND OF THE MIDNIGHT SUN. The Land of the Midnight Sun. Travels in Sweden, Norway, and Lapland, 1871-1877. By Paul B. Du Chaillu. 2 vols., 8vo, Cloth. (*In Press.*)

DU CHAILLU'S AFRICA. Explorations and Adventures in Equatorial Africa; with Accounts of the Manners and Customs of the People, and of the Chase of the Gorilla, the Crocodile, Leopard, Elephant, Hippopotamus, and other Animals. By Paul B. Du Chaillu. Illustrated. 8vo, Cloth, $5 00; Sheep, $5 50; Half Calf, $7 25.

DU CHAILLU'S ASHANGO LAND. A Journey to Ashango Land, and Further Penetration into Equatorial Africa. By Paul B. Du Chaillu. Illustrated. 8vo, Cloth, $5 00; Sheep, $5 50; Half Calf, $7 25.

WHITE'S MASSACRE OF ST. BARTHOLOMEW. The Massacre of St. Bartholomew: Preceded by a History of the Religious Wars in the Reign of Charles IX. By Henry White, M.A. With Illustrations. Crown 8vo, Cloth, $1 75.

WOOD'S HOMES WITHOUT HANDS. Homes Without Hands: being a Description of the Habitations of Animals, classed according to their Principle of Construction. By J. G. Wood, M.A., F.L.S. Illustrated. 8vo, Cloth, $4 50; Sheep or Roan, $5 00; Half Calf, $6 75; Full Morocco, $8 00.

DRAPER'S CIVIL WAR. History of the American Civil War. By John W. Draper, M.D., LL.D. 3 vols., 8vo, Cloth, Beveled Edges, $10 50; Sheep, $12 00; Half Calf, $17 25.

DRAPER'S INTELLECTUAL DEVELOPMENT OF EUROPE. A History of the Intellectual Development of Europe. By John W. Draper, M.D., LL.D. New Edition, Revised. 2 vols., 12mo, Cloth, $3 00; Half Calf, $6 50.

DRAPER'S AMERICAN CIVIL POLICY. Thoughts on the Future Civil Policy of America. By John W. Draper, M.D., LL.D. Crown 8vo, Cloth, $2 00; Half Morocco, $3 75.

DRAPER'S SCIENTIFIC MEMOIRS. Scientific Memoirs: being Experimental Contributions to a Knowledge of Radiant Energy. By John W. Draper, M.D., LL.D. 8vo, Cloth, $3 00.

THE CREEDS OF CHRISTENDOM. *Bibliotheca Symbolica Ecclesiæ Universalis.* The Creeds of Christendom, with a History and Critical Notes. By the Rev. Philip Schaff, D.D., LL.D., Professor of Biblical Literature in the Union Theological Seminary, N. Y. Three volumes. Vol. I. The History of Creeds. Vol. II. The Greek and Latin Creeds, with Translations. Vol. III. The Evangelical Protestant Creeds, with Translations. 8vo, Cloth, $15 00.

www.ingramcontent.com/pod-product-compliance
Lightning Source LLC
Chambersburg PA
CBHW051855300426
44117CB00006B/399